Modern Critical Views

Modern Critical Views

Katherine Mansfield
Christopher Marlowe
Andrew Marvell
Herman Melville
George Meredith
James Merrill
John Stuart Mill
Arthur Miller
Henry Miller
John Milton
Yukio Mishima
Molière
Michel de Montaigne
Eugenio Montale
Marianne Moore
Alberto Moravia
Toni Morrison
Alice Munro
Iris Murdoch
Robert Musil
Vladimir Nabokov
V. S. Naipaul
R. K. Narayan
Pablo Neruda
John Henry Newman
Friedrich Nietzsche
Frank Norris
Joyce Carol Oates
Sean O'Casey
Flannery O'Connor
Christopher Okigbo
Charles Olson
Eugene O'Neill
José Ortega y Gasset
Joe Orton
George Orwell
Ovid
Wilfred Owen
Amos Oz
Cynthia Ozick
Grace Paley
Blaise Pascal
Walter Pater
Octavio Paz
Walker Percy
Petrarch
Pindar
Harold Pinter
Luigi Pirandello
Sylvia Plath
Plato

Plautus
Edgar Allan Poe
Poets of Sensibility & the
  Sublime
Poets of the Nineties
Alexander Pope
Katherine Anne Porter
Ezra Pound
Anthony Powell
Pre-Raphaelite Poets
Marcel Proust
Manuel Puig
Alexander Pushkin
Thomas Pynchon
Francisco de Quevedo
François Rabelais
Jean Racine
Ishmael Reed
Adrienne Rich
Samuel Richardson
Mordecai Richler
Rainer Maria Rilke
Arthur Rimbaud
Edwin Arlington Robinson
Theodore Roethke
Philip Roth
Jean-Jacques Rousseau
John Ruskin
J. D. Salinger
Jean-Paul Sartre
Gershom Scholem
Sir Walter Scott
William Shakespeare
  Histories & Poems
  Comedies & Romances
  Tragedies
George Bernard Shaw
Mary Wollstonecraft
  Shelley
Percy Bysshe Shelley
Sam Shepard
Richard Brinsley Sheridan
Sir Philip Sidney
Isaac Bashevis Singer
Tobias Smollett
Alexander Solzhenitsyn
Sophocles
Wole Soyinka
Edmund Spenser
Gertrude Stein
John Steinbeck

Stendhal
Laurence Sterne
Wallace Stevens
Robert Louis Stevenson
Tom Stoppard
August Strindberg
Jonathan Swift
John Millington Synge
Alfred, Lord Tennyson
William Makepeace Thackeray
Dylan Thomas
Henry David Thoreau
James Thurber and S. J.
  Perelman
J. R. R. Tolkien
Leo Tolstoy
Jean Toomer
Lionel Trilling
Anthony Trollope
Ivan Turgenev
Mark Twain
Miguel de Unamuno
John Updike
Paul Valéry
Cesar Vallejo
Lope de Vega
Gore Vidal
Virgil
Voltaire
Kurt Vonnegut
Derek Walcott
Alice Walker
Robert Penn Warren
Evelyn Waugh
H. G. Wells
Eudora Welty
Nathanael West
Edith Wharton
Patrick White
Walt Whitman
Oscar Wilde
Tennessee Williams
William Carlos Williams
Thomas Wolfe
Virginia Woolf
William Wordsworth
Jay Wright
Richard Wright
William Butler Yeats
A. B. Yehoshua
Emile Zola

Modern Critical Views

WILLIAM
SHAKESPEARE
COMEDIES & ROMANCES

Modern Critical Views

WILLIAM
SHAKESPEARE
COMEDIES & ROMANCES

Edited with an introduction by

Harold Bloom

Sterling Professor of the Humanities
Yale University

CHELSEA HOUSE PUBLISHERS
New York
Philadelphia

PROJECT EDITORS: Emily Bestler, James Uebbing
ASSOCIATE EDITOR: Maria Behan
EDITORIAL COORDINATOR: Karyn Gullen Browne
EDITORIAL STAFF: Laura Ludwig, Linda Grossman, Perry King
DESIGN: Susan Lusk

Cover illustration by Kye Carbone

Library of Congress Cataloging in Publication Data

Shakespeare's comedies and romances.   (Modern critical views)
    Bibliography: p.
    Includes index.
    1. Shakespeare, William, 1564–1616—Comedies—Ad-
dresses, essays, lecutures.   2. Shakespeare, William,
1564–1616—Tragicomedies—Addresses, essays, lectures.
I. Bloom, Harold.   II. Series.
PR2981.B55   1986   822.3'.3   85-21314
ISBN 0-87754-664-9

Contents

Editor's Note

This volume brings together a representative selection of the best modern and contemporary critical essays that seek to illuminate Shakespeare's principal comedies and romances. They are arranged in the order of their publication, and range from Elmer Edgar Stoll's exemplary consideration of Shylock, revised from its original version of 1911, to A. D. Nuttall's important defense of Shylock as Shakespearean mimesis, published in 1983.

The editor's "Introduction" also centers upon Shylock as a mimesis of the Jew, and both builds upon and severely revises the very different readings of *The Merchant of Venice* by Stoll and Nuttall. These three interpretations of Shylock frame the volume, which also gives two essays or extracts each to *A Midsummer Night's Dream* and *The Tempest*, and at least one discussion to each of the other major comedies and romances, as well as an overview of many in Northrop Frye's general essay.

After Stoll's urgent refusal to sentimentalize Shylock, the volume's chronological sequence continues with G. Wilson Knight's reading of *Pericles* as a fair field of symbolic action. Muriel C. Bradbrook's study of the ethical structure of *All's Well that Ends Well* is complemented by Harold C. Goddard's deft moral analysis of *Measure for Measure*, a comedy as problematical as *The Merchant of Venice*.

With Reuben Brower's analogical reading of *The Tempest*, we continue in the complex critical quest to encompass the moral perplexities of Shakespearean representation. This emphasis is lightened in Anne Barton's intensely theatrical reading of *Love's Labour's Lost*, but then returns in a finer tone with John Hollander's examination of what he calls "the morality of indulgence" in the delightfully problematic *Twelfth Night*. A spirit akin to Hollander's is manifested in C. L. Barber's supple balancing of seriousness and levity in *As You Like It*, and can be apprehended, in a lesser mode, in A. P. Rossiter's reading of *Much Ado About Nothing*.

A new movement begins as we advance towards the critical present with Northrop Frye's synoptic overview of what he calls "the natural perspective" of Shakespearean comedy and romance. Frye's direct influence is reflected in Howard Felperin's meditation upon Prospero, which complements Reuben Brower's earlier interpretation of *The Tempest*. Rosalie Colie's reading of *The Winter's Tale*, itself providing a new perspective upon the pastoral convention, offers a useful contrast to Frye's mythopoeic approach.

René Girard, reacting antithetically both to Frye and to Freud, interprets myth and ritual in A Midsummer Night's Dream by contextualizing them in his own vision of sacred violence and the agon of the family romance. Juxtaposed with Girard, directly after him, is Alvin B. Kernan's corrective emphasis upon the role of the Elizabethan audience in A Midsummer Night's Dream. More in Kernan's mode than in Girard's, Ruth Nevo's reading of The Taming of the Shrew as farce also emphasizes the stagecraft of Shakespeare's art, particularly in Petruchio's flamboyant artifices.

With Meredith Skura's acute psychoanalytic interpretation of Cymbeline, we advance to a brilliant instance of both the present and the likely future of Shakespearean criticism. Current perspectives that are at once Freudian and feminist (in the subtlest sense) are then followed by the concluding essay, A. D. Nuttall's examination of The Merchant of Venice as a crucial instance of Shakespeare's new mimesis. Nuttall shrewdly opposes himself to the current post-Structuralist school of deconstructionism, with its Derrida-inspired questioning of the very possibility of the representation of human character and human action by language. Since Shakespeare remains the strongest instance of such a representation in all Western literature, it is appropriate that the volume end with a defense of the reality of that representation. We are thus returned full circle to where we began in the "Introduction," where the editor meditated both upon the strength of Shakespearean representation, and upon the unhappiness of Shylock's being the major instance of Shakespeare's rare refusal of originality.

Introduction

I

Shylock is to the world of the comedies and romances what Hamlet is to the tragedies, and Falstaff to the histories: a representation so original as to be perpetually bewildering to us. What is beyond us in Hamlet and Falstaff is a mode of vast consciousness crossed by wit, so that we know authentic disinterestedness only by knowing the Hamlet of Act V, and know the wit that enlarges existence best by knowing Falstaff before his rejection by King Henry V, who has replaced Hal. Shylock is not beyond us in any way, and yet he resembles Hamlet and Falstaff in one crucial regard; he is a much more problematical representation than even Shakespeare's art could have intended. Like Hamlet and Falstaff, he dwarfs his fellow characters. Portia, despite her aura, fades before him just as Claudius recedes in the clash of mighty opposites with Hamlet, and as Hotspur is dimmed by Falstaff.

I know of no legitimate way in which *The Merchant of Venice* ought to be regarded as other than an anti-Semitic text, agreeing in this with E. E. Stoll as against Harold Goddard, my favorite critic of Shakespeare. Goddard sees Antonio and Portia as self-betrayers, who should have done better. They seem to me perfectly adequate Christians, with Antonio's anti-Semitism being rather less judicious than Portia's, whose attitude approximates that of the T. S. Eliot of *After Strange Gods, The Idea of a Christian Society* and the earlier poems. If you accept the attitude towards the Jews of the Gospel of John, then you will behave towards Shylock as Portia does, or as Eliot doubtless would have behaved towards British Jewry, had the Nazis defeated and occupied Eliot's adopted country. To Portia, and to Eliot, the Jews were what they are called in the Gospel of John: descendants of Satan, rather than of Abraham.

There is no real reason to doubt that the historical Shakespeare would have agreed with his Portia. Shakespeare after all wrote what might as well be called *The Jew of Venice*, in clear rivalry with his precursor Marlowe's *The Jew of Malta*. Were I an actor, I would take great pleasure in the part of Barabas, and little or none in that of Shylock, but then I am a Jewish critic, and prefer the exuberance of Barabas to the wounded

· 1 ·

intensity of Shylock. There is nothing problematic about Barabas. We cannot imagine *him* asking: "If you prick us, do we not bleed?," anymore than we can imagine Shylock proclaiming: "As for myself, I walk abroad a-nights . . . and poison wells." Marlowe, subtly blasphemous and cunningly outrageous, gives us Christians and Muslims who are as reprehensible as Barabas, but who lack the Jew of Malta's superb delight in his own sublime villainy. Despite his moralizing scholars, Marlowe the poet is Barabas, or rhetorically so akin to his creation as to render the difference uninteresting. Shakespeare possibly intended to give us a pathetic monster in Shylock, but being Shakespeare, he gave us Shylock, concerning whom little can be said that will not be at least oxymoronic, if not indeed self-contradictory.

That Shylock got away from Shakespeare seems clear enough, but that is the scandal of Shakespearean representation; so strong is it that nearly all his creatures break out of the temporal trap of Elizabethan and Jacobean mimesis, and establish standards of imitation that do seem to be, not of an age, but for all time. Shylock also—like Hamlet, Falstaff, Cleopatra—compels us to see differences in reality we otherwise could not have seen. Marlowe is a great caricaturist; Barabas is grotesquely magnificent, and his extravagance mocks the Christian cartoon of the Jew as usurer and fiend. It hardly matters whether the mockery is involuntary, since inevitably the hyperbolic force of the Marlovian rhetoric raises word-consciousness to a level where everything joins in an over-reaching. In a cosmos where all is excessive, Barabas is no more a Jew than Tamburlaine is a Scythian or Faustus a Christian. It is much more troublesome to ask: Is Shylock a Jew? Does he not now represent something our culture regards as being essentially Jewish? So immense is the power of Shakespearean mimesis that its capacity for harm necessarily might be as substantial as its enabling force has been for augmenting cognition and for fostering psychoanalysis, despite all Freud's anxious assertions of his own originality.

II

Harold Goddard, nobly creating a Shakespeare in his own highly humane image, tried to persuade himself "that Shakespeare planned his play from the outset to enforce the irony of Portia's failure to be true to her inner self in the trial scene." E. E. Stoll, sensibly declaring that Shakespeare's contemporary audience set societal limits that Shakespeare himself would not have thought to transcend, reminds us that Jew-baiting was in effect little different than bear-baiting for that audience. I do not hope for a better critic of Shakespeare than Goddard. Like Freud, Goddard always looked for what Shakespeare shared with Dostoevsky, which seems to me rather more useful than searching for what Shakespeare shared with Kyd or even with Marlowe or Webster. Despite his authentic insistence that Shakespeare always was poet as well as playwright, Goddard's attempt to see *The Merchant of Venice* as other than anti-Semitic was misguided.

At his very best, Goddard antithetically demonstrates that the play's "spiritual argument" is quite simply unacceptable to us now:

> Shylock's conviction that Christianity and revenge are synonyms is confirmed. "If a Christian wrong a Jew, what should his sufferance be by Christian example? Why, revenge." The unforgettable speech from which that comes, together with Portia's on mercy, and Lorenzo's on the harmony of heaven, make up the spiritual argument of the play. Shylock asserts that a Jew is a man. Portia declares that man's duty to man is mercy—which comes from heaven. Lorenzo points to heaven but laments that the materialism of life insulates man from its harmonies. A celestial syllogism that puts to shame the logic of the courtroom.

Alas, the celestial syllogism is Goddard's, and Portia's logic is Shakespeare's. Goddard wanted to associate *The Merchant of Venice* with Chekhov's bittersweet "Rothschild's Fiddle," but Dostoevsky again would have been the right comparison. Shakespeare's indubitable anti-Semitism is no lovelier than Dostoevsky's, being compounded similarly out of xenophobia and The Gospel of John. Shylock's demand for justice, as contrasted to Portia's supposed mercy, is part of the endless consequence of the New Testament's slander against the Pharisees. But the authors of the New Testament, even Paul and John, were no match for the authors of the Hebrew Bible. Shakespeare, more even than Dostoevsky, is of another order, the order of the Yahwist, Homer, Dante, Chaucer, Cervantes, Tolstoi—the great masters of Western literary representation. Shylock is essentially a comic representation rendered something other than comic because of Shakespeare's preternatural ability to accomplish a super-mimesis of essential nature. Shakespeare's intellectual, Hamlet, is necessarily the paradigm of *the* intellectual, even as Falstaff is the model of wit, and Cleopatra the sublime of eros. Is Shakespeare's Jew fated to go on being the representation of *the* Jew?

"Yes and no," would be my answer, because of Shakespeare's own partial failure when he allows Shylock to invoke an even stronger representation of *the* Jew, the Yahwist's vision of the superbly tenacious Jacob tending the flocks of Laban and not directly taking interest. Something very odd is at work when Antonio denies Jacob's own efficacy:

> This was a venture, sir, that Jacob serv'd for;
> A thing not in his power to bring to pass,
> But sway'd and fashion'd by the hand of heaven.

That is certainly a Christian reading, though I do not assert necessarily it was Shakespeare's own. Good Christian merchant that he is, Antonio distinguishes his own profits from Shylock's Jewish usury, but Shylock, or rather the Yahwist, surely wins the point over Antonio, and perhaps over Shakespeare. If the Jewish "devil can cite Scripture for his purpose," so can the Christian devils, from John through Shakespeare, and the polemical point turns upon who wins the agon, the Yahwist or Shakespeare? Shakespeare certainly intended to show the Jew as caught in the repetition of a revenge morality masking itself as a demand for justice. That is the rhetorical force of Shylock's obsessive "I will have my bond," with all its dreadfully compulsive ironic plays upon "bond." But if Shylock, like the Yahwist's Jacob, is a strong representation of the Jew, then "bond" has a tenacity that Shakespeare himself may have underestimated. Shakespeare's most dubious irony, as little persuasive as the resolution of *Measure for Measure*, is that Portia triumphantly out-literalizes Shylock's literalism, since flesh cannot be separated from blood. But Shylock, however monstrously, has a true bond or covenant to assert, whether between himself and Antonio, or between Jacob and Laban, or ultimately between Israel and Yahweh. Portia invokes an unequal law, not a covenant or mutual obligation, but only another variant upon the age-old Christian insistence that Christians may shed Jewish blood, but never the reverse. Can it be said that we do not go on hearing Shylock's "I will have my bond," despite his forced conversion?

III

Shakespearean representation presents us with many perplexities throughout the comedies and romances: Angelo and Malvolio, among others, are perhaps as baffling as Shylock. What makes Shylock different may be a strength in the language he speaks that works against what elsewhere is Shakespeare's most original power. Shylock does not change by listening to himself speaking; he becomes only more what he always was. It is as though the Jew alone, in Shakespeare, lacks originality. Marlowe's Barabas *sounds* less original than Shylock does, and yet Marlowe employs Barabas to satirize Christian moral pretensions. The curious result is that Marlowe, just this once, seems "modern" in contrast to Shakespeare. What are we to do with Shylock's great outbursts of pathos when the play itself seems to give them no dignity or value in context? I do not find it possible to contravene E. E. Stoll's judgment in this regard:

> Shylock's disappointment is tragic to him, but good care is taken that it shall not be to us . . . The running fire assails him to the very moment—and beyond it—that Shylock says he is not well, and staggers out, amid Gratiano's jeers touching his baptism, to provoke in the audience the laughter of triumph and vengeance in his own day and bring tears to their eyes in ours. How can we here for a moment sympathize with Shylock unless at the same time we indignantly turn, not only against Gratiano, but against Portia, the Duke, and all Venice as well?

We cannot, unless we desire to read or see some other play. *The Merchant of Venice* demands what we cannot accept: Antonio's superior goodness, from the start, is to be demonstrated by his righteous scorn for Shylock, which is to say, Antonio most certainly represents what now is called a Jew-baiter. An honest production of the play, sensitive to its values, would now be intolerable in a Western country. The unhappy paradox is that *The Jew of Malta*, a ferocious farce, exposes the madness and hypocrisy of Jew-baiting, even though its Machiavel, Barabas, is the Jewish monster or Devil incarnate, while *The Merchant of Venice* is at once a comedy of delightful sophistication and a vicious Christian slander against the Jews.

In that one respect, Shakespeare was for an age, and not for all time. Bardolatry is not always an innocent disease, and produces odd judgments, as when J. Middleton Murry insisted: "*The Merchant of Venice* is not a problem play; it is a fairy story." For us, contemporary Jews and Gentiles alike, it had better be a problem play, and not a fairy story. Shylock, Murry admitted, was not "coherent," because a Shakespearean character had no need to be coherent. Yet Shylock is anything but incoherent. His palpable mimetic force enhances his rapacity and viciousness, and works to make an ancient bogeyman come dreadfully alive. For the reader or playgoer (though hardly the latter, in our time), Shylock is at once comic and frightening, a walking embodiment of the death drive.

We must not underestimate the power and influence of Shakespearean mimesis, even when it is *deliberately* unoriginal, as it is in Shylock. Hamlet and Falstaff contain us to our enrichment. Shylock has the strength to contain us to our destruction. Something of the same could be said for Angelo, in *Measure for Measure*, or of Malvolio, in *Twelfth Night*, or of nearly everyone in *Troilus*. History renders Shylock's strength as representation socially destructive, whereas Angelo and Malvolio inhabit the shadows of the individual consciousness. I conclude by noting that

Shakespeare's comedies and romances share in the paradox that Gershom Scholem said the writings of Kafka possessed. They have for us "something of the strong light of the canonical, of the perfection that destroys."

ELMER EDGAR STOLL

Shylock

To get at Shakespeare's intention (after a fashion) is, after all, not hard. As with popular drama, great or small, he who runs may read—he who yawns and scuffles in the pit may understand. The time is past for speaking of Shakespeare as utterly impartial or inscrutable: the study of his work and that of his fellows as an expression of Elizabethan ideas and technique is teaching us better. The puzzle whether the *Merchant of Venice* is not meant for tragedy, for instance, is cleared up when, as Professor Baker suggests, we forget Sir Henry Irving's acting, and remember that the title—and the hero—is not the 'Jew of Venice' as he would lead us to suppose; that this comedy is only like others, as *Measure for Measure* and *Much Ado*, not clear of the shadow of the fear of death; and that in closing with an act where Shylock and his knife are forgotten in the unravelling of the mystery between the lovers and the crowning of Antonio's happiness in theirs, it does not, from the Elizabethan point of view, perpetrate an anti-climax, but, like many another Elizabethan play, carries to completion what is a story for story's sake. 'Shylock is, and always has been the hero,' says Professor Schelling. But why, then, did Shakespeare drop his hero out of the play for good before the fourth act was over? It is a trick which he never repeated—a trick, I am persuaded, of which he was not capable.

Hero or not, Shylock is given a villain's due. His is the heaviest penalty to be found in all the pound of flesh stories, including that in *Il Pecorone*, which served as model for the play. Not in the Servian, the Persian, the African version, or even that of the *Cursor Mundi*, does the

From *Shakespeare Studies: Historical and Comparative in Method*. Copyright © 1927 by Macmillan Publishing Co.

money-lender suffer like Shylock—impoverishment, sentence of death, and an outrage done to his faith from which Jews were guarded even by decrees of German emperors and Roman pontiffs. It was in the old play, perhaps, source of the present one; but that Shakespeare retained it shows his indifference, at least, to the amenities, as regards either Jews or Judaism. In not a single heart do Shylock's griefs excite commiseration; indeed, as they press upon him they are barbed with gibes and jeers. Coriolanus is unfortunate and at fault, but we know that the poet is with him. We know that the poet is not with Shylock, for on that point, in this play as in every other, the impartial, inscrutable poet leaves little or nothing to suggestion or surmise. As is his custom elsewhere, by the comments of the good characters, by the methods pursued in the disposition of scenes, and by the downright avowals of soliloquy, he constantly sets us right.

As for the first of these artifices, all the people who come in contact with Shylock except Tubal—among them being those of his own house, his servant and his daughter—have a word or two to say on the subject of his character, and never a good one. And in the same breath they spend on Bassanio and Antonio, his enemies, nothing but words of praise. Praise or blame, moreover, is, after Shakespeare's fashion, usually in the nick of time to guide the hearer's judgment. Lest at his first appearance the Jew should make too favourable an impression by his Scripture quotations, Antonio is led to observe that the devil can cite Scripture for his purpose; lest the Jew's motive in foregoing interest (for once in his life) should seem like the kindness Antonio takes it to be, Bassanio avows that he likes not fair terms and a villain's mind; and once the Jew has caught the Christian on the hip, every one, from Duke to Gaoler, has words of horror or detestation for him and of compassion for his victim.

As for the second artifice, the ordering of the scenes is such as to enforce this contrast. First impressions, every playwright knows (and no one better than Shakespeare himself), are momentous, particularly for the purpose of ridicule. Launcelot and Jessica, in separate scenes, are introduced before Shylock reaches home, that, hearing their story, we may side with them, and, when the old curmudgeon appears, may be moved to laughter as he complains of Launcelot's gormandizing, sleeping, and rending apparel out, and as he is made game of by the young conspirators to his face. Here, as Mr. Poel has noticed, when there might be some danger of our sympathy becoming enlisted on Shylock's side because he is about to lose his daughter and some of his property, Shakespeare forestalls it. He lets Shylock, in his hesitation whether to go to the feast, take warning from a dream, but nevertheless, though he knows that they bid him not for love, decide to go in hate, in order to feed upon the prodigal Christian. And he lets him give up Launcelot, whom he has half a liking for, save that he is a huge feeder, to Bassanio—'to one that I would have him help to waste his borrowed purse.' Small credit these sentiments do him; little do they add to his pathos or dignity. Still more conspicuous is this care when Shylock laments over his daughter and his ducats. Lest then by any chance a stupid or tender-hearted audience should not laugh but grieve, Salanio reports his outcries—in part word for word—two scenes in advance, as matter of mirth to himself and all the boys in Venice. It is exactly the same method as that employed in *Twelfth Night*, Act III, scene ii, where Maria comes and tells not only Sir Toby, Sir Andrew, and Fabian, but, above all, the audience, how ridiculously Malvolio is acting, before they see it for themselves. The art of the theatre, but particularly the art of the comic theatre, is the art of preparations, else it is not securely comic. But the impression first of all imparted to us is of Shylock's villainy—an impression which, however comical he may become, we are not again allowed to lose. In the first scene in which he appears, the third in the play, there is one of the most remarkable instances in dramatic literature of a man saying one thing but thinking another and the audience made to see this. He prolongs the situation, keeps the Christians on tenterhooks, turns the terms of the contract over and over in his mind, as if he were considering the soundness of it and of the borrower, while all the time he is hoping, for once in his life, that his debtor may turn out not sound but bankrupt. He casts up Antonio's hard usage of him in the past, defends the practice of interest-taking, is at the point of stipulating what the rate this time shall be, and then—decides to be friends and take no interest at all. He seems, and is, loath to part for a time with three thousand ducats—' 'tis a good round sum!'—but at the bottom of his heart he is eager.

And as for the third artifice, that a sleepy audience may not make the mistake of the cautious critic and take the villain for the hero, Shakespeare is at pains to label the villain by an aside at the moment the hero appears on the boards:

> I hate him for he is a Christian,
> But more for that in low simplicity
> He lends out money gratis, and brings down
> The rate of usance here with us in Venice.

Those are his motives, later confessed repeatedly; and either one brands him as a villain more unmistakably in that day, as we shall see, than in ours. Of the indignities which he has endured he speaks also, and of revenge; but of none of these has he anything to say at the trial. There he pleads his oath, perjury to his soul should he break it, his 'lodged hate', or his 'humour'; further than that, 'I can give no reason nor I will not,'—for some reasons a man does not give; but here to himself and later to Tubal—'were he out of Venice I can make what merchandise I will'—he tells, in the thick of the action, the unvarnished truth. As with Shakespeare's villains generally—Aaron, Iago, or Richard III—only what they say concerning their purposes aside or to their confidants can be relied upon; and Shylock's oath and his horror of perjury are, as Dr Furness observes, belied by his clutching at thrice the principal when the pound of flesh escapes him, just as is his money-lender's ruse of pretending to borrow the cash from 'a friend' (avowed as such by Moses in the *School for Scandal*) by his going home 'to purse the ducats straight.'

His arguments, moreover, are given a specious, not to say a grotesque colouring. Similar ones used by the Jew in Silvayn's *Orator* (1596), probably known to Shakespeare, are there called 'sophisticall'. But Hazlitt and other critics strangely say that in argument Shylock has the best of it.

> What if my house be troubled with a rat
> And I be pleas'd to give *ten* thousand ducats
> To have it ban'd?

This particular rat is a human being; but the only thing to remark upon, in Shylock's opinion, is his willingness to squander ten thousand ducats on it instead of three. 'Hates any man the thing,' he cries (and there he is ticketed), 'he would not kill!' Even in Hazlitt's time, moreover, a choice of 'carrion flesh' in preference to ducats could not be plausibly compared as a 'humour'—the Jew's gross jesting here grates upon you—with an aversion to pigs or to the sound of the bag-pipe, or defended as a right by the analogy of holding slaves; nor could the practice of interest-taking find a warrant in Jacob's pastoral trickery while in the service of Laban; least of all in the day when Sir John Hawkins, who initiated the slave-trade, with the Earls of Pembroke and Leicester and the Queen herself for partners, bore on the arms which were granted him for his exploits a demi-Moor, proper, in chains, and in the day when the world at large still held interest-taking to be robbery. Very evidently, moreover, Shylock is discomfited by Antonio's question 'Did he take interest?' for he falters and stumbles in his reply—

> No, not take interest, not, as you would say,
> Directly, interest,—

and is worsted, in the eyes of the audience if not in his own, by the repeated use of the old Aristotelian argument of the essential barrenness of
money, still gospel in Shakespeare's day, in the second question,

> Or is your gold and silver ewes and rams?

For his answer is meant for nothing better than a piece of complacent
shamelessness:

> I cannot tell: I make it breed as fast.

Only twice does Shakespeare seem to follow Shylock's pleadings
and reasonings with any sympathy—'Hath a dog money?' in the first scene
in which he appears, and 'Hath not a Jew eyes?' in the third act—but a bit
too much has been made of this. Either plea ends in such fashion as to
alienate the audience. To Shylock's reproaches the admirable Antonio,
'one of the gentlest and humblest of all the men in Shakespeare's theatre,'
praised and honoured by everyone but Shylock, retorts, secure in his
virtue, that he is just as like to spit on him and spurn him again. And
Shylock's celebrated justification of his race runs headlong into a justification of his villainy: 'The villainy which you teach me I will execute, and
it shall go hard but I will better the instruction.' 'Hath not a Jew eyes?'
and he proceeds to show that your Jew is no less than a man, and as such
has a right, not to respect or compassion, as the critics for a century have
had it, but to revenge. Neither large nor lofty are his claims. The speech
begins with the answer to Salanio's question about the pound of flesh.
'Why, I am sure, if he forfeit, thou wilt not take his flesh. What's that
good for?' 'To bait fish withal,' he retorts in savage jest; 'if it will feed
nothing else it will feed my revenge;' and he goes on to complain of insults,
and of thwarted bargains to the tune of half a million, and to make a plea
for which he has already robbed himself of a hearing. Quite as vigorously
and (in that day) with as much reason, the detestable and abominable
Aaron defends his race and colour, and Edmund, the dignity of bastards.
The worst of his villains Shakespeare allows to plead their cause: their
confidences in soliloquy or aside, if not (as here) slight touches in the plea
itself, sufficiently counteract any too favourable impression. This, on the
face of it, is a plea for indulging in revenge with all its rigours; not a word
is put in for the nobler side of Jewish character; and in lending Shylock
his eloquence Shakespeare is but giving the devil his due.

II

By all the devices, then, of Shakespeare's dramaturgy Shylock is proclaimed, as by the triple repetition of a crier, to be the villain, though a comic villain or butt. Nor does the poet let pass any of the prejudices of that day which might heighten this impression. A miser, a money-lender, a Jew,—all three had from time immemorial been objects of popular detestation and ridicule, whether in life or on the stage. The union of them in one person is in Shakespeare's time the rule, both in plays and in 'character'-writing: to the popular imagination a money-lender was a sordid miser with a hooked nose. So it is in the acknowledged prototype of Shylock, Marlowe's 'bottle-nosed' monster, Barabas, the Jew of Malta. Though far more of a villain, he has the same traits of craft and cruelty, the same unctuous friendliness hiding a thirst for a Christian's blood, the same thirst for blood outreaching his greed for gold, and the same spirit of unrelieved egoism which thrusts aside the claims of his family, his nation, or even his faith. If Barabas fawns like a spaniel when he pleases, grins when he bites, heaves up his shoulders when they call him dog, Shylock, for his part, 'still bears it with a patient shrug', and 'grows kind', seeking the Christian's 'love' in the hypocritical fashion of Barabas with the suitors and the friars. If Barabas ignores the interests of his brother Jews, poisons his daughter, 'counts religion but a childish toy', and, in various forms, avows the wish that 'so I live perish may all the world', Shylock has no word for the generous soul but 'fool' and 'simpleton', and cries ('fervid patriot' that he is, 'martyr and avenger'): 'A diamond gone, cost me two thousand ducats in Frankfort! The curse never fell upon our nation until now. I never felt it till now.' Such is his love of his race, which, Professor Raleigh says, is 'deep as life'. And in the next breath he cries, as 'the affectionate father': 'Two thousand ducats in that, and other precious, precious jewels. I would my daughter were dead at my foot, and the jewels in her ear . . . and the ducats in her coffin.'

This alternation of daughter and ducats itself comes from Marlowe's play, as well as other ludicrous touches, such as your Jew's stinginess with food and horror of swine-eating, and the confounding of Jew and devil. This last is an old, wide-spread superstition: on the strength of holy writ the Fathers (with the suffrage in this century of Luther) held that the Jews were devils and the synagogue the house of Satan. In both plays in affords the standing joke, in the *Merchant of Venice* nine times repeated. 'Let me say Amen betimes,' exclaims Salanio in the midst of his good wishes for Antonio; 'lest the devil cross my prayer, for here he comes in the likeness of a Jew.' And in keeping with these notions Shylock's synagogue is, as Luther piously calls it, *ein Teuffels Nest*, the nest for hatching his plot once he and Tubal and the others of his 'tribe' can get together. 'Go, go, Tubal,' he cries in the unction of his guile, 'and meet me at our synagogue; go, good Tubal, at our synagogue, Tubal!' In any one such eagerness for the sanctuary is suspicious; but all the more in those times, when the congregation was of Jews and the business of a Christian's flesh. These sly and insinuating Oriental repetitions would of themselves have given the Saxon audience a shudder.

It is highly probable, moreover, that Shylock wore the red hair and beard, mentioned by Jordan, from the beginning, as well as the bottle-nose of Barabas. So Judas was made up from of old; and in their immemorial orange-tawny, high-crowned hats and 'Jewish gabardines,' the very looks of the two usurers provoked derision. In both plays the word Jew, itself a badge of opprobrium, is constantly in use instead of the proper name of the character and as a byword for cruelty and cunning. . . .

Those who will have it that Shylock, though bad, was made so, do violence to Shakespeare in two different ways. In the first place, they have recourse to an all-pervading irony. Antonio, gentlest and humblest of Shakespeare's heroes, kicking and spitting at Jews and thrusting salvation down their throats,—such, they say, is the spectacle of race-hatred pointed at by the poet. And those others who will have it that Shylock is a noble spirit brought to shame, carry the irony still further, into the characterization of Antonio and his friends. He, not Shylock, is the caricature: his virtues are but affectations and shams; his friends are parasites, spendthrifts, and fribbles! They make no effort to raise the three thousand ducats to save him, they do not even provide him with a surgeon against his need. That is, nothing is what it seems; a comedy ending in moonlight blandishments and badinage is a tragedy, and the play written for the customers of the Globe flies over their honest heads to the peaks of nineteenth-century criticism. Irony is surely unthinkable unless the author intends it, and here not the slightest trace of such an intention appears. Moreover, a play of Shakespeare's is self-contained; the irony is within it, so to speak, not underneath it. There is irony in the appearance of Banquo at the moment when Macbeth presumes hypocritically to wish for his presence at the feast; or, more obviously still, in the fulfilment of the Witches' riddling oracles; but there is no irony, as we have seen, such as Mr Yeats discovers in the success of Henry V and the failure of Richard II. There is irony in the situation of a king so powerful reduced to a state so pitiful, before he has 'shook off the regal thoughts wherewith he reigned'; but Shakespeare does not dream that to fail and be a Richard is better than to succeed and be a Henry—or an Antonio. He knows not the way of thinking which lightly sets the judgment of the world aside, nor the ways of modern artistic expression, which almost withholds the purport of the higher judgment from the world. No abysmal irony undermines his solid sense and straightforward meaning. Shylock is indeed condemned; Sir Henry Irving took no counsel of the poet when he made his exit from the ducal palace in pathetic triumph.

Nor is Jessica treated with malice, in mockery or irony, as, having forsaken him and robbed him and never since given him a regretful or pitying thought, she now revels in jest and sentiment, in moonlight and melody, at Belmont. What right has Signor Croce to call her ecstasy sensual? Since her father had made home a hell to her and Launcelot, and in robbing him she has acted with the approval of everybody, as did the son who robbed Harpagon, has she not a right, in the world where she now lives, to be really happy? Signor Croce may be horrified at Jessica as was Rousseau at the unfilial Cléante; but just as sympathy at the theatre traditionally is for the debtor and against the money-lender, so it is for the amorous son or eloping daughter and against the hard-hearted, stingy father. Thus it had been on the stage since the days of Plautus; cheating the old man was both sport for the slave and relief for the son's necessities. Either consideration gave pleasure in the comic theatre. It is not ideal justice—that is not the business of comedy; but as Monsieur Donnay says of Harpagon's gold, 'nous sommes enchantés que cet or, mal acquis, rentre dans la circulation. De tous les vices qui peuvent s'emparer d'un homme, l'avarice est certainement le plus détestable, et qui excite le moins notre pitié.'

And as for the Jew—' 'tis charity to undo a Jew,' both thought and said the age. Indeed, is not Jessica what might have been taken for a true daughter of her tribe, like Rachel, who 'stole the images that were her father's' before she fled; and like the daughters of Israel, who before they went up out of the land of Egypt, 'borrowed' of their neighbours jewels of silver and jewels of gold? 'And they spoiled the Egyptians,' adds naïvely and complacently the ancient chronicler; and, having turned Christian, why should not Jessica spoil the Jew? the Christians will be likely to ask. But here, as in Antonio's notion of conversion, or the Duke's notion of clemency to Jews, is the irony of history, not of art. Shakespeare's thought is as simple and sincere as is the old hagiographer's about the balancing of Jews' ledgers by royal edict—*pacem operatur justicia.*

In the second place, they do violence to Shakespeare, as Mr Hudson observes, in representing Shylock as the product of his environment. The thoughts of men had hardly begun to run in such channels; the ancient rigours of retribution held fast; men still believed in heaven and hell, in villains and heroes. Though in Shakespeare there is little of George Eliot's moral austerity, as brought to bear on Tito Melema, for instance, Mr Yeats errs, I think, in the opinion that his plays are, like all great literature, 'written in the spirit of the Forgiveness of Sin.' Macbeth is not forgiven, nor is Othello. Richard III and Iago were damned even in the making. Though the shortcomings of Falstaff, Bardolph, Pistol, and Nym serve a while as food for mirth, Shakespeare is in full accord with Henry V as he casts his fellows out of his company and out of his mind, to meet their end, maybe, in the brothel or on the gallows. And he is in full accord with Portia and the Duke in the judgement scene. Except in comedy, he has not the spirit of forgiveness which, like Uncle Toby's towards the Devil, comes of mere kindness of heart; and neither in comedy nor in tragedy has he the forgiveness of our psychological and social drama and novel, where both villains and heroes are no more, which comes of fulness of knowledge. Thus he deals with poverty, the hard-hearted, greasy, foul-smelling, ignorant and ungrateful multitude, for which he so often utters his aversion; and thus he deals with the kindred subject of heredity. If a scoundrel is a bastard, or is mean of birth, the fact is not viewed as an extenuating circumstance, but is turned to a reproach. It may in a sense explain his depravity, but never explain it away. It sets the seal upon it. It confirms the prejudice that there is a difference between noble blood and that of low degree. So, though our hearts are softened by Shylock's recital of the indignities he has suffered, the hearts of the Elizabethans, by a simpler way of thinking, are hardened. It confirms the prejudice that there is a difference betwixt Christian and Jew. The Fathers, Protestant theologians like Luther, seventeenth-century lawyers like Coke and Prynne, review the pitiful story of the Jews in Europe grimly, with at best a momentary and furtive pathos. It proves their notion of the curse. What else, in an age when it was the universal belief that Jew and Gentile alike took upon their heads the curse of Adam's sin on issuing from the mother's womb? Even to-day a man who is abused in the street is supposed, by bystanders, to deserve it: the world barks at rags and poverty like the dogs: and everyone knows that there are certain scars (as of branding) and certain diseases (though poeple without them may be equally guilty) which a canny man does not complain of or betray. And how much more in the days of literary and theological bludgeoning; when the reformers were to the common enemy, and to one another, dogs, hogs, and asses; when Shakespeare himself let one of his noblest characters cast it up to another that he possessed but one trunk of clothes; when Milton was reviled, in scholarly Latin, for his blindness and (in defiance of fact) for his guttering eyelids; and when Dryden never heard the last of the beating he got at the instigation of a fellow poet in a London street. For everything there is someone to blame, is the point of view, and who so much as he who has the worst of it?

> And every loss the men of Jebus bore,
> They still were thought God's enemies the more!

Such is the logic of Luther as he puts to the Jews the crushing question (naïvely exhorting Christians, if they must speak to Jews at all, to do likewise, and 'not to quarrel with them'): 'Hear'st thou, Jew, dost thou know that Jerusalem, your temple, and your priesthood have been destroyed now over fourteen hundred and sixty years?' Even at the end of the seventeenth century Robert South, as he considers the universal detestation in which, through the ages, Jews have been held, must conclude that there is 'some peculiar vileness essentially fixed in the genius of this people.' That no one is to blame does not occur to him, or that the cause of the detestation lies in race-hatred, the incompatibility of temperament and customs. 'What's his reason?' cries Shylock. It is the reason which Antonio—that is Shakespeare—is not analytical enough to recognize or cynical enough to avow. Steadily the Jewishness of Shylock is kept before us; like Barabas, he loses his name in his nationality—'the Jew,' 'the dog Jew,' 'the villain Jew,' 'his Jewish heart';—and it is not merely according to the measure of his villainy that at the end and throughout the play he suffers. With Robert South Shakespeare himself might have said that the reason was his 'essential Jewish *vileness*'; but we, who, in the light of modern psychology and the history of society, are aware that no man and no age can render adequately the reason why they themselves do anything, recognize that the famous reason given by Shylock himself, in the heat of his *ex parte* pleading with which Shakespeare so little sympathizes, curiously enough hits the mark.

. . . Then there is inversion, the tables turned. 'L'histoire du persécuteur victime de sa persécution, du dupeur dupé, du voleur volé, fait le fond de bien des comédies.' The trial scene is an example. To most critics Shylock has here seemed to be more or less pathetic, despite the fact that, as I take it, Shakespeare has employed almost every possible means to produce a contrary, quite incompatible effect.

Professor Baker holds that Shakespeare evinces a sense of dramatic values in presenting Shylock's disappointment as tragic in his own eyes, amusing in Gratiano's. How is the tragic value presented? By the miser and usurer's prostrate prayer to the Duke to take his life if he would take his wealth, or by the plea that he is not well? The biter bitten, is the gibe cast at him at the end of *Il Pecorone*; and that, exactly, is the spirit of the scene. It is the same spirit and almost the same situation as at the close of Sheridan's *Duenna*, where another Jew, not nearly so culpable as Shylock, having now been fast married to the dragon herself, not, as he thinks, to the maiden that she guards, is jeered at for it, while one of the characters gives the reason,—that 'there is not a fairer subject for contempt and ridicule than a knave become the dupe of his own art.' Shylock's disappointment is tragic to him, but good care is taken that it shall not be to us. Shakespeare is less intent on values than on the conduct and direction of our sympathies through the scene. This he manages both by the action and the comment. The scene is a rise and a fall, a triumph turned into a defeat, an apparent tragedy into a comedy; and the defeat is made to repeat the stages of the triumph so as to bring home to us the fact—the comic fact—of retribution. When fortune turns, almost all the steps of the ladder whereby Shylock with scales and knife had climbed to clutch the fruit of revenge he must now descend empty-handed and in bitterness; and what had been offered to him and refused by him, he is now, when he demands it again, refused. With the course of the action the comment is in perfect accord and unison, marking and signalizing the stages of Shylock's fall. The outcries against the Jew and his stony heart, of the Duke, Bassanio, and Gratiano—protested against by Antonio as futile—give place to the jeers of Gratiano and the irony of the fair judge. Gratiano is not the only one to crow. 'Thou shalt have justice, more than thou desir'st—Soft! The Jew shall have all justice—Why doth the Jew pause? Take thy forfeiture—Tarry, Jew; the law hath yet another hold on you—Art thou contented, Jew? What dost thou say?' Aimed at Shylock as he pleads and squirms, these words fall from lips which had a moment before extolled the heavenly qualities of mercy! But for more than the meagre mercy which Shylock is shown there is neither time nor place, the crowing fits the latter part of the action as perfectly as the indignant comment had fitted the earlier, and we must equally accept it or divest the scene of meaning and sense. The Jew's very words are echoed by Portia and Gratiano as they jeer, and at every turn that the course of justice takes (welcomed by Shylock, while it was in his favour, with hoarse cries of gloating and triumph) there are now peals and shouts of laughter, such laughter as arises when Tartuffe the hypocrite is caught by Orgon,—'un rire se lève de tous les coins de la salle, un rire de vengeance si vous voulez, un rire amer, un rire violent.' The running fire assails him to the very moment—and beyond it—that Shylock says he is not well, and staggers out, amid Gratiano's jeers touching his baptism, to provoke in the audience the laughter of triumph and vengeance in his own day and bring tears to their eyes in ours. How can we here for a moment sympathize with Shylock unless at the same time we indignantly turn, not only against Gratiano, but against Portia, the Duke, and all Venice as well? But Shakespeare's scene it is—Shakespeare's comedy,—not ours or Hazlitt's.

One reason why the critics have, despite all, even in this scene, found pathos in Shylock, is that they well know that comic effects may keep company with the pathetic, in Shakespeare as in Dostoevsky and Chekhov. They remember Mercutio's last words, Mrs Quickly's report of Falstaff's death, or the Fool's babblings in *King Lear*. Laughter may indeed blend with tears when the character is treated tenderly; but here and in the daughter-ducats scene it is, as I have said, only the laughter of derision. In the judgment scene, moreover, there is—very clearly marked—the spirit of retaliation; it is a harsh and vindictive laughter; and if Shakespeare had here intended any minor and momentary pathetic effects such as critics nowadays discover, he simply overwhelms them. Professor Matthews says that Shakespeare meant the spectators to hate Shylock and also to laugh at him, and yet made him pathetic—supremely pathetic too. The combination seems to me impossible, at least in a comedy, and Professor Matthews seems to me to be talking metaphysics and forgetting the stage which he knows so well. If hateful, Shylock would provoke in the audience the *rire de vengeance*, an echo of Gratiano's jeer; if pathetic also, he would—and should—provoke no laughter (at least of such kind as is known to me) at all. In comedy, at any rate, things must be simple and clear-cut; a character which is to provoke laughter cannot be kept, like Buridan's ass, in equilibrium, exciting, at the same time, both sympathy and hatred. For then the audience will keep its equilibrium too.

G. WILSON KNIGHT

The Writing of ''Pericles''

The problems raised by *Pericles* are unique. In no other Shakespearian play do we find to stark a contrast of (i) scenes of supreme power and beauty with (ii) scenes which no one can accept as Shakespeare's without disquietude. Two more facts must be faced: the first, that the play seems to have been extremely popular; the second, that it alone of the accepted canon was omitted from the First Folio.

The most questionable scenes, which occur early, are strange both in matter and in manner. The first, showing Pericles' suit for the hand of Antiochus' daughter and his reading of the riddle, is peculiar enough; what dramatic interest is raised sags soon after and it is hard to follow his later fears and successive flights with the requisite interest. The verse, too, is troublesome. The thought is clear and pointed, but the language seems weak; at the best, it lacks colloquial grip and condensed power and at the worst sounds like apprentice work; there are few striking metaphors, and rhyme bulks large. One begins by suspecting another hand, or wondering if Shakespeare is revising a script of his own dating back to the time of *The Two Gentlemen of Verona*, a manner suggested by Pericles' first lines:

> I have, Antiochus, and, with a soul
> Embolden'd with the glory of her praise,
> Think death no hazard in this enterprise.
> (I. i. 3)

Often one suspects the text which may be faulty. And yet, as against these suspicions, we are forced to recognize that everything is organic in

From *The Crown of Life*. Copyright © 1948 by Methuen & Co., Ltd.

story-value; more, that each scene, indeed the early scenes as a single unit, are imaginatively coherent, and the peculiar manner, on the whole, sustained. Moreover, little occurs that is indisputably unauthentic, and the thoughts at least, and even the action, recall other Shakespearian plays. Occasionally we meet lines that sound like late writing of the normal kind. Later, we have long sequences of apparently mature Shakespeare between work of the doubtful sort. The court scenes at Tarsus and Pentapolis are full of strange, often rhymed, rather formal, verse, but Pericles' arrival on the shore of Pentapolis in Act II, with its accompanying storm-poetry and fisherman's talk, has the Shakespearian stamp. Even the queer scenes seem to grow in power, perhaps because one gets acclimatized; after Act I one is less inclined to doubt, and from Act III onwards there is little but superlative, even for Shakespeare, strength. Finally, after a number of re-readings one begins to suspect some especial purpose in the passages of stilted verse, lending themselves, as they do, to semi-didactic comment and generalized statement. The style is often gnomic.

. . . The events are linked by Gower who directs us with a series of choric speeches, the story of *Pericles* having been contained in Gower's *Confessio Amantis*. How far the attempts at archaic phraseology are successful may be questioned; and so may the poetic value of these speeches in general; but, since their quaintness is clearly deliberate, and since they are crammed with typical Shakespearian imagery of tempests and wreck in association with 'fortune', they may be allowed to pass.

We start with Pericles' suit for Antiochus' daughter, who enters 'apparell'd like the spring' and appears a dazzling creature of intelligence, virtue and honour (I. i. 12–14). Pericles' praise is extravagant. But there is in it something a trifle feverish; it is the result more of fascination, almost lust, than love, resembling Orsino's passion for Olivia:

> You gods, that made me man, and sway in love,
> That hath inflam'd desire in my breast
> To taste the fruit of yon celestial tree
> Or die in the adventure, be my helps,
> As I am son and servant to your will,
> To compass such a boundless happiness!
>
> (I. i. 19)

The weak conclusion is certainly reminiscent of Shakespeare's early writing, but the speech is subtle enough. Notice the speaker's self-defence, not unusual in lust, attributing it, with some justice, to instinct divinely implanted. The image in the third line recalls certain passages in Dante, so fine an expert in the subtleties of the good and evil in human desire. The thing aimed at is specifically dangerous. Antiochus warns Pericles that the lady is a 'fair Hesperides' with 'golden fruit', guarded by 'death-like dragons' (I. i. 27–9). He continues with reminders of former suitors whose 'dead cheeks'—like those in Keats' *Belle Dame Sans Merci*—advise him to 'desist' from this mad engagement with death (I. i. 34–40). Pericles' suit is to depend on his solving of a riddle and failure means death; so, as it turns out, does success too, since the riddle concerns the lady's incestuous relationship with her father, a powerful and wicked king who will not tolerate his secret's discovery.

Our hero's adventure is a plunge into sin and death closely associated with ravishing desire. He has not actively sinned, except in giving way to a lustful and cheating fantasy, but the result is immersion into an experience of evil with accompanying disgust and danger. It is a fall in the theological sense. His eyes are now opened to 'this glorious casket stor'd with ill'; he has found 'sin' within the thing of beauty:

> You're a fair viol, and your sense the strings,
> Who, finger'd to make men his lawful music,
> Would draw heaven down and all the gods to hearken;
> But being play'd upon before your time,
> Hell only danceth at so harsh a chime.
>
> (I. i. 76–85)

The phraseology is intensely impregnated with moral and theological concepts ('lawful', 'heaven', 'gods', 'hell'). The evil exposed is a denial of a 'lawful music'; of the harmony of human marriage and procreation defined in Sonnet VIII, where father, mother, and child are described as making a single music. The creative order has been mutilated and hence the oblique confusions of the riddle itself:

> I am no viper, yet I feed
> On mother's flesh which did me breed;
> I sought a husband, in which labour
> I found that kindness in a father.
> He's father, son, and husband mild,
> I mother, wife, and yet his child.
> How they may be and yet in two,
> As you will live, resolve it you.
>
> (I. i. 64)

Shakespeare's final work is aptly heralded by this inversion of that creative mystery which is to be from now on its emphatic and repeated theme. The poetry denounces this obscenity with thoughts of 'foul incest' (I. i. 126)

and 'serpents' who breed poison and sweet flowers (I. i. 132–3). The black
evil suggests *Lucrece* and *Macbeth*:

> Murder's as near to lust as flame to smoke
> Poison and treason are the hands of sin . . .
> (I. i. 138)

So Pericles flees from Antioch to escape the King's vengeance.

The short scene is clearly important. Though the verse may at
moments recall Shakespeare's early manner, the philosophical impact lies
clearly in advance of it. Moreover, the rhymed or otherwise stilted
sequences suit the intention of the miniature 'morality'. The meaning is
generalized: the King is less man than ogre, the lady less a lady than a
ravishing *thing*: she is not even given a name, and her entry to music is
correspondingly formal. The whole scene is a moral on the dangers
attending visual lust and recalls the moral undertones of the casket-scene
in *The Merchant of Venice*, with its song on 'fancy' bred 'in the eyes' (*The
Merchant of Venice*, III. ii. 63; cp. 'eye' in our *Pericles* scene at I. i. 32), the
lesson there of the golden casket containing a skull corresponding here to
'this glorious casket stor'd with ill' (I. i. 77). In both plays failure to read
the riddles concerned is to be punished, the penalty in *Pericles* being death.
The scene is impregnated with a grimness of intention surpassing anything in the earlier play, the antinomy of good and evil transcended in
Antony and Cleopatra being now again powerfully distinct: the unity has
fallen apart, as is, in the new style of myth-making, necessary, since that
fine immediacy and coalescence is to be henceforth strung out again into
narrative sequence. A further, semi-social, criticism of Antiochus as tyrant
gives us a line or two of Shakespeare's mature best:

> The blind mole casts
> Copp'd hills towards heaven, to tell the earth is throng'd
> By man's oppression; and the poor worm doth die for't.
> (I. i. 100)

The speech continues with gnomic rhymes: we have no choice but to
accept the poetic amalgam as it stands.

After escaping to Tyre, Pericles is struck down with melan-
cholia. He has had a blasting experience, not unlike Hamlet's, both
suffering through knowledge of incest in one they love and falling into
a mysterious gloom:

> Why should this change of thoughts
> The sad companion, dull-ey'd melancholy,
> Be my so us'd a guest, as not an hour

In the day's glorious walk or peaceful night—
The tomb where grief should sleep—can breed me quiet ?

(I. ii. 1)

Pleasures 'court' his eye, but, like Hamlet ('I have of late, but wherefore I know not . . .'—*Hamlet*, II. ii. 313), he cannot enjoy them. His fear of Antiochus is, he half knows, irrational; and yet he realizes that his silence will be, like Hamlet's, an ever-living threat: Antiochus 'will think me speaking though I swear to silence' (I. ii. 19). His vague foreboding (like the Queen's at *Richard II*, II. ii. 1–72), burdened by fear and horror, expresses itself in such phrases as 'black as incest' (1. ii. 76) and ' his bed of blackness' (I. ii. 89). He seems to feel guilt, yet is uncertain how far the 'offence' is his own (I. ii. 92). The experience transmitted is both subtle and powerful, though the verse often remains, comparatively, weak:

And what may make him blush in being known,
He'll stop the course by which it might be known . . .

(I. ii. 22)

That does not sound like late Shakespeare. There is a dialogue between Pericles and Helicanus containing typical Shakespearian thoughts on flattery, but couched in a poetry at its best recalling the early histories:

If there be such a dart in princes' frowns
How durst thy tongue move anger to our face?

(I. ii. 53)

However, the sequence of emotions and events moves with steady assurance.

So Pericles sets out on his journeys. His first action is to be one of charity: he seems to make deliberately for Tarsus (I. iv. 88), which is suffering from a severe famine, with ships laden with provisions. Before his arrival we meet Cleon and Dionyza, the king and queen, moralizing on their misfortunes:

CLEON: This Tarsus, o'er which I have the government,
    A city on whom plenty held full hand,
    For riches strew'd herself even in the streets;
    Whose towers bore heads so high they kiss'd the
                                                clouds,
    And strangers ne'er beheld but wonder'd at;
    Whose men and dames so jetted and adorn'd,
    Like one another's glass to trim them by:
    Their tables were stor'd full to glad the sight,
    And not so much to feed on as delight;
    All poverty was scorn'd, and pride so great,
    The name of help grew odious to repeat.

DIONYZA: O! 'tis too true.
CLEON: But see what heaven can do! . . .
(I. iv. 21)

He continues with an extraordinary account of past luxuries and present necessity, saying how parents are ready to eat their erstwhile pampered babies, the passage driving home a contrast of superficial luxury and basic need. Such is heaven's judgement on man's wickedness:

O! let those cities that of plenty's cup
And her prosperities so largely taste,
With their superfluous riots hear these tears:
The misery of Tarsus may be theirs.
(I. iv. 52)

'Superfluous' directly reminds us of Lear's

Take physic, pomp;
Expose thyself to feel what wretches feel,
That thou may'st shake the superflux to them,
And show the heavens more just.
(*King Lear*, III. iv. 33)

or Gloucester's:

Heavens, deal so still!
Let the superfluous and lust-dieted man,
That slaves your ordinance, that will not see
Because he does not feel, feel your power quickly.
(*King Lear*, IV. i. 67)

The similarity in thought is as striking as the divergence in style: we are aware of profundity crudely expressed. Here the semi-gnomic stiffness suggests the kind of weakness critics have complained of in the verse Shakespeare allows to his gods and goddesses (e.g. Hymen, Hecate, Diana, Jupiter); which raises yet further possibilities.

On Pericles' appearance, they fear that his ships signify some hostile invasion taking advantage of their own weakness, but instead find an act of pure charity, Pericles disclaiming all protestations of 'reverence' and asking only for 'love' (I. iv. 99). Gratitude is poured on him and a statue set up in his honour (II. chor. 14). His own misfortunes have been used to relieve the sufferings of others (cp. *Romeo and Juliet*, V. i. 84 and V. iii. 42; *King Lear*, IV. i. 65–72). The scene, moralistic from the start, has turned into a little morality drama on the theme of good works and indeed recalls the parable of the ungrateful man in the New Testament; for, after being let off by Providence functioning through Pericles' charity, Cleon and Dionyza are to prove criminally ungrateful.

News of Antiochus' continued persecution makes a longer stay unsafe and Pericles leaves Tarsus. We have already in typical Shakespearian manner been introduced to tempests. A tyrant's revenge was a 'tempest' at I. ii. 98. Sea-voyages are here considered all but suicidal. Pericles when setting out from Tyre was spoken of as putting himself

> unto the shipman's toil
> With whom each minute threatens life or death.
> (I. iii. 24)

Thaliard, commissioned to murder him, takes it for granted that he has 'scap'd the land to perish at the sea' (I. iii. 29). Now, when Pericles again dares the waters, Fortune, in spite of his recent good works, is cruel. Gower describes how he puts forth into the dangers of ocean and is stricken by a thunderous tempest and roaring seas; how his ship is 'wrack'd and split' and the 'good prince' driven from shore to shore till the spite of 'Fortune' is satiated (II. chor. 27–38). Through the attempt at archaic language a typically Shakespearian range of thought, imagery, and phraseology is apparent. Pericles is cast up at Pentapolis.

The opening of Act II brings us closer than ever before to the Shakespearian tempest: we have, as it were, a close-up of this persistent terror that has for so long burdened the poet's imagination. Pericles enters 'wet' and speaks in the usual tradition:

> Yet cease your ire, you angry stars of heaven!
> Wind, rain, and thunder, remember, earthly man
> Is but a substance that must yield to you.
> Alas! the sea hath cast me on the rocks,
> Wash'd me from shore to shore, and left me breath
> Nothing to think on but ensuing death:
> Let it suffice the greatness of your powers
> To have bereft a prince of all his fortunes;
> And having thrown him from your watery grave,
> Here to have death in peace is all he'll crave.
> (II. i. 1)

The accent is clearly Shakespearian, though even here the virile tempest-verse tails off into rhyme. Notice that the elements are directly humanized as divine powers. We are made to feel that the hero has endured a series of trials and buffetings; in him mortality is getting a rough passage. The implications are again general. The speech says crisply in Shakespearian terms, 'Tragedy': that is its function.

The following fishermen's dialogue preserves, in a different vein, the high standard of the opening. . . .

THIRD FISHERMAN: Faith, master, I am thinking of the poor men that
  were cast away before us even now.
FIRST FISHERMAN: Alas! poor souls; it grieved my heart to hear what
  pitiful cries they made to us to help them, when, well-a-day, we
  could scarce help ourselves.

(II. i. 18)

The simple men are philosophical as well as sympathetic, and their
humour shows a moralizing depth unknown to Shakespeare's earlier prose
rustics. One of them, marvelling 'how the fishes live in the sea', is
answered:

Why, as men do a-land; the great ones eat up the little ones; I can
compare our rich misers to nothing so fitly as to a whale; a' plays and
tumbles, driving the poor fry before him, and at last devours them all
at a mouthful. Such whales have I heard on o' the land, who never
leave gaping till they've swallowed the whole parish, church, steeple,
bells and all.

(II. i. 31)

'A pretty moral', says Pericles, aside (II. i. 39), and continues with a comment that would, with the necessary adaptation, have well suited the
gardener's comparison in *Richard II* (III. iv.) of state-affairs to his own
humble profession, perhaps our nearest equivalent to this scene, though
there given verse, partly to suit the wholly serious intention. This is
Pericles' remark:

How from the finny subject of the sea
These fishers tell the infirmities of men;
And from their watery empire recollect
All that men may approve or men detect!
(II. i. 53)

Notice again the stiff, gnomic, rhyme, here clearly fused with a Shakespearian comment in a purely Shakespearian scene.

Pericles introduces himself in terms of the clearest tragic generality as

A man whom both the waters and the wind,
In that vast tennis-court, have made the ball
For them to play upon, entreats you pity him;
He asks of you that never us'd to beg.
(II. i. 64)

The metaphor (to which the nearest Shakespearian equivalent occurs at
King Lear, IV. i. 36–7) is that of *The Duchess of Malfi*:

> We are merely the stars' tennis-balls, struck and bandied
> Which way please them.
>
> (IV. iv. 63)

There follows more satire from the Fishermen on those (like Autolycus in *The Winnter's Tale*) who make a better living out of begging than any workers, with comic play on the words 'beg' and 'crave'. Pericles speaks lines of strongest sinew:

> A man throng'd up with cold, my veins are chill,
> And have no more of life than may suffice
> To give my tongue that heat to ask your help . . .
>
> (II. i. 78)

which again, however, tail off into a limp couplet. The warmhearted men invite him to share their simple life and its homely comforts, the general warmth and kindliness overtopping both humour and satire. Sometimes Shakespearian comedy is dull, the play on words tedious, the satiric arrows too particular for a later age; here the humour is obvious and the thrusts general. Pericles words for us a natural response: 'How well this honest mirth becomes their labour!' (II. i. 102). The scene is more than comic relief; its social philosophy is organic to the play's moralistic thinking. The king here is 'the good Simonides' (II. i. 107):

> PERICLES: The good King Simonides do you call him?
> FIRST FISHERMAN: Ay, sir; and he deserves to be so called for his
>   peaceable reign and good government.
> PERICLES: He is a happy king, since he gains from his subjects the name
>   of good by his government.
>
> (II. i. 108)

The statement serves to crystallize the sense already transmitted of simple honesty and wisdom: we are in a good community. The society is not levelled, but the men are as happy and rich-hearted in their station as the King in his. This one always feels about Shakespeare's rustics, but never before was the expression so purposeful.

Pericles hears of the tournament to be held for the hand of the King's daughter, and there follows the chance discovery in the fishermen's net of Pericles' armour:

> Help, master, help! here's a fish hangs in the net, like a poor man's right
> in the law; 'twil hardly come out. Ha! bots on't, 'tis come at last, and
> 'tis turned to a rusy armour.
>
> (II. i. 126)

It is poetically important that these simple fisher-folk are the means of
Pericles' retrieving of his fortune and that the sea itself should so mysteri-
ously redeem its cruelty by this sudden shift of favour. The equation
sea-fortune, hinted throughout Shakespeare, is in *Pericles* emphatic and
obvious. The rhythm of events, nearly all concerned with 'fortune' and
the sea, is a pretty clear reading of the shifts of chance in human
existence:

> Thanks, Fortune, yet, that after all my crosses
> Thou giv'st me somewhat to repair myself . . .
>   (II. i. 131)

Again:

> It kept where I kept, I so dearly lov'd it;
> Till the rough seas, that spare not any man,
> Took it in rage, though calm'd they have given't again.
> I thank thee for't; my shipwrack now's no ill
> Since I have here my father's gift in's will.
>   (II. i. 140)

The accent is Shakespearian (cp. 'though calm'd . . . again' with *The
Tempest*, II. i. 259) though the end rhyme, as before, falls limp. Pericles
decides to try his luck at court. There is a last happy touch in the
Fisherman's hint:

> Ay, but hark you, my friend; 'twas we that made up this garment
> through the rough seams of the water; there are certain condolements,
> certain vails [-gratuities]. I hope, sir, if you thrive, you'll remember from
> whence you had it.
>   (II. i. 160)

Pericles' concluding words, though picturesque, are rather trivial:

> Unto thy value will I mount myself
> Upon a courser whose *delightful* steps
> Shall make the gazer joy to see him tread.
>   (II. i. 169)

The weak adjectival emphasis—noticeable elsewhere in these early scenes—
might be Greene's, or even Marlowe's, or from a young Shakespeare,
younger than any of which we have record, in imitation; or again, they
may conceivably be mature Shakespeare, looking, in this tentative play,
for new things, setting himself in a new-old manner for some specific
purpose.

   The court of the good Simonides scarcely offers anything of equivalent interest to the Fishermen's conversation, but its atmosphere is well realized, and the events important. The verse, and much else, is formal and the rhymes often awkward. The stage-formality itself seems here more important than the verse; as when the various knights pass across with their devices and mottoes. The importance of such ceremonial grows throughout Shakespeare's final period, its nature being here satisfactorily captured by Malone's direction:

> A Public Way. Platform leading to the Lists. A Pavilion near it, for the reception of the King, Princess, Ladies, Lords, etc.
>
> (II. ii)

The jousting is done off-stage, as in *Richard II*, and we move to feasting, music and dance after the manner of *Romeo and Juliet* and *Timon of Athens*.

We are continually pointed to Pericles' appearance of lowness and poverty. The other knights' blazonings are spectacular: a 'black Ethiop' against a 'sun', a knight pictured as overthrown by a lady, a 'wreath of chivalry', 'a burning torch', a hand surrounded by clouds and holding gold. Pericles' 'present' (probably the actual thing, not merely a device) is 'a wither'd branch, that's only green on top' (II. ii. 16–44). The courtiers remark on his rusty armour and rude appearance, suggesting that he seems more at home with the 'whipstock' than the lance (II. ii. 51). He is at the best 'a country gentlemen' (II. iii. 33), regarded rather as is Posthumus in *Cymbeline*, though he meets a worthier acceptance, for the good Simonides is, unlike Cymbeline, not to be deceived by appearances:

> Opinion's but a fool, that makes us scan
> The outward habit by the inward man.
> (II. ii. 56)

Where the thought is clear enough, whatever may be wrong with the seemingly transposed phraseology. Others take their example from the King:

> Contend not, sir; for we are gentlemen
> That neither in our hearts nor outward eyes
> Envy the great nor do the low despise.
> (II. iii. 24)

King Simonides is always moralizing, often in gnomic rhyme, warning his daughter Thaisa of the duties incumbent on princes if they are to hold their subjects' respect (II. ii. 10–13), and asserting the importance of honour, that is, the interchange of courtesies after the fashion of Timon:

KNIGHTS: We are honour'd much by good Simonides.
SIMONIDES: Your presence glads our days; honour we love;
For who hates honour, hates the gods above.
(II. iii. 20)

Simonides' sentiments, in both substance and manner of expression, are directly in line with those of the King's speech on true and false honour in *All's Well that Ends Well* (II. iii. 124–51), a play whose early scenes abound in gnomic sequences very like those in *Pericles*. A near equivalent to Simonides' court will also be found in the early scenes of *Timon of Athens*, where there are more analogies to the strangely stilted language of *Pericles*, both in Timon's moralizing and Apemantus' proverb-like commentary. In both plays we have a firm sense of (i) true worth as independent of social rank and (ii) the duties incumbent on high position: our court scenes follow organically on the fishermen's talk. The thought, too, recalls the two contrasted uses of gold in the early and late acts of *Timon*, and its two directions (the casket and wealthy heiress) in *The Merchant of Venice*. Simonides' remark on the folly of reading worth by outward appearances is directly in line with Bassanio's:

So may the outward shows he least themselves;
The world is still deceived by ornament.
(*The Merchant of Venice*, II. ii. 73)

This truth, which is indeed a central truth throughout Shakespeare, is here dramatically lived before us, since Pericles, poor as he appears, is really a king.

Indeed, the most insistent impressionistic recurrence in *Pericles*, except for the sea-voyages, concerns the balancing of true and false values. We started with Pericles' infatuation for a deceptive beauty compared to the golden apples of the Hesperides (I. i. 27) and turning out to be, like Morocco's choice, a 'glorious casket stor'd with ill' (I. i. 77). We moved next to the paradox of Tarsus once so wealthy with people overdressed and bejewelled and their food arranged more to please the eye—cp. again 'eyes' in the Fancy-song of the *Merchant of Venice* (III. ii. 63)—than the taste (I. iv. 21–9), but now brought low by savage hunger; brought, that is, to realize its ultimate dependence; brought up against basic fact; such fact as is the natural air breathed by the admirable fishermen of Pentapolis.

Always in Shakespeare riches (gold, jewels, rich clothes, etc.) have two possible meanings: they may be shown as in themselves deceptive or they may, by metaphor, be used to reflect an essential good. So the rusty armour that had so often defended Pericles' father is compared to a 'jewel' (II. i. 168) and princes are like 'jewels' which need keeping bright to deserve respect (II. ii. 12). And now—since we have brought our list up to date—when Thaisa begins to fall in love with Pericles she says: 'To me he seems like diamond to glass' (II. iii. 36). The comparison of a loved person to a rich stone is, of course, among the most frequent of Shakespeare's habitual correspondences (e.g. *Romeo and Juliet*, I. v. 50; *Troilus and Cressida*, I. i. 105; *Othello*, V. ii. 346). Later—to push ahead in our narrative—courtiers round a sovereign are as 'diamonds' about a 'crown' (II. iv. 53). There is, too, a peculiarly interesting example of the reverse, ironic, use, when the 'high gods', sick of Antiochus' wickedness, let loose their 'vengeance':

> Even in the height and pride of all his glory,
> When he was seated in a chariot
> Of an inestimable value, and his daughter with him,
> A fire from heaven came and shrivell'd up
> Their bodies, even to loathing; for they so stunk,
> That all those eyes ador'd them ere their fall
> Scorn now their hand should give them burial.
>
> (II. iv. 6)

The passage renders actual the contrast of glorious appearance with inward pollution which first started Pericles on his wanderings. Of all our moralizings this passage, so strongly reminiscent of Greek tragedy, is the crown.

To return to Pericles' fortunes at the court of Simonides. Having proved victorious in the tournament, he is crowned with 'a wreath of victory' (II. iii. 10) by Thaisa who functions as 'queen o' the feast' (II. iii. 17), like Perdita in *The Winter's Tale*, with Simonides playing the kindly over-lord, and reminding her, as her father reminds Perdita, of her duties. Pericles remains very quiet—he is now extraordinarily humble—and meditative, comparing the King to his own father, once just such a 'sun' surrounded by star-princes, though he himself has fallen to the glimmerings of a 'glow-worm', and drawing therefrom the moral:

> Whereby I see that Time's the king of men;
> He's both their parent, and he is their grave,
> And gives them what he will, not what they crave.
>
> (II. iii. 37–45)

Twice (II. iii. 54, 91) Pericles' especial melancholy is noted. Simonides, a jovial host after the manner of Old Capulet and Wolsey, is worried, and urges on Thaisa her responsibilities:

> Princes in this should live like gods above,
> Who freely give to every one that comes
> To honour them . . .
>
> (II. iii. 59)

Prompted by her father she questions Pericles, with whom she has fallen in love: her bashfulness in approach is delicately managed. The scene works up to a dance. The whole situation is dominated by Simonides: kingly, courteous, moralistic, and jovial.

Simonides next dismisses all the suitors but Pericles, telling them that Thaisa has sworn 'by the eye of Cynthia' (II. v. 11) that she will wear 'Diana's livery' (II. v. 10) for a whole year: our first mention of the goddess, who is to assume such importance later. Simonides enjoys not only his ruse but also his daughter's self-willed determination, expressed in a letter, to marry Pericles or no one, the long story of Shakespeare's tyrannic fathers from Capulet to Lear being most delightfully reversed. Simonides admires the stranger-knight who is clearly a man trained 'in arts and arms' (II. iii. 82), winning the tournament and showing himself both a skillful dancer (II. iii. 102–9) and a skilled musician:

> I am beholding to you
> For your sweet music this last night; I do
> Protest my ears were never better fed
> With such delightful pleasing harmony.
>
> (II. v. 25)

True, the adjectival verse sounds most unlike late Shakespeare, but it is followed at once by:

PERICLES: It is your Grace's pleasure to commend, Not my desert.
SIMONIDES: Sir, you are music's master.
PERICLES: The worst of all her scholars, my good lord.

> (II. v. 29)

Which no one will question. Pericles is conceived as the perfect courtier (as defined by Castiglione) and even his tourneying praised as art:

> In framing an artist art hath thus decreed,
> To make some good, but others to exceed,
> And you're her labour'd scholar.
>
> (II. iii. 15)

Music is regularly in Shakespeare the antagonist to tempests; and Simonides' peaceful court thinks automatically in artistic terms. Indeed, there are in *Pericles* many noticeable artistic emphases, some of a new sort to be observed later; and all blend with the moralistic tone of thought, the ceremonious directions, and even the stilted, and often questionable, formality of the verse. Art, as such, seems to be getting a more self-conscious attention than is usual; which is scarcely surprising in a play where the myth-making fantasy seems, as in the recurring voyages, to be functioning with a new freedom.

Pericles remains humble, and when confronted with Thaisa's letter by the supposedly irate father asserts that he never dreamed of aiming so high. Like Prospero, Simonides keeps up the pretence of harshness, accusing him, as Ferdinand is accused, of treachery. So the scene is driven to its delightful conclusion:

> Therefore, hear you, mistress; either frame
> Your will to mine; and you, sir, hear you—
> Either be ruled by me or I will make you—
> Man and wife.
>
> (II. v. 81)

Simonides is a grand person and the scenes at his court, though blemished seriously by old play incorporations, bits of immature or hurried writing, faulty texts or evidences of genius at a loss—exact decision is impossible—remain of the highest Shakespearian standard in stage-organization, human delineation (Simonides and Thaisa), and the depicting of a chivalrous society (after the pattern of Theseus in A Midsummer Night's Dream and Timon in Timon of Athens). The neat, semi-humorous overturning of a tragic situation to reveal kindliness and joy is a clear precurser of other more important reversals in Pericles and later plays: while the rewarding of Pericles' humility forecasts the fortunes of Cranmer in Henry VIII.

Pericles' story has clearly been forming itself into a significant design. His first adventure was one of semi-adolescent fantasy bringing him up sharply against disillusion and a realization of evil; he next won merit by charitable deeds; was again rebuffed by fortune, only to find himself on the shores of a hospitable community rich in social wisdom and artistic feeling; and so to a love affair characterized not by daring and aspiration (as was the other) but by a profound humility and crowned with unexpected success. We are watching something like a parable of human fortune, with strong moral import at every turn.

Act III is introduced by a striking chorus, describing the still house after the marriage-banquet, the silence broken only by heavy snores and crickets at the 'oven's mouth':

> The cat, with eyne of burning coal,
> Now couches fore the mouse's hole . . .
>
> (III. chor. 5–8)

The association of marriage-feast, midnight and the sleeping house recalls the final scene of A Midsummer Night's Dream, though nothing there quite

touches the warm realism of our short passage, which has a fine Shakespearian ring. The bride is 'brought to bed' by 'Hymen' (III. chor. 9). There
follows a dumb-show depicting Thaisa 'with child'. After revealing his
royal identity Pericles sets sail, with his queen, for home; but the voyage is
ill-starred:

> And so to sea. Their vessel shakes
> On Neptune's billow; half the flood
> Hath their keel cut; but Fortune's mood
> Varies again; the grisled north
> Disgorges such a tempest forth,
> That, as a duck for life that dives,
> So up and down the poor ship drives.
>
> (III. chor. 44)

The action next opens with Pericles on ship-board addressing the storm.
Sea-tempest, so long a favourite image, and brought so near to us in Act
II, has become at last the focus of dramatic action, and never before was it
given such poetic thunder as in Pericles' opening lines:

> Thou God of this great vast, rebuke these surges,
> Which wash both heaven and hell; and thou, that hast
> Upon the winds command, bind them in brass,
> Having call'd them from the deep. O! still
> Thy deafening, dreadful thunders; gently quench
> Thy nimble, sulphurous flashes. O! how Lychorida,
> How does my queen? Thou stormest venomously;
> Wilt thou spit all thyself? The seaman's whistle
> Is as a whisper in the ears of death,
> Unheard. Lychorida! Lucina, O!
> Divinest patroness, and midwife gentle
> To those that cry by night, convey thy deity
> Aboard our dancing boat; make swift the pangs
> Of my queen's travails!
>
> (III. i. 1)

The nurse brings the child with news of its mother's death:

> O you gods!
> Why do you make us love your goodly gifts,
> And snatch them straight away?
>
> (III. i. 22)

Continually we are pointed to these seemingly meaningless shifts of
fortune which characterise the action. Pericles now speaks to the child
born, as it were, amid a living death, commenting on its rude welcome to
the stage of life:

Thou hast as chiding a nativity
As fire, air, water, earth, and heaven can make,
To herald thee from the womb; even at the first
Thy loss is more than can thy portage quit
With all thou can'st find here.

(III. i. 32)

Observe the exact mention of the elements, natural and divine. The
storm is generalized; the child's birth shown as an entry into the turmoils
of nature, widely understood, an entry into storm-tossed mortality recalling the crying child of old Lear's lunatic sermon (*King Lear*, IV. vi. 187);
and when the child is called 'this fresh new sea-farer' (III. i. 41) only a
response most insensitive to Shakespeare's storm-poetry in general, and
his use of it in *Pericles* in particular, will limit the meaning to the
immediate occasion. As again in *The Winter's Tale*, the association of
child and tempest holds a general, if unemphasized, implication.

The superstitious sea-men insist that Thaisa be immediately buried
at sea and Pericles, with another passage of supreme poetry, gives way:

A terrible child-bed hast thou had, my dear;
No light, no fire: the unfriendly elements
Forgot thee utterly; nor have I time
To give thee hallow'd to thy grave, but straight
Must cast thee, scarcely coffin'd, in the ooze;
Where, for a monument upon thy bones,
And aye-remaining lamps, the belching whale
And humming water must o'erwhelm thy corpse,
Lying with simple shells!

(III. i. 57)

Nowhere else does Shakespeare's sea-poetry move with quite so superb an
ease, the one word 'humming' doing more than long passages of earlier
description; as though, in this extraordinary story, with all the normal
restrictions gone, except indeed for the necessity of prime concentration
on this favourite theme, his deepest genius were enjoying a liberty hitherto unknown. Perhaps only whilst desultorily working over an old plot in
which he scarce half-believed could such unsought-for excellence have
matured. Notice that the text, when Shakespeare's hand is indisputably at
work, seems remarkably pure.

Pericles asks for spices, his 'casket' and 'jewels' (III. i. 66), and
includes them, with some writing, in the coffin, which is cast overboard.
The ship makes for Tarsus.

We move to Ephesus, where we meet Cerimon, a descendant of
Friar Laurence in *Romeo and Juliet*, deeply versed in the understanding of

mineral and vegetable properties, and indeed at home with the inmost 'disturbances that nature works and of her cures' (III. ii. 37). He is a magician, of 'secret art' (III. ii. 32), like Prospero in *The Tempest*. He is, too, noble, a man of Timon-like lustre, renowned for his generosity, who has, like Timon, 'poured forth' his charity, till 'hundreds' are indebted to his skill, personal labours, and 'purse' (III. ii. 43–8). He defines his own life-wisdom for us:

> I hold it ever,
> Virtue and cunning were endowments greater
> Than nobleness and riches; careless heirs
> May the two latter darken and expend,
> But immortality attends the former,
> Making a man a god.
>
> (III. ii. 26)

His art holds a deeper content

> Than to be thirsty after tottering honour
> Or tie my treasure up in silken bags
> To please the fool and death.
>
> (III. ii. 40)

The contrast already suggested between the substantial and the ephemeral, the real and the deceptive, is here more sharply defined and given a personal centre. Cerimon is an almost superhuman figure living out a truth expressed throughout the New Testament, as in the parable of the rich man summoned by death, and such phrases as 'the body is more than clothes', 'consider the lilies of the field'.

We meet him at night-time, called from his rest to help shipwrecked mariners, while people comment on the storm in the usual Shakespearian manner, saying how it exceeds all previous experience. When servants bring in Thaisa's coffin, Cerimon's wryly humorous comment recalls the sea's throwing up of Pericles' armour at Pentapolis:

> If the sea's stomach be o'ercharg'd with gold,
> 'Tis a good constraint of fortune it belches upon us . . .
>
> (III. ii. 54)

Gold is present, in spite of Cerimon's former repudiation, as a preliminary to the sudden disclosure of wondrous riches enclosing the sparkling richness of the supreme jewel, Thaisa. The chest has a marvellous scent: it smells 'most sweetly', with a 'delicate odour' (III. ii. 60–1), phrases pointing on to *The Winter's Tale*, III. i. 1; and *The Tempest*, II. i. 44, 49. The body itself is

> Shrouded in cloth of state; balm'd and entreasur'd
> With full bags of spices.
>
> (III. ii. 65)

Pericles' written message asks that 'this queen worth all our mundane cost' be buried in return for the 'treasure' enclosed, and for charity's sake (III. ii. 70–5). Notice how Thaisa is surrounded by clustering impressions of wealth: they are to continue.

Cerimon sets to recover her with the help of 'fire' and 'music'. He gives his orders busily, in language aptly broken by colloquial pauses:

> Death may usurp on nature many hours,
> And yet the fire of life kindle again
> The overpress'd spirits. I heard
> Of an Egyptian, that had nine hours lien dead,
> Who was by good appliances recover'd.
>
> (III. ii. 82)

The reference to an Egyptian is peculiarly apt in a scene so strongly reminiscent of the magic for which ancient Egypt was renowned. The miracle is now worked before our eyes:

> Well said, well said; the fire and cloths.
> The rough and woeful music that we have,
> Cause it to sound, beseech you.
> The viol once more;—how thou stirr'st, thou block!
> The music there! I pray you, give her air.
> Gentlemen,
> This queen will live; nature awakes, a warmth
> Breathes out of her; she hath not been entranc'd
> Above five hours. See! how she 'gins to blow
> Into life's flower again.
>
> (III. ii. 87)

Music, for so long Shakespeare's normal dramatic antithesis to tempestuous death, becomes directly implemental; and will be so again, in *The Winter's Tale*, as the agent of Hermione's release. Cerimon's skill goes beyond science, in the modern sense, resembling rather the raising of the dead in the New Testament, a reading borne out by the reaction of those who attend:

> The heavens
> Through you increase our wonder and set up
> Your fame for ever.
>
> (III. ii. 96)

Cerimon's next words mark the culmination of the imagery of jewels and riches so persistent throughout *Pericles*:

> She is alive! behold,
> Her eyelids, cases to those heavenly jewels
> Which Pericles hath lost,
> Begin to part their fringes of bright gold:
> The diamonds of a most praised water
> Do appear to make the world twice rich. Live,
> And make us weep to hear your fate, fair creature,
> Rare as you seem to be!
>
>   (III. ii. 98)

'Rare': the word is to characterize everything most wondrous in this and later plays. The original direction—pointing on, as did 'warmth' earlier, to *The Winter's Tale*—is 'she moves'. The poetic excitement is breathlessly intense: we are watching the key-incident that unlocks the whole range of Shakespeare's later work. His imagery, his poetry, dictates the action. From his earliest plays he has been deeply engaged with sea-tempests and death; with true and false appearance; with riches, real and unreal, in relation to love; and with wealth strewn on the sea's floor, the treasures it has gorged; and more than once with a jewel thrown into the sea, as a symbol of love, for ever lost; and, continually, with music as an almost mystical accompaniment of love, reunion, and joy. All are together here, as the supreme jewel, Thaisa, is given back.

Her first words are, 'O dear Diana!' (III. ii. 105). She wonders, like Lear waking after madness, where she is: 'What world is this?' (III. ii. 106). The watchers marvel at the strangeness of the act, this miracle 'most rare' (III. iii. 107). But Cerimon hushes their exclamations of wonder and removes Thaisa to a chamber of rest. Later he gives her the jewels from the chest and she, despairing of seeing her lord again, decides to take on a 'vestal livery' (III. iv. 10), and is accordingly introduced by Cerimon to Diana's temple.

We have moved very far beyond gnomic rhymes and moral precepts; beyond psychological lessons and social comment; have advanced beyond ethic altogether to a dramatic disclosure metaphysical rather than moral, indeed visionary rather than metaphysical, as we watch life blossom and glow from the very jaws of death, warmed into renewed existence by Cerimon's fire and music. This is the new thing that has come, spontaneously, from Shakespeare's novel attempt in free narrative; something quite unlike any previous incident; which yet could not, perhaps, have been born before *Antony and Cleopatra*; but which, once touched, insists on re-expression till the end.

Pericles leaves his child, called Marina because she was born at sea (III. iii. 13), with Cleon and his queen Dionyza. Cleon grieves for the 'shafts of fortune' that have so mortally attacked their former benefactor, and Pericles answers:

> We cannot but obey
> The powers above us. Could I rage and roar
> As doth the sea she lies in, yet the end
> Must be as 'tis.
>
> (III. iii. 9)

Thaisa's death is no peculiar misfortune, but rather the general fate and fact of mortality. Pericles, worn with disaster, vows 'by bright Diana', who has by now become the play's presiding deity, to leave his hair 'unscissor'd' until his daughter's marriage (III. iii. 27–9); and departs, after being recommended by Cleon to 'the mask'd Neptune and the gentlest winds of heaven' (III. iii. 36). The verse continues to maintain a high Shakespearian standard.

Marina's education at Tarsus is described in the chorus to Act IV. She is trained in both music and letters, and becomes so generally admired that she rouses the queen's jealousy on behalf of her own daughter, Philoten. The two girls work in rivalry:

> Be't when she weav'd the sleided silk
> With fingers long, small, white as milk,
> Or when she would with sharp neeld wound
> The cambric, which she made more sound
> By hurting it; when to the lute
> She sung, and made the night-bird mute,
> That still records with moan; or when
> She would with rich and constant pen
> Vail to her mistress Dian, still
> This Philoten contends in skill
> With absolute Marina . . .
>
> (IV. chor. 21)

The lines recall earlier remarks on Pericles' musical skill and dancing. Music and poetry are normal Shakespearian interests, but the emphasis on needlework is both new and, as we shall see, important. Now, jealous of Marina's excellences, the wicked mother (a forecast of the Queen in *Cymbeline*, Philoten corresponding to Cloten) engages Leonine to murder her.

Marina enters, grieving for the death of her nurse Lychorida. She bears 'a basket of flowers' and speaks lines pointing on to Perdita in *The Winter's Tale* and the burial of Fidele in *Cymbeline*:

> No, I will rob Tellus of her weed,
> To strew thy green with flowers; the yellows, blues,
> The purple violets, and marigolds,

> Shall as a carpet hang upon thy grave,
> While summer days do last. Ay me! poor maid,
> Born in a tempest, when my mother died,
> This world to me is like a lasting storm,
> Whirring me from my friends.
>
> (IV. i. 13)

'Carpet' may be tentatively referred to the new interest in arts of design that gives us Marina's needlework. The generalizing of a usual thought in the concluding lines is plain—no finer example occurs in Shakespeare—with death envisaged as the supreme separator, and therefore as tempest, tempests being continually felt elsewhere as the separators and antagonists of love. As the moment of Marina's own death seems to be approaching (she is talking with Leonine by the sea-shore) she wistfully recalls her birth:

> MARINA: Is this wind westerly that blows?
> LEONINE: South-west.
> MARINA: When I was born the wind was north.
> LEONINE: Was't so?
>
> (IV. i. 50)

She describes the storm; how Pericles galled his kingly hands at the ropes, the loss of life, the cries, the confusion. Asked again when this happened, she answers, 'When I was born' (IV. i. 58). The association of birth and tempest continues to exert strong poetic radiations.

Leonine reveals his murderous intentions, offering her, as Othello offers Desdemona, a space for prayer. The short following dialogue is rich with a peculiarly Shakespearian poignancy of emotional realism as Marina asserts her innocence and pleads for life, appalled at Leonine's impossibly wicked intention:

> I saw you lately
> When you caught hurt in parting two that fought . . .
>
> (V. i. 86)

It reminds us of Arthur and Hubert in *King John*. The situation is saved by the Pirates, whom the dramatist uses as cavalierly as he uses the bear in *The Winter's Tale*. Leonine reports to the Queen that the murder has been performed.

Dionyza is a fine study, showing the same hard-headed, unsentimental approach to crime as Lady Macbeth and Goneril. Cleon is distracted at the supposed murder, remembering Marina's virtues:

> a princess
> To equal any single crown o' the earth
> I' the justice of compare.
>
> (IV. iii. 7)

What, he asks, will his wife tell Pericles? Her reply is terse and uncompromising:

> DIONYZA: That she is dead. Nurses are not the fates
>   To foster it, nor ever to preserve.
>   She died at night; I'll say so. Who can cross it?
>   Unless you play the pious innocent,
>   And for an honest attribute cry out
>   'She died by foul play'.
> CLEON: O! go to. Well, well,
>   Of all the faults beneath the heavens, the gods
>   Do like this worst.
> DIONYZA: Be one of those that think
>   The pretty wrens of Tarsus will fly hence,
>   And open this to Pericles. I do shame
>   To think of what a noble strain you are,
>   And of how coward a spirit.
>
>   (IV. iii. 14)

Cleon answers exactly as does Macbeth when similarly taxed. The dialogue recalls, too, Goneril's scene with Albany (*King Lear*, IV. ii.), though it even exceeds earlier plays in its condensed, clarity and psychological pith. How subtly, for example, Cleon's weakness of will shows through his conscience-stricken protestations ('Well, well'.) Every phrase tells, psychologically and dramatically, till the close:

> CLEON: Thou art like the harpy,
>   Which, to betray, dost with thine angel's face,
>   Seize with thine eagle's talons.
> DIONYZA: You are like one that superstitiously
>   Doth swear to the gods that winter kills the flies;
>   But yet I know you'll do as I advise.
>
>   (IV. iii. 46)

A formal ending, perhaps; but with what a deadly formality!

In dumb-show we see Pericles coming to Tarsus, where he hears of Marina's supposed death, and reads Dionyza's hypocritical inscription, on the carefully devised monument, in the 'glittering golden characters' (IV. iii. 44) with which she disguises her 'black villainy' (IV. iv. 44): as before, we have a golden falsity and Pericles is again deceived. He suspects nothing; receives this as but another stroke of fate; vows never now to cut his hair, 'puts on sackcloth', and sets out to sea (IV. iv. 28–9). His endurance reaches its limit:

>   He bears
>   A tempest, which his mortal vessel tears,
>   And yet he rides it out.
>
>   (IV. iv. 29)

Utterly broken, he now leaves his course to 'Lady Fortune' (IV. iv. 48).

There is less necessity to speak at length of the brothel scenes at Mitylene, since their merits have been generally recognized. They recall *Measure for Measure*, with the stark contrast of purity and vice rendered sharper by bringing Marina, who corresponds (with many differences) to Isabella, actually inside the brothel and threatening her integrity. The harsh, yet often richly amusing, satire is of the finest and the persons of the Pandar, the Bawd and Boult generously realized. To this sink of iniquity Marina is sold by the pirates. The play's presiding deity, Diana, is aptly invoked:

> MARINA: If fires be hot, knives sharp, or waters deep,
> Untied I still my virgin knot will keep.
> Diana, aid my purpose!
> BAWD: What have we to do with Diana?
>
> (IV. ii. 162)

The incongruity dramatized by Marina's hideous situation is painful, but even so a fine humour matures from it. Rather like Timon with the Bandits, she converts her would-be customers, who retreat shame-faced:

> FIRST GENTLEMAN: But to have divinity preached there! Did you ever dream of such a thing?
> SECOND GENTLEMAN: No, no. Come, I am for no more bawdy-houses. Shall's go hear the vestals sing?
>
> (IV. v. 4)

She speedily ruins trade, to her employer's exasperation.

Lysimachus' visit is given a detailed presentation. He is governor of Mitylene and enters with an unpleasant bearing, but there seems no evidence that he is (as has been suggested) playing a spy-part like the Duke in *Measure for Measure*, to nose out the city's vice: rather he is a loose young man, like Bertram in *All's Well that Ends Well*, of enough wealth and power to gratify his desires at will. Marina's talk, however, soon enough converts him to a shame-faced, though untrue, asseveration:

> I did not think
> Thou couldst have spoke so well; ne'er dream'd
> thou could'st.
> Had I brought hither a corrupted mind,
> Thy speech had altered it.
>
> (IV. vi. 112)

He asserts that he 'came with no ill intent' and that to him now 'the very doors and windows savour vilely' (IV. vi. 120). Notice the emphasis on

Marina's 'speech': good-breeding in a prostitute is considered unthinkable. The incident's handling clearly assumes a conventional ethic which makes sharp distinction between masculine laxity and feminine impurity:

BOULT: ·The nobleman would have dealt with her like a nobleman, and she sent him away as cold as a snow-ball; saying his prayers too.

(IV. vi. 152)

Even Boult, left alone with Marina and charged to break down her defences, succumbs to her withering scorn. Finally she urges (in a speech whose nervous broken rhythms serve a clear purpose) her real value:

> O! that the gods
> Would safely deliver me from this place.
> Here, here's gold for thee.
> If that thy master would gain by me,
> Proclaim that I can sing, weave, sew, and dance,
> With other virtues which I'll keep from boast . . .
>
> (IV. vi. 195)

Her offer to teach succeeds triumphantly: though recalling Viola's in *Twelfth Night* (I. ii. 55–7), her profession of skill is here far more important, since Marina is, as it were, art incarnate, an emphasis already strong and now driven home by the following chorus:

> She sings like one immortal, and she dances
> As goddess-like to her admired lays;
> Deep clerks she dumbs; and with her neeld composes
> Nature's own shape, of bud, bird, branch, or berry,
> That even her art sisters the natural roses;
> Her inkle, silk, twin with the rubied cherry . . .
>
> (V. chor. 3)

Images both of melody and of design are included.

The play's last movement starts on 'God Neptune's annual feast' (V. chor. 17); an occasion, that is, or propitiation to the controlling powers. Pericles arrives on a ship with 'banners sable, trimm'd with rich expense' (V. chor. 19), recalling former imagery of riches and textile art. Malone provides an exquisitely appropriate direction:

On board Pericles' ship off Mitylene. A pavilion on deck, with a curtain before it; Pericles within it, reclined on a couch. A barge lying beside the Tyrian vessel.

(V. 1)

The contrast of peace with our earlier storm-scenes is strong. Pericles, who has not spoken for months, is in sack-cloth, with hair unshaven, fasting; a figure of grief, perhaps, in some undefined fashion, of remorse, for the fact of mortality in a universe that has robbed him of wife and child. Lysimachus sends for Marina, now famed in Mitylene for her arts and charm, to see if she can restore him.

The following action is another pinnacle of Shakespeare's art. Marina is brought to cure Pericles, as Helena cures the King in *All's Well that Ends Well*. Though she is no intentional magician, we are pointed, as with Cerimon, to a blend of divinity and art: she is to pit both her 'sacred physic' and 'utmost skill' (V. i. 74–6) against Pericles' stonelike, frozen immobility, his living death. She sings.

When Pericles awakes from his trance, she touches on her own sufferings, saying how she herself has 'endur'd a grief' that might well equal his (V. i. 88); how she is descended from a kingly stock, though brought low by 'wayward Fortune' (V. i. 90–2). Pericles, half-awake, stammeringly repeats her strange phrases. He looks in her eyes; something he half recognizes, but breaks off. We watch a re-enactment of Lear's waking to music into the presence of Cordelia. Questioned, Marina asserts that no 'shores' (i.e. land) can claim her birth, though she was 'mortally brought forth' (V. i. 104); an assurance dramatically serving to emphasize her momentary function of enacting, like Cordelia, a super-mortal presence (cp. 'Thou art a soul in bliss . . .' *King Lear*, IV. vii. 46) invading mortal grief. Pericles' interest is roused:

> I am great with woe, and shall deliver weeping.
> My dearest wife was like this maid, and such a one
> My daughter might have been: my queen's square brows;
> Her stature to an inch; as wand-like straight;
> As silver-voic'd; her eyes as jewel-like,
> And cased as richly; in pace another Juno;
> Who starves the ears she feeds, and makes them hungry,
> The more she gives them speech.
>
> (V. i. 106)

Such riches-imagery ('silver' and 'jewel') we have already discussed: the last lines descend from *Antony and Cleopatra* (II. ii. 245).

Marina incorporates both the poetic worth of Thaisa and the sacred magic of Cerimon; she is, as we have seen, all but art personified. She is that to which all art aspires, which it seeks to express:

> Prithee, speak;
> Falseness cannot come from thee, for thou look'st
> Modest as justice, and thou seem'st a palace
> For the crown'd truth to dwell in.
>
> (V. i. 121)

How finely is limned for us this spiritualized royalty, one with that delicate power, or beauty, lying behind all Shakespeare's royalistic tonings and reaching its subtlest flowering in his last works. Marina incorporates an eternal essence of personified Truth and Justice, able to awake belief in things elsewise 'impossible'; for she is herself, as Pericles observes, an image of one formerly 'lov'd', but now miraculously, it would seem, alive (V. i. 124–7).

Our lines have already suggested a painting, or, more probably, a statue, a work of still, yet pulsing, intellectual, life; Yeats' 'monuments of unaging intellect' in *Sailing to Byzantium*. Monumental art is Shakespeare's normal approach to eternity, though his earlier use of it has been sparing and tentative. We have already had two statues here; one to honour Pericles (II. chor. 14) and another with an inscription of 'glittering golden characters' in memory of Marina (IV. iii. 44; iv. 34), both at Tarsus. Yet more potent was the heart-seizing transference of 'monument' and 'aye-remaining lamps' to the glimmering ocean depths of Thaisa's burial (III. i. 62–3). And now comes the supreme and final expression:

> Tell thy story;
> If thine consider'd prove the thousandth part
> Of my endurance, thou art a man, and I
> Have suffer'd like a girl; yet thou dost look
> Like Patience gazing on kings' graves, and smiling
> Extremity out of act.
>
> (V. i. 136)

We remember Viola's 'Patience on a monument smiling at grief' (*Twelfth Night*, II. iv. 116); but these lines hold a deeper penetration. The whole world of great tragedy ('kings graves') is subdued to an over-watching figure, like Cordelia's love by the bedside of Lear's sleep. 'Extremity', that is disaster in all its finality (with perhaps a further suggestion of endless time), is therefore negated, put out of action, by a serene assurance corresponding to St. Paul's certainty in 'O death, where is thy sting?' Patience is here an all-enduring calm seeing *through* tragedy to the end; smiling through endless death to ever-living eternity.

And yet there is nothing inflexible, inhuman, about Marina: she remains at every instant a natural girl. Learning her name, Pericles, again like Lear, thinks he is being mocked, fears lest some 'incensed god' aims to make the world 'laugh' at him (V. i. 145). The paradox grows more intense. This amazing presence is yet human, a living girl:

> But are you flesh and blood?
> Have you a working pulse? and are no fairy?

> Motion!—Well; speak on. Where were you born?
> And wherefore call'd Marina?
>
> (V. i. 154)

Life, as in Hermione in *The Winter's Tale*, breathes from the statued calm. There is more talk of her birth at sea (V. i. 158). Pericles thinks it all a deceitful dream (like that described so poignantly by Caliban in *The Tempest*):

> O! Stop there a little.
> This is the rarest dream that e'er dull sleep
> Did mock sad fools withal; this cannot be.
> My daughter's buried . . .
>
> (V. i. 162)

He controls himself; asks her to continue; tries, with an effort, to talk reasonably. She recounts the attempt to murder her and her subsequent adventures. Her survival is, of course, given a perfectly water-tight realism. On the plane of logical statement nothing unique has occurred, but such logic has at best a secondary importance in drama. It is what we momentarily live, not what we remember, that counts. Here the experience dramatized is one of a gradual unfurling; an awakening to discovery of life where death seemed certain. The plot has been manipulated specifically to generate this peculiar experience, which next quite bursts its boundaries, and, expanding beyond, automatically clothes itself in semi-transcendental phraseology. The story is, anyway, a fiction; its threaded events, even less than in most stories, count for little; all depends on what the poet makes of them. The most realistic tension in the whole play comes at these moments of amazing tragic reversal, at the restoration of Thaisa by Cerimon and the amazing impact of Marina's survival. In both we attend the unveiling of death from off the features of life: this it is which generates the unique excitement. The discovery is elaborately delayed, expanded, played upon, allowed to grow more and more certain till no doubt remains:

> O Helicanus! strike me, honour'd sir;
> Give me a gash, put me to present pain,
> Lest this great sea of joys rushing upon me
> O'erbear the shores of my mortality,
> And drown me with their sweetness. O! come hither,
> Thou that begett'st him that did thee beget;
> Thou that wast born at sea, buried at Tarsus,
> And found at sea again. O Helicanus!
> Down on thy knees, thank the holy gods as loud
> As thunder threatens us; this is Marina.
>
> (V. i. 192)

The sea is now a 'sea of joys'; and notice the triple reference of birth, death, and restoration 'at sea'; while we may recall that our action is set on a barge, in calm water, on the occasion of Neptune's feast. The new joy is proportional to the tragedy ('as loud . . . threatens us') being reversed.

Marina's self-discovery has clearly something divine about it. In all her words she has 'been god-like perfect'; she has brought Pericles 'another life' (V. i. 208). Pericles calls for his garments; notices Lysimachus for the first time; and, after somewhat perfunctorily greeting him, returns to his joy:

> PERICLES: Give me my robes. I am wild in my beholding.
> O heavens, bless my girl! But, hark! what music?
> Tell Helicanus, my Marina, tell him
> O'er, point by point, for yet he seems to doubt,
> How sure you are my daughter. But, what music?
> HELICANUS: My lord, I hear none.
> PERICLES: None!
> The music of the spheres! List, my Marina.
> LYSIMACHUS: It is not good to cross him; give him way.
> PERICLES: Rarest sounds! Do ye not hear?
> LYSIMACHUS: My lord, I hear.
> PERICLES: Most heavenly music!
> It nips me unto listening, and thick slumber
> Hangs upon mine eyes; let me rest. (*Sleeps*)
>   (V. i. 224)

The scene closes, as it started, in sleep, or trance: there is a double awakening, from sleeping to waking and from waking to some yet higher apprehension; we attend a dramatized awakening which culminates, beyond discovery and recognition, in the hearing of those heavenly harmonies which were contrasted, in *The Merchant of Venice*, with the 'muddy vesture of decay' (V. i. 64) preventing their reception. The scene enacts the breaking of those boundaries, an adventure into that music, or the irruption of that music into human life.

Pericles' sleep leads on to a direct theophany, or divine appearance, the first (except for Hymen and Hecate) in Shakespeare. Diana appears to Pericles as in a vision (V. i. 240) and directs him to Ephesus, where he is to sacrifice with her 'maiden priests' (V. i. 243) before all the people and recount his wife's death 'at sea' (V. i. 245)—the emphasis persists—and all his and his daughter's sufferings:

> Perform my bidding, or thou liv'st in woe;
> Do it, and happy; by my silver bow!
> Awake, and tell thy dream!
>   (V. i. 248)

Pericles starts up, crying:

> Celestial Dian, goddess argentine,
> I will obey thee!
>
> (V. i. 251)

He immediately gives directions for the next, and final, voyage.

There follows first much 'pageantry' and 'minstrelsy' at Mitylene (V. ii. 6, 7), and then they all sail for Ephesus:

> In feather'd briefness sails are fill'd,
> And wishes fall out as they're will'd.
>
> (V. ii. 15)

The couplet neatly drives home the old metaphoric equivalence, almost identity, of sea and soul.

Malone's final stage-direction is:

> The Temple of Diana at Ephesus; Thaisa, standing near the altar, as high priestess; a number of Virgins on each side.
>
> (V. iii)

Cerimon is present. Pericles formally presents his account to Diana, with the usual emphasis on death and birth 'at sea' (V. iii. 5). Marina, he says, 'wears yet thy silver livery' (V. iii. 7), a phrase recalling Diana's 'silver bow' (V. i. 249), and blending with earlier imagery of rich metals.

Hearing his account, Thaisa, now called a 'nun' (V. iii. 15) by strange Christian transference (cp. *A Midsummer Night's Dream*, I. i. 70–8, 89–90), faints, and Cerimon explains her identity to Pericles, recounting how he himself opened her coffin filled with 'jewels' (V. iii. 24). Thaisa recovers:

> O! my lord,
> Are you not Pericles? Like him you speak,
> Like him you are. Did you not name a tempest,
> A birth, and death?
>
> (V. iii. 31)

How precise and yet with what generalized, universal reverberations is this ringing of the changes on birth and death in tempest. Our second reunion works up more swiftly than the first to its climax. Pericles recognizes the hand of divinity, crying 'Immortal Dian!' (V. iii. 37) and even half-wishing, as did Othello before him, to dissolve at this high moment:

> This, this: no more, you gods! your present kindness
> Makes my past miseries sport: you shall do well,
> That on the touching of her lips I may

Melt and no more be seen. O! come, be buried
A second time within these arms.

(V. iii. 40)

All old questions of fortune and the gods are caught up into this miraculous reversal which, glancing back, makes tragedy in its short illusion a game, melted in the sun of union.

Marina, her 'burden at the sea' (V. iii. 47), is introduced to her mother: 'Bless'd, and mine own' (V. iii. 48) says Thaisa. The phraseology throughout these reunions is saturated in religious suggestion: this, our final scene, is aptly staged outside a temple, with Thaisa as high priestess. Cerimon, too, is regarded as a divine instrument, functioning very precisely as Chist Himself in the Christian scheme:

> PERICLES: Now do I long to hear how you were found,
> How possibly preserv'd, and whom to thank,
> Besides the gods, for this great miracle.
> THAISA: *Lord Cerimon, my lord; this man,*
> *Through whom the gods have shown their power;*
> *that can*
> *From first to last resolve you.*
> PERICLES: Reverend sir,
> The gods can have no mortal officer
> More like a god than you. Will you deliver
> How this dead queen re-lives?
> CERIMON: I will, my lord.

(V. iii. 56)

'The gods', 'great miracle', 'power', a 'god': the impressions are piled on. We are directed to feel that a dead person 'relives', and though Cerimon promises, as does Paulina in *The Winter's Tale*, an explanation, we do not hear it, in either play. We are left with a sense of wonder.

. . . The structural elements in *Pericles* are not all new; but the treatment gives them fresh, and explicitly transcendental, meaning. Instead of a happy-ending romance, or ritual, in the tradition of Lyly, with whatever validity such fictions may be considered to hold—and it is probable that they hold more than we normally suppose—we are here confronted by some extra dimension of validity. The depth and realism of tragedy are present within the structure of romance. The two extremes, happy and sad, of Shakespearian art coalesce to house a new, and seemingly impossible, truth; as though the experiences behind or within the composition of *King Lear* and *Timon of Athens* were found not necessarily antithetical to the happy ending but rather reached therein their perfect fulfilment. Hence the sense of breath-taking surprise, of wonder and reverence, in the reunions, and the cogent presentation of the miracle-worker, Cerimon.

Pericles might be called a Shakespearian morality play. The epilogue asserts as much, though it does no justice to the more important scenes, which so tower above the rest and which it would be a great error to relate too sharply to any known type of drama. These, whatever we think of them, are spontaneous, new creations. And yet, in spite of their superiority, they cannot be isolated: *Pericles* is too thoroughly organic a play for that, with all its running coherences of idea, image, and event. These demand a short retrospective comment.

There are the continual references to 'fortune' personified at IV. iv. 48 as 'Lady Fortune' (cp. *Timon of Athens*, I. i. 64), variously entwined with the sequence of sad and happy adventures and used rather as in *Antony and Cleopatra* with strong suggestion of 'chance'. The gods are referred to as in *King Lear*, though with a greater sense of their reality, beneficence, and intervention; as in 'you most potent gods' (III. ii. 63); the 'powers that give heaven countless eyes to view men's acts' (I. i. 72); 'we cannot but obey the powers above us' (III. iii. 9). The 'most high gods' quickly punish, with 'heaven's shaft', the wicked (II. iv. 3, 15), but are otherwise conceived as kindly (II. iii. 59). Such deities counter the chance-like concept of 'fortune'. Somewhat sterner are the Destinies, conventionally supposed as cutting the thread of life (I. ii. 108), and also the typically Shakespearian conception:

> Time's the king of men,
> He's both their parent and he is their grave.
> (II. iii. 45)

Religious reverence crystallizes into the personal deities of Neptune and Diana; the first to be related to our voyages and tempests, the latter of high importance at the end.

To pass to the more human essences. There are a number of variations concerning true and false value played on riches (gold, silver and jewels) following, as we have noted, the use of riches in *The Merchant of Venice* and *Timon of Athens*. Now in *Timon of Athens* the gold of the later action may be related to the aristocratic essence, the spiritual fineness of Timon himself; and something similar happens in *Pericles*. For our glitter of jewels and other riches blends naturally into the play's royalism, where again we have a divergence of directions, with distinctions drawn between the wicked and good princes (Antiochus, Cleon and Dionyza against Pericles and Simonides); the former tyrannous (I. ii. 103) and regarding conscience as unworthy of noble blood (IV. iii. 23–5); the others, chivalrous and relating princely honour to charity (I. iv. 85–96; II. iii. 24–6; 59–61).

Here we may approach a new subtlety creeping into Shakespeare's royalism: his emphasis on the discovery (by the owner or someone else) of a child's royal birth (in Marina, Perdita, Guiderius, Arviragus, Miranda). Royal blood is felt mystically, spiritually, with Marina as a palace 'for the crowned Truth to dwell in' (V. i. 124). We are reminded of Wordsworth's child forgetting 'the glories he hath known and that imperial palace whence he came' (in the *Ode on Intimations of Immortality*); and of Coleridge's remarkable play *Zapolya*, specifically written on the pattern of Shakespeare's last plays, where the spiritual connotations of the discovery of royal blood are vividly felt. Where the later poets witness a 'spiritual' reality, Shakespeare works from a firmer basis of Tudor royalism: but he invariably develops that, as in his manipulation of Timon's innate aristocracy, into something more spiritual, chivalric, or Christian, with stress on generosity and humility (as with Theseus in *A Midsummer Night's Dream*). This development reaches its finest results in his semi-mystic approach to the royal children from *Pericles to Henry VIII*; and may delicately be referred to some yet more universal intimation of concerning the royal birth and destinies of the individual human soul, widely understood; for the royal protagonist of drama is always primarily an objectification of the spectator's individual self; his 'I'; and certainly in *Pericles* the greatest moments are weighted by a sense of man's universal destiny. So, whatever our political principles, we find the royalistic image of radiating its lines of force: and it is precisely this princeliness that renders the rich, kindly and even humorous (III. ii. 54–5) Lord Cerimon, on whom sits the aristocratic lustre of Timon, more attractive than his great descendant Prospero, who, though of ducal status, is more coldly conceived. Indeed, both *Pericles* and *The Winter's Tale* hold a certain freshness that the later, more coherent, play lacks. Something is lost as miracle becomes assured.

These imaginative strands are all Shakespearian favourites; but their use is new. They are newly actualized: what was formerly imagery becomes dramatic fact. The old image of storm gives us 'enter Pericles, wet'; that of bark-in-storm becomes a stage-setting, with Pericles 'on shipboard'; the old association love = jewel is built into a personal sense of Thaisa's and Marina's jewel-like worth; the love-image of jewel-thrown-into-the-sea (see *The Shakespearian Tempest*, pp. 64–9; 222–3) becomes Thaisa in her jewel-stored coffin (like Portia's picture in the casket) thrown overboard. Shakespeare's continual reference to pagan deities works up to the 'feast of Neptune' and actual appearance of Diana. Finally, music, for so long a dramatic accompaniment to scenes of love and reunion, becomes an active force in Cerimon's magic and explicitly mystical in Pericles' 'music of the spheres' (V. i. 231). . . . Pericles is the result of no sudden vision: it is Shakespeare's total poetry on the brink of self-knowledge.

It is accordingly not strange that art, as such, should be given greater emphasis than hitherto; in stage-conception, ceremonious procession (as of the tourneying knights) and ritual quality; in dumb-show; in monumental inscriptions, and metaphors; in musical accomplishment (Pericles' and Marina's); in Marina's dancing and decorative needlework. The arts least emphasized in Shakespeare, the static arts of design, assume a new prominence, giving us the exquisite descriptions of Marina in monumental terms. Shakespeare's drama is aspiring towards the eternal harmony and the eternal pattern.

The new excellences are bought at a cost. Pericles himself is a passive figure, quite unlike Shakespeare's usual dynamic protagonists. He himself does nothing crucial; his fall is purely an awareness of evil, like Hamlet's, his good acts are perfunctorily set down, his repentance in sack-cloth and unshaven hair a repentance for no guilt of his own but rather for the fact of mortality in a harsh universe. He is here for things to happen to and forges little or nothing for himself; his most original actions are a series of escapes or departures; he is too humble to press his suit for Thaisa. He is, indeed, less a realized person than man, almost 'every man', in the morality sense, as the epilogue suggests. We can, however, improve on the epilogue by seeing the whole as a panorama of life from adolescent fantasy and a consequent fall, through good works to a sensible and fruitful marriage, and thence into tragedy, with a reemergence beyond mortal appearances into some higher recognition and rehabilitation. The medium is myth or parable supposedly, of course, realistic: we must not expect death to be totally negated; Thaisa's father dies (V. iii. 78); Cerimon cannot restore everyone (III. ii. 7). But, as in parable always, it is the central person, or persons, that count; and here the deaths of Thaisa and Marina are shown, in the fiction, as false, though with an intensity surpassing fiction.

Having worked through the play like this, we may well question whether it is not as authentic as any of Shakespeare's works. . . . The high standard of authenticity demanded by the Folio editors is witnessed alike by their own preface and the massive and detailed coherence of the material they published: such things do not happen by chance. But neither can the internal coherence of Pericles, far more precise than that of many a more famous Shakespearian work, be dismissed. Nothing is here forgotten: Antiochus' wickedness, Pericles' relief of the famine, the crime of Dionyza and Cleon, all are exactly remembered long after their purpose in the narrative sequence has been fulfilled; from first to last the Gower speeches have the whole action in mind; the various imagistic correspondences, cutting across divergences of style, knit the narrative into a unity. Every line, good or bad, serves a purpose: there are probably less extravagant irrelevancies than, say, in *Hamlet* or *King Lear* (e.g. the weak elaboration of *Hamlet*, I. ii. 79–81, and what might be called the delaying bombast of *King Lear*, I. iv. 299–311). The play appears to be carefully and critically composed: witness Gower's laboured apologies for the disrespect shown to the unities and even for the employment of a single language for different places (IV. iv. 7). Whatever we think of certain parts, the whole, as we have it, is unquestionably dominated by a single mind; that mind is very clearly Shakespeare's; and Shakespeare's, too, in process of an advance unique in literature.

M.C. BRADBROOK

Virtue is the True Nobility:
A Study of the Structure of
"All's Well that Ends Well"

All's Well that Ends Well might have
as its subtitle "Two Plays in One." In this [essay] I shall be concerned with
one of the plays only—the play that is revealed by the structure and the
plot. Such a partial and one-sided approach is justified because, I believe,
it reveals the governing idea of the whole composition. This is perhaps a
dangerous assumption, for

> in attempting to isolate the idea that governs a play we run the risk of
> fixing it and deadening it, especially when the idea discerned is expressed
> as a philosophical proposition and stated in a sentence or two.

The governing idea of this particular play is one which I believe
belongs rather to Shakespeare's age than to all time. To display it therefore requires what may seem a humorless and over-detailed study of the
background of ideas. The method by which the idea is presented is not
quite Shakespeare's usual one, though not unlike that discerned by modern critics elsewhere in his work. No one could dare to suggest that
Shakespeare took a moral idea and dressed it up in human terms; yet the
allegorical mode of thought and the conception that literature should
promote good actions were still very much alive in his day. They were not
secure. Shakespeare himself, in that period of the mid-nineties when he
more or less has the stage to himself—the period between the death of

From *The Review of English Studies* 26 (1950). Copyright © 1965 by Prentice-Hall, Inc.

Marlowe and the arrival of Jonson—transformed the conception of dramatic art and produced those ripe and humane works which for ever made impossible such plays as Robert Wilson's.

The modern reader of *All's Well*—"the new Cambridge production is the first for many years"—may feel that the play contains one superb character study, that of Bertram; and at least one speech of great poetic power, Helena's confession to the Countess. Seen through Helena's eyes Bertram is handsome, brave, "the glass of fashion and the mould of form": seen through the eyes of the older characters he is a degenerate son, an undutiful subject, a silly boy. The two images blend in the action, as we see him sinking from irresponsibility to deceit, but making a name for himself in the wars. He ends in an abject position, yet Helena's devotion continues undiminished. Her medieval counterpart, patient Griselda, whose virtues are passive, is not called on for more than obedience, and the audience need not stop to wonder what kind of a person the Marquis could be, whether such barbarity could be justified as an assay of virtue, and how the final revelation could leave his wife with any palate for his company. As a character, he exists only to demonstrate Griselda's patience. But Bertram is not "blacked out" in this way. The connection of his character and Helena's feelings with the general theme can be explained, but they are not identified with it.

In *All's Well* the juxtaposition of the social problem of high birth versus native merit and the human problem of unrequited love recalls the story of the Sonnets; the speeches of Helena contain echoes from the Sonnets, but the story to which her great speeches are loosely tied does not suit their dramatic expression. It illustrates the nature of social distinctions, of which the personal situation serves only as example. It might be hazarded that this first tempted Shakespeare, who then found himself saying more, or saying other, than his purely structural purpose could justify. Helena's speech to the Countess is the poetic center of the play, but the structural center is the King's judgment on virtue and nobility. For once, the dramatist and the poet in Shakespeare were pulling different ways. *All's Well that Ends Well* expresses in its title a hope that is not fulfilled; all did not end well, and it is not a successful play.

My contention is that *All's Well* fails because Shakespeare was trying to write a moral play, a play which he proposed to treat with the gravity proper, for example, to "a moral history." He was not writing allegorically but his characters have a symbolic and extra-personal significance. To write such a play the writer must be detached and in complete control of his material; and Shakespeare was not happy when he was theorizing. Here he is not driven to bitter or cynical or despairing comment on the filth that lies below the surface of life. Instead of the stews of Vienna, the activities of Pandarus and Thersites, we have the highly moral comments of the young Lords on Bertram. Yet compared with *Measure for Measure*—to which it is most closely linked by similarities of plot—the play appears more confused in purpose, more drab and depressing, if less squalid. Both are concerned with what Bacon called Great Place; the one with the nature and use of power, the other with the nature and grounds of true nobility. The characters are occasionally stiffened into types: the King becomes *Vox Dei*, which means that he is merely a voice. Yet at other times, but chiefly in soliloquy, deep personal feeling breaks through. Angelo's temptations and Helena's love are not completely adjusted to the stories which contain them. These feelings burst out irrepressibly, and in a sense irrelevantly, though they are the best things in the plays.

To compare *Measure for Measure* with its source play, *Promos and Cassandra*, is to see the shaping process of imagination at work: to compare *All's Well* with Painter's translation of Boccaccio is at least revealing. The alterations are perfectly consistent, tending to greater dependence, humility, and enslavement on Helena's part and greater weakness and falsehood on Bertram's. New characters are added to voice Helena's claims to virtue and dignity—this is the chief purpose of the Countess, Lafeu, and the additions to the King's part—while others are created to stigmatize Bertram. An outline of Painter will make this clear.

Giletta of Narbonne is brought up with Beltramo and several other children; though not noble she is rich, and refuses many suitors for love of him. After his departure she waits some time—years are implied—before following him, and she sees him before she seeks the King. The conditions of her bargain are that she cures the King in eight days or she offers to be burnt, the King spontaneously adding that he will give her a husband if she succeeds. She asks the right to choose and, somewhat to the royal chagrin, names Beltramo. The King almost apologizes to the firmly protesting Count, but pleads that he has given his royal word. After the wedding Giletta goes to Rossiglione, puts the estate in order, tells the people the whole story and goes away openly with a kinsman and a good deal of treasure. She reaches Florence, ferrets out Beltramo's mistress, plans the substitution and eventually gives birth to twin sons. At her leisure she returns, and entering on a day of feast, presents her two sons; Beltramo, to honor his word, and to please his subjects and the ladies, his guests who make suit to him, receives her as his wife.

These shrewd, unsentimental, vigorous Italians, who come to terms after a brisk skirmish, resemble Benedick and Beatrice rather than their own Shakespearian descendants. Two principal characters, the Countess and Parolles, have been added by Shakespeare, and two lesser ones, Lafeu and the Fool. The climaxes are heightened, and in the last scene Bertram is in danger of the law. Shakespeare's hero is a very young man, highly conscious of his birth. He is handsome, courageous in battle, winning in manners: he is also an inveterate liar.

The Elizabethan code of honor supposed a gentleman to be absolutely incapable of a lie. In law his word without an oath was in some places held to be sufficient. To give the lie was the deadliest of all insults and could not be wiped out except in blood. Honor was irretrievably lost only by lies or cowardice. These were more disgraceful than any crimes of violence. Alone among Shakespeare's heroes Bertram is guilty of the lie. Claudio, in *Much Ado*, is clear, and Bassanio, though he thinks of a lie to get himself out of an awkward situation at the end of the play, does not utter it. By such conduct Bertram forfeits his claims to gentility: a gentleman, as Touchstone remembered, swore by his troth, as a knight by his honor. For this he is shamed and rebuked openly, not only by his elders but by his contemporaries and even by his inferiors. The feelings of a modern audience towards Claudio or Bassanio may be due to a change in social standards, but Bertram is roundly condemned.

The fault, however, is not entirely his, for like Richard II, Prince Hal, and all other great ones in search of an excuse, he can shelter behind ill company. Parolles, or Wordy, a character of Shakespeare's own invention, is perceived in the end by Bertram himself to be the Lie incarnate. From the beginning the Countess had known him as

> a verie tainted fellow, and full of wickedness,
> My sonne corrupts a well-derived nature
> With his inducement
>
> (III. ii. 90–2)

whilst Helena describes him before he appears as "a notorious Liar," "a great way foole, solie a coward." It is not till the final scene that Bertram too acknowledges him

> a most perfidious slave . . .
> Whose nature sickens: but to speake a truth.
> (V. iii. 207–9)

In the earlier part of the play he is completely gulled by Parolles, who gains his ends by flattery. To the Elizabethan, the flatterer was the chief danger of noble youth, and his ways were exposed in most of the manuals of conduct. In Stefano Guazzo's *Civile Conversation*, a book of manners designed for the lesser nobility, much of Book II is taken up with the subject. Shakespeare in his comedy makes little use of the figure of the flatterer, and this differentiates him from Chapman, Jonson, and Middleton, who took the parasite of ancient comedy and furnished him with the latest tricks of the coney-catcher. Falstaff is in some sense a flatterer, but he is never more deceived than when he thinks to govern his sweet Hal.

Flattery thrives on detraction, and Parolles's evil speaking, which finally exposes him, has been anticipated by his double-dealing with Helena and Lafeu. His cowardice is of no power to infect Bertram, but his lying is contagious, and in the last scene the count shows how deeply he is tainted. The unmasking of Bertram re-echoes the unmasking of Parolles.

Shakespeare is unlikely to have felt deeply about the minutiae of social procedure, the punctilio of a modern and Frenchified fashion like the duel, or the niceties of address. Saviolo's discourse on the lie is put into the mouth of Touchstone, Segar's observations on Adam *armigero* are given to the First Gravedigger, and Falstaff has the longest if not the last word on Honor. But the question "Wherein lies true honor and nobility?" was older than the new and fantastic codes of honor, or the new ideas of what constituted a gentleman. It is the theme of the first English secular drama, *Fulgens and Lucres* (c. 1490), where Medwall gave the lady's verdict for the worthy commoner against the unworthy nobleman, thereby proving his independence of his original, Buonaccorso, who in *De Vere Nobilitate* had left the matter open. In 1525, Rastell, *Of Gentylnes & Nobylyte*, treated the same subject, and it was an obvious theme for secular moralities. The question of blood and descent had been touched on by Shakespeare in *King John* in the triple contrast of Arthur, the legal successor, John the King *de facto*, and Richard the Bastard, whose royalty of nature makes him the natural leader. Civil nobility seen in relation to courtly life was a different aspect of the same problem and it is with this that Shakespeare is concerned in *All's Well*.

When at the turn of the fifteenth century, the ruling caste had ceased also to be a fighting caste, there remained for the elder and wiser the role of statesman or politician and for the younger sort that of courtier. The feudal tenant-in-chief had derived his standing from his military prowess and his local territorial responsibilities of delegated rule. Although the military profession was no longer paramount, the young noble was trained in war. The perfect courtier was required to be witty, full of counsel and of jests, skilled in music and poetry, a horseman, a patron of all noble science. Such arts of living could be learned only at the court. He should be ambitious of honor—like Hotspur and Prince Hal—truthful and loyal, kindly and modest. His life was devoted to glory, and his reward was good fame. Such employments as the professions afforded—of which that of physician was held least worthy, as too close to the barber and the apothecary—were the refuge of impoverished families and of younger sons. As the king was the fount of honor, the young noble's place was at court; but the vanity and corruption of court life were especially dangerous for the young. In actuality, the scramble for preferment was a dangerous game in which the player might lose his all. Warnings against the court had been set forth in literature for more than a century. Spenser's *Colin Clout's Come Home Again* depicts both the glories and miseries of the court. A sick or aging ruler left the courtiers exposed to all the natural dangers of the place without restraint. Such a situation is depicted at the beginning of *All's Well*. The metaphor of the sick King was always something more than a metaphor for Shakespeare. The Countess bids farewell to her "unseason'd courtier" with open misgivings, and Helena, too, is openly afraid of the influence of the court on Bertram: Parolles's description is not inviting, and even the clown is not improved by it. When the court is reached, all the virtuous characters turn out to be elderly. The King describes the perfect courtier in the person of Bertram's father, recalled to his mind by the young man's likeness (a resemblance already twice commented on):

> Youth, thou bear'st thy Father's face,
> Franke Nature rather curious then in hast
> Hath well compos'd thee: Thy Father's morall parts
> Maist thou inherit too.
>
> (I. ii. 18–21)

The elder Rousillon is but lately dead when the play opens. In an extensive picture or mirror of his father, the King sets up to Bertram that model which had already been recommended to him by his mother. It constitutes one of the main statements of the play, embodying the idea of true nobility.

> He did look farre
> Into the service of the time, and was
> Discipled of the bravest . . . in his youth
> He had the wit, which I can well observe
> To day in our young Lords: but they may jest
> Till their owne scorne returne to them unnoted
> Ere they can hide their levitie in honour:
> So like a Courtier, contempt nor bitternesse
> Were in his pride, or sharpnesse; if they were,
> His equall had awak'd them, and his honour
> Clocke to it selfe, knew the true minute when

> Exception bid him speake: and at this time
> His tongue obeyd his hand. Who were below him,
> He us'd as creatures of another place,
> And bow'd his eminent top to their low rankes,
> Making them proud of his humilitie,
> In their poor praise he humbled. . . .
>
> (I. ii. 26 ff.)

The model which Bertram actually takes is very antithesis of this. Parolles claims to be both courtier and soldier, but his courtliness is entirely speech, as his soldiership is entirely dress. Even the clown calls Parolles knave and fool to his face (II. iv). He is ready to play the pander and to tempt Bertram ("a filthy Officer he is in those suggestions for the young Earle," III. v. 17–18), yet at the end he crawls to the protection of old Lafeu, who had been the first to meet with provocative insults the challenge of the "counterfeit."

Affability to inferiors was indeed not always recommended: Elyot held that courtesy consisted in giving every man his due, whilst Guazzo thought "to be too popular and plausible, were to make largesse of the treasures of his courtesie, to abase himself, and to shew a sign of folly or flatterie." Yet on the other hand, Theseus's gracious kindness to the tradesmen, or Hamlet's sharp answer to Polonius's "I will use them according to their desert"—

> God's bodkin, man, much better. Use everie man after his desert, and
> who should scape whipping: use them after your own Honor and Dignity.
> The lesse they deserve, the more merit is in your bountie

illustrate the same virtue which the King praised in the elder Rousillon.

The arts of speech were indeed in themselves the very stuff of which a courtier was made. Guazzo describes first of all the speech and bearing to be cultivated, and then the truthfulness, fair speaking, and modesty which should characterize the matter of discourse. Hence the ungraciousness of Bertram's petulance. "A poore Physition's daughter my wife?" did not perhaps sound quite so outrageous as it does now, for marriage out of one's degree was a debasing of the blood which blemished successive heirs. But Helena is of gentle, though not of noble blood, and all the other young nobles who have been offered to her have been ready to accept her.

The question that is raised by Bertram's pride and the King's act is one central to all discussion on the nature of nobility.

> One standard commonplace on nobility took shape: that lineage alone
> was not enough, but that the son of a noble family should increase and
> not degrade the glory of his ancestors.

Aristotle had said that Nobility consisted in virtue and ancient riches. Lord Burghley, a potent authority in his day, lopped the phrase down: "Nobility is nothing but ancient riches." Whilst it was admitted that the King could confer nobility upon anyone, gentility was sometimes held to be conferred only by descent; hence the saying, "The King cannot make a gentleman." At the court of Elizabeth, herself the granddaughter of a London citizen and surrounded by new nobility, the more rigid views were not likely to prevail. Nevertheless "nobility native" was inevitably preferable to "nobility dative." Through inheritance it conferred a disposition to virtue, and even the degenerate were shielded in some manner by their descent, "the fame and wealth of their ancestors serves to cover them as long as it can, as a thing once gilded, though it be copper within, till the gilt be worn away." Education and the example of his ancestors would also help the nobleman, though a bad education might corrupt him entirely. The debate on old and new titles in Osorio's *Discourse of Civil and Christian Nobility* went in favour of blood, while Nenna's *Il Nennio* supported the lowly born. But all would agree with Mulcaster: 'The well-born and virtuous doth well deserve double honor among men . . . where desert for virtue is coupled with descent in blood.'

Desert for virtue is Helena's claim, and the two words echo significantly throughout the play. The causes for ennobling the simple were headed by "virtue public," i.e. some great public service, and this it is which ennobles her. Learning and riches were other causes. Elyot declared that nobility is "only the prayse and surname of virtue" and set forth the eleven moral virtues of Aristotle as the model for his Governor. The essentially competitive nature of honour, while it was recognized, was not stressed.

In Helena and Bertram, the true and the false nobility are in contest. Helena seeks recognition: Bertram denies it. The King, with the Countess and Lafeu, whom Shakespeare created to act as arbiters, are all doubly ennobled by birth and virtue and therefore judge dispassionately. By these three judges the young people are compared at intervals throughout the play, to the increasing disadvantage of Bertram. In the first scene, the Countess introduces Helena as inheriting virtue and yet improving on it. The technical terms of honor emphasize her point:

> I have those hopes of her good, that her education promises: her dispositions shee inherits, which makes faire gifts fairer . . . she derives her honestie, and atcheeves her goodnesse
>
> (I. i. 47 ff.)

Of Bertram she cherishes hopes less assured, but wishes that his blood and virtue may contend for precedence, and his goodness share with his birthright.

By making his social climber a woman, Shakespeare took a good deal of the sting out of the situation. Helena's virtues were derived from her father and from heaven, to whose intervention she ascribes all her power to cure the King. She protests she is richest in being simply a maid, and the King offers her to Bertram with the words

> Vertue and shee
> Is her owne dower: Honour and wealth, from mee.

The promotion of a modest but dignified young woman is far from arousing jealousy. Helena had been conscious of her lowliness and in her first soliloquy she almost despairs:

> Twere all one,
> That I should love a bright particuler starre,
> And think to wed it, he is so above me.
> (I. i. 97–9)

To the Countess, before making her confession, she says:

> I am from humble, he from honored name:
> No note upon my Parents, his all noble,
> My Master, my deere Lorde he is, and I
> His servant live, and will his vassall die.
> (I. iii. 164–7)

These words are not retracted by her confession for she protests that she does not follow him by any token of presumptuous suit: "Nor would I have him till I doe deserve him" (I. iii. 199). At her first encounter with the King, Helena is almost driven off by her first rebuff. In stately couplets which mark out the solemnity of the moment she suddenly returns and offers herself as "the weakest minister" of heaven. She frankly claims "inspired Merit" and warns the King that it is presumption to think Heaven cannot work through the humble. "Of heaven, not me, make an experiment." The King recognizes the power of something greater than herself in Helena's voice and he submits. She is "undoubted blest."

Such claims shift the ground of Helena's nobility. To fail to recognize her as already ennobled in a superior way by the choice of heaven is an aggravation of Bertram's offence in refusing the consummation of the marriage—itself a religious duty as Diana reminds him (IV. ii. 12–13). The countess feels nothing but indignation with the "rash and unbridled boy," for

> the misprising of a Maide too vertuous
> For the contempt of Empire.
> (III. ii. 27–8)

Even before the journey to court she had loved Helena as her own child (I. iii. 98, 143–4) and now she prefers her, disclaiming her proper son (III. ii. 68–9), who in rejecting such a wife has lost more honor than he can ever win with his sword. Helena's penitential pilgrimage raises her yet higher in the Countess's estimation, and finally, with the report of her death, she becomes "the most vertuous gentlewoman, that ever Nature had praise for creating" (IV. v. 9–10).

In bestowing a wife on one of the royal wards, the King was certainly doing no more than Elizabeth and James had done. Much lesser persons regarded their wards as legitimate matrimonial prizes. The customary formula (which the King uses): "Can you like of this man?" "Can you like of this maid?" did not imply love but only the ability to live harmoniously together. Bertram, who is succinctly described by Lafeu as an "asse," has, it is clear from the first scene, no dislike to Helena, but he knows her as his mother's servant and "I cannot *love* her, nor will strive to doo't." Only later does the brilliant idea occur to him that he was really in love with Lafeu's daughter. His seduction of Diana "contrives against his owne Nobilitie," and his responsibility for the death of Helena means that "the great dignitie that his valour hath here acquir'd for him (i.e. in Florence), shal at home be encountred with a shame as ample" (IV. iii. 25–30, 79–82).

Bertram's "folly," though excused as the fault of Parolles's ill counsel (IV. ii. 1), and as "Naturall rebellion, done i' th blaze of youth" (V. iii. 6), remains in the eyes of Lafeu a blot upon his honor. However much Bertram wronged his King, his mother, and his wife, he wronged himself much more (V. iii. 12–19). Lafeu champions Helena's memory rather in the way in which Paulina champions Hermoine's, and the rapidity with which the King jumps to thoughts of murder when he sees the royal gem offered as "an amorous token for fair *Maudlin*" is a proof of his feeling for Helena no less than of his well-merited distrust of Bertram. Like the rings of Bassanio and Portia, the jewels which are bandied about in the last scene are symbolic of a contract and an estate of life. The King's gem derived from him to Helena, and Bertram neither knows nor cares what it is. His own monumental ring symbolizes all that he has thrown away:

> an honour longing to our house,
> Bequeathed downe from manie Ancestors,
> Which were the greatest obloquie i' th world,
> In me to loose.
>
> (IV. ii. 42–5)

This jewel, with which he had taunted Helena, is found at the end in her keeping.

Nevertheless, though Helena is wise and Bertram foolish, though she is humble and he is proud, his final acknowledgment of her would constitute a strong ending. When Brachiano marries Vittoria, or when in *A Woman Killed with Kindness*, Sir Francis marries Susan, the condescension of the noble partner is matter for astonishment. Even in realistic comedy, such as *Eastward Ho!*, the marriage of court and city provides grounds for satire and for farce. Helena's success would lose all point if it were not a great exception. If this suggests that social theory enabled the judicious spectator both to eat his cake and have it, the answer is that the same dilemma lies at the center of the play, and is expounded by the king in a full account of the nature of title and dignity—a speech which had tradition behind it, but which is sharply at variance with the nigglers who measured whether honor came with the first or third generation of a new title.

> Tis onely title thou disdainst in her, the which
> I can build up: strange is it that our bloods
> Of Colour, waight and heat, pour'd all together,
> Would quite confound distinction: yet stands off
> In differences so mightie. If she bee
> All that is vertuous (save what thou dislikst),
> A poore Phisitian's daughter, thou dislikst
> Of vertue for the name: but doe not so:,
> From lowest place, whence vertuous things proceed,
> The place is dignified by th' doers' deede.
> When great addition swells, and vertue none,
> It is a dropsied honour. Good alone,
> Is good without a name. Vilenesse is so:
> The propertie by what it is, should go,
> Not by the title. She is young, wise, faire,
> In these, to Nature shee's immediate heire:
> And these breed honour: that is honour's scorne,
> Which challenges it selfe as honour's borne,
> And is not like the sire: Honour's thrive
> When rather from our acts we them derive
> Then our fore-goers: the meere words a slave
> Deboshed on everie tombe, on everie grave:
> A lying Trophee, and as ofte is dumbe,
> Where dust, and damn'd oblivion is the Tombe
> Of Honour'd bones indeed. . . .
>
> (II. iii. 124 ff.)

Helena already possesses the essential attributes and therefore the potentiality of honor, which the King by his recognition of her claims will bestow. "The name and not the thing" is vanity.

Medieval tradition recognized three classes of nobility. Christian, natural, and civil. Pre-eminence must be given to sanctity, but the saints included poor fishers, even slaves. Natural nobility or perfection of kind might be ascribed to animals, and a noble falcon justly so termed. The writers of books of honor often mentioned these two classes but pointed out that they could not discuss them. One of the fullest treatments of the subject is by Dante in his *Convivio*. He denies civil nobility any real value. Nobility, he says, cannot be defined by riches, which in themselves are vile, or by time, because all men ultimately derive from a common stock, but only by its effects. The necessary outcome or effect of Nobility is Virtue: where Virtue exists, Nobility must therefore exist as its cause. Nobility descends upon an individual by the grace of God (*Convivio*, IV. XV) and is "the seed of blessedness dropped by God into a rightly placed soul." Dante goes on to expound the eleven moral virtues (much like Elyot). The claim to nobility by descent is then refuted, natural and Christian nobility identified, and civil nobility wiped out. Dante's Third Ode, upon which this section of the *Convivio* provides a commentary, is addressed to Beatrice, who, like Helena, is an example of active virtue, received by a direct infusion of grace. The language of religion is used with particular frequency by Shakespeare in this play, and the gravest words of all are spoken by the Clown (IV. V. 50–9) when he describes how "the Prince of this world" entices nobility "into his court."

> I am for the house with the narrow gate, which I take to be too little for pompe to enter: some that humble themselves may, but the manie will be too chill and tender, and theyll bee for the flowrie way that leads to the broad gate, and the great fire.

Helena is "a Jewell" (V. iii. 1) which Bertram throws away. His rejection of her must be seen not in isolation but as linked with his choice of Parolles. The first dialogue of Helena and Parolles, the Liar and Vertue as she herself has labelled them, must be seen as the encounter of Bertram's good and evil angels, who, if this were a morality, would contend for his soul in open debate. In the final scene Parolles turns the tables on Bertram, and though the King dismisses the informer with contempt, an elaborate and inexorable shaming of the now utterly silenced young man proceeds. This last scene, in which Shakespeare completely forsakes his original, has the closest affinities with *Measure for Measure*. It is a judgment scene with charge and countercharge piled up in bewildering contradiction till they are resolved as if by miracle in the sudden appearance of the central figure. In this scene the King appears as the fount of justice: he deprives Bertram of all honor (V. iii. 184–6), though the revenges with which he threatens the young man should not be taken in any personal sense. Such a finale, with a royal judgment, and a distribution of rewards and punishments, was a well-established comic convention, though it is difficult to resist the thought that in offering Diana a husband, the King shows some inability to profit by experience. The riddles with which Diana led up to the *dénouement* recall those in which Portia swore she lay with Doctor Balthazar to obtain the ring, and they are not to modern taste.

Bertram's conversion must be reckoned among Helena's miracles. What is well ended is her struggle for recognition, which he concedes her. Her devotion, tinged for the first time with bitterness, requires another mode of expression than the last dozen lines allow. She has been acknowledged by her lord: that her personal happiness is simply irrelevant, and the ending therefore neither hypocritical nor cynical, can be granted only if the play is seen as a study of the question of "Wherein lies true honor and nobility?"

HAROLD C. GODDARD

"*Measure for Measure*"

"**W**ould you know a man? Give him power." History sometimes seems little else than an extended comment on that ancient maxim. Our own day has elucidated it on a colossal scale. *Measure for Measure* might have been expressly written to drive home its truth. It is little wonder, then, that the play of Shakespeare's in which the word "authority" occurs more often than in any other should have an extraordinary pertinence for a century in which the word "authoritarian" is on so many lips. The central male figure of the drama is one of the most searching studies ever made of the effect of power upon character.

Measure for Measure, like *Troilus and Cressida*, is closely bound to *Hamlet*. It is as if Shakespeare, having exposed in that masterpiece and the plays that culminated in it the futility of revenge as a method of requiting wrong, asked: what then? How, when men fail to keep the peace, shall their quarrels be settled, their misconduct penalized, without resort to personal violence? To that question the all but universal reply of the wiser part of human experience seems to have been: by law. In place of revenge—justice. Instead of personal retaliation—legal adjudication. "A government of laws and not of men": that is the historic answer of those peoples at least who have some freedom. And there is the imposing body of common and statute law to back it up. Trial by jury. Equality before the law. The advance of civilization that these concepts and conquests register cannot be overestimated. Under their spell men are even tempted to the syllogism:

From *The Meaning of Shakespeare*. Copyright © 1951 by The University of Chicago. The University of Chicago Press.

> Quarrels are settled by law.
> Wars are just larger quarrels.
> Therefore: wars can be settled by law.

Recent history is little more than the story of the world's disillusionment with regard to this conclusion. The weakness of the syllogism lies in its major premise. "A government of laws and not of men." It sounds august. But there never was, there is not, and there never will be, any such thing. If only laws would construe, administer, and enforce themselves! But until they do, they will rise no nearer justice than the justice in the minds and hearts of their very human agents and instruments. Those with power may sedulously inculcate in subjects the illusion that there is a necessary connection between law and justice as the very cement of the state, without which the political structure would collapse (as well it might); but, philosophically, any mental structure erected on this illusion is built on quicksand. Disillusionment on this subject, if it comes at all, usually comes gradually. We cling to the older and more comforting notion here as we do to infantile ideas of God. When at last we realize that the blessings of the law (which cannot be exaggerated) are due to the wisdom and goodness of man, and its horrors (which also cannot be exaggerated) to his cruelty and greed, we have grasped the fact that law is just an instrument—no more good or bad in itself than the stone we use as a hammer or a missile—and we will never again be guilty of thinking of law and war as opposites, or of confusing peace with the reign of law. Whether the horrors of war are greater or less than the horrors of law may be debated. Shelley, for one, put "legal crime" at the nadir of human baseness. In cowardice, at any rate, it ranks below open violence. *Measure for Measure* records, possibly, Shakespeare's first full disillusionment on this subject.

> It is the law, not I, condemn your brother.

The entire play might be said to have been written just to italicize that lie. The angle-villain tries to hide behind it as behind a shield. So-called civilization tries to do the same. But civilization—as Emerson remarked—crowed too soon.

II

For fourteen years Vienna has suffered from so lax an enforcement of the laws that the very babies have taken to beating their nurses, and a visitor from outside the city might actually

> have seen corruption boil and bubble
> Till it o'er-run the stew: laws for all faults,
> But faults so countenanc'd, that the strong statutes
> Stand like the forfeits in a barber's shop,
> As much in mock as mark.

The ruling Duke decides that, with such a reputation for lenity, he is not the one to rein in a steed that has known no curb. He will delegate his power to a sterner hand and let justice get a fresh start under a new regime. At least, such seems his motive on the surface. But the Duke is a curious character—"the old fantastical Duke of dark corners"—whether born so or made so by the exigencies of Shakespeare's plot. He is as fond of experimenting on human beings and inquiring into their inner workings as a vivisector is of cutting up guinea pigs. And when he retires not for a trip to Poland, as he gives out, but to return, disguised as a friar, to note the results of his temporary abdication, his motive seems less political and social than psychological. He is really not so much giving up his power as increasing it by retaining it in secret form. The Duke is as introspective as Hamlet, "one that, above all other strifes, contended especially to know himself," and his theatrical instinct also reminds us of the Prince of Denmark, though in his fondness for dazzling his audience he is more like Hal. In spite of his professed love of retirement and hatred of crowds and applause, he is the very reverse of a hermit, and intends (though he doesn't announce the fact in advance and may even be unconscious of it) to burst forth out of the clouds of disguise in full dramatic glory, as he does in the fifth act. His whole plan may be viewed as a sort of play witnin a play to catch the conscience of his deputy—and of the city. Moreover, he does not intend to miss the performance of his play any more than Hamlet did. The proof that his impulse is melodramatic, or at best psychological, is the fact that he knows at the time he appoints his deputy of a previous act of turpitude on his part. Angelo—for so the deputy is ironically named—deserted the girl to whom he was betrothed when her worldly prospects were wrecked, and slandered her into the bargain to escape the world's censure. He succeeded. His reputation for virtue and austerity is unimpeached. He can be reckoned on to put the screws on all offenders. It is as if the Duke were saying to himself: "Granted that my dispensation has been too lenient; I'll show you what will happen under a paragon of strictness. See how you like it then!" If he had not been more bent on proving his point than on the public welfare, why did he pick out a man whose secret vices he knew? How often have men been given temporary power precisely in order to prove them unworthy of it! Lord Angelo, says the Duke in the first act,

> is precise;
> Stands at a guard with envy; scarce confesses
> That his blood flows, or that his appetite
> Is more to bread than stone; *hence shall we see,*
> *If power change purpose, what our seemers be.*

That last is tolerably explicit. And that there may be no doubt as to what the Duke has in mind. Shakespeare has him again call him "this well-seeming Angelo," when, much later in the play, he reveals his outrageous treatment of Mariana.

III

So Angelo comes to power—ostensibly in association with the kindly and humane but weak-kneed Escalus, who, however, is chiefly a figurehead. The new ruler's hammer comes down first on Claudio, who, under an obsolete blue law, is condemned to death for anticipating the state of marriage with the girl to whom he was betrothed. The judgment is the more reprehensible because the worldly circumstances of the guilty pair demanded a certain concealment, their union was a marriage in fact if not in law, and no question of premeditated infidelity or broken vows was involved. The moral superiority of Claudio to the man who is to judge him is sufficiently pointed. Isabella, Claudio's chaste and virtuous sister, who is about to enter a nunnery, in spite of her reluctance to condone any laxity, intercedes with Angelo on Claudio's behalf. Angelo, at first, will do nothing but repeat "he must die," but as Isabella's beauty mounts with her ardor, the Deputy, who prides himself on being above all such appetites, is suddenly aware of a passion for her, his attitude alters, and he says, with a new sensation at his heart:

> I will bethink me. Come again tomorrow.
> Hark how I'll bribe you;

retorts Isabella, carried beyond discretion by her sense of coming victory.

> How! bribe me?

cries Angelo, startled by a word that fits with deadly accuracy a criminal thought he has not dared confess to himself. He can fairly see him turn on his heel and grow pale.

> Ay, with such gifts that heaven shall share with you,

the innocent Isabella replies. But what other Isabella, or what devil within the innocent one, had put that fatally uncharacteristic and inopportune word "bribe" on her tongue? It is one of those single words on which worlds turn that Shakespeare was growing steadily more fond of.

Isabella returns the next day, and Angelo, after hints that produce as little effect as did Edward IV's on Lady Grey, makes the open shameful proposal that the sister herself be the "bribe" to save her brother. Isabella, spurning the infamous suggestion, cries that she will proclaim him to the world if he does not give her an instant pardon for her brother. But when he reminds her that his impeccable reputation will protect him like a wall, she realizes it is true, and goes to report her failure to Claudio and to prepare him for death.

The scene between brother and sister (on which the disguised Duke eavesdrops) is one of the dramatic and poetic pinnacles of Shakespeare, and we scarcely need to except anything even in *Hamlet* when we say that few scenes in his works elicit from different readers more diametrically opposite reactions. Is Isabella to be admired or despised? Some think her almost divine in her virtue; others almost beneath contempt in her self-righteousness. You could fancy the two parties were talking about two different Isabellas. They are. There are two Isabellas.

Hamlet acquaints us with the psychological proximity of heaven and hell. This play goes on to demonstrate that, despite their polarity, the distance between them can be traversed in just about one-fortieth of the time it took Puck to put a girdle round about the earth.

A pendulum is ascending. It reaches the limit gravity will permit and instantly it is descending. A ball is sailing through the air. It touches the bound interposed by a wall and instantly it is sailing in the opposite direction. And even when the reaction is not instantaneous the same principle holds: everything breeds within itself the seed of its contrary. Human passion is no exception to the rule. At the extremity, it too turns the other way around, upside down, or inside out.

"Why, how now, Claudio!" cries Lucio, meeting his friend under arrest and on his way to jail, "whence comes this restraint?"

> CLAUD.: From too much liberty, my Lucio, liberty:
> As surfeit is the father of much fast,
> So every scope by the immoderate use
> Turns to restraint. Our natures do pursue—
> Like rats that ravin down their proper bane,—
> A thirsty evil, and when we drink we die.

To which Lucio, ever the wit, replies: "I had as lief have the foppery of freedom as the morality of imprisonment." The play is saturated with antitheses like that, and abounds in examples that recall Claudio's rat.

There is a woman in it, a bawd and keeper of a brothel, Mistress Overdone, almost the double in marital virtue of Chaucer's Wife of Bath.

Hath she had any more than one husband?

Escalus inquires of Pompey, her tapster, and the loyal Pompey proudly replies:

Nine, sir; Overdone by the last.

Overdone! it might be the name of most of the leading characters of the play. Each of them is too something-or-other. And what they do is likewise overdone. Good and evil get inextricably mixed throughout *Measure for Measure*, for virtue is no exception to the rule, and, pushed to the limit, it turns into vice.

Which brings us back to the two Isabellas.

Whatever it may be to an inveterately twentieth-century mind, the question for Shakespeare does not concern Isabella's rejection of Angelo's advances and her refusal to save her brother at such a price. Any one of his greater heroines—Imogen, Cordelia, Desdemona, Rosalind—in the same position would have decided, instantly, as she did. Who will doubt it? The notion that Isabella is just a self-righteous prude guarding her precious chastity simply will not stand up to the text. Lucio's attitude toward her alone is enough to put it out of court. Her presence can sober this jesting "fantastic" and elicit poetry and sincerity from his loose lips:

> I hold you as a thing ensky'd and sainted,
> By your renouncement in immortal spirit,
> And to be talk'd with in sincerity,
> As with a saint.

Prudes do not produce such effects on libertines and jesters.

The question rather concerns what follows. The sister comes to the brother religiously exalted by a consciousness of the righteousness of what she had done—ever a dangerous aftermath of righteousness. The brother catches something of her uplifted mood.

> CLAUD.:   If I must die,
> I will encounter darkness as a bride,
> And hug it in mine arms.
>   There spake my brother,

the sister, thrilled, replies. And there indeed the noblest Claudio did speak, or Shakespeare would never have put such poetry on his lips. But Isabella, whom we interrupted, has instantly gone on:

> there my father's grave
> Did utter forth a voice. Yes, thou must die.

What a flash of illumination! *Is there a ghost in this play too?*

And when Isabella reveals the terrible price that Angelo has put on his life, Claudio is equal to that too—or he and his sister's spirit are together. Pushed to his limit by that spirit, his instantaneous reaction—it cannot be marked too strongly—is exactly hers:

> O heavens! it cannot be,

and, again,

> Thou shalt not do't.

If it were my life, Isabella cries, I would throw it down like a pin. And she would have *at that moment*, as Claudio perceives:

> Thanks, dear Isabel.

But Claudio is made of more human stuff than his sister, and, held as she has held him to an extremity of courage and resolution almost beyond his nature, the law of reaction asserts itself and he drops into fear:

> Death is a fearful thing.

And then follows that terrific Dantesque-Miltonic picture of life after death with its "viewless winds" and "thrilling region of thick-ribbed ice" that leaves even Hamlet's similar speculations nowhere—nowhere in appalling power at least. Obscurity made vivid.

> Sweet sister, let me live.

And what does the sweet sister reply?

> O you beast!

Imagine Desdemona saying that! Claudio has said, or done, nothing to deserve such a term. A weak wretch on the threshold of execution, yes. But surely no "beast." What has happened? What always happens. What happened a few seconds before Claudio himself in another fashion. The overstretched string of Isabella's righteous passion snaps. She has herself dropped from saintliness to beastliness—and projects her own beastliness on her brother. "Isabella—beastly!" her defenders will cry. Why not? There is both beast and saint in every one of us, and whoever will not admit it had better close his Shakespeare once for all, or, rather, open it afresh and learn to change his mind. It is now, not before, that those who have harsh things to say about Isabella may have their innings. Drunk with self-righteousness, she who but a moment ago was offering her life for her brother cries:

Die, perish! Might but my bending down.
Reprieve thee from thy fate, it should proceed.
I'll pray a thousand prayers for thy death,
No word to save thee.

This is religion turned infernal. And it is the worse because of her allusion, in her scene with Angelo, to Christ's atonement:

Alas, alas!
Why, all the souls that were were forfeit once;
And He that might the vantage best have took
Found out the remedy. How would you be,
If He, which is the top of judgement, should
But judge you as you are? O, think on that;
And mercy then will breathe within your lips,
Like man new made.

And then, "O you beast!"

What is there to question is this psychology? Is there any human being who cannot confirm it—on however diminished a scale—from his own experience? Who in the midst of making a speech, performing a part, or carrying a point, realizing with delight that it is "coming off," has not paused for a fraction of a second to pat himself on the back, and then—it was indeed all "off" in another sense! The whole thing collapsed, instantly or gradually according to the degree of the complacency.

Commentators have wondered at the pure Isabella's quick acquiescence in the disguised Duke's scheme for having her go back and seem to consent to Angelo's proposal while he arranges to substitute the rejected Mariana, once the Deputy's betrothed, at the rendezvous. You may call the Duke's strategem vile, shady, or inspired, as you will, and Isabella's reaction to it laudable or damnable. Commendable or not, her conduct is one thing at any rate: credible. It is just the next swing of the pendulum. Conscious, or underconscious, of the fearful injustice she did her brother in that final outburst, she now seeks to set the balance straight. She would not have turned a hand to save him: *therefore*, she will now do anything to save him. Whatever we say, and whatever the Elizabethans said, to the morality of this much debated point, the psychology of it at any rate is sound. Shakespeare's part was done when he showed how a girl made like Isabella would act in those circumstances. And her conduct here coheres perfectly with another bone of contention at the end of the play: her apparent abandonment of getting herself to a nunnery in favor of getting a husband to herself—or at least taking one when offered. Her religious fervor at the outset—with which the ghost of her father plainly had something to do—was "overdone."

And that prospective husband, the Friar—otherwise the Duke? He is tarred with the same brush of excess. He professes to affect retirement and shun publicity. But it is not solitude that he loves. Whatever he was as a ruler, he becomes a moral meddler as a friar, as intoxicated over the human puppet-show whose strings he is pulling as Angelo is in another way over the moral-social drama of which he is manager. He will lie right and left, and even make innocence suffer cruelly (as in his concealing from Isabella the fact that her brother is not dead), merely for the sake of squeezing the last drops of drama or melodrama from the situation. And we must admit that it *is* a situation indeed, a dozen situations in one, in that last act. *Measure for Measure* has been widely criticized as an example of Shakespeare's own too great concession to theatrical effect. The point is in one sense well taken. But the author very shrewdly shifts the responsibility from himself to the Duke by making the man who was guilty of the worst offenses of that sort just the sort of man who would have been guilty of them. The man who made the great speech beginning:

> Heaven doth with us as we with torches do,
> Not light them for themselves,

had rare insight. It is Shakespeare's own ideal of going forth from ourselves and shining in, and being reflected from, the lives of others. But torches can serve the incendiary as well as the illuminator, and while the Duke did not go quite that far, if we reread the fifth act—with special attention to his part—the verdict will be: "Overdone by the last."

The only way to make the Duke morally acceptable is frankly to take the whole piece as a morality play with the Duke in the role of God, omniscient and unseen, looking down on the world. As has often been pointed out, there is one passage that suggests this specifically:

> O my dread lord,

cries the exposed Angelo, when the Duke at last throws off his disguise,

> I should be guiltier than my guiltiness,
> To think I can be undiscernible,
> *When I perceive your Grace, like power divine,*
> *Hath look'd upon my passes.*

The title of the play—the most "moral" one Shakespeare used—gives some warrant to the suggestion, as does the general tone of forgiveness at the end. But if the Duke is God, he is at first a very lax and later a very interfering God, and both the atmosphere and the characterization of the play are too intensely realistic to make that way out of the difficulty entirely satisfactory. If Shakespeare wants us to take it so, the execution of his intention is not especially successful. But we may at any rate say there is a morality play lurking behind *Measure for Measure*.

IV

And this brings us to the apex of the triangle, or the pyramid, Angelo, for the illumination of whom almost everything in the play seems expressly inserted.

Angelo is one of the clearest demonstrations in literature of the intoxicating nature of power as such. Power means unbounded opportunity, and opportunity acts on the criminal potentialities in man as gravitation does on an apple. Shakespeare wrote his *Rape of Lucrece* around this theme (and came back to it in *Macbeth*), and the stanzas on Opportunity in that poem are the best of glosses on *Measure for Measure*, such lines, to cull out just a few, as

> O Opportunity, thy guilt is great! . . .
> Thou sett'st the wolf where he the lamb may get . . .
> And in thy shady cell, where none may spy him,
> Sits Sin, to seize the souls that wander by him . . .
> Thou blow'st the fire when temperance is thaw'd . . .
> Thou foul abettor! thou notorious bawd!

This is why power as such is so often synonymous with crime. "Power as such," said Emerson, "is not known to the angels." But it was known to Angelo.

Angelo, in spite of his treatment of his betrothed, Mariana, was not an intentional villain or tyrant. His affinities are not with Pandulph and Richard III, but with Edward IV and Claudius. His soliloquy, on his knees,

> When I would pray and think, I think and pray
> To several subjects. Heaven hath my empty words,

looks back to Hamlet's uncle, as his

> Would yet he had liv'd!

when he supposes Claudio is dead at his command looks forward to
Macbeth. But his case is in a way worse than theirs, for, supposing himself
a mountain of virtue, when the temptation—and with it a sensation he
has never experienced—comes, he rolls almost instantly into the abyss.
Spiritual pride erects no defenses.

> ANG.:   I have begun,
> And now I give my sensual race the rein.

He loathes himself:

> The tempter or the tempted: who sins most?
> Ha!
> Not she; nor doth she tempt: but it is I
> That, lying by the violet in the sun,
> Do as the carrion does, . . . *Most dangerous*
> *Is that temptation that doth goad us on*
> *To sin in loving virtue.*

In loving Isabella, he thinks he means. But how much profounder the
second construction that the sentence bears, which makes it embrace both
intending violator and intended victim! Though poles apart, the virtuous
maid and the respected head of the state are here identical. Their vulnerable spot is the same: the sin of loving their own virtue.

There are few passages in Shakespeare that give a more inescapable
impression of coming from the poet himself than Isabella's great speech to
Angelo on power. It is the speech perhaps above any other in his works
that seems written to the twentieth century and that the twentieth
century should know by heart. The spectacle of

> man, proud man,
> Dress'd in a little brief authority,

"like an angry ape" playing "fantastic tricks before high heaven" made
Shakespeare as well as the angels weep. But her words recoil too perfectly
on Isabella's own head not to make them also perfectly in character:

> Merciful Heaven!
> Thou rather with thy sharp and sulphurous bolt
> Split'st the unwedgeable and gnarled oak
> Than the soft myrtle.

This shaft is aimed at the man who would make the soft Claudio a public
example of the moral austerity of his regime. But how about Isabella
herself, who is shortly to launch thunderbolts against the same weakling
in the scene where she calls him beast?—not to mention what she is doing

at the moment, for Angelo in strength is nearer the myrtle than the oak he considers himself. *Tu quoque!* Shakespeare perceives that spiritual power is quite as open to abuse as political power. The sheer theatrical effectiveness of his astonishing scene can easily blind us to the tangle of moral ironies and boomerangs it involves. This retiring girl, who had fairly to be pushed into the encounter by Lucio, finally standing up with audacity to the first man of the state is thrilling drama. But unfortunately Isabella gets an inkling of that fact herself.

> Go to your bosom,

she cautions Angelo,

> Knock there, and ask your heart what it doth know
> That's like my brother's fault.

If only she could have said those lines to herself, substituting for the last one,

> That's like this man's offence,

she never would have let slip from her lips that fatal word that ties some unplumbed sensual element in her own nature to the very corruption of justice and virtue she is condemning.

But Angelo's blackest act is not his sin of sensuality against Isabella, which he commits in wish and as he thinks in fact. Nor is it even the prostitution of his office that that involves. It is his acceptance of Isabella's sacrifice of herself and his then sending Claudio to death nevertheless. This final infamy—completed in intention though defeated in fact—ranks with John of Lancaster's treachery to the rebels in *II Henry IV*. Nothing worse need be said of it than that.

> Alack! when once our grace we have forgot,
> Nothing goes right,

Angelo cries, in anguish at what he has done. He might just as well have said,

> Alack! when once our power is unbounded,
> Nothing goes right,

for his are the typical sins and crimes of unlimited authority.

"Power is poison."

What power is has never been more tersely summed up than in those three words of Henry Adams in the section of the *Education* in which he analyzes its effect on Presidents of the United States, as he had observed it in Washington.

Power is poison. Its effect on Presidents had been always tragic, chiefly as an almost insane excitement at first, and a worse reaction afterwards; but also because no mind is so well balanced as to bear the strain of seizing unlimited force without habit or knowledge of it; and finding it disputed with him by hungry packs of wolves and hounds whose lives depend on snatching the carrion. . . . *The effect of unlimited power on limited mind is worth noting in Presidents because it must represent the same process in society, and the power of self-control must have limit somewhere in face of the control of the infinite.*

Shakespeare was saying precisely that, I think, in *Measure for Measure*. If concentration of authority in time of "peace" can let loose such demons of Opportunity in those who possess power, and transform their subjects either into pelting petty officers, hungry packs of wolves and hounds, or into their victims, what will the same thing do in time of war? In "peace" such unadulterated authority is at least not "necessary." It is the crowning infamy of war that it does make it essential. Victory demands efficiency, and efficiency calls for undisputed unity of command. War is authority—overdone.

V

The underplot of this play is unsavory. But of its kind it is a masterpiece of the first order, both in itself and in its integration with the main plot and its themes. Mistress Overdone, the keeper of a Viennese brothel, Abhorson, the executioner in a Viennese prison, and Barnardine, a con-demned murderer, may be said to be its symbolic triad. A prison is presumably a place where Justice is done. Pompey, Mistress Overdone's tapster, is struck rather by its resemblance to his employer's establishment.

"I am as well acquainted here as I was in our house of profession: one would think it were Mistress Overdone's own house, for here be many of her old customers. First, here's young Master Rash . . ." and foregoing acquaintance with the rest of the inmates whom Pompey goes on to introduce, we are sent back in astonished recognition, by that name "Master Rash," to Hamlet (and his "prais'd be rashness") who first made known to us the idea that the world is a prison. This play carries Hamlet's analogy a step further, and continually suggests the resemblance of the main world, not so much to a prison—though it is that too—as to a house of ill fame, where men and women sell their honors in a dozen senses.

Lucio, for instance, mentions "the sanctimonious pirate, that went to sea with the Ten Commandments, but scraped one out of the table."

If this is not an oblique, if a bit blunt, hit at Angelo (on Shakespeare's part of course, not Lucio's), then a cap that fits should never be put on. It was "Thou shalt not steal," of course, that the pirate scraped out. We know which one of the ten Angelo eliminated, if, indeed, it was not half-a-dozen of them. It would be interesting, taking Lucio's hint, to run through the cast and ask which and how many of the Commandments each character discarded. Isabella certainly could close her eyes to the first one. But without taking time for the experiment, one thing is certain. There would be no perfect scores—either way. The man in ermine in this play casts wanton eyes on the same woman whom the libertine looks on as a saint. That is typical of almost everything in it.

" 'Twas never merry world," declares Pompey, comparing his profession with a more respectable one, "since, of two usuries, the merriest was put down, and the worser allowed by order of law a furred gown to keep him warm; and furred with fox and lambskins too, to signify that craft, being richer than innocency, stands for the facing." This might be dismissed as the irresponsible chatter of the barroom, did not the main plot so dreadfully confirm it and Angelo himself confess it in soliloquy:

> Thieves for their robbery have authority
> When judges steal themselves.

If it will help any ultramodern person to understand Pompey's "usuries," read "rackets" in their place.

When the Provost tells this same Pompey, then in prison, that he may earn his freedom if he will act as assistant to the executioner, Shakespeare gives us another of his deadly parallels between the world of law and the world of lawbreakers. Pompey jumps at the chance: "Sir, I have been an unlawful bawd time out of mind; but yet I will be content to be a lawful hangman." But Abhorson, who is proud of his calling, is scandalized at the suggestion: "A bawd, sir? Fie upon him! he will discredit our mystery." To which the Provost replies: "A feather will turn the scale." (Between being bawd and executioner, he means, of course.) As to what Shakespeare thought, we get a hint when we remember the Duke's tribute:

> This is a gentle Provost: seldom when
> The steeled gaoler is the friend of men.

So recklessly does Shakespeare go on heaping up analogies between persons and things of low and those of high estate that when Elbow, the Constable, who must have been Dogberry's cousin, brings Froth and Pompey before Angelo and Escalus in judicial session, and introduces his prisoners as "two notorious benefactors," we begin to wonder, in the general topsy-turvydom, whether there may not be relative truth in his malapropism. At any rate, the upperworld characters are guilty of far worse moral and mental, if not verbal, confusions. "Which is the wiser here," asks Escalus, "Justice or Iniquity?"

And you shall have your bosom on this wretch,

cries the disguised Duke to Isabella, when Angelo's infamy becomes known to him,

> Grace of the Duke, revenges to your heart,
> And general honour.

An odd idea of honor for a supposed friar to impart to a prospective nun: the time-worn notion that it consists in having all your old scores settled. And when he hears that "a most notorious pirate" has just died in prison of a fever, thus supplying a head that can be sent to Angelo in place of Claudio's, he exclaims:

> O, 'tis an accident that Heaven provides!

—an equally odd idea of Heaven. But he far exceeds these lapses. At the end of the play, in an atmosphere of general pardon, Lucio, who—unwittingly but not unwittily—has abused the Duke to his face when disguised as a friar, does not escape. The Duke orders him married to the mother of his illegitimate child, and, the ceremony over, whipped and hanged. "I beseech your Highness," Lucio protests, "do not marry me to a whore." And the Duke relents to the extent of remitting the last two but not the first of the three penalties.

The emphasis on this incident at the very end brings to mind the moment when Lucio pulls off the Duke's hood:

> DUKE: Thou art the first knave that e'er mad'st a duke . . .
> Come hither, Mariana.
> Say, wast thou e'er contracted to this woman?
> ANG.: I was, my lord.
> DUKE: Go take her hence, and marry her instantly.

Poor Mariana's willingness, in contrast with Lucio, to marry *her* "knave" makes the parallelism more rather than less pointed.

Measure for Measure—once one gives the underplot its due—fairly bristles with disconcerting analogies and moral paradoxes like this last one. Only a hopelessly complacent person will not be challenged by it. And whoever will be honest with himself will confess, I believe, to a

strange cumulative effect that it produces. Barring Escalus and the Provost, who are put in to show that not all judges are harsh nor all jailers
hardhearted, we are more in love in the end with the disreputable than
with the reputable characters. Overworld and underworld threaten to
change places.

Whether *Measure for Measure* was a favorite play of Samuel Butler's
I do not know. It ought to have been. In it Shakespeare certainly proves
himself a good Butlerian, an adherent to the principle that "every proposi-
tion has got a skeleton in its cupboard." Many entries in the *Note-Books*
might have been composed to illuminate Shakespeare's play:

> God is not so white as he painted, and he gets on better with the Devil
> than people think. The Devil is too useful for him to wish him ill and, in
> like manner, half the Devil's trade would be at an end should any great
> mishap bring God well down in the world. . . . The conception of them
> as the one absolutely void of evil and the other of good is a vulgar notion
> taken from science whose priests have ever sought to get every idea and
> every substance pure of all alloy.
>
> God and the Devil are about as four to three. There is enough
> preponderance of God to make it far safer to be on his side than on the
> Devil's, but the excess is not so great as his professional *claqueurs*
> pretend it is.

What is this but the repentant Angelo's

> Let's write good angel on the devil's horn,

slightly expanded?

Quite in conformity with Butler's dicta, I am not sure that honest
readers do not find Barnardine, the condemned murderer, the most delec-
table character in *Measure for Measure*—he who for God knows how long
has defied the efforts of the prison authorities to execute him. We like him
so well that we do not wish to inquire too curiously into his past. For my
part, I am certain the murder he did—if he really did it—was an emi-
nently good-natured one. "Thank you kindly for your attention," he says
in effect, when they come to hale him to the gallows, "but I simply
cannot be a party to any such proceeding. I am too busy—sleeping." Let
him sleep. Let anyone sleep to his heart's content who puts to rout one
Abhorson. He has earned his nap.

Like Falstaff, Barnardine tempts the imagination to play around
him. No higher tribute can be paid to a character in a play, as none can
to a person in life. The fascination he has for us—he, and, in less degree,
the rest of the underworld of which he is a member—is partly because
these men and women, being sinners, have some tolerance for sin. And

some humor, which comes to much the same thing. *Judge not:* they come vastly nearer obeying that injunction (of which *Measure for Measure* sometimes seems a mere amplification) than do their betters. Never will anyone say of them as Escalus said of Angelo: "my brother justice have I found so severe, that he hath forced me to tell him he is indeed Justice." They are not forever riding the moral high horse. They make no pretensions. They mind their own business, bad as it is, instead of telling, or compelling, other people to mind *theirs* or to act in *their* way. It is a relief to find somebody of whom that is true. "Our house of profession." No, Pompey is wrong. It is not the establishment to which he is bawd and tapster, but the main world, that better deserves that name. For everybody with power—save a few Abraham Lincolns—is, *ipso facto*, professing and pretending all day long. "I am convinced, almost instinctively," says Stendhal, "that as soon as he opens his mouth every man in power begins to lie, and so much the more when he writes." It is a strong statement, and Shakespeare would certainly have inserted an "almost" in his version of it, but there are his works, from the History Plays on, to show his substantial agreement with it. Why does Authority always lie? Because it perpetuates itself by lies and thereby saves itself from the trouble of crude force: costumes and parades for the childish, decorations and degrees for the vain and envious, positions for the ambitious, propaganda for the docile and gullible, orders for the goosesteppers, fine words (like "loyalty" and "co-operation") for the foolishly unselfish—to distract, to extort awe, to flatter and gratify inferiority, as the case may be. Dr. Johnson ought to have amended his famous saying. Patriotism is only one of the last refuges of a scoundrel.

Angelo and the Duke, if anyone, ought to know, and in their hearts they agree exactly. Hear them in soliloquy. The identity is not accidental.

> ANG.:   O place, O form,
>   How often dost thou with thy case, thy habit,
>   Wrench awe from fools and tie the wiser souls
>   To thy false seeming!

> DUKE: O place and greatness! millions of false eyes
>   Are stuck upon thee. Volumes of report
>   Run with these false and most contrarious quests
>   Upon thy doings; thousand escapes of wit
>   Make thee the father of their idle dream
>   And rack thee in their fancies.

The effect of power on those who do not possess it but wish that they did, Shakespeare concludes, is scarcely better than on those who do.

And here is the deepest reason—is it not?—why we prefer the "populace" in this play to the powers-that-be. The vices of the two ends of "society" turn out under examination to be much alike. But the lower stratum has one virtue to which the possessors and pursuers of power, for all their pretensions, cannot pretend: namely, lack of pretension. Here is a genuine basis for envying the dispossessed. Revolutions by the down-trodden, abortive or successful, to regain their share of power have occurred throughout history. The world awaits a revolution by the power-ful to gain relief from the insincerities to which their privileges and position forever condemn them. Thoreau staged a one-man revolution based on a kindred principle. If this is what it implies, *Measure for Measure* may yet be banned by the authorites. . . . But no! it is as safe as the music of Beethoven. "The authorities" will never understand it.

VI

If we do not want a world presided over by a thundering Jove—this play seems to say—and under him a million pelting petty officers and their understudies, and under *them* millions of their victims, we must renounce Power as our god—Power and all his ways. And not just in the political and military worlds, there the evils of autocracy with its inevitable bureau-cracy of fawning yes-men, while obvious to all but autocratic or servile eyes, may be more or less "necessary." It is the more insidiously personal bondages to power that should concern us first. Revolution against authority—as Isabella, for all her great speech, did not perceive, and as Barnardine did—begins at home. Let men in sufficient numbers turn into Barnardines, who want to run no one else but will not *be* run by anyone, even to the gallows, and what would be left for the pelting petty officers, and finally for Jove himself, but to follow suit? There would be a revolu-tion indeed. The more we meditate on Barnardine the more he acquires the character of a vast symbol, the key perhaps to all our troubles. Granted, with Hamlet, that the world is a prison. We need not despair with Hamlet. We may growl rather with Barnardine at all intruders on our daydreams, and learn with him that even in a prison life may be lived—independently. Why wait, as modern gospels preach, until we are out of prison before beginning to live? "Now is a time."

Approximately three hundred years before the twentieth century, *Measure for Measure* made clear the truths that it has taken two world wars to burn into the consciousness of our own generation: that Power lives by Authority and that Authority is always backed by two things, the physical force that tears bodies and the mental violence that mutilates brains:

> In every cry of every Man,
> In every Infant's cry of fear,
> In every voice, in every ban,
> The mind-forg'd manacles I hear.

The two—dynamite and propaganda, to use modern terms—are always found together. "By skilful and sustained propaganda," said Hitler, "an entire people can be made to see even heaven as hell and the most miserable life as paradise." Where there is an Angelo on the bench, there will always be an Abhorson in the cellar. And how well Shakespeare liked Abhorson, his name proclaims.

> O, it is excellent.
> To have a giant's strength; but it is tyrannous
> To use it like a giant. . . .
> Could great men thunder
> As Jove himself does, Jove would ne'er be quiet;
> For every pelting, petty officer
> Would use his heaven for thunder,
> Nothing but thunder! Merciful Heaven!
> Thou rather with thy sharp and sulphurous bolt
> Split'st the unwedgeable and gnarled oak
> Than the soft myrtle; but man, proud man,
> Dress'd in a little brief authority,
> Most ignorant of what he's most assur'd,
> His glassy essence, like an angry ape,
> Plays such fantastic tricks before high heaven
> As make the angels weep; who, with our spleens,
> Would all themselves laugh mortal.

REUBEN BROWER

The Mirror of Analogy:
"The Tempest"

Of *The Tempest*, we may say what
Ferdinand said of the masque,

> This is a most majestic vision, and
> Harmonious charmingly.

The harmony of the play lies in its metaphorical design, in the closeness
and completeness with which its rich and varied elements are linked
through almost inexhaustible analogies. It is hard to pick a speech at
random without coming on an expression that brings us by analogy into
direct contact with elements that seem remote because of their place in
the action or because of the type of experience they symbolize. Opening
the play at the second act we read,

> Four legs and two voices; a most delicate monster!

The last phrase is comic enough as used of Caliban and as issuing from the
lips of Stephano, a 'most foul' speaker. But 'delicate' evokes a more subtle
incongruity by recalling characters and a world we might suppose were
forgotten. Stephano is parodying Prospero when he rebukes Ariel as 'a
spirit too delicate / To act her [Sycorax's] earthy and abhorr'd commands'
and when he says,

> delicate Ariel,
> I'll set thee free for this!

From *The Fields of Light: An Experiment in Critical Reading.* Copyright © 1951 by Oxford
University Press.

We have in Stephano's words not only the familiar Shakespearean balancing of comic and serious, but a counterpointing of analogies that run throughout the play. 'Delicate' as the antithesis of 'earth' points to the opposition of Ariel and Caliban and to the often recurring earth-air symbolism of *The Tempest*. 'Delicate' used of this remarkable island creature echoes also the 'delicate temperance' of which the courtiers spoke and 'the air' that 'breathes . . . here most sweetly.' 'Monster'—almost another name for Caliban—balances these airy suggestions with an allusion to 'the people of the island . . . of monstrous shape' and thereby to the strain of fantastic sea lore in *The Tempest*, which is being parodied in this scene.

So viewed, Shakespeare's analogies may perhaps seem too much like exploding nebulae in an expanding though hardly ordered universe. But Shakespeare does not 'multiply variety in a wilderness of mirrors'; he makes use of a few fairly constant analogies that can be traced through expressions sometimes the same and sometimes extraordinarily varied. And the recurrent anologies (or continuities) are linked through a key metaphor into a single metaphorical design. Shakespeare is continually prodding us—often in ways of which we are barely conscious—to relate the passing dialogue with other dialogues into and through a super-design of metaphor.

In concentrating on how the design is built up, I am not forgetting that it is a metaphorical design in a *drama*, that we are interested in how Shakespeare has linked stages in a presentation of changing human relationships. Toward the end of the [essay] I hope to show how wonderfully the metaphorical design is related to the main dramatic sequence of *The Tempest*, especially in the climactic speeches of Acts IV and V.

The play moves forward, we should remember, from a scene of tempest to final promise of 'calm seas, auspicious gales,' and through a series of punishments or trails to a series of reconciliations and restorations. Although, as Dr. Johnson might say, there is a 'concatenation of events' running through Prospero's 'project' and though the play has a curiously exact time schedule, there is often little chronological or logical connection between successive dialogues or bits of action. To be sure Shakespeare has the Elizabethan conventions on his side, but the freedom of his dramatic composition in *The Tempest* never seems merely conventional or capricious because the linkage of analogy is so varied and so pervasive.

The surest proof of the pervasiveness of Shakespeare's design lies in the mere number of continuities that can be discovered in the play. But some are more important than others because they can be traced through more expressions or in more scenes and because they express analogies more closely related to the key metaphor. The six main continuities, roughly labelled to indicate their character, are: 'strange-wondrous,' 'sleep-and-dream,' 'sea-tempest,' 'music-and-noise,' 'earth-air,' 'slavery-freedom,' and 'sovereignty-conspiracy.'

All of these continuities appear during the second scene of Act I, which is an exposition of Shakespeare's metaphorical and dramatic designs for the entire play. Near the close of the scene, Ariel's two songs offer wonderfully concentrated expressions of both designs. 'Come unto these yellow sands' calms the 'fury' of the waves and Ferdinand's 'passion,' thus charting in brief the course of the action. 'Full fathom five' is anticipatory in a very different fashion. It presents in miniature the main lines of the metaphorical design and sounds the key note of 'sea-change,' Shakespeare's most direct expression of the key metaphor of *The Tempest*.

The central portion of the scene follows:

ACT I, *scene* ii
Enter PROSPERO *and* MIRANDA

MIRANDA: If by your art, my dearest father, you have
    Put the wild waters in this roar, allay them.
    The sky, it seems, would pour down stinking pitch,
    But that the sea, mounting to th' welkin's cheek,
    Dashes the fire out. O! I have suffer'd
    With those that I saw suffer: a brave vessel,
    Who had, no doubt, some noble creatures in her,
    Dash'd all to pieces. O! the cry did knock
    Against my very heart. Poor souls, they perish'd.
    Had I been any god of power, I would
    Have sunk the sea within the earth, or e'er
    It should the good ship so have swallow'd and
    The fraughting souls within her.
PROSPERO: Be collected:
    No more amazement. Tell your piteous heart
    There 's no harm done.
MIRANDA: O, woe the day!
PROSPERO: No harm.
    I have done nothing but in care of thee,—
    Of thee, my dear one! thee, my daughter!—who
    Art ignorant of what thou art, nought knowing
    Of whence I am: nor that I am more better
    Than Prospero, master of a full poor cell,
    And thy no greater father,
MIRANDA: More to know
    Did never meddle with my thoughts.
PROSPERO: 'Tis time
    I should inform thee further. Lend thy hand,

And pluck my magic garment from me.—So:

                                                   [*Lays down his mantle.*]

Lie there, my art.—Wipe thou thine eyes; have comfort.
The direful spectacle of the wrack, which touch'd
The very virtue of compassion in thee,
I have with such provision in mine art
So safely order'd, that there is no soul—
No, not so much perdition as an hair,
Betid to any creature in the vessel
Which thou heard'st cry, which thou saw'st sink. Sit down;
For thou must now know further.

MIRANDA: You have often
Begun to tell me what I am, but stopp'd,
And left me to a bootless inquisition,
Concluding, 'Stay; not yet.'

PROSPERO: The hour's now come,
The very minute bids thee ope thine ear;
Obey and be attentive. Canst thou remember
A time before we came unto this cell?
I do not think thou canst, for then thou wast not
Out three years old.

MIRANDA: Certainly, sir, I can.

PROSPERO: By what? by any other house or person?
Of anything the image tell me, that
Hath kept with thy remembrance.

MIRANDA: 'Tis far off;
And rather like a dream than an assurance
That my remembrance warrants. Had I not
Four or five women once that tended me?

PROSPERO: Thou hadst, and more, Miranda. But how is it
That this lives in thy mind? What seest thou else
In the dark backward and abysm of time?
If thou remember'st aught ere thou cam'st here,
How thou cam'st here, thou may'st.

MIRANDA: But that I do not.

PROSPERO: Twelve year since, Miranda, twelve year since,
Thy father was the Duke of Milan and
A prince of power.

MIRANDA: Sir, are not you my father?

PROSPERO: Thy mother was a piece of virtue, and
She said thou wast my daugther; and thy father
Was Duke of Milan, and his only heir
A princess,—no worse issued.

MIRANDA: O, the heavens!
What foul play had we that we came from thence?
Or blessed was 't we did?

PROSPERO: Both, both, my girl:
    By foul play, as thou say'st, were we heav'd thence:
    But blessedly holp hither.
MIRANDA: O! my heart bleeds
    To think o' the teen that I have turn'd you to,
    Which is from my remembrance. Please you, further.
PROSPERO: My brother and thy uncle, call'd Antonio,—
    I pray thee, mark me,—that a brother should
    Be so perfidious!—he whom next thyself,
    Of all the world I lov'd, and to him put
    The manage of my state; as at that time
    Through all the signiories it was the first,
    And Prospero the prime duke; being so reputed
    In dignity, and for the liberal arts,
    Without a parallel: those being all my study,
    The government I cast upon my brother,
    And to my state grew stranger, being transported
    And rapt in secret studies. Thy false uncle—
    Dost thou attend me?
MIRANDA: Sir, most heedfully.
PROSPERO: Being once perfected how to grant suits,
    How to deny them, who t' advance, and who
    To trash for over-topping; new created
    The creatures that were mine, I say, or chang'd 'em,
    Or else new form'd 'em: having both the key
    Of officer and office, set all hearts i' the state
    To what tune pleas'd his ear; that now he was
    The ivy which had hid my princely trunk,
    And suck'd my verdure out on't.—Thou attend'st not.
MIRANDA: O, good sir! I do.
PROSPERO: I pray thee, mark me.
    I, thus neglecting worldly ends, all dedicated
    To closeness and the bettering of my mind
    With that, which, but by being so retir'd,
    O'erpriz'd all popular rate, in my false brother
    Awak'd an evil nature; and my trust,
    Like a good parent, did beget of him
    A falsehood in its contrary as great
    As my trust was; which had, indeed no limit,
    A confidence sans bound. He being thus lorded,
    Not only with what my revenue yielded,
    But what my power might else exact,—like one,
    Who having, into truth, by telling of it,
    Made such a sinner of his memory,
    To credit his own lie,—he did believe
    He was indeed the duke; out o' the substitution,

And executing th' outward face of royalty,
With all prerogative:—Hence his ambition growing,—
Dost thou hear?
MIRANDA: Your tale, sir, would cure deafness.
PROSPERO: To have no screen between this part he play'd
And him he play'd it for, he needs will be
Absolute Milan. Me, poor man,—my library
Was dukedom large enough: of temporal royalties
He thinks me now incapable; confederates,—
So dry he was for sway,—wi' the king of Naples
To give him annual tribute, do him homage;
Subject his coronet to his crown, and bend
The dukedom, yet unbow'd,—alas, poor Milan!—
To most ignoble stooping.
MIRANDA: O the heavens!
PROSPERO: Mark his condition and the event; then tell me
If this might be a brother.
MIRANDA: I should sin
To think but nobly of my grandmother:
Good wombs have borne bad sons.
PROSPERO: Now the condition.
This King of Naples, being an enemy
To me inveterate, hearkens my brother's suit;
Which was, that he, in lieu o' the premises
Of homage and I know not how much tribute,
Should presently extirpate me and mine
Out of the dukedom, and confer fair Milan,
With all the honours on my brother: whereon,
A treacherous army levied, one midnight
Fated to the purpose did Antonio open
The gates of Milan; and, i' the dead of darkness,
The ministers for the purpose hurried thence
Me and thy crying self
MIRANDA: Alack, for pity!
I, not rememb'ring how I cried out then,
Will cry it o'er again: it is a hint,
That wrings mine eyes to 't.
PROSPERO: Hear a little further,
And then I'll bring thee to the present business
Which now 's upon us; without the which this story
Were most impertinent.
MIRANDA: Wherefore did they not
That hour destroy us?
PROSPERO: Well demanded, wench:
My tale provokes that question. Dear, they durst not,
So dear the love my people bore me, nor set

A mark so bloody on the business; but
With colours fairer painted their foul ends.
In few, they hurried us aboard a bark,
Bore us some leagues to sea; where they prepar'd
A rotten carcass of a boat, not rigg'd,
Nor tackle, sail, nor mast; the very rats
Instinctively have quit it: there they hoist us,
To cry to the sea that roar'd to us; to sigh
To the winds whose pity, sighing back again.
Did us but loving wrong.

MIRANDA: Alack! what trouble
Was I then to you!

PROSPERO: O, a cherubin
Thou wast, that did preserve me! Thou didst smile,
Infused with a fortitude from heaven,
When I have deck'd the sea with drops full salt,
Under my burden groan'd; which rais'd in me
An undergoing stomach, to bear up
Against what should ensue.

MIRANDA: How came we ashore?

PROSPERO: By Providence divine.
Some food we had and some fresh water that
A noble Neapolitan, Gonzalo,
Out of his charity,—who being then appointed
Master of this design,—did give us, with
Rich garments, linens, stuffs, and necessaries,
Which since have steaded much; so, of his gentleness,
Knowing I lov'd my books, he furnish'd me,
From mine own library with volumes that
I prize above my dukedom.

MIRANDA: Would I might
But ever see that man!

PROSPERO: Now I arise:—   [*Resumes his mantle.*]
Sit still, and hear the last of our sea-sorrow.
Here in this island we arriv'd; and here
Have I, thy schoolmaster, made thee more profit
Than other princes can, that have more time
For vainer hours and tutors not so careful.

MIRANDA: Heavens thank you for 't! And now, I pray you, sir.—
For still 'tis beating in my mind,—your reason
For raising this sea-storm?

PROSPERO: Know thus far forth.
By accident most strange, bountiful Fortune,
Now my dear lady, hath mine enemies
Brought to this shore; and by my prescience
I find my zenith doth depend upon

> A most auspicious star, whose influence
> If now I court not but omit, my fortunes
> Will ever after droop. Here cease more questions;
> Thou art inclin'd to sleep; 'tis a good dulness,
> And give it way;—I know thou canst not choose.

As we trace the first two continuities ('strange-wondrous,' 'sleep-and-dream'), the reader can appreciate how unobtrusively they emerge from the developing dramatic pattern. Prospero's narrative, with which the scene opens, tells us of the past and describes the present situation while symbolizing the quality of *The Tempest* world. Prospero explains that his enemies have come to this shore 'by accident most strange,' and Miranda, who falls to sleep at the end of his tale, accounts for her lapse of saying,

> The strangeness of your story put
> Heaviness in me.

Prospero's tale was strange indeed: it included a ruler 'rapt in secret studies,' a 'false uncle' who 'new created / The creatures' of the state, the miraculous voyage of Prospero and Miranda (who was 'a cherubin') and their safe arrival 'by Providence divine.' This 'strangeness' is best defined by Alonso's remarks near the end of the play:

> These are not natural events; they strengthen
> From strange to stranger . . .

> This is as strange a maze as e'er men trod;
> And there is in this business more than nature
> Was ever conduct of . . .

They are 'unnatural' in a broad seventeenth-century sense of the term; that is, outside the order which includes all created things. The theme is almost constantly being played on: 'strange,' 'strangely,' or 'strangeness' occur altogether some seventeen times, and similar meanings are echoed in 'wondrous,' 'monstrous,' 'divine.'

Of all the analogies of the play this is probably the vaguest, the nearest in effect to the atmospheric unity of nineteenth-century Romantic poetry. But a more precise metaphor of strangeness appears, the 'strange-ness' of 'new created creatures.' From the 'accident most strange' of the shipwreck we come to Alonso's ponderous woe:

> O thou, mine heir
> Of Naples and of Milan! what strange fish
> Hath made his meal on thee?

and then to Trinculo's discovery of Caliban—'A strange fish!' With a similar comic antiphony, Miranda finds Ferdinand 'a thing divine,' and Ferdinand replies, 'O you wonder'; while a little later Caliban hails Trinculo as his god and cries, 'Thou wondrous man.' The full significance of these strange births will appear later.

The vague 'strangeness' of the island world is closely allied to a state of sleep, both continuities appearing in Miranda's remark about the 'heaviness' that came over her while listening to Prospero's story. The feeling that we are entering on an experience of sleep-and-dream arises beautifully out of the dramatic and rhythmic texture of the opening dialogue between father and daughter. The movement of these speeches with their oddly rocking repetitions is in key with the sleepy incredibility of the events about to be described: 'Canst thou remember . . . thou canst . . . I can . . . thy remembrance . . . my remembrance . . . thou remember'st . . . Twelve year since, Miranda, twelve year since . . .' Throughout the story Prospero is continually reminding Miranda to 'attend' to the telling, and it seems perfectly natural that at the end she should be 'inclin'd to sleep.' (Note in passing how neatly Shakespeare has broken a long narrative into dialogue and also given a distinct impression of Prospero's firmness and of Miranda's innocent dependence.) Miranda's images of the past come back to her 'rather like a dream,' and Prospero seems to be drawing their story from a world of sleep, 'the dark backward and abysm of time.'

With the next scene (the mourning King and his courtiers) we meet one of Shakespeare's typical analogical progressions. The sleep which affects the courtiers is, like Miranda's, a strange 'heaviness.' Their dialogue runs down, psychologically and rhythmically, through three echoes of Miranda's words:

> GONZALO: Will you laugh me asleep, for I am very heavy? . . .
> SEBASTIAN: Do not omit the heavy offer of it . . .
> ALONSO: Thank you. Wondrous heavy.
> SEBASTIAN: What a strange drowsiness possesses them!

The conversation that follows between the conspirators shows how Shakespeare uses an analogy to move to a new level of action and experience and to make them harmonious with what precedes and follows. Sebastian and Antonio begin by talking about actual sleep and waking: why are they not drowsy like the others? Then Antonio shifts to talking of sleepiness and alertness of mind, and from that to imagining that he sees 'a crown dropping' upon Sebastian's head. The wit becomes more complex as Sebastian describes Antonio's talk as 'sleepy language'—without meaning—though indicating that it does have meaning, 'There's meaning in thy snores.' This dialogue, which readers are liable to dismiss as so much Elizabethan wit, has its place within the play's metaphorical pattern. The plotting takes on a preposterous dreamy-sleepy character like that of Prospero's narrative and Miranda's recollections. Through such verbal trifling Shakespeare maintains the continuous quality of his imagined world.

References to similar wakings and sleepings, to dreams and dreamlike states, abound from here to the end of the play, where the sailors are 'brought moping . . . even in a dream,' and the grand awakening of all the characters is completed. But up to that point confusion between waking and sleep is the rule, being awake is never far from sleep or dream. In *The Tempest* sleep is always imminent, and more than once action ends in sleep or trance.

The witty talk of the conspirators glides from conceits of 'sleep' to conceits of 'the sea,' to talk of 'standing water' and 'flowing' and 'ebbing.' The 'good Gonzalo,' in consoling the King, speaks in similar figures:

> It is foul weather in us all, good sir,
> When you are cloudy.

Recurrent expressions of 'sea and tempest,' like those of 'sleep and dream,' are numerous and have a similar atmospheric value of not letting us forget the special quality of life on Prospero's island. But they also have far more important effects, for many of them become metaphors which are more precisely and more variously symbolic and which link more kinds of experience together.

By tracing two groups of 'tempest' expressions, metaphors of 'seaswallowing' and images of 'clouds,' we may understand how these more complex analogies are built up. We may also see how Shakespeare moves from narrative fact to metaphor, from image or metaphor referring only to narrative fact to metaphor rich in moral and psychological implications. As in creating the analogies of 'strangeness' and 'sleep,' Shakespeare starts from a dramatic necessity: the audience must be told what the situation was in the storm scene with which the play opens, and they must learn through an actor (Miranda) how they are to take it. . . . Although there is a hint of magic in Miranda's vision of the tempest, she pictures it as a violent actuality:

> Had I been any god of power, I would
> Have sunk the sea within the earth, or e'er
> It should the good ship so have swallow'd and
> The fraughting souls within her.

As if there were an inner rhythm in these responses, this metaphor, like others we have been tracing, recurs in the plotting episode. Antonio is speaking of his sister Claribel, left behind in Tunis:

> she that from whom
> We all were sea-swallow'd, though some cast again,
> And by that destiny to perform an act
> Whereof what 's past is prologue, what to come
> In yours and my discharge.

In this new context 'sea-swallowed' does several things at once. It brings back Miranda's horrified impression; but the magical nature of the storm now being known, the phrase reminds us that there was no 'sea-swallowing,' no actual sinking of 'fraughting souls.' Next, with a curiously Shakespearean 'glide and a jump' via the pun on 'cast,' 'sea-swallowed' merges into another metaphor (they are now 'cast' as actors in destiny's drama). 'Sea-swallowing' has become a metaphor that expresses destiny's extraordinary way of bringing Sebastian to the throne.

The irony of Antonio's words, which is clear to the audience, is made explicit later in the solemn speech in which Ariel explains the purpose of the tempest:

> You are three men of sin, whom Destiny—
> That hath to instrument this lower world
> And what is in 't,—the never-surfeited sea
> Hath caused to belch up you . . .

Few passages could show better how Shakespeare carries his analogies along and at the same time completely renews them. The 'belching up' recalls the wreck and the casting ashore and the earlier connection with destiny. But the sea's action is now described in much grosser terms and with grim sarcasm, while the oddly compact grammar makes 'the never-surfeited sea' very nearly a synonym for 'Destiny.' The violence though increased is now religious and moral; the imagery has become expressive of the strenuous punishment and purification of 'three men of sin' [Alonso, Antonio, Sebastian]. So by the continuity of his varying metaphor Shakespeare has expressed an unbroken transition from actual storm to the storm of the soul. This sequence, which expresses both physical and metaphysical transformations, points very clearly to the key metaphor of *The Tempest*.

The recurrent cloud images present a similar sequence as they take on various symbolic meanings in the course of the play. 'Cloud' does not actually occur in the opening storm scene, but when Trinculo sees 'another storm brewing' and speaks of a 'black cloud,' we are reminded of the original tempest. The cloud undergoes an appropriate change in Trinculo's speech; it 'looks like a foul bombard that would shed his liquor.' This comic cloud is very different from 'the curl'd clouds' on which Ariel rides, though they too are associated with storms. The clouds of Caliban's exquisite speech are those of Ariel and the deities of the masque:

>   and then, in dreaming,
> The clouds methought would open and show riches
> Ready to drop upon me . . .

Clouds—here linked with magical riches—become in Prospero's 'cloud-capp'd towers' speech a symbol for the unsubstantial splendor of the world. One of the subordinate metaphors there, the 'melting into air' and the 'dissolving' of the clouds, is picked up in Prospero's later words about the courtiers:

>   The charm dissolves apace;
> And as the morning steals upon the night,
> Melting the darkness, so their rising senses
> Begin to chase the ignorant fumes that mantle
> Their clearer reason.

This dissolution of night clouds (suggested also by 'fumes') is a figure for the change from madness to sanity, from evil ignorance to the clear perceptions of reason. Although the cloud images of the play are so varied, they have a common symbolic value, for whether they are clouds of tempest or of visionary riches or of the soul, they are always magically unsubstantial. The reader is led to feel some touch of likeness among experiences as different as a storm at sea, a bit of drunken whimsy, a vision of heavenly and earthly beauty, and a spiritual regeneration. The cloud sequence, as an arc of metaphor, is in perfect relation to the gradual dramatic movement from tempest and punishment to fair weather and reconciliation, the images having meanings more and more remote from any actual storm.

The 'cloud-like' change in the distracted souls of the guilty nobles was induced (as if in reminiscence of Plato) by *Solemn music*—

> A solemn air and the best comforter
> To an unsettled fancy.

Many of the expressions referring to music, like the stage direction above, are not explicitly metaphorical, but along with the continuities of 'sleep' and 'strangeness' they help maintain the magical character of the action.

The music is always the music of spirits and always a sign of more than natural events.

The one fairly constant musical metaphor in *The Tempest* is the symbolic opposition of confused noises, especially storm sounds, and harmonious music. The key word and the central impression of the opening scene is certainly 'noise' in the modern sense. The impression is carried over in the first words of the next scene:

> If by your art, my dearest father, you have
> Put the wild waters in this roar, allay them.

Miranda's request is soon answered by Ariel's first song, 'the wild waves' are 'whist.' The *solemn and strange music* heard when the *strange Shapes* bring a banquet to the courtiers makes Alonso say, 'What harmony is this? my good friends, hark!' Gonzalo replies: 'Marvellous sweet music!' By contrast, when Ariel enters shortly after, in order to inform the 'three men of sin' of their punishment by the storm, there is an off-stage sound of *Thunder and lightning*. The masque vision which Ferdinand finds 'harmoniously charmingly' is rudely interrupted by *a strange, hollow, and confused noise* which symbolizes the stormy anger expressed by Prospero in the speeches that follow. When in the next scene he prepares to forgive his enemies, he abjures the 'rough magic' by which he

> call'd forth the mutinous winds,
> And 'twixt the green sea and the azur'd vault
> Set roaring war . . .

As the *solemn music* is played the clouds of ignorance 'dissolve,' and so the musical metaphor, like the sea metaphor, has moved from outer to inner weather.

The music analogy has some close links with the earth-air continuity which we glanced at in the introductory chapter of the book. Ferdinand, following Ariel's 'yellow sands' song, asks, 'Where should this music be? i' th' air, or th' earth?' And a little later:

> This is no mortal business, nor no sound
> That the earth owes: I hear it now above me.

The connection of air and music can never be long forgotten: Ariel and his spirits of 'thin air' are the musicians of the island.

The earth-air, Caliban-Ariel antithesis coincides at points with what we might call a slavery-freedom continuity, for Caliban is in Prospero's words both 'slave' and 'earth.' Ariel too is called a 'slave' by Prospero, and for the time of the play he is as much a slave as Caliban. He is always asking for his freedom, which is at last granted, his release being symbolically expressed in the airy rovings of his final song. He flies into perpetual summer and, like air, becomes merged with the elements. By contrast, the 'high-day, freedom!' of which Caliban sings is ironically enough simply a change of masters.

The 'slaves' and 'servants' of the play suffer various kinds of imprisonment, from Ariel in his 'cloven pine' to Ferdinand's mild confinement, and before the end of Act IV everyone except Prospero and Miranda has been imprisoned in one way or another. During the course of Act V all the prisoners except Ferdinand (who has already been released) are set free, each of them by Prospero's special command.

A sovereignty-conspiracy analogy parallels very closely the slavery-freedom analogy, some of the same persons, e.g. Ferdinand and Caliban, appearing as both slaves and conspirators. 'That foul conspiracy / Of the beast Caliban, and his confederates' is of course a parody version of the 'Open-ey'd Conspiracy' of Sebastian and Antonio. Ferdinand, too, is charged fantastically by Prospero with plotting against his island rule. Talk of kings and royalty turns up in many scenes, being connected usually with the denial of kingship, as in 'good Gonzalo's' speech on his golden age commonwealth where 'he would be king' and yet have 'no sovereignty.' Though no single explicit metaphor for conspiracy or usurpation is often repeated, Shakespeare rings many changes on the theme as he moves, from plot to plot. Prospero's brother, we recall, is said to have 'new created the creatures' of state. Alonso's seizure of power is called a 'substitution': 'crediting his own lies,' he began to believe 'he was indeed the duke,' and from merely playing a part he went on to become 'absolute Milan.' The figure is picked up in the somnolent dialogue of Sebastian and Antonio:

> I remember
> You did supplant your brother Prospero.

In the second of the scenes in which Caliban and his fellows plot to overthrow the island 'tyrant,' Sebastian's 'supplant' is recalled with a difference:

CALIBAN: I would my valiant master would destroy thee; I do not lie.
STEPHANO: Trinculo, if you trouble him any more in his tale, by this hand,
   I will supplant some of your teeth.

The figure recurs a little later in more serious context:

> . . . you three
> From Milan did supplant good Prospero.

In Act V after various supplantings, serious and comic, accomplished or merely projected, all true kings are restored and all false ones dethroned.

The two continuities, sovereignty-conspiracy and slavery-freedom, are also alike in the fact that their metaphorical force is expressed through scenes that are just one step removed from allegory. The more serious of the restorations and releases convey similar kinds of moral meaning. Ferdinand's release from 'wooden slavery' signifies that he is a true lover and a true prince. In being freed from madness Alonso has escaped from 'heart-sorrow' and regained his rightful rank and a 'clear life ensuing.' Both continuities convey an impression of topsy-turvydom in the order of things, an unnatural interchange of status among creatures of every kind. Both express a return to stability after a disturbance of degree.

What then is the key metaphor through which the various continuities are linked, and how are they connected through it? Shakespeare's most direct expression of his key metaphor is 'sea-change,' the key phrase of Ariel's song. But what does Shakespeare mean by 'sea-change'? Ariel sings of 'bones' being made into 'coral' and of 'eyes' becoming 'pearls.' 'A change into something rich and strange,' we now understand, is a change 'out of nature.' 'Sea-change' is a metaphor for 'magical transformation,' for metamorphosis. The key metaphor of the play is 'change' in this special sense, and 'change' is the analogy common to all of the continuities we have been tracing. (I am not forgetting that they are also expressive of many other relationships, or that Shakespeare is often playing with two or three metaphors at once, as in the various figures of 'sea-swallowing.' But all are at least expressive of change, or changeableness.)

Through the first rather vague analogies we traced, of 'strangeness' and 'sleep-and-dream,' numerous events and persons in the play are qualified as belonging to a realm where anything may happen. Expressions of 'strangeness' and 'sleep,' like many of the references to sea and music, suggest 'far other Worlds and other Seas,' where magical change is to be expected. A more particular metaphor of change is expressed through the stress on the 'strangeness' of 'new creations' and on the confusion between sleep and dream and waking. The island is a world of fluid, merging states of being and forms of life. This lack of dependable boundaries between states is also expressed by the many instances of confusion between natural and divine. Miranda says that she might call Ferdinand

> A thing divine; for nothing natural
> I ever saw so noble.

Ferdinand cannot be sure whether she is a goddess or a maid, and Caliban takes Trinculo for a 'brave god.' There is a further comic variation on this theme in Trinculo's difficulty in deciding whether to classify Caliban as fish or man, monster or devil.

But 'change' is most clearly and richly expressed through the sequence of tempest images (especially 'cloud' and 'sea-swallowed') and through the noise-music antithesis. All kinds of sounds, harmonious and ugly, like the manifestations of sea and storm, are expressive of magical transformation. 'The fire and cracks / Of sulphurous roaring' (imagery in which both storm and sound analogies are blended) 'infects' the courtiers' 'reason,' and *solemn music* induces the 'clearing' of their understanding. The 'music' and the 'tempest' continuities, taken together as metaphors of 'sea-change,' are perhaps the most extensive of all the analogies in their organizing power. They recur often, they connect a wide diversity of experiences, and they express in symbolic form some of the main steps in the drama, in particular, the climactic moments of inner change: Ariel's revelation to the courtiers of their guilt, Alonso's first show of remorse, and the final purification.

The earth-air or Caliban-Ariel antithesis may seem to have very little to do with metamorphosis. But the relation of this theme to the key metaphor is clear and important. Air, Ariel, and his music are a blended symbol of change as against the unchanging Caliban, 'the thing of darkness.' He can be punished, but hardly humanized; he is, says Prospero,

> A devil, a born devil, on whose nature
> Nurture can never stick; on whom my pains,
> Humanely taken, are all lost, quite lost.

The other continuities parallel to earth-air, of slavery-freedom and conspiracy-sovereignty, are frequently expressive of major and minor changes of status among the inhabitants and temporary visitors on Prospero's island.

But the interconnection of Shakespeare's analogies through the key metaphor cannot be adequately described, since we are able to speak of only one point of relationship at a time. We can get a better sense of the felt union of various lines of analogy in *The Tempest* by looking at the two passages where Shakespeare expresses his key metaphor most completely, the 'Full fathom five' song and Prospero's 'cloud-capp'd towers' speech.

Rereading Ariel's song at this point we can see how many of the main continuities are alluded to and related in the description of 'sea-change' and how the song anticipates the metaphorical design that emerges through the dialogue of the whole play. The total metaphorical pattern is to an amazing degree an efflorescence from this single crystal:

> Full fathom five thy father lies;
> Of his bones are coral made:
> Those are pearls that were his eyes:
> Nothing of him that doth fade,
> But doth suffer a sea-change
> Into something rich and strange.
> Sea-nymphs hourly ring his knell:
> BURTHEN: 'Ding-dong!'
> Hark! now I hear them—Ding-dong bell.

In addition to the more obvious references to the deep sea and its powers and to the 'strangeness' of this drowning, there are indirect anticipations of other analogies. 'Fade' prefigures the 'dissolving cloud' metaphor and the theme of tempest changes, outer and inner. 'Rich,' along with 'coral' and 'pearls,' anticipates the opulent imagery of the dream-world passages and scenes, the 'riches ready to drop' on Caliban and the expressions of wealth and plenty in the masque. The song closes with the nymphs tolling the bell, the transformation and the 'sea sorrow' are expressed through sea-music. Ferdinand's comment reminds us that the song has connections with two other lines of analogy:

> The ditty does remember my drown'd father.
> This is no mortal business, nor no sound
> That the earth owes:—I hear it now above me.

The song convinces Ferdinand that he is now King of Naples (the first of the interchanges of sovereignty), and it is a 'ditty' belonging not to the 'earth,' but to the 'air.'

The sense of relationship between the many continuities is still more vividly felt in the lines of Prospero's most memorable speech:

> You do look, my son, in a mov'd sort,
> As if you were dismay'd: be cheerful, sir:
> Our revels now are ended. These our actors,
> As I foretold you, were all spirits and
> Are melted into air, into thin air:
> And, like the baseless fabric of this vision,
> The cloud-capp'd towers, the gorgeous palaces,
> The solemn temples, the great globe itself,
> Yea, all which it inherit, shall dissolve
> And, like this insubstantial pageant faded,
> Leave not a rack behind. We are such stuff
> As dreams are made on, and our little life
> Is rounded with a sleep.

In Prospero's words Shakespeare has gathered all the lights of analogy into a single metaphor which sums up the metaphorical design and the essential meaning of *The Tempest*. The language evokes nearly every continuity that we have traced. 'Melted into air,' 'dissolve,' 'cloud,' and 'rack' bring us immediately to Ariel and tempest changes, while 'vision,' 'dream' and 'sleep' recall other familiar continuities. 'Revels,' 'gorgeous palaces,' and 'pageant' (for Elizabethans closely associated with royalty) are echoes of the kingly theme; and 'solemn' is associated particularly with the soft music of change. The 'stuff' of dreams is at once cloud-stuff (air) and cloth, both images being finely compressed in 'baseless fabric.' Taken with 'faded' these images refer obliquely to the garments so miraculously 'new-dyed . . . with salt water,' one of the first signs of 'sea-change' noted by Gonzalo. Within the metaphor of tempest-clearing and of cloud-like transformation, Shakespeare has included allusions to every important analogy of change in the play.

But it is through the twofold progress of the whole figure that the change metaphor is experienced and its most general meaning fully understood. We read first: that like the actors and scenery of the vision, earth's glories and man shall vanish into nothingness. Through a happy mistake we also read otherwise. By the time we have passed through 'dissolve,' 'insubstantial,' and 'faded,' and reached 'leave not a rack behind,' we are reading 'cloud-capped towers' in reverse as a metaphor for tower-like clouds. 'Towers,' 'palaces,' 'temples,' 'the great globe,' 'all which it inherit' are now taken for cloud forms. Through a sort of Proustian merging of icon and subject, we experience the blending of states of being, of substantial and unsubstantial, or real and unreal, which is the essence of *The Tempest* metamorphosis.

Similar meanings are expressed through the closing dream figure, which grows equally out of the metaphorical context of the speech and the play. 'Rounded,' we should take with Kittredge as 'surrounded,' but without losing the force of round, as in Donne's 'surrounded with tears.' 'Our little life' is more than sentimental, it is our little life (microcosm) in contrast with 'the great globe' (macrocosm). There may also be an over-image in 'surrounded' of the world in classical myth and geography with its encircling ocean, sleep being the stream that 'rounds' the lesser world. In relation to the metaphorical design of the play, 'rounded with a sleep' and the notion of life ending in dreams express again the sense of confusion between sleep and dream and waking. This metaphor which completes the figure of cloud-change is Shakespeare's most perfect symbol for the closeness of states that to our daylight sense are easily separable. Although the vision here expressed goes far beyond the play, it is still a natural extension of the dramatic moment and a fulfilment of the metaphor that has been implicit since the noisy opening lines of *The Tempest*.

But if Shakespeare's total metaphor is in a sense present everywhere, it is also a design that develops in close relation to the main dramatic movement of the play. As we have noted more than once, a particular metaphor will be varied to fit a new dramatic situation and so serve to express the situation more fully and to anticipate the next step in the development of the drama. The best example of this adaptation of metaphor comes in a speech in which Shakespeare seems to be playing capriciously with his noise-music theme. At first sight the passage seems inconsistent with the symbolic contrast between storm noise and music:

> ALONSO: O, it is monstrous! monstrous!
> Methought the billows spoke and told me of it;
> The winds did sing it to me; and the thunder,
> That deep and dreadful organ-pipe, pronounc'd
> The name of Prosper: it did bass my trespass.

It is admittedly odd that the confused noise of the tempest should, in Alonso's soul, compose a harmony—however gloomy—but the paradox fits in perfectly with the developing structure of the play. Alonso has just been told by Ariel that the storm had a purpose as an instrument of Destiny. Since at this moment remorse first appears in the play and the inner clearing begins, it is exactly right that the storm sounds should seem harmonious and so point forward to the events of the fourth and fifth acts. No use of metaphor in *The Tempest* reveals more clearly Shakespeare's exact sense of the movement of his drama, of the changing human relations and feelings he is presenting.

In building up his metaphorical design, Shakespeare prepares us for the moment in *The Tempest* when the major shift in dramatic relationships takes place. The moment comes in the speech in which Prospero describes the behavior of the King and the courtiers as they slowly return from madness to sanity. The first important step toward this climax, Alonso's acknowledgment of his guilt, was expressed through a metaphor combining both sea and musical changes. The next step, Ferdinand's release from his tempest-trials and from dream-like enchantment, is expressed through the masque, which is an elaborate dramatization of metamorphosis, Ariel's 'meaner fellows,' 'the rabble,' being now transformed into majestic Olympian goddesses. Once again, familiar continuities appear, and again they are transformed to fit a new occasion. 'Earth,' for example, is no longer 'barren place and fertile,' but the earth enriched by human cultivation and symbolized now by Ceres—not by Caliban, who is 'nature resisting nurture.' Iris summons this new Earth in the gorgeous speech beginning 'Ceres, most bounteous lady, thy rich leas . . . ,' lines in which we hear a quite new majesty of tone and movement. The couplet form sets the dialogue apart from human speech, while the longer periods, the added stresses, the phrasal balancings are especially appropriate to 'that large utterance of the early gods.' (Here is one of many instances of how Shakespeare adapts his sound patterns to his metaphorical and dramatic designs.) Prospero's visionary speech that ends 'the revels' is not simply a concentration of metaphor without reference to the dramatic development. It announces the changes to come, it gives a rich expression of their meaning, and it anticipates the dream-like flux of the psychological events of the last act.

If we now read Prospero's words in Act V, in which he describes the great changes as they take place, we see many references back to Shakespeare's metaphorical preparation for this moment. We also realize that various lines of action and various lines of analogy are converging almost simultaneously. The speech opens with Prospero's farewell to his art, after which he turns his thoughts to 'restoring the senses' of the courtiers, whom Ariel has just gone to release:

> A solemn air and the best comforter
> To an unsettled fancy, cure thy brains,
> Now useless, boil'd within thy skull! There stand,
> For you are spell-stopp'd.
> Holy Gonzalo, honourable man,
> Mine eyes, even sociable to the show of thine,
> Fall fellowly drops. The charm dissolves apace;
> And as the morning steals upon the night,
> Melting the darkness, so their rising senses
> Begin to chase the ignorant fumes that mantle
> Their clearer reason.—O good Gonzalo!
> My true preserver, and a loyal sir
> To him thou follow'st, I will pay thy graces
> Home, both in word and deed.—Most cruelly
> Didst thou, Alonso, use me and my daughter:
> Thy brother was a furtherer in the act:—
> Thou'rt pinch'd for 't now, Sebastian.—Flesh and blood,
> You, brother mine, that entertain'd ambition,
> Expell'd remorse and nature; who, with Sebastian,—
> Whose inward pinches therefore are most strong,—
> Would here have kill'd your king: I do forgive thee,
> Unnatural though thou art!—Their understanding
> Begins to swell, and the approaching tide
> Will shortly fill the reasonable shores

That now lie foul and muddy. Not one of them
That yet looks on me, or would know me.—Ariel,
Fetch me the hat and rapier in my cell:—[Exit Ariel]
I will discase me, and myself present,
As I was sometime Milan.—Quickly, spirit;
Thou shalt ere long be free.

If this is a climactic moment, what changes in dramatic relationships are taking place, what is happening dramatically? The 'men of sin,'
like Ferdinand, have come to the end of the trials which began with the
storm and continued through various 'distractions.' Now, as Prospero
explains, they are undergoing a moral as well as a mental regeneration,
they are 'pinch'd' with remorse and are being forgiven. The twofold
regeneration is further dramatized in the speeches that follow: 'th' afflic-
tion of Alonso's mind amends,' he resigns Prospero's dukedom and 'entreats'
him to pardon his 'wrongs.'

But these are the prose facts, the bare bones of the changes in
dramatic relationships. We cannot feel the peculiar quality of what is
taking place or grasp its meaning apart from the metaphorical language
through which it is being expressed. And the expressions acquire their
force and precision from the whole metaphorical preparation we have
been tracing. The courtiers' senses are restored by 'an airy charm,' by
magic similar to that which was worked by Ariel and his spirits. The
allusions to 'heavenly music' and 'a solemn air,' in contrast to the 'rough
magic' that Prospero has abjured, remind us that these changes will be
musically harmonious, like the songs of Ariel, and not noisy and confused
like the storm sent to punish these men and reveal their 'monstrous' guilt.
Toward the end of the speech, the imagery recalls the tempest metaphor,
but it is altered so as to express the mental and moral change that is
taking place. The return of understanding is like an approaching tide that
covers the evidence of a storm (both 'foul' and 'muddy' have storm
associations from earlier occurrences).

But the metaphor that best expresses this clearing is the one for
which the preparation has been most complete:

The charm dissolves apace;
And as the morning steals upon the night,
Melting the darkness, so their rising senses
Begin to chase the ignorant fumes that mantle
Their clearer reason.

'Dissolving' and 'melting' and 'fumes' take us back at once to the grand
transformations of the masque speech, to the earlier cloud transformations

both serious and comic; and they take us back further to the association of clouds with magical tempests, inner storms, and clearing weather. We read of the moral and psychological transformations with a present sense of these analogies. They are qualified for us as a dream-like dissolution of tempest clouds, as events in the 'insubstantial' region where reality and unreality merge.

It is through such links that Shakespeare concentrates at this climactic moment the fullest meaning of his key metaphor. There is of course no separation in the reader's experience between the dramatic fact and the metaphorical qualification. The images that recur in Prospero's speech take us back to felt qualities, but to felt qualities embedded in particular dramatic contexts. 'Melting,' for example, carries us to the spirit-like dissolution of 'spirits . . . melted into air, into thin air'; but it also reminds us of the masque pageantry and of Prospero's calming of Ferdinand's fears. We hear Prospero's soothing and mysterious tone in both the earlier and later uses of the word. The dramatic links and the analogical links are experienced at once, which is to say that metaphorical design and dramatic design are perfectly integrated.

We can now realize that metamorphosis is truly the key metaphor to the *drama*, and not the key metaphor to a detachable design of decorative analogies. Through the echoes in Prospero's speech of various lines of analogy, Shakespeare makes us feel each shift in dramatic relationships as a magical transformation, whether it is the courtiers' return to sanity, or Prospero's restoration to his dukedom, or Ariel's flight into perpetual summer. While all of the 'slaves' and 'prisoners' are being freed, and while all of the 'sovereigns' are being restored, the sense of magical change is never wholly lost. The union of drama and metaphor in *The Tempest* is nowhere more complete than in the last act of the play.

The larger meaning of Shakespeare's total design, which was anticipated in the cloud and dream metaphor of Prospero's visionary speech, is most clearly and fully expressed in these final transformations. In a world where everything may become something else, doubts naturally arise, and in the swift flow of change the confusion about what is and what is not becomes fairly acute. When Prospero 'discases' himself and appears as Duke of Milan, Gonzalo says with understandable caution:

> Whether this be,
> Or be not, I'll not swear.

And Prospero answers:

> You do yet taste
> Some subtilties o' the isle, that will not let you
> Believe things certain.

Whereas in the earlier acts the characters had often accepted the unreal as real (spirits, shipwrecks, drownings, visions), they now find it difficult to accept the real as truly real. The play concludes with their acceptance of the unexpected change to reality. But for the spectator there remains the heightened sense of the 'thin partitions' that 'do divide' these states. The world that common sense regards as real, of order in nature and society and of sanity in the individual, is a shimmering transformation of disorder. 'We shall all be changed, in a moment, in the twinkling of an eye.' (This or something like it is as near as we can dome to describing the total attitude conveyed by *The Tempest.*)

Thus *The Tempest* is, like Marvell's 'Garden,' a Metaphysical poem of metamorphosis, though the meaning of change is quite different for the two writers. It is worth noting too that Shakespeare 'had Ovid in his eye,' a fact that is obvious from the echoes of Goldings' famous translation. There could be no better proof of Shakespeare's maturity than the contrast between the 'sweet witty' Ovidianism of 'Venus and Adonis' and the metaphorical design of *The Tempest*, which gives philosophic meaning to a drama of Ovidian metamorphosis. We remember 'a lily prison'd in a gaol of snow' as an isolated 'beauty,' but hardly as an apt symbol of the amorous relations of Venus and Adonis, or as symbolic of some larger meaning in their story. (Indeed a 'gaol of snow' is rather inept for the fervid goddess of the poem) 'Those were pearls that were his eyes' revives Ariel's sea-music, Ferdinand's melancholy, and a world of fantasy and transshifting states of being. The increased concentration in meaning of the image from *The Tempest* is a sign of a growth in the command of language which is command of life for a poet. As Arnold said of Wordsworth, Shakespeare now 'deals with more of *life*' and 'he deals with *life*, as a whole, more powerfully.' His maturity and power appear in the variety of experience so perfectly harmonized through the imaginative design of *The Tempest*.

ANNE BARTON

"Love's Labour's Lost"

In a sense the play has ended; an epilogue has been spoken by Berowne and that haunting and beautiful kingdom created by the marriage of reality with illusion destroyed, seemingly beyond recall. In the person of Marcade, the world outside the circuit of the park has at last broken through the gates, involving the people of the play in its sorrows and grim actualities, the plague-houses and desolate retreats, the mourning cities and courts of that vaster country overshadowing the tents and the fantastic towers of Navarre. Yet before the final dissolution of that minute and once isolated kingdom of the play, when some of the characters seem already to have disappeared and the others are preparing sadly to journey into the realms beyond the walls of the royal close, there is granted suddenly a little moment of grace. In the waning afternoon, all the people of the play return to the stage and stand quietly together to hear the song which "the two learned men have compiled in praise of the Owl and the Cuckoo," a song into which the whole of that now-vanished world of Love's Labour's Lost seems to have passed, its brilliance, its strange mingling of the artificial and the real, its loveliness and laughter gathered together for the last time to speak to us in the form of a single strain of music.

> When daisies pied and violets blue
> And lady-smocks all silver-white
> And Cuckoo-buds of yellow hue
> Do paint the meadows with delight. . . .

It is the landscape of the royal park that lies outstretched before us, a little world of thickets and smooth lawns, meadows and wooded hills. In

---

From *Shakespeare Quarterly* 4 (1953). Copyright © 1953 by Folger Shakespeare Library.

the foreground, their appearance and speech as decorative and charming as the setting in which they have met to solemnize their vows of asceticism and study, stand four young men, Berowne, Dumain, Longaville, and that ruler of Navarre whose slender kingdom of foresters and dairy-maids, courtiers, pedants, and fools seems bounded by the park and its single, rustic village. Mannered and artificial, reflecting an Elizabethan delight in patterned and intricate language, Navarre's lines at the beginning of the play are nevertheless curiously urgent and intense.

> Let fame, that all hunt after in their lives,
> Live regist'red upon our brazen tombs,
> And then grace us in the disgrace of death;
> When, spite of cormorant devouring Time,
> Th' endeavour of this present breath may buy
> That honour which shall bate his scythe's keen edge,
> And make us heirs of all eternity.

With the King's first words, an expression of that peculiarly Renaissance relationship of the idea of Fame with that of Time and Death, a shadow darkens for a moment the delicate dream landscape of the park. Touched by this shadow, affected by its reality, the four central characters of *Love's Labour's Lost* enter the world of the play.

Fantastic and contrived as they are, those absurd vows to which the four friends commit themselves in the initial scene spring from a recognition of the tragic brevity and impermanence of life that is peculiarly Renaissance. For the people of the sixteenth century, the world was no longer the mere shadow of a greater Reality, the imperfect image of that City of God whose towers and golden spires had dominated the universe of the Middle Ages. While the thought of Death was acquiring a new poignancy in its contrast with man's increasing sense of the value and loveliness of life in this world, Immortality tended to become, for Renaissance minds, a vague and even a somewhat dubious gift unless it could be connected in some way with the earth itself, and the affairs of human life there. Thus there arose among the humanist writers of Italy that intense and sometimes anguished longing, voiced by Navarre at the beginning of *Love's Labour's Lost*, to attain "an immortality of glory, survival in the minds of men by the record of great deeds or of intellectual excellence. . . ." At the very heart of the plan for an Academe lies the reality of Death, the Renaissance desire to inherit, through remarkable devotion to learning, an eternity of Fame, and thus to insure some continuity of personal existence, however slight, against the ravages of "cormorant devouring Time."

It is obvious, however, from the very beginning of the play, that the Academe and the idea of immorality which it embodies must fail. Less remote and docile than Dumain and Longaville, existing upon a deeper level of reality within the play, the brilliant and sensitive Berowne, a Chorus character throughout, first realizes how unnatural the vows are, how seriously they trespass, despite their three-year limit, against the normal laws of life and reality. The paradox of the Academe and the reason why its failure is not only understandable but absolutely necessary lie in the fact that this elaborate scheme which intends to enhance life and extend it through Fame even beyond the boundaries of the grave would in reality, if successfully carried out, result in the limitation of life and, ultimately, in its complete denial. In their very attempt to retain hold upon life, the King and his companions, as Berowne alone understands, are cutting themselves off from it, from love, and the beauty of women, from all those simple sensuous pleasures of the world which have prompted the establishment of the Academe in the first place by making the "too much loved earth more lovely," and the thought of its loss in Death so unbearably grim.

Long before the appearance of those two delightful but sobering characters, Holofernes and Nathanial, Berowne has seen the barrenness of learning that is divorced from life, the tragedy of industrious men of science who find a name for every star in the western skies and yet "have no more profit of their shining nights / Than those that walk and wot not what they are." Even in the first scene of the play, before his love for Rosaline has made his perception deeper and more sensitive, Berowne realizes in some sense that the only way to deal with the bleak reality of Death and Time is to accept it, to experience as much of life's sensory loveliness as possible while the opportunity is still given. Implicit in his earliest lines is the knowledge, related somehow to the first group of the "Sonnets," that "we cannot cross the cause why we were born," and although he agrees at last to take the oath, it is through him that we first sense the conviction expressed by the play as a whole that this idea of intellectual glory is an essentially sterile one, that the price exacted is too great to pay for a fame and a memory on earth that will soon be lost in the unimagined reaches of Time.

It was one of Walter Pater's most famous dictums that "All art constantly aspires towards the condition of music," and in his beautiful essay on "Shakespeare's English Kings" he asserted more particularly that "into the unity of a choric song the perfect drama ever tends to return, its intellectual scope deepened, complicated, enlarged, but still with an unmistakable singleness, or identity, in its impression on the mind." Such a unity is evident throughout *Love's Labour's Lost*, and, indeed, the quality of the whole is very much that of a musical composition, an inexorable movement forward, the appearance and reappearance in the fabric of the play of certain important themes, forcing the harmony into a series of coherent resolutions consistent with each other and with the drama as a whole. Berowne has scarcely finished speaking before his assertion that "every man with his affects is born, / Not by might mast'red, but by special grace" is echoed in the structure of the comedy itself, with the entrance of Constable Dull and the reluctant Costard, the first to disobey the edicts of the new Academe.

The little episode which follows is not only significant of the trend of future action but, in itself, one of the most delightful moments of the play. As the King reads Armado's incredible accusation and Costard tries feebly to avert impending doom by making Navarre laugh, it becomes obvious for the first time how much enchantment the play holds for the ear, how subtly it combines highly individual idioms of speech into a single conversation. *Love's Labour's Lost* is a play of many voices, and much of its beauty grows from the sheer music of their rise and fall, the exploitation of their differences of quality and tone, accent and complication. Here in the first scene, the frank simplicity of Dull, the awed monosyllables of Costard, are placed by Shakespeare in a deliberate musical relationship with the studied sentences of Longaville, the fantastic style of Armado, and the more attractive elegance of Berowne, and the whole episode is given the quality of a polyphonic composition half artificial and half real.

Beyond its humor and fascination of language, the Costard scene has, of course, a more serious purpose in the play, a purpose virtually identical with that fulfilled by a scene in *Measure for Measure*. In the later comedy, Angelo appears in the opening scene of the second act in a role analogous to Navarre's in *Love's Labour's Lost*, and the old counsellor Escalus in one similar to Berowne's. The scheme of justice which Angelo would enforce in Vienna is as ridiculously inflexible, as ignorant of the nature of human beings as Navarre's Academe, and it is protested by Escalus. Not, however, until the sudden entrance of Constable Elbow, an Austrian cousin of Dull's, and Pompey, who can in some measure be compared to Costard, does it become completely obvious how impractical the system is, how helpless its high-minded idealism when forced to deal with real individuals, their private standards of morality and unpredictable human weaknesses. The fate of Angelo's justice is settled even before he himself has sinned against it, in the process of that riotous contention between Elbow, Froth, and Pompey, and in the same way, Navarre's

Academe has failed before he and his friends are actually forsworn, from the moment that the real and intensely individual figures of Costard and Dull appear in their respective roles as transgressor and upholder. Among the lower social levels of the park, life itself destroys the King's scheme almost in the moment of its foundation.

Walter Pater found *Love's Labour's Lost* particularly charming in its changing "series of pictorial groups, in which the same figures reappear, in different combinations but on the same background," a composition, for him, like that of some ancient tapestry, studied, and not a little fantastic. The grouping of the characters into scenes would appear, however, to have been dictated by a purpose far more serious than the mere creation of such patterns; it is one of the ways in which Shakespeare maintains the balance of the play world between the artificial and the real, and indicates the final outcome of the comedy.

There are, of course, huge differences in the reality of the people who walk and speak together within the limits of the royal park. From the artificial and virtually indistinguishable figures of Dumain and Longaville, never really more than fashionable voices, the scale of reality rises gradually towards Berowne, in whom the marriage of a certain remote and fantastic quality with the delightful realism which first recognized the flaws in the Academe reflects the comedy as a whole, and reaches its apogee in the utter substantiality and prosaic charm of Constable Dull, who could never in any sense be accused of retreating into unreality, or affecting an elegant pose. Again and again, characters from different levels along this scale are grouped into scenes in a manner that helps to maintain the delicate balance of the play world; thus, in the first scene, with the incredible idea of the Academe and the sophisticated dialogue of Berowne and Longaville, Costard and the bewildered Dull are employed in much the same way that the mocking voice of the cuckoo is in the glowing spring landscape of the closing song, to keep the play in touch with a more familiar and real world, as well as to indicate the ultimate victory of reality over artifice and illusion.

As the first act ends, this theme is repeated again, and the inevitability of future events made even more clear with the abandonment of the edicts of the Academe by the very individual who was responsible for the deliverance of Costard into the righteous hands of Dull, the intense and serious Armado. The grave figure of the Spanish traveller is one of the most interesting and in a sense enigmatic to appear in *Love's Labour's Lost*, and his sudden love for Jaquenetta certainly the strangest of the five romances which develop within the park. Like Berowne, Armado is a very real person who is playing a part, but in his case it is far more difficult to separate the actor from the man underneath, and the pose itself is more complex than the fashionable role of Berowne. Even in his soliloquies, Armado seems to be acting to some invisible audience, and it is only in one moment at the end of the play that we are granted a glimpse of the man without the mask.

Romantic and proud, intensely imaginative, he has retreated into illusion much further than has Berowne, creating a world of his own within the world of the park, a world peopled with the heroes of the past, Samson and Hercules, Hector and the knights of Spain. Somehow, it is among these long-dead heroes that Armado really exists, rather than among the people of the play itself, and his bizarre language, so strange and artificial when placed beside the homely speech of Costard, was created for that remote, imaginative environment and possesses there a peculiar beauty and aptness of its own. A character with some of the isolation of Jacques, always separated from the gibes and chatter of Moth, he falls in love with Jaquenetta without accepting her as the real country-wench she is, but creates a little drama about the object of his passion in which his is the central role, and Jaquenetta appears in any likeness that he pleases, Delilah or Deianira. The illusion in which the real character of Armado lives has its own beauty and charm, but as the play progresses it becomes evident that this illusion is not strong enough to withstand the pressure of reality and must in the end be destroyed.

With the coming into the King's park of the Princess of France and her companions a new stage in the development of *Love's Labour's Lost* has been reached, and a theme we have not heard before begins slowly to rise in the musical structure of the play. Before the arrival of the ladies, it has been made clear that the Academe must fail, and it is no surprise when in the opening scene of the second act we find each of the four friends stealing back alone after the initial meeting to learn the name of his love from the obliging Boyet. As life itself breaks swiftly through the artificial scholarship of the court, the vitality of the play rises to an amazing height; the Academe is kept constantly before us, the reasons for its failure elaborated and made more plain, but at the same time, while the world of the royal park becomes more and more delightful, while masque and pageantry, sensuous beauty and laughter flower within the walls, it becomes slowly obvious that more than the Academe will be destroyed by the entrance of the ladies. Not only its scholarship, but the entire world of the play, the balance of artifice and reality of which it was formed, must also be demolished by forces from without the walls.

The Princess and her little retinue represent the first penetration of the park by the normal world beyond, a world composed of different and colder elements than the fairy-tale environment within. Through them, in some sense, the voice of Reality speaks, and although they seem to fit perfectly into the landscape of the park, indulge in highly formal, elaborate skirmishes of wit with each other and with the men, they are somehow detached from this world of illusion and artificiality in a way that none of its original inhabitants are. The contrived and fashionable poses which they adopt are in a sense less serious, more playful than those of the other characters, and they are conscious all the time, as even Berowne is not, that these attitudes are merely poses, and that Reality is something quite different. With them into the park they bring past time and a disturbing reminder of the world outside, and from them come the first objective criticisms which pass beyond the scheme of the Academe to attack the men who have formed it. Maria, remembering Longaville as she saw him once before in Normandy, criticizes in her first speech the unreality with which the four friends have surrounded themselves, and points out for the first time in the play the danger of attitudes which develop without regard for the feelings of others, of wit that exercises itself thoughtlessly upon all.

In the wit of the ladies themselves, it is a certain edge of reality, an uncompromising logic, which cuts through the pleasant webs of artifice, the courtly jests and elaborations in the humor of the men, and emerges victorious with an unfailing regularity. Unlike the women, the King and his companions play, not with facts themselves, but with words, with nice phrases and antithetical statements, and when their embroidered language itself has been attacked, their courteous offers disdained as mere euphemisms, they can only retire discomfited. Even Berowne is utterly defeated when he approaches Rosaline with his graceful conceits.

> BER: Lady, I will commend you to mine own heart.
> ROS: Pray you, do my commendations;
>   I would be glad to see it.
> BER: I would you heard it groan.
> ROS: Is the fool sick?
> BER: Sick at the heart.
> ROS: Alack, let it blood.
> BER: Would that do it good?
> ROS: My physic says "ay."

Witty as Berowne, as agile of mind, Rosaline attacks his conventional protestations with a wit based on realism, a ridicule springing from a consciousness of the absurdity of artifice. That Berowne could be expressing a real passion in these artificial terms never enters her mind; he is merely mocking her, and she defends herself in the most effective way she can.

Berowne is, however, like the King, Dumain, and Longaville, suddenly and genuinely in love. The Academe has been thoroughly demolished and now, in the fourth act, Shakespeare introduces, in the characters of Holofernes and Nathaniel, reminders of what such a scheme might have led to, examples of the sterility of learning that is unrelated to life. As usual, Dull, surely the most delightful of that illustrious Shakespearian series of dim-witted but officious representatives of constabulary law, appears with them as the realistic element in the scene, the voice of the cuckoo which mocks, unconsciously, the intricate speech of the two pedants. Bewildered as usual, Dull shows here a quality of stubbornness we had not quite expected in him, maintaining stolidly against the fantastic perorations of Holofernes and Nathaniel that the deer killed by the Princess was "not a haud credo; 'twas a pricket." It is one of the most charming of his infrequent appearances, matched only by that little scene later in the play in which, utterly stupefied by the conversation which he has endured from Holofernes and Nathanial at dinner, he sits mute and quiescent through all the arrangements for the pageant of the Nine Worthies, only at the very last, when roused by another character, entering the dialogue at all to offer us a personal performance upon the tabor, a talent as engaging and unexpected in Dull as song is in the Justice Silence of 2 Henry IV.

Unlike Dull, the schoolmaster and the curate are in some sense mere types, elements of a satire, but Shakespeare is after all not writing a treatise, and even though their absurdity is emphasized, the two have a certain charm of their own, and their interminable quibblings a faint and grotesque beauty. On a lower, less refined level, they reflect the love of words themselves that is visible throughout the play, reveling, not like Armado in the romance and wonder of the past, but in Latin verbs and bits of forgotten erudition, spare and abstract. As Moth says, "They have been at a great feast of languages and stol'n the scraps," and in their conversation the wisdom of ages past appears in a strangely mutilated form, the life drained from it, curiously haphazard and remote.

When in the third scene of Act Four, Berowne appears alone on the stage, we move from the two pedants to a higher level of reality, but one in which artifice is still present. Berowne's love for Rosaline is becoming increasingly intense, and although he seems at first only to be adopting another pose, that of melancholy lover, he is slowly becoming, as the play progresses, a more convincing and attractive figure, and his love more real.

> By heaven, I do love; and it hath taught me to rhyme and to be melancholy; and here is part of my rhyme, and here my melancholy. Well, she hath one of my sonnets already; the clown bore it, the fool sent it, and the lady hath it; sweet clown, sweeter fool, sweetest lady.

Often, beneath ornament and convention the Elizabethans disguised genuine emotion. Berowne's love for Rosaline is as sincere as Philip Sidney's for Stella, his longing as real as that of the unknown Elizabethan lover in Nicholas Hillyarde's strangest and most haunting miniature who stands in the attitude of a familiar poetic conceit, gaunt and disheveled, against a background of flames.

The episode which follows Berowne's introductory soliloquy is, of course, one of the finest in the entire play. It is the first of three scenes in *Love's Labour's Lost* which possess the quality of a play within the play, formal in construction, somehow contrived, always beautifully handled. Here, above the whole scene, Berowne acts as spectator and as Chorus, establishing the play atmosphere in his various asides, crying out upon the entrance of Longaville, "Why, he comes in like a perjure, wearing papers," or in a more general affirmation,

> "All hid, all hid"—an old infant play,
> Like a demigod here sit I in the sky,
> And wretched fools' secrets heedfully o'er-eye.

Throughout *Love's Labour's Lost*, the play is a symbol of illusion, of unreality, as it is in *A Midsummer Night's Dream*, and here it is employed to render the artificiality, the convenient but obvious device of having each of the four lovers appear alone upon the stage, read aloud the poem addressed to his lady, and step aside for the advance of the next one, not only acceptable, but completely delightful. In this play environment, a level of unreality beyond that of the comedy as a whole, the multiple discoveries are perfectly convincing, and the songs and sonnets read by the lovers the charming testimonies of a passion that is not to be questioned.

Through the comments of the spectator, Berowne, the scene is still, however, kept in touch with reality. From his wonderful, rocketing line upon the entrance of the King, "Shot, by heaven!" to the moment when he steps from his concealment in all the splendor of outraged virtue, Berowne's role is again analogous to that of the cuckoo in the closing song, mocking the lovers "enamelling with pied flowers their thoughts of gold," maintaining the balance of the play. When he actually appears among his shamefaced friends to chide them for this "scene of fool'ry," the play within the play ends, as the spectator becomes actor, and we return, with his beautifully sanctimonious sermon, to the more usual level of reality.

The sheer delight of the scene rises now towards its peak as, only a few lines after the close of the play scene, another and even more effective climax is built up. Costard appears with Berowne's own sonnet written to Rosaline, and suddenly the play rises into magnificence. "Guilty, my lord, guilty. I confess, I confess." Berowne has become more real and brilliant than ever before, and at the same time, his speech attains a power and a radiance new in the comedy, an utterance still fastidious, still choice, but less self-conscious, as he sums up for Navarre, Dumain, and Longaville all that Shakespeare has been saying long before, in the Costard scene, in the fall from grace of Don Armado.

> Sweet lords, sweet lovers, O let us embrace!
> As true we are as flesh and blood can be.
> The sea will ebb and flow, heaven show his face;
> Young blood doth not obey an old decree.
> We cannot cross the cause why we were born,
> Therefore of all hands must be we forsworn.

Following these lines, there is a deliberate slackening of intensity, and the scene descends for a moment into a completely artificial duel of wits among the King, Berowne, and Longaville, on a somewhat hackneyed conceit. Berowne's toying with the various meanings of dark and light is as artificial and contrived as anything we have heard from him earlier in the play, but from these lines the scene suddenly rises to its final climax in that speech justifying the breaking of the vows, which is without doubt the most beautiful in the entire play. "Have at you then, affection's men-at-arms." Finally and completely, the Academe has crumbled, and it is Berowne, as is perfectly proper, who sums up all that the play has been saying up to this point in his exquisite peroration upon earthly love.

"Other slow arts entirely keep the brain, / And therefore, finding barren practisers, / Scarce show a harvest of their heavy toil." Holofernes and Nathaniel are indirectly brought before us, the symbols of learning divorced from life, and having thus disposed of scholarship, Berowne passes on to speak of Love itself, and the task of justifying his own perjury and that of his three friends. Gradually, his speech rises to a lyrical height unequalled in the rest of the play, his customary eloquence and delicacy of language transfigured and made splendid, the sincerity perfectly blended with the surviving mannerism. "And when Love speaks, the voice of all the gods / Make heaven drowsy with the harmony." With these two lines, the final climax of the scene has been reached, lines of an almost incredible beauty, sensuous and languid, their exact meaning a little puzzling perhaps, but communicating all that is necessary, in a realm beyond precise explanation.

After these lines, the speech loses something of its beauty, but its intensity remains and fires the King, Dumain, and Longaville. The action flares up suddenly in great, vibrant lines; "Shall we resolve to woo these girls of France?" "Saint Cupid, then! and, soldiers, to the field," and in a whirlwind of vitality and excitement the scene moves toward its close. "For revels, dances, masks, and merry hours, / Forerun fair Love, strewing her way with flowers." Yet, as is customary with Shakespeare, the scene ends quietly, with two thoughtful, foreboding lines which are prophetic of what is to come in the next act. As though he turned back for a second, musingly, in the act of going off with the others, Berowne, as Chorus, remarks more to himself and that deserted little glade which was the scene of the play within the play than to his retreating friends, "Light wenches may prove plagues to men forsworn; / If so, our copper buys no better treasure," lines which despite their apparent gaiety are curiously disturbing.

With the beginning of that long, last act, a turning point in the action of the play has been reached. The Academe defeated by life itself on all levels of the park, one might except that *Love's Labour's Lost* would move now, as *Much Ado About Nothing* does in its final act, into an untroubled close, a romantic ending like that of the Beatrice-Benedick plot. As we have in some sense been told by the title, and by the comments of the ladies, such as ending is, in this case, impossible. From the Academe theme the play turns now to the destruction of the half-real world within the royal park, a destruction which, in the actual moment in which it is accomplished, is unexpected and shocking, and yet has been prepared for and justified by previous events within the comedy. As we enter the Fifth Act, shadows begin to fall across the play world. Life within the park, its brilliance and laughter, mounts higher and higher, yet it is the winter stanzas of the closing song that this act suggests, and a new darkness, a strange intensity forces the harmony of the play into unforeseen resolutions. Vanished now are the untroubled meadows of spring, and the landscape acquires a realism that is somehow a little harsh.

> When icicles hang by the wall,
> And Dick the shepherd blows his nail,

And Tom bears logs into the hall,
And milk comes frozen home in pail,
When blood is nipp'd and ways be foul. . . .

With Act Five, the thought of Death enters the park. The play opened, of course, under the shadow of death, the great motivation of the Academe, but after that opening speech of Navarre's, it vanished altogether, never appearing again even in the imagery of the play until the entrance of the ladies. Significantly, it is they, the intruders from the outside world of reality, who first, in Act Three, bring death into the park itself. In this act, the Princess kills a deer, but in the lines in which the hunt is spoken of, those of Holofernes and the Princess herself, the animal's death is carefully robbed of any disturbing reality. After Holofernes has told us how "The preyful Princess pierc'd and pricked / A pretty, pleasing pricket," the fate of the deer is as unreal as the wooded landscape over which it ran. It might just as well have sprung to its feet and gamboled off when the forester's back was turned.

Not until Act Five does the death image become real and disturbing, and even here, until the final entrance of Marcade, it is allowed to appear only in the imagery, or else in the recollection by some character of a time and a place beyond the scope of the play itself, the country of France where Katherine's sister died of her melancholy and longing, or that forgotten antiquity in which the bones of Hector were laid to rest. Appearing thus softened, kept in the background of the comedy, it is neverthless a curiously troubling image, and as it rises slowly through the fabric of the play, the key of the entire final movement is altered. In the mask scene, Berowne, half-serious about his love and that of the King, Dumain, and Longaville, cries to the ladies,

Write "Lord have mercy on us" on those three;
They are infected; in their hearts it lies;
They have the plague, and caught it of your eyes.
These lords are visited; you are not free,
For the Lord's tokens on you I do see.

and while the image is playfully treated still, it is surely a curious and grotesque figure, this marriage of love, the symbol throughout the comedy of life itself, with death. One cannot imagine such an image appearing earlier in the play, before the outside world, the echoes of its great plague bells sounding through desolate streets, the lugubrious cries of the watchmen marking the doors of the infected houses, began to filter obscurely through the little kingdom of the park.

It is the tremendous reality of death which will destroy the illusory world of Navarre as thoroughly as the gentler forces of life destroyed the Academe and the artificial scheme it represented, earlier in the play. At the very beginning of the Fifth Act, it is made apparent why this must happen, why it is completely necessary for the world of the comedy, despite its beauty and grace, to be demolished. The Princes and her gentlewomen have been discussing the favors and the promises showered upon them by the King and his courtiers, laughing and mocking one another gently. Suddenly, the atmosphere of the entire scene is altered with a single, curious comment, a kind of overheard aside, made by Katherine, upon the real nature of Love. Rosaline turns to her, and as she remembers past time and a tragedy for which the god of Love was responsible then, the scene suddenly becomes filled with the presence of death.

> ROS: You'll ne'er be friends with him: 'a kill'd your sister.
> KATH: He made her melancholy, sad, and heavy;
>   And so she died. Had she been light, like you,
>   Of such a merry, nimble, stirring spirit,
>   She might have been a grandam ere she died.
>   And so may you; for a light heart lives long.

Against such a memory of the reality of love, the Princess and her three companions place the fantastic protestations of Navarre, Berowne, Dumain, and Longaville. As we have seen, their love is genuine; it has made the character of Berowne immeasurably more attractive, caused him no little anguish of spirit, created that great speech of his at the end of Act Four. Beneath the delicate language, the elegance and the gaiety, lies a real passion, but the women from the world outside, where love has been coupled for them with death and reality, see only artifice and pose. The artificiality which has become natural to the four friends and the environment in which they live holds them from the accomplishment of their desire, for the ladies, hearing from Boyet of the masque in which their lovers intend to declare themselves, are unable to perceive in the scheme anything but attempted mockery, and in defending themselves, frustrate the serious purpose of the entertainment.

> They do it but in mocking merriment,
> And mock for mock is only my intent. . . .
> There's no such sport as sport by sport o'erthrown,
> To make theirs ours, and ours none but our own;
> So shall we stay, mocking intended game,
> And they well mock'd depart away with shame.

This masque scene is, of course, the second of the plays within the play, less delightful than the one before it, but immensely significant, the part of audience and commentator played in this instance by Boyet. As usual, the men are completely defeated by the ladies, the delicate fabric of their wit and artifice destroyed by the realistic humour of their opponents. Berowne, approaching the supposed Rosaline with a courteous request, "White-handed mistress, one sweet word with thee," is mercilessly re-buffed by the Princess—"Honey, and milk, and sugar; there is three" —and the charming illusion of the masque itself ruined by the satiric comments of Boyet who, unlike Berowne in the earlier play scene, actu-ally insinuates himself into the unreal world of the entertainment, and totally upsets it.

Even when the exposure is complete and the men have asked pardon from their loves, the women think only that they have defeated a mocking jest directed against them, not that they have prevented their lovers from expressing a genuine passion. For the first time, Berowne reaches utter simplicity and humbleness in his love; his declaration to Rosaline at the end of the masque scene is touching and deeply sincere, but for her, this passion is still unbelievable, a momentary affectation, and she continues to mock her lover and the sentiments he expresses.

> BER: I am a fool, and full of poverty.
> ROS: But that you take what doth to you belong,
>   It were a fault to snatch words from my tongue.
> BER: O, I am yours, and all that I possess.
> ROS: All the fool mine?

More sensitive, gifted with a deeper perception of reality than his com-panions, Berowne seems to guess what is wrong, and he forswears "Taffeta phrases, silken terms precise, / Three pil'd hyperboles, spruce affectation, / Figures pedantical . . . ," at least to Rosaline, but the rejection itself is somewhat artificial, and he remains afterwards with more than "a trick of the old rage."

The masque has failed, and Berowne's more direct attempt to announce to the ladies the purpose behind the performance and detect in them an answering passion has been turned away by the unbelieving Princess. At this point, Costard enters to announce that Holofernes and Nathaniel, Moth and Armado are at hand to present the pageant of the Nine Worthies, and the third and last of the plays within the play begins. As we enter this play scene, the vitality and force of the comedy reaches its apogee, but in its laughter there rings now a discordant note that we have not heard before. The actors themselves are, after all, no less sincere than Bottom and his troupe in A Midsummer Night's Dream, and they are a great deal more sensitive and easy to hurt. They are real people whose intentions are of the very best, their loyalty to their King unquestioned, and although their performance is unintentionally humorous, one would expect the audience to behave with something of the sympathy and forbearance exhibited by Duke Theseus and the Athenians.

The only civil members of the audience in *Love's Labour's Lost*, however, are the ladies. The Princess cannot resist one sarcasm upon the entrance of Armado, but it is addressed quietly to Berowne, before the play itself begins, while Armado is engrossed with the King and obviously does not hear. Thereafter, every one of her comments to the players is one of interest or pity: "Great thanks, great Pompey," "Alas, poor Maccabaeus, how hath he been baited," "Speak, brave Hector; we are much delighted." The players have only the Princess to appeal to in the storm of hilarity which assails them, and it is only she, realistic as she is, who understands that a play is an illusion, that it is to be taken as such and respected in some sense for itself, regardless of its quality. Like Theseus in A *Midsummer Night's Dream*, she realizes somehow that "the best in this kind are but shadows; and the worst are no worse, if imagination amend them," and when she addresses the players she is wise and sensitive enough to do so not by their own names, which she has read on the playbill, but by the names of those whom they portray, thus helping them to sustain that illusion which is the very heart of a play.

In contrast to that of the Princess, the behaviour of the men is incredibly unattractive, particularly that of Berowne. It is difficult to believe that this is the same man who spoke so eloquently a short time ago about the soft and sensible feelings of love, and promised Rosaline to mend his ways. Costard manages to finish his part before the deluge, and Nathaniel, although unkindly treated, is not personally humiliated. Only with the appearance of Holofernes as Judas Maccabaeus and Armado as Hector is the full force of the ridicule released, and it is precisely with these two characters that the infliction of abuse must be most painful. Costard, after all, is a mere fool; he takes part in the baiting of the others with no compunction at all, and Nathanial throughout the comedy has been little more than a foil for Holofernes, but the village pedagogue is a more sensitive soul, and not at all unsympathetic.

Holofernes has his own reality, his own sense of the apt and the beautiful which, though perverse, is meaningful enough for him, and it is exceedingly painful to see him stand here on the smooth grass of the lawn, his whole subjective world under merciless attack, a storm of personal epithets exploding about him.

DUM: The head of a bodkin.
BER: A death's face in a ring
LONG: The face of an old Roman coin, scarce seen.
BOYET: The pommel of Caesar's falchion.
DUM: The carv'd bone face on a flask.
BER: Saint George's half-cheek in a brooch.

The laughter is unattractive, wild, and somehow discordant, made curiously harsh by the introduction of Berowne's "death's face," and it has little resemblance to the laughter which we have heard in the play before this, delicate, sophisticated, sometimes hearty, but never really unkind. When Holofernes cries at the last, "This is not generous, not gentle, not humble," he becomes a figure of real dignity and stature, restrained and courteous in the face of the most appalling incivility.

Meanwhile, around the pedagogue and his little audience the afternoon has been waning slowly into evening, long shadows falling horizontally across the lawn, and Boyet calls after the retreating Holofernes in a strangely haunting line, "A light for Monsieur Judas. It grows dark, he may stumble." A kind of wildness grips all the men, and though Dumain says in a weird and prophetic line, "Though my mocks come home by me, I will now be merry," Armado faces a jeering throng ever before he has begun to speak. Of all the players, Armado is the one for whom we have perhaps the most sympathy. He is a member of the court itself, has had some reason to pride himself upon the King's favor, and has been good enough to arrange the pageant in the first place. The people represented in it are those who inhabit that strange world of his fancy, and one knows that his anguish is not alone for his personal humiliation, but for that of the long-dead hero he portrays, when he cries, "The sweet war-man is dead and rotten; sweet chucks, beat not the bones of the buried; when he breathed, he was a man." A little grotesque, as Armado's sentences always are, the line is nevertheless infinitely moving in its summoning up of great spaces of time, its ironic relation to the idea of immortality through fame expressed in the opening speech of the comedy. Not since the reference to Katherine's sister have we had such a powerful and disturbing image of death brought before us, death real and inescapable although still related to a world and a time beyond the play itself.

In the remaining moments of the play scene, the hilarity rises to its climax, a climax becoming increasingly harsh. During the altercation between Costard and Armado which results from Berowne's ingenious but unattractive trick, images of death begin to hammer through the fabric of the play. The painfulness of the realism grows as Armado, poor, but immensely proud, is finally shamed and humbled before all the other characters. For the first time in the play, the mask falls from Armado's face, and the man beneath it is revealed, his romanticism, his touching personal pride, the agony for him of the confession that in his poverty he wears no shirt beneath his doublet. Still acting, he tries feebly to pass off this lack as some mysterious and romantic penance, but the other characters know the truth; Armado knows they do, and the knowledge is intensely humiliating. The illusion of the role he has played throughout *Love's Labour's Lost* is destroyed for others as well as for himself, and he stands miserably among the jeers of Dumain and Boyet while complete reality breaks over him, and the little personal world which he has built up around himself so carefully shatters at his feet.

The other people in the play are so concerned with Armado's predicament that no one notices that someone, in a sense Something, has joined them. His entrance unremarked by any of the other characters, materializing silently from those shadows which now lie deep along the landscape of the royal park, the Messenger has entered the play world.

> MAR: I am sorry, madam, for the news I bring
>   Is heavy in my tongue. The King your father—
> PRIN: Dead, for my life!
> MAR: Even so; my tale is told.

There is perhaps nothing like this moment in the whole range of Elizabethan drama. In the space of four lines the entire world of the play, its delicate balance of reality and illusion, all the hilarity and overwhelming life of its last scene has been swept away and destroyed, as Death itself actually enters the park, for the first time, in the person of Marcade. Only in one Elizabethan madrigal, Orlando Gibbons' magnificent "What Is Our Life?" is there a change of harmony and mood almost as swift and great as this one, and it occurs under precisely the same circumstances, the sudden appearance among the images of life in Raleigh's lyric of "the graves that hide us from the searching sun" the memory of the inescapable and tremendous reality of Death.

Clumsy, as one always is in the presence of sudden grief, the King can think of nothing to say but to ask the Princess "How fares your Majesty?" a question to which she, from the depths of her sorrow and bewilderment, gives no reply, but prepares with the dignity characteristic of her to leave for France. Now, the men come forward uncertainly, and first the King and then Berowne, clinging still to a world no longer existing, attempt to express their love in terms which had been appropriate to that world, terms at first still incomprehensible to the women and then, at last, understood, but not altogether trusted.

As vows had begun the play, so vows end it. The King is assigned as his symbol of reality a "forlorn and naked hermitage" without the walls of the royal park, in the real world itself, in which he must try for a twelvemonth if this love conceived in the sunlit landscape of Navarre can persist in the colder light of actuality. For Dumain and Longaville, those shadowy figures, penances more vague but of a similar duration are assigned, and then at last, Berowne, shaken and moved to the depths of his being, inquires from Rosaline, who has been standing a little apart from the others, lost in thought,

> Studies my lady? Mistress, look on me;
> Behold the window of my heart, mine eye,
> What humble suit attends thy answer there.
> Impose some service on me for thy love.

Slowly, speaking with great care, Rosaline answers, and in the strangest and most grotesque of the penances, Berowne is condemned to haunt the hospitals and plague-houses of the world outside the park, to exercise his wit upon the "speechless sick," and try the power of his past role, the old artificiality that had no concern for the feelings of others, that humiliated Armado in the play scene, the careless mocks of the old world, upon the reality of the ailing and the dying. "A jest's prosperity lies in the ear / Of him that hears it, never in the tongue / Of him that makes it." It was this reality of actual living that Berowne was unconscious of when he led the unthinking merriment of the play scene just past. Yet, at the end of the year, love's labors will be won for Berowne, and he will receive Rosaline's love, not in the half real world of the park, but in the actuality outside its walls. Thus the play which began with a paradox, that of the Academe, closes with one as well. Only through the acceptance of the reality of Death are life and love in their fullest sense made possible for the people of the play.

The world of the play past has now become vague and unreal, and it is not distressing that Berowne, in a little speech that is really a kind of epilogue, should refer to all the action before the entrance of Marcade, the people who took part in that action and the kingdom they inhabited and in a sense created, as having been only the elements of a play. It is a play outside which the characters now stand, bewildered, a little lost in the sudden glare of actuality, looking back upon that world of mingled artifice and reality a trifle wistfully before they separate in the vaster realm beyond the royal park. Through *Love's Labour's Lost*, the play has been a symbol of illusion, of delightful unreality, the masque of the Muscovites, or the pageant of the Nine Worthies, and now it becomes apparent that there was a further level of illusion above that of the plays within the play. The world of that illusion has enchanted us; it has been possessed of a haunting beauty, the clear loveliness of those landscapes in the closing song, but Shakespeare insists that it cannot take the place of reality itself, and should not be made to. Always, beyond the charming, frost-etched countryside of the pastoral winter, like the background of some Flemish Book of Hours, lies the reality of the greasy kitchen-maid and her pot, a reality which must sooner or later break through and destroy the charm of the artificial and the illusory.

For us, however, knowing how Shakespeare's later work developed, and how the play image itself took on another meaning for him, there is a strange poignancy in this closing moment, with its confident assertion of the concrete reality of the world into which the characters are about to journey, the necessity for them to adjust themselves to that reality. Later, in *As You Like It* and *Hamlet* Shakespeare would begin to think of the play as the symbol, not of illusion, but of the world itself and its actuality, in *Macbeth* and *King Lear* as the symbol of the futility and tragic nature of that actuality, "that great stage of fools." Yet he must always have kept in mind the image as it had appeared years before in the early comedy of *Love's Labour's Lost*, for returning to it at the very last, he joined that earlier idea of the play as illusion with its later meaning as a symbol of the real world, and so created the final play image of *The Tempest* in which illusion and reality have become one and the same, and there is no longer any distinction possible between them. The world itself into which Berowne and his companions travel to seek out reality will become for Shakespeare at the last merely another stage, a play briefly enacted,

> And, like the baseless fabric of this vision,
> The cloud-capp'd towers, the gorgeous palaces,
> The solemn temples, the great globe itself,
> Yea, all which it inherit, shall dissolve,
> And, like this insubstantial pageant faded,
> Leave not a rack behind. We are such stuff
> As dreams are made on; and our little life
> Is rounded with a sleep.

JOHN HOLLANDER

"Twelfth Night" and the Morality of Indulgence

To say that a play is "moral" would seem to imply that it represents an action which concretizes certain ethical elements of human experience, without actually moralizing at any point, and without having any of the characters in it state univocally a dogma, precept, or value that would coincide completely with the play's own moral intention. It was just this univocal didacticism, however, which characterized what was becoming in 1600 a prevailing comic tradition. The moral intent of the Jonsonian "comedy of humours" was direct and didactic; its purpose was to show

> the times deformitie
> Anatomiz'd in euery nerue and sinnew
> With constant courage, and contempt of feare.

For moral purposes, a humour is an identifying emblem of a man's moral nature, graven ineradicably onto his physiological one. In the world of a play, a humour could be caricatured to such a degree that it would practically predestine a character's behaviour. It was made to

> . . . so possesse a man, that it doth draw
> All his affects, his spirits and his powers,
> In their confluctions, all to runne one way,
> This may be truly said to be a Humour.

From *The Sewanee Review* 2, vol. 68 (1959). Copyright © 1959 by The University of the South.

The emblematic character of the humour, and the necessity for its use, were affirmed even more directly by Sidney, whose dramatic theory Jonson seems to have greatly admired:

> Now, as in Geometry the oblique must bee knowne as wel as the right, and in Arithmeticke the odde as well as the euen, so in the actions of our life who seeth not the filthiness of euil wanteth a great foile to perceiue the beauty of vertue. This doth the Comedy handle so in our priuate and domestical matters, as with hearing it we get as it were an experience, what is to be looked for of a nigardly *Demea*, of a crafty *Dauus*, of a flattering *Gnato*, of a vaine glorious *Thraso*, and not onely to know what effects are to be expected, but to know who be such, by the signifying badge giuen them by the Comedian.

Now *Every Man In His Humour* was first acted in 1598, and it is known that Shakespeare appeared in it. He seems in *Twelfth Night* (for which I accept the traditional date of 1600–1601) to have attempted to write a kind of moral comedy diametrically opposed to that of Jonson, in which "the times deformitie" was not to be "anatomiz'd," but represented in the core of an action. For a static and deterministic Humour, Shakespeare substituted a kinetic, governing Appetite in the action, rather than in the bowels, of his major characters. In his plot and language, he insists continually on the fact and importance of the substitution. Characters in a comedy of humours tend to become caricatures, and caricatures tend to become beasts, inhuman personifications of moral distortions that are identified with psyiological ones. I believe that it was Shakespeare's intention in *Twelfth Night* to obviate the necessity of this dehumanization by substituting what one might call a moral process for a moral system. While it is true that the play contains quite a bit of interesting discussion of humours as such, and that there is some correspondence between appetites and humours, it is equally true that the only person in the play who believes in the validity of humourous classifications, who, indeed, lives by them, is himself a moral invalid. I will have more to say about this later. At this point I merely wish to suggest that the primary effective difference between Shakespeare's and Jonson's techniques in making moral comedy is the difference between what is merely a display of anatomy, and a dramatization of a metaphor, the difference between a Pageant and an Action.

II

The Action of *Twelfth Night* is indeed that of a Revels, a suspension of mundane affairs during a brief epoch in a temporary world of indulgence, a land full of food, drink, love, play, disguise and music. But parties end, and the reveller eventually becomes satiated and drops heavily into his worldly self again. The fact that plays were categorized as "revells" for institutional purposes may have appealed to Shakespeare; he seems at any rate to have analyzed the dramatic and moral nature of feasting, and to have made it the subject of his play. His analysis is schematized in Orsino's opening speech.

The essential action of a revels is: To so surfeit the Appetite upon excess that it "may sicken and so die." It is the Appetite, not the whole Self, however, which is surfeited: the Self will emerge at the conclusion of the action from where it has been hidden. The movement of the play is toward this emergence of humanity from behind a mask of comic type.

Act I, Scene i, is very important as a statement of the nature of this movement. Orsino's opening line contains the play's three dominant images:

> If music be the food of love, play on.
> Give me excess of it, that, surfeiting,
> The appetite may sicken, and so die.
> (I. i. 1–3)

Love, eating, and music are the components of the revelry, then. And in order that there be no mistake about the meaning of the action, we get a miniature rehearsal of it following immediately:

> That strain again! It had a dying fall.
> Oh, it came o'er my ear like the sweet sound
> That breathes upon a bank of violets
> Stealing and giving odor! Enough, no more.
> 'Tis not so sweet now as it was before.
> O spirit of love, how quick and fresh art thou!
> That, notwithstanding thy capacity
> Receiveth as the sea, naught enters there,
> Of what validity and pitch soe'er,
> But falls into abatement and low price,
> Even in a minute! So full of shapes is fancy
> That it alone is high fantastical.
> (I. i. 4–15)

A bit of surfeiting is actually accomplished here; what we are getting is a proem to the whole play, and a brief treatment of love as an appetite. The substance of a feast will always fall into "abatement and low price" at the conclusion of the feasting, for no appetite remains to demand it. We also think of Viola in connection with the "violets / Stealing and giving odor," for her actual position as go-between-turned-lover is one of both inadvertent thief and giver. The Duke's rhetoric is all-embracing, however, and he immediately comments significantly upon his own condition.

> Oh, when mine eyes did see Olivia first,
> Methought she purged the air of pestilence!
> That instant was I turned into a hart,
> And my desired, like fell and cruel hounds,
> E'er since pursue me.
>
> (I. i. 19–23)

Like Actaeon, he is the hunter hunted; the active desirer pursued by his own desires. As embodying this overpowering appetite for romantic love, he serves as a host of the revels.

The other host is Olivia, the subject of his desire. We see almost at once that her self-indulgence is almost too big to be encompassed by Orsino's. Valentine, reporting on the failure of his mission, describes her state as follows:

> So please my lord, I might not be admitted,
> But from her handmaid do return this answer:
> The element itself, till seven years' heat,
> Shall not behold her face at ample view;
> But, like a cloistress, she will veiled walk
> And water once a day her chamber round
> With eye-offending brine—all this to season
> A brother's dead love, which she would keep fresh
> And lasting in her sad remembrance.
>
> (I. i. 24–32)

"To season a brother's dead love": she is gorging herself on this fragrant herb, and though she has denied herself the world, she is no true anchorite, but, despite herself, a private glutton. The Duke looks forward to the end of her feast of grief,

> . . . when liver, brain, and heart,
> These sovereign thrones, are all supplied, and filled
> Her sweet perfections with one self king!
>
> (I. i. 37–39)

The trinitarian overtone is no blasphemy, but a statement of the play's teleology. When everyone is supplied with "one self king," the action will have been completed.

The first three scenes of the play stand together as a general prologue, in which the major characters are introduced and their active natures noted. Viola is juxtaposed to Olivia here; she is not one to drown her own life in a travesty of mourning. It is true that she is tempted to "serve that lady" (as indeed she does, in a different way). But her end in so doing would be the whole play's action in microcosm; the immersion in committed self-indulgence would result in the revelation of her self:

And might not be delivered to the world
Till I had made mine own occasion mellow,
What my estate is.

(I. ii. 42–44)

She will serve the Duke instead, and use her persuasive talents to accomplish the ends to which his own self-celebrating rhetoric can provide no access. "I can sing," she says, "and speak to him in many sorts of music." Her sense of his character has been verified; the Captain tells her that his name is as his nature. And "what is his name?" she asks. "Orsino," answers the Captain. Orsino—the bear, the ravenous and clumsy devourer. Her own name suggests active, affective music; and the mention of Arion, the Orpheus-like enchanter of waves and dolphins with his music, points up the connotation. Orsino's "music," on the other hand, is a static well of emotion to which he allows his own rhetoric to submerge; Viola's is more essentially instrumental, effective, and convincing.

The third scene of Act I complete the prologue by further equating the moral and pysiological. Here we first encounter the world of what Malvolio calls "Sir Toby and the lighter people" (it is indeed true that there is none of Malvolio's element of "earth" in them). The continued joking about *dryness* that pervades the wit here in Olivia's house, both above and below stairs, is introduced here, in contrast to Olivia's floods of welling and self-indulgent tears. The idea behind the joking in this and the following scenes is that drinking and merriment will moisten and fulfill a dry nature. As Feste says later on, "Give the dry fool drink, then the fool is not dry." Toby's sanguine temperament and Aguecheek's somewhat phlegmatic one are here unveiled. They are never identified as such, however; and none of the wit that is turned on the associations of "humours," "elements," and "waters," though it runs throughout the play, ever refers to a motivating order in the universe, except insofar as Malvolio believes in it.

What is most important is that neither Feste, the feaster embodying not the spirit but the action of revelry, nor Malvolio, the ill-wisher (and the *bad appetite* as well), his polar opposite, appears in these introductory scenes. It is only upstairs in Olivia's house (I. v.) that the action as such commences. The revels opens with Feste's exchange with Maria in which she attempts three times to insist on innocent interpretations of "well-hanged" and "points." But Feste is resolute in his ribaldry. Thus Olivia, momentarily voicing Malvolio's invariable position, calls Feste a "dry fool," and "dishonest"; Malvolio himself refers to him as a "barren rascal." From here on in it will be Feste who dances attendance on the revelry, singing, matching wit with Viola, and being paid by almost everyone for his presence. To a certain degree he remains outside the action, not participating in it because he represents its very nature; occasionally serving as a comic angel or messenger, he is nevertheless unmotivated by any appetite, and is never sated of his fooling. His insights into the action are continuous, and his every remark is telling. "*Cucullus non facit monachum.* That's as much as to say I wear not motley in my brain." Indeed, he does not, but more important is the fact that his robe and beard are not to make him a *real* priest later on. And neither he as Sir Thopas, nor Olivia as a "cloistress," nor Malvolio in his black suit or travestied virtue, nor the transvestite Viola is what he appears to be. No one will be revealed in his true dress until he has doffed his mask of feasting. And although neither Feste nor Malvolio will change in this respect, it is for completely opposite reasons that they will not do so.

Every character in the play, however, is granted some degree of insight into the nature of the others. It is almost as if everyone were masked with the black side of his vizard turned inwards; he sees more clearly past the *persona* of another than he can past his own. Valentine, for the Duke, comments on Olivia, as we have seen before. Even Malvolio is granted such an insight. Olivia asks him "What manner of man" Caesario is; unwittingly, his carping, over self-conscious and intellectualized answer cuts straight to the heart of Viola's disguise: "Not yet old enough for a man, nor young enough for a boy, as a squash is before 'tis a peascod, or a codling when 'tis almost an apple. 'Tis with him in standing water, between boy and man. He is very well-favored and he speaks very shrewishly. One would think his mother's milk were scarce out of him" (I. v. 165–171).

The puns on "cod" and "codling" insist on being heard here, and as with the inadvertently delivered obscenity about Olivia's "great P's" and their source in the letter scene, Malvolio does not know what he is saying. The point is that Malvolio asserts, for an audience that knows the real facts, that Viola can scarcely be a male creature.

A more significant case of this hide-and-seek is Olivia's retort to Malvolio in the same scene: "O you are sick of self-love, Malvolio, and taste with a distempered appetite"; it provides the key to his physiological-moral nature. "Sick of self-love" means "sick with a moral infection called self-love," but it can also mean "already surfeited, or fed up with your own ego as an object of appetite." Malvolio's "distempered appetite" results from the fact that he alone is not possessed of a craving directed outward, towards some object on which it can surfeit and die; he alone cannot morally benefit from a period of self-indulgence. Actually this distemper manifests itself in terms of transitory desires on his part for status and for virtue, but these desires consume him in their fruitlessness; he is aware of the nature of neither of them. This is a brilliant analysis of the character of a melancholic, and Shakespeare's association of the melancholy, puritanic, and status-seeking characters in Malvolio throws considerable light on all of them. The moral nature of the plot of *Twelfth Night* can be easily approached through the character of Malvolio, and this, I think, is what Lamb and his followers missed completely in their egalitarian sympathy for his being no "more than steward." For Malvolio's attachment to self-advancement is not being either aristrocratically ridiculed or praised as an example of righteous bourgeois opposition to medieval hierarchies. In the context of the play's moral physiology, his disease is shown forth as a case of indigestion due to his self-love, the result of a perverted, rather than an excessive appetite. In the world of feasting, the values of the commercial society outside the walls of the party go topsy-turvey: Feste is given money for making verbal fools of the donors thereof; everyone's desire is fulfilled in an unexpected way; and revellers are shown to rise through realms of unreality, disguise, and luxurious self-deception. We are seduced, by the revelling, away from seeing the malice in the plot to undo Malvolio. But whatever malice there is remains peculiarly just. It is only Malvolio who bears any ill will, and only he upon whom ill will can appear to be directed. He makes for himself a hell of the worldly heaven of festivity, and when Toby and Maria put him into darkness, into a counterfeit hell, they are merely representing in play a condition that he has already achieved.

The plot against Malvolio, then, is no more than an attempt to let him surfeit on himself, to present him with those self-centered, "time-pleasing" objects upon which his appetite is fixed. In essence, he is led to a feast in which his own vision of himself is spread before him, and commanded to eat it. The puritan concern with witchcraft and the satanic, and its associations of them with madness are carried to a logical extreme; and once Malvolio has been permitted to indulge in his self-interest by means of the letter episode, he is only treated as he would himself treat anyone whom he believed to be mad. His puritanism is mocked by allusions to his praying made by Toby and Maria; a priest (and a false, dissembling one at that, the answer to a puritan's prayer) is sent to him; and the implications of the darkness are eventually fulfilled as his prison becomes his hell.

It is interesting to notice how carefully Shakespeare analyzed another characteristic of the melancholic in his treatment of Malvolio. L. C. Knights has suggested that the vogue of melancholy at the turn of the seventeenth century was occasioned to some degree by the actual presence in England of a large number of *"intellectuels en chômage"* (in Denis de Rougement's words), unemployed, university-trained men whose humanistic education had not fitted them for any suitable role in society. Malvolio is no patent and transparent university intellectual (like Holofernes, for example). He contrives, however, to over-rationalize his point (where the Duke will over-sentimentalize it) on almost every occasion. Even his first introduction of Viola, as has been seen before, is archly over-reasoned. His venture into exegesis of a text is almost telling.

It is not merely self-interest, I think, that colors the scrutiny of Maria's letter. His reading is indeed a close one: he observes that, after the first snatch of doggerel, "The numbers altered." But Malvolio is incapable of playing the party-game and guessing the riddle. Of "M,O,A,I doth sway my life," he can only say "And yet to crush this a little it would bow to me, for every one of these letters are in my name." He even avoids the reading that should, by all rights, appeal to him: Leslie Hotson has suggested that "M,O,A,I" probably stands for *Mare, Orbis, Aer,* and *Ignis,* the four elements to which Malvolio so often refers. Malvolio himself fails as a critic, following a "cold scent" that, as Fabian indicates, is "as rank as a fox" for him in that it tantalizes his ambition.

But he continues to aspire to scholarship. In order to let his tongue tang with arguments of state, he intends to "read politic authors." His intrusion on the scene of Toby's and Andrew's merry-making involves a most significant remark: "Is there no respect of persons, time, or place in you?", he asks. In other words, "Do you not observe even the dramatic unities in your revelling? Can you not apply even the values that govern things as frivolous as plays to your lives?" Coming from Malvolio, the ethical theorist, the remark feels very different from the remark made to Sir Toby by Maria, the practical moralist: "Aye, but you must confine yourself within the modest levels of order." Maria, presiding over the festivities, would keep things from getting out of hand. It is not only the spirit in which Malvolio's comment is uttered that accounts for this difference, however. I think that one of the implications is quite clearly the fact that Jonson's ordered, would-be-classic, but static and didactic comedy would disapprove of *Twelfth Night* as a moral play, and mistake its intention for a purely frivolous one.

The prank played on Malvolio is not merely an "interwoven" second story, but a fully developed double-plot. Like the Belmont episodes in *The Merchant of Venice,* it is a condensed representation of the action of the entire play. In *Twelfth Night,* however, it operates in reverse, to show the other side of the coin, as it were. For Malvolio there can be no fulfillment in "one self king." His story effectively and ironically underlines the progress towards this fulfillment in everybody else, and helps to delineate the limitations of the moral domain of the whole play. In contrast to Feste, who appears in the action at times as an abstracted spirit of revelry, Malvolio is a model of the sinner.

The whole play abounds in such contrasts and parallels of character, and the players form and regroup continually with respect to these, much in the manner of changing figurations in a suite of *branles*. Viola herself indulges in the festivities in a most delicate and (literally) charming way. She is almost too good a musician, too effective an Orpheus: "Heaven forbid my outside have not charmed her," she complains after her first encounter with Olivia. But as soon as she realizes that she is part of the game, she commits herself to it with redoubled force. If her "outside" is directed toward Olivia, her real identity and her own will are concentrated even more strongly on Orsino. In the most ironic of the love scenes she all but supplants Olivia in the Duke's affections. Orsino, glutting himself in his own version of romantic love, allows himself to make the most extravagant and self-deceptive statements about it:

> Come hither, boy. If ever thou shalt love,
> In the sweet pangs of it remember me;
> For such as I am all true lovers are,
> Unstaid and skittish in all motions else
> Save in the constant image of the creature
> That is beloved.
>
> (II. iv. 15–20)

This skittishness, beneath the mask of the ravenous and constant bear, is obvious to Feste at least: "Now, the melancholy god protect thee, and the tailor make thy doublet of changeable taffeta, for thy mind is a very opal. I would have men of such constancy put to sea, that their business might be everything and their intent everywhere; for that's it that always makes a good voyage of nothing." (II. iv. 75–80)

Orsino also gives us a curious version of the physiology of the passions on which the plot is based; it is only relatively accurate, of course, for he will be the last of the revellers to feel stuffed, to push away from him his heaping dish.

> There is no woman's sides
> Can bide the beating of so strong a passion
> As love doth give my heart, no woman's heart
> So big to hold so much. They lack retention.
> Alas, their love may be called appetite—
> No motion of the liver, but the palate—

> They suffer surfeit, cloyment and revolt.
> But mine is all as hungry as the sea
> And can digest as much.
>   (II. iv. 96–104)

Viola has been giving him her "inside" throughout the scene, and were he not still ravenous for Olivia's love he could see her for what she is: a woman with a constancy in love (for himself and her brother) that he can only imagine himself to possess. She is indeed an Allegory of Patience on some baroque tomb at this point. She is ironically distinguished from Olivia in that her "smiling at grief" is a disguising "outside" for her real sorrow, whereas Olivia's is a real self-indulgent pleasure taken at a grief outworn. It is as if Olivia had misread Scripture and taken the letter of "Blessed are they that mourn" for the spirit of it. Her grief is purely ceremonial.

The "lighter people," too, are engaged in carrying out the action in their own way, and they have more business in the play than merely to make a gull of Malvolio. Toby's huge stomach for food and drink parallels the Duke's ravenous capacity for sentiment. The drinking scene is in one sense the heart of the play. It starts out by declaring itself in no uncertain terms. "Does not our life consist of the four elements?" catechizes Sir Toby. "Faith, so they say," replies Andrew, "but I think it rather consists of eating and drinking." No one but Feste, perhaps, really knows the extent to which this is true, for Andrew is actually saying "We are not merely comic types, mind you, being manipulated by a dramatist of the humours. The essence of our lives lies in a movement from hunger to satiety that we share with all of nature."

When Toby and Andrew cry out for a love song, Feste obliges them, not with the raucous bawdy thing that one would expect, but instead, with a direct appeal to their actual hostess, Olivia. This is all the more remarkable in that it is made on behalf of everyone in the play. "O Mistress Mine" undercuts the Duke's overwhelming but ineffectual mouthings. Viola's effective but necessarily misdirected charming, and, of course, Aguecheek's absolute incompetence as a suitor. The argument is couched in purely naturalistic terms: "This feast will have to end, and so will all of our lives. You are not getting younger ('sweet and twenty' is the contemporaneous equivalent of 'sweet and thirty,' at least). Give up this inconstant roaming; your little game had better end in your marriage, anyway." The true love "that can sing both high and low" is Viola-Sebastian, the master-mistress of Orsino's and Olivia's passion. (Sebastian has just been introduced in the previous scene, and there are overtones here of his being invoked as Olivia's husband.) Sebastian has, aside from a certain decorative but benign courtly manner, no real identity apart from Viola. He is the fulfillment of her longing (for she has thought him dead) and the transformation into reality of the part she is playing in the *ludus amoris*. The prognostication is borne out by Sebastian's own remark: "You are betrothed both to a man and maid." He is himself characterized by an elegance hardly virile; and, finally, we must keep in mind the fact that Viola was played by a boy actor to begin with, and that Shakespeare's audience seemed to be always ready for an intricate irony of this kind.

But if Viola and Sebastian are really the same, "One face, one voice, one habit, and two persons, A natural perspective that is and is not," there is an interesting parallel between Viola and Aguecheek as well. Both are suitors for Olivia's hand: Andrew, ineffectively, for himself; Viola for Orsino, and (effectively) for Sebastian. Their confrontation in the arranged duel is all the more ironic in that Andrew is an effective pawn in Toby's game (Toby is swindling him), whereas Viola is an ineffective one in the Duke's (she is swindling him of Olivia's love).

Feste's other songs differ radically from "O Mistress Mine." He sings for the Duke a kind of languorous ayre, similar to so many that one finds in the songbook. It is aimed at Orsino in the very extravagance of its complaint. It is his own song, really, if we imagine him suddenly dying of love, being just as ceremoniously elaborate in his funeral instructions as he has been in his suit of Olivia. And Feste's bit of handy-dandy to Malvolio in his prison is a rough-and-tumble sort of thing, intended to suggest in its measures a scrap from a Morality, plainly invoking Malvolio in darkness as a devil in hell. Feste shows himself throughout the play to be a master of every convention of fooling.

If Feste's purpose is to serve as a symbol of the revels, however, he must also take a clear and necessary part in the all-important conclusion. *Twelfth Night* itself, the feast of the Epiphany, celebrates the discovery of the "True King" in the manger by the Wise Men. "Those wits," says Feste in Act I, Scene v, "that think they have thee [wit] do very oft prove fools, and I that am sure I lack thee many pass for a wise man." And so it is that under his influence the true Caesario, the "one self king," is revealed. The whole of Act V might be taken, in connection with "the plot" in a trivial sense, to the other *epiphany*, the perception that follows the *anagnorisis* or discovery of classic dramaturgy. But we have been dealing with the Action on *Twelfth Night* as representing the killing off of excessive appetite through indulgence of it, leading to the rebirth of the unencumbered self. The long final scene, then, serves to show forth the Caesario-King, and to unmask, discover, and reveal the fulfilled selves in the major characters.

The appearance of the priest (a real one, this time) serves more than the simple purpose of a proving the existence of a marriage between Olivia and "Caesario." It is a simple but firm intrusion into the world of the play of a way of life that has remained outside of it so far. The straightforward solemnity of the priest's rhetoric is also something new; suggestions of its undivided purpose have appeared before only in Antonio's speeches. The priest declares that Olivia and her husband have been properly married:

> And all the ceremony of this compact
> Sealed in my function, by my testimony.
> Since when, my watch hath told me, toward my grave
> I have travelled but two hours.
>
> (V. i. 163–166)

It is possible that the original performances had actually taken about two hours to reach this point. At any rate, the sombre acknowledgment of the passage of time in a real world is there. Antonio has prepared the way earlier in the scene; his straightforward confusion is that of the unwitting intruder in a masquerade who has been accused of mistaking the identities of two of the masquers.

That the surfeiting has gradually begun to occur, however, has become evident earlier. In the prison scene, Sir Toby has already begun to tire: "I would we were well rid of this knavery." He gives as his excuse for this the fact that he is already in enough trouble with Olivia, but such as this has not deterred him in the past. And, in the last scene, very drunk as he must be, he replies to Orsino's inquiry as to his condition that he hates the surgeon, "a drunken rogue." Self-knowledge has touched Sir Toby. He could not have said this earlier.

As the scene plays itself out, Malvolio alone is left unaccounted for. There is no accounting for him here, though; he remains a bad taste in the mouth. "Alas poor fool," says Olivia, "How have they baffled thee!" And thus, in Feste's words, "the whirligig of time brings in his revenges." Malvolio has become the fool, the "barren rascal." He leaves in a frenzy, to "be revenged," he shouts, "on the whole pack of you." He departs from the world of this play to resume a role in another, perhaps. His reincarnation might be as Middleton's De Flores, rather than even Jaques. His business has never been with the feasting to begin with, and now that it is over, and the revellers normalized, he is revealed as the true madman. He is "The Madly-Used Malvolio" to the additional degree that his own uses have been madness.

For Orsino and Viola the end has also arrived. She will be "Orsino's mistress and his fancy's queen." He has been surfeited of his misdirected voracity; the rich golden shaft, in his own words, "hath killed the flock of all affections else" that live in him. "Liver, brain and heart" are indeed all supplied; for both Olivia and himself, there has been fulfillment in "one self king." And, lest there be no mistake, each is to be married to a Caesario or king. Again, "Liver, brain and heart" seems to encompass everybody: Toby and Maria are married, Aguecheek chastened, etc.

At the end of the scene, all exit. Only Feste, the pure fact of feasting, remains. His final song is a summation of the play in many ways at once. Its formal structure seems to be a kind of quick rehearsal of the Ages of Man. In youth, "A foolish thing was but a toy"; the fool's bauble, emblematic of both his *membrum virile* and his trickery, is a trivial fancy. But in "man's estate," the bauble represents a threat of knavery and thievery to respectable society, who shuts its owner out of doors. The "swaggering" and incessant drunkenness of the following strophes bring Man into prime and dotage, respectively. Lechery, trickery, dissembling, and drunkenness, inevitable and desperate in mundane existence, however, are just those activities which, mingled together in a world of feasting, serve to purge Man of the desire for them. The wind and the rain accompany him throughout his life, keeping him indoors with "dreams and imaginations" as a boy, pounding and drenching him unmercifully, when he is locked out of doors, remaining eternal and inevitable throughout his pride in desiring to perpetuate himself. The wind and the rain are the most desperate of elements, that pound the walls and batter the roof of the warm house that shuts them out, while, inside it, the revels are in progress. Only after the party is ended can Man face them without desperation.

It is a metaphor of the rain that lasts longest, though, and it recapitulates the images of water, elements and humours that have pervaded the entire play. Feste himself, who tires of nothing, addresses Viola: "Who you are and what you would are out of my welkin—I might say 'element' but the word is overworn." He adroitly comments on Malvolio's line "Go to; I am not of your element" by substituting a Saxon word for a Latin one. The additional association of the four elements with the humours cannot be overlooked. It is only Malvolio, of course, who uses the word "humour" with any seriousness: "And then to have the humour of State," he muses, as he imagines himself "Count Malvolio." Humours are also waters, however. And *waters*, or fluids of all kinds, are continually being forced on our attention. Wine, tears, seawater, even urine, are in evidence from the first scene on, and they are always being metaphorically identified with one another. They are all fluids, bathing the world of the play in possibilities for change as the humours do the body. Feste's answer to Maria in the prison scene has puzzled many editors; if we realize, however, that Feste is probably hysterically laughing at what he has just been up to. "Nay, I'm for all waters" may have the additional meaning that he is on the verge of losing control of himself. He is "for all waters" primarily in that he represents the fluidity of revelling celebration. And finally, when all is done, "The rain it raineth every day," and Feste reverts to gnomic utterance in a full and final seriousness. Water is rain that falls to us from Heaven. The world goes on. Our revels now are ended, but the actors solidify into humanity, in this case. "But that's all one, our play is done / And we'll strive to please you every day."

III

In this interpretation of *Twelfth Night*, I have in no sense meant to infer that Malvolio is to be identified as Ben Jonson, or that the play functioned in any systematic way in the war of the theatres. There are, of course, a number of propitious coincidences: Marston's *What You Will*, coming some six or seven years after *Twelfth Night*, devotes much effort to lampooning Jonson. What could have been meant by the title, however, as well as Shakespeare's real intention in his subtitle, remains obscure. Perhaps they both remain as the first part of some forgotten proverb to the effect that what you will (want) may come to you in an unexpected form. Perhaps they are both merely throwaway comments to the effect that the play is really "what you may call it." (It has been frequently suggested that it is a translation of Rabelais' "*Fay ce que vouldras.*") Then there is the dig, in *Every Man Out of His Humour*, at a comedy with a romantic (Italian- ate) plot more than vaguely resembling that of *Twelfth Night*. *Every Man Out* has been dated in 1599, but the idea that Shakespeare may have chosen just such a "romantic" story with which to oppose Jonson's comic theories is not inconceivable.

My point, however, is that *Twelfth Night* is opposed by its very nature to the kind of comedy that Jonson was not only writing, but advocating at the time; that is a moral comedy, representing human experience in terms of a fully dramatized metaphor rather than a static emblematic correspondence; and, finally, that it operates to refute the moral validity of comedy of humours in its insistence on the active metaphor of surfeiting the appetite, upon which the whole plot is con- structed. It is only romantic in that it shares, with *As You Like It* (and with *Love's Labour's Lost*, too, for that matter), a hint of the world of transformation of the last plays. Its moral vision is as intense as that of the problem comedies.

C. L. BARBER

The Alliance of Seriousness and Levity in "As You Like It"

Shakespeare's next venture in comedy after *The Merchant of Venice* was probably in the Henry IV plays, which were probably written in 1597–98. Thus the Falstaff comedy comes right in the middle of the period, from about 1594 to 1600 or 1601, when Shakespeare produced festive comedy. *Much Ado About Nothing, As You Like It*, and *Twelfth Night* were written at the close of the period, *Twelfth Night* perhaps after *Hamlet*. *The Merry Wives of Windsor*, where Shakespeare's creative powers were less fully engaged, was produced sometime between 1598 and 1602, and it is not impossible that *All's Well That Ends Well* and even perhaps *Measure for Measure* were produced around the turn of the century, despite that difference in tone that has led to their being grouped with *Hamlet* and *Troilus and Cressida* . . .

As You Like It is very similar in the way it moves to *A Midsummer Night's Dream* and *Love's Labour's Lost*, despite the fact that its plot is taken over almost entirely from Lodge's *Rosalynde*. As I have suggested [elsewhere], the reality we feel about the experience of love in the play, reality which is not in the pleasant little prose romance, comes from presenting what was sentimental extremity as impulsive extravagance and so leaving judgment free to mock what the heart embraces. The Forest of Arden, like the Wood outside Athens, is a region defined by an attitude of

From *Shakespeare's Festive Comedies.* Copyright © 1959 by Princeton University Press.

liberty from ordinary limitations, a festive place where the folly of romance can have its day. The first half of As You Like It, beginning with tyrant brother and tyrant Duke and moving out into the forest, is chiefly concerned with establishing this sense of freedom; the traditional contrast of court and country is developed in a way that is shaped by the contrast between everyday and holiday, as that antithesis has become part of Shakespeare's art and sensibility. Once we are securely in the golden world where the good Duke and "a many merry men . . . fleet the time carelessly," the pastoral motif as such drops into the background; Rosalind finds Orlando's verses in the second scene of Act III, and the rest of the play deals with love. This second movement is like a musical theme with imitative variations, developing much more tightly the sort of construction which played off Costard's and Armado's amorous affairs against those of the nobles in Navarre, and which set Bottom's imagination in juxtaposition with other shaping fantasies. The love affairs of Silvius and Phebe, Touchstone and Audrey, Orlando and Rosalind succeed one another in the easy-going sequence of scenes, while the dramatist deftly plays each off against the others.

THE LIBERTY OF ARDEN

The thing that asks for explanation about the Forest of Arden is how this version of pastoral can feel so free when the Duke and his company are so high-minded. Partly the feeling of freedom comes from release from the tension established in the first act at the jealous court:

> Now go we in content
> To liberty, and not to banishment.
> (I.iii.139–140)

Several brief court scenes serve to keep this contrast alive. So does Orlando's entrance, sword in hand, to interrupt the Duke's gracious banquet by his threatening demand for food. Such behavior on his part is quite out of character (in Lodge he is most courteous); but his brandishing entrance gives Shakespeare occasion to resolve the attitude of struggle once again, this time by a lyric invocation of "what 'tis to pity and be pitied" (II.vii.117).

But the liberty we enjoy in Arden, though it includes relief from anxiety in brotherliness confirmed "at good men's feasts," is somehow easier than brotherliness usually is. The easiness comes from a witty redefinition of the human situation which makes conflict seem for the moment superfluous. Early in the play, when Celia and Rosalind are talking of ways of being merry by devising sports, Celia's proposal is "Let us sit and mock the good housewife Fortune from her wheel" (I.ii. 34–35). The two go on with a "chase" of wit that goes "from Fortune's office to Nature's" (I.ii.43), whirling the two goddesses through many variations; distinctions between them were running in Shakespeare's mind. In Act II, the witty poetry which establishes the greenwood mood of freedom repeatedly mocks Fortune from her wheel by an act of mind which goes from Fortune to Nature:

> A fool, a fool! I met a fool i' th' forest, . . .
> Who laid him down and bask'd him in the sun
> And rail'd on Lady Fortune in good terms, . . .
> "Good morrow, fool," quoth I. "No, sir," quoth he,
> "Call me not fool till heaven hath sent me fortune."
> And then he drew a dial from his poke,
> And looking on it with lack-lustre eye,
> Says very wisely, "It is ten o'clock.
> Thus we may see." quoth he, "how the world wags.
> 'Tis but an hour ago since it was nine,
> And after one more hour 'twill be eleven;
> And so, from hour to hour, we ripe and ripe,
> And then, from hour to hour, we rot and rot;
> And thereby hangs a tale."
>
> (II.vii.12–28)

Why does Jaques, in his stylish way, say that his lungs "began to crow like chanticleer" to hear the fool "thus moral on the time," when the moral concludes in "rot and rot"? Why do we, who are not "melancholy," feel such large and free delight? Because the fool "finds," with wonderfully bland wit, that nothing whatever happens under the aegis of Fortune. ("Fortune reigns in gifts of the world," said Rosalind at I.ii.44.) The almost tautological inevitability of nine, ten, eleven, says that all we do is ripe and ripe and rot and rot. And so there is no reason not to bask in the sun and "lose and neglect the creeping hours of time" (II.vii.112). . . . Touchstone's "deep contemplative" moral makes the same statement as the spring song towards the close of the play: "How that a life was but a flower." When they draw the moral, the lover and his lass are only thinking of the "spring time" as they take "the present time" when "love is crowned with the prime." (The refrain mocks them a little for their obliviousness, by its tinkling "the only pretty ring time.") But Touchstone's festive gesture is *not* oblivious.

The extraordinary thing about the poised liberty of the second act is that the reduction of life to the natural and seasonal and physical works all the more convincingly as a festive release by including a recognition that the physical can be unpleasant. The good Duke, in his opening speech, can "translate the stubbornness of fortune" into a benefit: he does it by the witty shift which makes the "icy fang / And churlish chiding of the winter wind" into "counsellors / That feelingly persuade me what I am" (II.i.6–11). The two songs make the same gesture of welcoming physical pain in place of moral pain:

> Come hither, come hither, come hither!
>   Here shall he see
>   No enemy
> But winter and rough weather.
>   (II.v.5–8)

They are patterned on holiday drinking songs . . . and they convey the free solidarity of a group who, since they relax in physical pleasures together, need not fear the fact that "Most friendship is feigning, most loving mere folly."

Jaques speech on the seven ages of man, which comes at the end of Act II, just before "Blow, Blow, thou winter wind," is another version of the liberating talk about time; it expands Touchstone's "And thereby hangs a tale." The simplification, "All the world's a stage," has such imaginative reach that we are as much astonished as amused, as with Touchstone's summary ripe and rot. But simplication it is, nevertheless; quotations (and recitations) often represent it as though it were dramatist Shakespeare's "philosophy," his last word, or one of them, about what life really comes to. To take it this way is sentimental, puts a part in place of the whole. For it only is *one* aspect of the truth that the roles we play in life are settled by the cycle of growth and decline. To face this part of the truth, to insist on it, brings the kind of relief that goes with accepting folly—indeed this speech is praise of folly, superbly generalized, praise of the folly of living in time (or is it festive abuse? the poise is such that relish and mockery are indistinguishable). Sentimental readings ignore the wit that keeps reducing social roles to caricatures and suggesting that meanings really are only physical relations beyond the control of mind or spirit:

> Then a soldier, . . .
> Seeking the bubble reputation
> Even in the cannon's mouth. And then the justice,
> In fair round belly with good capon lin'd . . .
>   (III.vii.149–154)

Looking back at time and society in this way, we have a detachment and sense of mastery similar to that established by Titania and Oberon's outside view of "the human mortals" and their weather.

COUNTERSTATEMENTS

That Touchstone and Jaques should at moments turn and mock pastoral contentment is consistent with the way it is presented; their mockery makes explicit the partiality, the displacement of normal emphasis, which is implicit in the witty advocacy of it.

> If it do come to pass
> That any man turn ass,
> Leaving his wealth and ease
> A stubborn will to please . . .
> (II.v.52–55)

The folly of going to Arden has something about it of Christian humility, brotherliness and unworldliness ("Consider the lilies of the field . . ."), but one can also turn it upside down by "a Greek invocation to call fools into a circle" and find it stubbornness. Touchstone brings out another kind of latent irony about pastoral joys when he plays the role of a discontented exile from the court:

> CORIN: And how like you this shepherd's life, Master Touchstone?
> TOUCHSTONE: Truly, shepherd, in respect of itself, it is a good life; but in respect that it is a shepherd's life, it is naught. In respect that it is solitary, I like it very well; but in respect that it is private, it is a very vile life. Now in respect it is in the fields, it pleaseth me well; but in respect it is not in the court, it is tedious. As it is a spare life, look you, it fits my humour well; but as there is no more plenty in it, it goes much against my stomach.
> (III.ii.12–22)

Under the apparent nonsense of his self-contradictions, Touchstone mocks the contradictory nature of the desires ideally resolved by pastoral life, to be at once at court and in the fields, to enjoy both the fat advantages of rank and the spare advantages of the mean and sure estate. The humor goes to the heart of the pastoral convention and shows how very clearly Shakespeare understood it.

The fact that he created both Jaques and Touchstone out of whole cloth, adding them to the story as it appears in Lodge's *Rosalynde*, is an index to what he did in dramatizing the prose romance. Lodge, though he has a light touch, treats the idyllic material at face value. He never makes fun of its assumptions, but stays safely within the convention, because he has no securely grounded attitude towards it, not being sure of its relation to reality. Shakespeare scarcely changes the story at all, but where in Lodge it is presented in the flat, he brings alive the dimension of its relation to life as a whole. The control of this dimension makes his version solid as well as delicate.

Although both Jaques and Touchstone are connected with the action well enough at the level of plot, their real position is generally mediate between the audience and something in the play, the same position Nashe assigns to the court fool, Will Summers, in *Summer's Last Will and Testament*. Once Jaques stands almost outside the play, when he responds to Orlando's romantic greeting: "Good day and happiness, dear Rosalind!" with "Nay then, God b'wi'you, and you talk in blank verse!" (IV.i.31). Jaques' factitious melancholy, which critics have made too much of as a "psychology," serves primarily to set him at odds both with society and with Arden and so motivate contemplative mockery. Touchstone is put outside by his special status as a fool. As a fool, incapable, at least for professional purposes, of doing anything right, he is beyond the pale of normal achievements. In anything he tries to do he is comically disabled, as, for example, in falling in love. All he achieves is a burlesque of love. So he has none of the illusions of those who try to be ideal, and is in a position to make a business of being dryly objective. "Call me not fool till heaven hath sent me fortune." Heaven sends him Audrey instead, "an ill-favour'd thing, sir, but mine own" (V.iv.60)—not a mistress to generate illusions. In *As You Like It* the court fool for the first time takes over the work of comic commentary and burlesque from the clown of the earlier plays; in Jaques' praise of Touchstone and the corrective virtues of fooling, Shakespeare can be heard crowing with delight at his discovery. The figure of the jester, with his recognized social role and rich traditional meaning, enabled the dramatist to embody in a character and his relations with other characters the comedy's purpose of maintaining objectivity.

The satirist presents life as it is and ridicules it because it is not ideal, as we would like it to be and as it should be. Shakespeare goes the other way about: he represents or evokes ideal life, and then makes fun of it because it does not square with life as it ordinarily is. If we look for social satire in *As You Like It*, all we find are a few set pieces about such stock figures as the traveller and the duelist. And these figures seem to be described rather to enjoy their extravagance than to rebuke their folly. Jaques, in response to a topical interest at the time when the play appeared, talks a good deal about satire, and proposes to "cleanse the foul body of th' infected world" (II.vii.60) with the fool's medicine of ridicule. But neither Jaques, the amateur fool, nor Touchstone, the professional, ever really gets around to doing the satirist's work of ridiculing life as it is, "deeds, and language, such as men do use." After all, they are in Arden, not in Jonson's London: the infected body of the world is far away, out of range. What they make fun of instead is what they can find in Arden— pastoral innocence and romantic love, life as it might be, lived "in a holiday humour." Similar comic presentation of what is not ideal in man is characteristic of medieval fool humor, where the humorist, by his gift of long ears to the long-robed dignitaries, makes the point that, despite their pageant perfection, they are human too, that "stultorum numerus infinitus est." Such humor is very different from modern satire, for its basic affirmation is not man's possible perfection but his certain imperfection. It was a function of the pervasively formal and ideal cast of medieval culture, where what should be was more present to the mind than what is: the humorists' natural recourse was to burlesque the pageant of perfection, presenting it as a procession of fools, in crowns, mitres, caps, and gowns. Shakespeare's point of view was not medieval. But his clown and fool comedy is a response, a counter-movement, to artistic idealization, as medieval burlesque was a response to the ingrained idealism of the culture.

"ALL NATURE IN LOVE MORTAL IN FOLLY"

I have quoted [previously] a riddling comment of Touchstone which moves from acknowledging mortality to accepting the folly of love:

> We that are true lovers run into strange capers; but as all is mortal in nature, so is all nature in love mortal in folly.
>
> (II.iv.53–56)

The lovers who in the second half of the play present "nature in love" each exhibit a kind of folly. In each there is a different version of the incongruity between reality and the illusions (in poetry, the hyperboles) which love generates and by which it is expressed. The comic variations are centered around the seriously-felt love of Rosalind and Orlando. The final effect is to enhance the reality of this love by making it independent of illusions, whose incongruity with life is recognized and laughed off. We can see this at closer range by examining each affair in turn.

All-suffering Silvius and his tyrannical little Phebe are a bit of Lodge's version taken over, outwardly intact, and set in a wholly new perspective. A "courting eglogue" between them, in the mode of Lodge, is exhibited almost as a formal spectacle, with Corin for presenter and Rosalind and Celia for audience. It is announced as

> a pageant truly play'd
> Between the pale complexion of true love
> And the red glow of scorn and proud disdain.
> (III.iv.55–57)

What we then watch is played "truly"—according to the best current convention: Silvius, employing a familiar gambit, asks for pity; Phebe refuses to believe in love's invisible wound, with exactly the literal-mindedness about hyperbole which the sonneteers imputed to their mistresses. In Lodge's version, the unqualified Petrarchan sentiments of the pair are presented as valid and admirable. Shakespeare lets us feel the charm of the form; but then he has Rosalind break up their pretty pageant. She reminds them that they are nature's creatures, and that love's purposes are contradicted by too absolute a cultivation of romantic liking or loathing: "I must tell you friendly in your ear, / Sell when you can! you are not for all markets" (III.v.59–60). Her exaggerated downrightness humorously underscores the exaggerations of conventional sentiment. And Shakespeare's treatment breaks down Phebe's stereotyped attitudes to a human reality: he lightly suggests an adolescent perversity underlying her resistance to love. The imagery she uses in disputing with Silvius is masterfully squeamish, at once preoccupied with touch and shrinking from it:

> 'Tis pretty, sure, and very probable
> That eyes, which are the frail'st and softest things,
> Who shut their coward gates on atomies,
> Should be call'd tyrants, butchers, murtherers!
> . . . lean but upon a rush,
> The cicatrice and capable impressure
> Thy palm some moment keeps; but now mine eyes,
> Which I have darted at thee, hurt thee not, . . .
> (III.v.11–25)

Rosalind, before whom this resistance melts, appears in her boy's disguise "like a ripe sister," and the qualities Phebe picks out to praise are feminine. She has, in effect, a girlish crush on the femininity which shows through Rosalind's disguise; the aberrant affection is happily got over when Rosalind reveals her identity and makes it manifest that Phebe has been loving a woman. "Nature to her bias drew in that" is the comment in *Twelfth Night* when Olivia is fortunately extricated from a similar mistaken affection.

Touchstone's affair with Audrey complements the spectacle of exaggerated sentiment by showing love reduced to its lowest common denominator, without any sentiment at all. The fool is detached, objective and resigned when the true-blue lover should be

> All made of passion, and all made of wishes,
> All adoration, duty, and observance.
> (v.ii.101–102)

He explains to Jaques his reluctant reasons for getting married:

JAQUES: Will you be married, motley?
TOUCHSTONE: As the ox hath his bow, sir, the horse his curb, and the falcon her bells, so man hath his desires; and as pigeons bill, so wedlock would be nibbling.

> (III.iii.79–83)

This reverses the relation between desire and its object, as experienced by the other lovers. They are first overwhelmed by the beauty of their mistresses, then impelled by that beauty to desire them. With Touchstone, matters go the other way about: he discovers that man has his troublesome desires, as the horse his curb; then he decides to cope with the situation by marrying Audrey:

> Come, sweet Audrey.
> We must be married, or we must live in bawdry.
> (III.iii.98–99)

Like all the motives which Touchstone acknowledges, this priority of desire to attraction is degrading and humiliating. One of the hall-marks of chivalric and Petrarchan idealism is, of course, the high valuation of the lover's mistress, the assumption that his desire springs entirely from her beauty. This attitude of the poets has contributed to that progressively-increasing respect for women so fruitful in modern culture. But to assume that only one girl will do is, after all, an extreme, an ideal attitude: the other half of the truth, which lies to wait to mock sublimity, is instinct—the need of a woman, even if she be an Audrey, because "as pigeons bill, so wedlock would be nibbling." As Touchstone put it on another occasion:

> If the cat will after kind,
> So be sure will Rosalinde.
> (III.ii.109–110)

The result of including in Touchstone a representative of what in love is unromantic is not, however, to undercut the play's romance: on the contrary, the fool's cynicism, or one-sided realism, forestalls the cynicism with which the audience might greet a play where his sort of realism had been ignored. We have a sympathy for his downright point of view, not only in connection with love but also in his acknowledgment of the vain and self-gratifying desires excluded by pastoral humility; he embodies the part of ourselves which resists the play's reigning idealism. But he does not do so in a fashion to set himself up in opposition to the play. Romantic commentators construed him as "Hamlet in motely," a devastating critic. They forgot, characteristically, that he is ridiculous: he makes his attitudes preposterous when he values rank and comfort above humility, or follows biology rather than beauty. In laughing at him, we reject the tendency in ourselves which he for the moment represents. The net effect of the fool's part is thus to consolidate the hold of the serious themes by exorcising opposition. The final Shakespearean touch is to make the fool aware that in humiliating himself he is performing a public service. He goes through his part with an irony founded on the fact (and it is a fact) that he is only making manifest the folly which others, including the audience, hide from themselves.

Romantic participation in love and humorous detachment from its follies, the two polar attitudes which are balanced against each other in the action as a whole, meet and are reconciled in Rosalind's personality. Because she remains always aware of love's illusions while she herself is swept along by its deepest currents, she possesses as an attribute of character the power of combining wholehearted feeling and undistorted judgment which gives the play its value. She plays the mocking reveller's role which Berowne played in *Love's Labour's Lost*, with the advantage of disguise. Shakespeare exploits her disguise to permit her to furnish the humorous commentary on her own ardent love affair, thus keeping comic and serious actions going at the same time. In her pretended role of saucy shepherd youth, she can mock at romance and burlesque its gestures while playing the game of putting Orlando through his paces as a suitor, to "cure" him of love. But for the audience, her disguise is transparent, and through it they see the very ardor which she mocks. When, for example, she stages a gayly overdone take-off of the conventional impatience of the lover, her own real impatience comes through the burlesque; yet the fact that she makes fun of exaggerations of the feeling conveys an awareness that it has limits, that there is a difference between romantic hyperbole and human nature:

> ORLANDO: For these two hours, Rosalind, I will leave thee.
> ROSALIND: Alas, dear love, I cannot lack thee two hours!
> ORLANDO: I must attend the Duke at dinner. By two o'clock I will be with thee again.

ROSALIND: Ay, go your ways, go your ways! I knew what you would prove. My friends told me as much, and I thought no less. That flattering tongue of yours won me. 'Tis but one cast away, and so, come death! Two o'clock is your hour?

(IV.i.181–190)

One effect of this indirect, humorous method of conveying feeling is that Rosalind is not committed to the conventional language and attitudes of love, loaded as these inevitably are with sentimentality. Silvius and Phebe are her foils in this: they take their conventional language and their conventional feelings perfectly seriously, with nothing in reserve. As a result they seem naïve and rather trivial. They are no more than what they say, until Rosalind comes forward to realize their personalities for the audience by suggesting what they humanly are beneath what they romantically think themselves. By contrast, the heroine in expressing her own love conveys by her humorous tone a valuation of her sentiments, and so realizes her own personality for herself, without being indebted to another for the favor. She uses the convention where Phebe, being unaware of its exaggerations, abuses it, and Silvius, equally naïve about hyperbole, lets it abuse him. This control of tone is one of the great contributions of Shakespeare's comedy to his dramatic art as a whole. The discipline of comedy in controlling the humorous potentialities of a remark enables the dramatist to express the relation of a speaker to his lines, including the relation of naïveté. The focus of attention is not on the outward action of saying something but on the shifting, uncrystallized life which motivates what is said.

The particular feeling of headlong delight in Rosalind's encounters with Orlando goes with the prose of these scenes, a medium which can put imaginative effects of a very high order to the service of humor and wit. The comic prose of this period is first developed to its full range in Falstaff's part, and steals the show for Benedict and Beatrice in *Much Ado About Nothing*. It combines the extravagant linguistic reach of the early clowns' prose with the sophisticated wit which in the earlier plays was usually cast, less flexibly, in verse. Highly patterned, it is built up of balanced and serial clauses, with everything linked together by alliteration and kicked along by puns. Yet it avoids a stilted, Euphuistic effect because regular patterns are set going only to be broken to underscore humor by asymmetry. The speaker can rock back and forth on antitheses, or climb "a pair of stairs" (V.ii.42) to a climax, then slow down meaningly, or stop dead, and so punctuate a pithy reduction, bizarre exaggeration or broad allusion. T. S. Eliot has observed that we often forget that it was Shakespeare who wrote the greatest prose in the language. Some of it is in *As*

You Like It. His control permits him to convey the constant shifting of attitude and point of view which expresses Rosalind's excitement and her poise. Such writing, like the brushwork and line of great painters, is in one sense everything. But the whole design supports each stroke, as each stroke supports the whole design.

The expression of Rosalind's attitude towards being in love, in the great scene of disguised wooing, fulfills the whole movement of the play. The climax comes when Rosalind is able, in the midst of her golden moment, to look beyond it and mock its illusions, including the master illusion that love is an ultimate and final experience, a matter of life and death. Ideally, love should be final, and Orlando is romantically convinced that his is so, that he would die if Rosalind refused him. But Rosalind humorously corrects him, from behind her page's disguise:

> . . . Am I not your Rosalind?
> ORLANDO: I take some joy to say you are, because I would be talking of her.
> ROSALIND: Well, in her person, I say I will not have you.
> ORLANDO: Then, in mine own person, I die.
> ROSALIND: No, faith, die by attorney. The poor world is almost six thousand years old, and in all this time there was not any man died in his own person, videlicet, in a love cause. Troilus had his brains dash'd out with a Grecian club; yet he did what he could to die before, and he is one of the patterns of love. Leander, he would have liv'd many a fair year though Hero had turn'd nun, if it had not been for a hot midsummer night; for (good youth) he went but forth to wash him in the Hellespont, and being taken with the cramp, was drown'd; and the foolish chroniclers of that age found it was 'Hero of Sestos.' But these are all lies. Men have died from time to time, and worms have eaten them, but not for love.
> ORLANDO: I would not have my right Rosalind of this mind, for I protest her frown might kill me.
> ROSALIND: By this hand, it will not kill a fly!

(IV.i.90–108)

A note almost of sadness comes through Rosalind's mockery towards the end. It is not sorrow that men die from time to time, but that they do not die for love, that love is not so final as romance would have it. For a moment we experience as pathos the tension between feeling and judgment which is behind all the laughter. The same pathos of objectivity is expressed by Chaucer in the sad smile of Pandarus as he contemplates the illusions of Troilus' love. But in *As You Like It* the mood is dominant only in the moment when the last resistance of feeling to judgment is being surmounted: the illusions thrown up by feeling are mastered by laughter and so love is reconciled with judgment. This resolution is complete by the close of the wooing scene. As Rosalind rides the crest of a wave of happy fulfillment (for Orlando's behavior to the pretended Rosalind has made it perfectly plain that he loves the real one) we find her describing with delight, almost in triumph, not the virtues of marriage, but its fallibility:

> Say 'a day' without the 'ever.' No, no, Orlando! Men are April when they woo, December when they wed. Maids are May when they are maids, but the sky changes when they are wives.
>
> (IV.i.146–150)

Ordinarily, these would be strange sentiments to proclaim with joy at such a time. But as Rosalind says them, they clinch the achievement of the humor's purpose. (The wry, retarding change from the expected cadence at "but the sky changes" is one of those brush strokes that fulfill the large design.) Love has been made independent of illusions without becoming any the less intense; it is therefore inoculated against life's unromantic contradictions. To emphasize by humor the limitations of the experience has become a way of asserting its reality. The scenes which follow move rapidly and deftly to complete the consummation of the love affairs on the level of plot. The treatment becomes more and more frankly artificial, to end with a masque. But the lack of realism in presentation does not matter, because a much more important realism in our attitude towards the substance of romance has been achieved already by the action of the comedy.

In writing of Marvell and the metaphysical poets, T. S. Eliot spoke of an "alliance of levity and seriousness (by which the seriousness is intensified)." What he has said about the contribution of wit to this poetry is strikingly applicable to the function of Shakespeare's comedy in *As You Like It*: that wit conveys "a recognition, implicit in the expression of every experience, of other kinds of experience which are possible. The likeness does not consist simply in the fact that the wit of certain of Shakespeare's characters at times is like the wit of the metaphysicals. The crucial similarity is in the way the humor functions in the play as a whole to implement a wider awareness, maintaining proportion where less disciplined and coherent art falsifies by presenting a part as though it were the whole. The dramatic form is very different from the lyric: Shakespeare does not have or need the sustained, inclusive poise of metaphysical poetry when, at its rare best, it fulfills Cowley's ideal:

> In a true piece of Wit all things must be
> Yet all things there agree.

The dramatist tends to show us one thing at a time, and to realize that one thing, in its moment, to the full; his characters go to extremes, comical as well as serious; and no character, not even a Rosalind, is in a position to see all around the play and so be completely poised, for if this were so the play would cease to be dramatic. Shakespeare, moreover, has an Elizabethan delight in extremes for their own sake, beyond the requirements of his form and sometimes damaging to it, an expansiveness which was subordinated later by the seventeenth century's conscious need for coherence. But his extremes, where his art is at its best, are balanced in the whole work. He uses his broad-stroked, wide-swung comedy for the same end that the seventeenth-century poets achieved by their wire-drawn wit. In Silvius and Phebe he exhibits the ridiculous (and perverse) possibilities of that exaggerated romanticism which the metaphysicals so often mocked in their serious love poems. In Touchstone he includes a representative of just those aspects of love which are not romantic, hypostatizing as a character what in direct lyric expression would be an irony:

> Love's not so pure and abstract as they use
> To say who have no mistress but their muse.

By Rosalind's mockery a sense of love's limitations is kept alive at the very moments when we most feel its power:

> But at my back I always hear
> Time's winged chariot hurrying near.

The fundamental common characteristic is that the humor is not directed at "some outside sentimentality or stupidity," but is an agency for achieving proportion of judgment and feeling about a seriously felt experience.

As You Like It seems to me the most perfect expression Shakespeare or anyone else achieved of a poise which was possible because a traditional way of living connected different kinds of experience to each other. The play articulates fully the feeling for the rhythms of life which we have seen supporting Nashe's strong but imperfect art in his seasonal pageant. Talboys Dimoke and his friends had a similar sense of times and places when they let holiday lead them to making merry with the Earl of Lincoln; by contrast, the Puritan and/or time-serving partisans of Lincoln could not or would not recognize that holiday gave a license and also set a limit. An inclusive poise such as Shakespeare exhibits in Rosalind was not, doubtless, easy to achieve in any age; no culture was ever so "organic" that it would do men's living for them. What Yeats called Unity of Being became more and more difficult as the Renaissance progressed; indeed, the increasing difficulty of poise must have been a cause of the period's increasing power to express conflict and order it in art. We have seen this from our special standpoint in the fact that the everyday-holiday antithesis was most fully expressed in art when the keeping of holidays was declining.

The humorous recognition, in *As You Like It* and other products of this tradition, of the limits of nature's moment, reflects not only the growing consciousness necessary to enjoy holiday attitudes with poise, but also the fact that in English Christian culture saturnalia was never fully enfranchised. Saturnalian customs existed along with the courtly tradition of romantic love and an ambient disillusion about nature stemming from Christianity. In dramatizing love's intensity as the release of a festive moment, Shakespeare keeps that part of the romantic tradition which makes love an experience of the whole personality, even though he ridicules the wishful absolutes of doctrinaire romantic love. He does not found his comedy on the sort of saturalian simplification which equates love with sensual gratification. He includes spokesmen for this sort of release in reduction; but they are never given an unqualified predominance, though they contribute to the atmosphere of liberty within which the aristocratic lovers find love. It is the latter who hold the balance near the center. And what gives the predominance to figures like Berowne, Benedict and Beatrice, or Rosalind, is that they enter nature's whirl consciously, with humor that recognizes it as only part of life and places their own extravagance by moving back and forth between holiday and everyday perspectives. Aristophanes provides a revealing contrast here. His comedies present experience entirely polarized by saturnalia; there is little *within* the play to qualify that perspective. Instead, an irony attaches to the whole performance which went with the accepted place of comedy in the Dionysia. Because no such clear-cut role for saturnalia or saturnalian comedy existed within Shakespeare's culture, the play itself had to place that pole of life in relation to life as a whole. Shakespeare had the art to make this necessity into an opportunity for a fuller expression, a more inclusive consciousness.

A.P. ROSSITER

"Much Ado About Nothing"

The play's date (1598 seems secure) invites one of two general approaches to interpretation. *Either* this is all trivial, however clever: the author is totally disengaged throughout, and we are foolish to look for anything in any way deep, ourselves solemnly making ado about nothing; *or* it is a brilliantly superficial and deliberately limited 'Italian' love-fantasia on the theme of deception by appearances (all sorts of deceptions, by several sorts of appearances): and we remember that seeming and being will provide plots in very different tones from this, in the plays that Shakespeare goes on to write in 1599 and later.

In 1923 (*Much Ado:* New Cambridge ed.) Dover Wilson advanced the hypothesis of an Old Play in verse, put through 'prose revision' which left loose tags and oddments that no longer had meaning, as well as 'verse fossils'. This revision made the most of the Benedick-Beatrice sub-plot; less of Hero and Claudio; and reduced the original Borachio-Margaret 'sub-sub-plot' (on the parallel loves of the serving-man and maid pattern) to next to nothing. Undeniably there are some discrepancies in the text which this hypothesis explains away nicely. But on one important point I have my objections. In II.ii. Borachio, sketching the defamation-scheme, says that 'instances' will be offered: he is to be seen at Hero's window, and they are to 'hear me call Margaret Hero, hear Margaret term me Claudio'. On pp. 105–7 of 'The Note on the Copy', Dover Wilson makes this 'slip' the one certain evidence for the existence of a Borachio-Margaret sub-plot in 'the unrevised text', which Shakespeare here repeated accidentally: aware only that in the old play 'Margaret was deceived as well as the

From *Angel with Horns: Fifteen Lectures on Shakespeare*, edited by Graham Storey. Copyright © 1961 by Longman Group Ltd. Theatre Arts Books.

Prince and Claudio', when vanity would make her dress as Hero, and welcoming 'Borachio' would look like Hero's being faithless with him. Theobald substituted 'Borachio' for 'Claudio': the original Cambridge editors were not satisfied. Theobald wanted to know how it could displease Claudio to hear his mistress using *his* name tenderly; and the Cambridge editors commented that 'Hero's supposed offence would not be enhanced by calling one lover by the name of another'. With respect, I find both attitudes obtuse. It *would* offend Claudio to hear his name misused (and to a servant); and while adultery-in-advance is a severe offence to any bridegroom, it *is* made more offensive if the morrow's marriage is mocked in the meeting of the guilty lovers. The Cambridge editors went on to suggest that Shakespeare may have meant Borachio to persuade Margaret to play, 'as children say, at being Hero and Claudio'; but they did not see that this was a *sufficient* explanation, which it surely is. The use of Hero's name would have convinced the onlookers that what they saw was not just her dress; and that of Claudio's would have the most powerful effect on those who knew the real Claudio was with them. It would seem the acme of jadishness. Indeed, all Borachio need do is to deliver the names in a mocking tone of soupy infatuation.

If this convinces, the difficulty vanishes; and the best evidence for the Borachio-Margaret sub-plot with it. Shakespeare had a reasonably clear idea of how he *could* present the scene (which he never did); and it is not significant enough, as Dover Wilson claims, that 'we are not informed' of the 'detail' of 'Margaret in Hero's garments' till V.i.232. It shows what was in Shakespeare's mind: if he *had* written the scene to be played out, then we do not need informing of what we *see* (for Margaret must, obviously, have appeared in whatever Hero had worn before: probably the ball-dress from II.i.).

This weakens the Old Play hypothesis: although it remains possible that the 1598 composition may have been from an earlier draft (perhaps a mere sketch); and true that writing of distinguishably different sorts is juxtaposed in it, together with the uncertainties and dead-ends which result from quick composition. Detective-story consistency, and the elimination of all redundancies and contradictions, are not to be expected of an Elizabethan and especially not of a dramatist. In short, the slight internal contradictions seen on reading do not signify (if Shakespeare saw them); and do not matter much, if we do. The 'old' matter (if it was old) suited certain contrasts which Shakespeare wanted to draw around 1598, and gave the 'main' plot the right lack of emphasis for the task in hand. There is no reason to doubt that the emphasis on Benedick and Beatrice is deliberate, whether he worked from a draft, a sketch, or in some other way. Nor, I think, can we fail to observe that in the 'main' plot *some* passages of a tone too disturbed or disturbing for the 'Old Play', or for early work, 'arrived' in the course of writing out, because there were already in his mind feelings and reflections on, say, 'what men daily do, not knowing what they do': feelings which were, after 1598, to lead his work towards tragicomedy (of a sort that this play is *not*).

Deception by appearances in *love* is patently what most of *Much Ado* is 'about'. As Hero puts it:

> Of this matter
> Is little Cupid's crafty arrow made,
> That only wounds by hearsay . . .
> (III.i.21–3)

Cupid is not responsible for calumny; but 'hearsay' is a main force in both love-plots: each is about its effects on proud, self-willed, self-centred and self-admiring creatures, whose comedy is at bottom that of imperfect self-knowledge, which leads them on to fool themselves. Is it exaggeration to bring even Dogberry into this pattern? to point to his manifest self-admiration ('a fellow that hath had losses; and one that hath two gowns, and everything handsome about him'), and to hint that the little arrow that wounds *him* 'by hearsay' is magnificent language and 'wit'? Are not words and wisdom his Cupids? No doubt that stretches 'love' too far. But self-love is a common term to all three of the splendid comedians of the piece.

The play's wit has been justly praised and is worth some examination in detail. It is of several distinguishable sorts: the simpler important only in so far as contributing to the cumulative effect, one of impetuous exuberance, a kind of competitive vitality, expressing itself in quick manipulations of language. The Messinans have dancing minds, and make words dance or caper to their unpremeditated tunes. At its simplest level, it is mere quibble: where A has used a word capable of two meanings in different contexts, and B shows his awareness of both, by displacing it. This may be no more than a conventional game, 'comic wit degenerating into clenches'; and though editors explain them, 'the mind', as Johnson says, 'is refrigerated by interruption'. *Much Ado* suffers but little from this. It may, again, be an elaboration of that: when A and B are the same person, as when Beatrice 'takes herself up' on Claudio: 'The Count is neither sad, nor sick, nor merry, nor well; but civil count—civil as an orange, and something of that jealous complexion.' (II.i.262–4). That is exactly at the point where mere verbal cleverness, non-significant quibble, passes over into relevant wit: evocative here either of Beatrice's vitality (the 'character' view), or of the exuberant quality of lively minds which strike fire by scoring off each other: the quality I called *competitive* vitality, as of a 'college of wit-crackers'.

In the wit-game Benedick and Beatrice rightly regard themselves as 'seeded' players. Beatrice makes this clear in the scene in Hero's apartment before the wedding (III.iv.), when Margaret scores off her for once. Shown Hero's new gloves, she is not interested (her mind is bothered with Benedick), and unguardedly pretends to have a cold:

> I am stuff'd, cousin, I cannot smell.
> MARGARET: A maid and stuff'd! There's goodly catching of cold.
> BEATRICE: O, God help me! God help me! How long have you profess'd apprehension?

('Since when have you been a wit-cracker in this line?'—which Beatrice regards, with good reason, as her own.) Beatrice gets more of her own medicine later, over the prescription of 'Carduus Benedictus': here the wit is both verbal and something more—we might call it the wit of situation. No precise *double-entendre* is made; but Beatrice's state of mind is such that she feels (like Benedick before her) 'there's a double meaning in that'; and she lays herself open to another laugh by again using the wrong word:

> Benedictus! why Benedictus? You have some moral in this 'Benedictus'.
> MARGARET: Moral? No, by my troth, I have no moral meaning.

It is a notable point in Shakespeare's contrivance that he gives both wits their off-day, as soon as love has disturbed their freedom.

As a rule, bawdy quibble outlives its contemporaries—simply because of 'human nature'; or because the fundamental situation is practically constant. In this play, jesting about sex is apposite: its subjects are sex-opposition, wooing, wedding, wiving (with due attention to the dangers of the last in making sport of a man). The audience certainly laughed at Benedick's 'Well, a horn for my money, when all's done' (II.iii.56), the *second* time they saw the play. It becomes comic dramatic irony, if you read Elizabethanly. Yet, quite often, I see no great gain by doing so. There is something pathetic in the detailed scholarship which laboriously strives to conjure from its grave every ghost of an expired laugh. 'Lighthearted bawdry' has its point in *Much Ado* (as in Mercutio); but only the best of points can stand heavy-handed annotation. Much of it turns on obsolete phrases: the fuse of the whole firework has to be replaced with a dry note; and the verbal transaction, by losing all its speed, loses nearly all its crack.

Quibble in slow-motion ceases to be witty. None the less, by noticing or examining the dexterities of verbal switch required, we are speeded up to a better awareness of the Elizabethan manipulations of language; and, at the same time, made more conscious of the vitality evoked individually by characters, and cumulatively by quibble, pun and jest together.

Shakespeare's wit in devising the linguistic mishaps and semantic excesses of Dogberry is the other side to the flat and despised 'mere quibble'. Dogberry exaggerates, by accident and in self-satisfied ignorance, the processes by which the true wits divert the meanings of words deliberately, knowingly, and with pride in their craft. But the one is the antithesis to the other; and both sides could be told, 'Thou hast frighted the word out of his right sense, so forcible is thy wit' (Benedick to Beatrice, V.ii.48). Wit and nitwit share a common obsessive delight in the wonders of words. This is largely what makes Dogberry the apposite farce-fool for a play in which all three plots turn on understandings and misunderstandings: quite apart from his being a marvel of the official numbskull's capacity to make extreme ado about genuine nothing.

But has the 'Malaprop' had its day? It took the stage in *Woodstock* (? 1594), was cornered by Sheridan, survived to Dickens. It is perhaps funniest in hierarchical societies, where clever and witty management (or mismanagement) of language distinguishes the *élite*; and aping this makes the linguistic lower orders flatteringly absurd. My impression is that Malaprops are only comic nowadays to over-language-conscious schoolmasters; or, of course, when bawdily Dogburian: when the right idea comes out in very much the wrong word. But, unless I mistake, Dogberry's skids are never improper. Impropriety in this play is the privilege of the educated.

The wit that does *not* turn on word-play is best shown by examples. Essentially it is the exuberance which leaps beyond expectation in 'improving the occasion'. Not only Benedick and Beatrice have this hyperbolic comic inventiveness: the former his strokes of Falstaffian invention, the latter her alarming opportunism (she is likely to score suddenly off anyone, at any time). The qualities of swiftness and unexpectedness are just as neatly shown by old Leonato's perfectly timed shot at Benedick. Don Pedro asks if Hero is Leonato's daughter. 'Her mother hath many times told me so', is the conventional formula in reply. 'Were you in doubt, sir, that you ask'd her?' asks Benedick. 'Signior Benedick, no; for then were you a child' (a palpable hit). They appear equally in Beatrice's magnificent impertinence to Don Pedro. She must cry 'Heigh ho for a husband!'—

DON PEDRO: Lady Beatrice, I will get you one.
BEATRICE: I would rather have one of your father's getting. . . .

And the quality of 'comic inventiveness' is shown immediately after, when he teasingly offers himself, and she says she will not have him unless she can have another for working-days: he is so costly she would have to keep him for best.

Both quickness of repartee and comic inventiveness (hyperbolic feats of exaggeration and elaboration) are intrinsic to the attitudes of self-dramatization upon which the comedy of character depends. Energy is delight and accomplished dexterity a pleasure to watch. Benedick and Beatrice have both: all the more because they are playing a part before themselves, and playing it high in an infectious sort of daring: figures of pride, which is at once humanly splendid, and 'goes before a fall'. There is no need to repeat what others have said of their proud hearts as a source of misogamy, because marriage means submission and commonplaceness. Benedick shows a more delicately amusing self-conceit than this in, for example, the admirable lines (V.ii.63ff.), where the two mock-solemnly agree (a) that they are too wise to woo peaceably, and (b) that not one, wise man among twenty will praise himself. Benedick then hits the high note impeccably with 'Therefore is it most expedient for the wise, if Don Worm, his conscience, find no impediment to the contrary, to be the trumpet of his own virtues, as I am to myself'—a pause, to let the conceit of it shock all modest minds; then he goes one better—'So much for praising myself, who, I myself will bear witness, is praiseworthy.' Here he is playing the Falstaffian game of carrying outrageousness as far as it will go. The *other* side of this self-conceit is in II.iii.200ff., his solemn resolutions to profit morally by what he has overheard on his character: 'I must not seem proud; happy are they that hear their detractions and can put them to mending'; and the heroic resolve to make the supreme sacrifice: 'No; the world must be peopled.' There, he is magnificently *absurd*, and totally unaware of himself. I stress the point to bring out the unappreciated fact that the common distinction between persons we laugh *at* and those we laugh *with* is too naïve and crude, at any rate for Shakespeare. Benedick's subsequent efforts to extract a double meaning from two snubbing sentences of Beatrice's repeat this vista of ingenious absurdity. Besides being excellent comedy of mistaken meanings, the last speech in II.iii. is a perfect miniature sample of love-humour racing a man past himself: 'I will go get her picture.' (*Exit*)

It may seem a wantonly paradoxical view, in so verbally brilliant a piece, but I would contend that some of the wittiest work is to be found in the interrelations and inter-inanimations of the plots. Of the three, the one that takes attention foremost is technically a sub-plot. We hardly notice that it gets going before the 'main' plot, but Beatrice is 'at' Benedick before Claudio appears; and this sex-antagonism in a fencing match between experts with sharp words is musically 'the first subject'. The comedy of this Benedick and Beatrice plot is not the simple, sentimental indulgence of the 'boy meets girl' pattern, although that is included; rather it lies in the entertaining, good-natured, critically aware contemplation of the bents in human nature shown in (a) their antagonism (their incapacity to leave one another alone); (b) their deception by contrived intrigue; (c) the revelations which spring from this, under the pressure of circumstances (that arise from the main plot): leading to (d) reversal of all their first positions. The audience is always in a slightly superior position, *not* identifying itself with either of them, though sympathetic. When all the analysers have anatomized, and perhaps reconstructed Benedick and Beatrice, they remain 'just representations of general nature', and hence, as Johnson says, 'please many and please long'.

If I were to answer in a word what the Benedick and Beatrice plot turns on, I should say *misprision*. Benedick and Beatrice misapprehend both each other *and* themselves: each misprizes the other sex, and misapprehends the possibility of a complete agreement between them, as individuals, on what causes that misprision: love of freedom and a superior conceit of themselves as 'wise' where others are fools; as 'free' and untied; and as having a right to enjoy kicking over other people's traces. They fancy they are quite different *from*, and quite indifferent *to* each other. Indifferent they are not; and the audience is 'superior' in seeing their humours *as* humours; and in being aware that the opposite to love (as passionate, obsessive interest) is not hate (another passionate interest), but cool or unnoting indifference. How little Beatrice's 'disdain' for Benedick is truly disdainful is shown in her immediately thinking of him as a measure for Don John (II.i.6ff.).

Because the mind of each runs on the other, they can both be simply gulled by hearsay; provided that it is overheard and includes the sort of freedom of comment we all use on absent friends: mildly malicious in tone, unspiteful in intent, and near enough true on their recognizable oddities and shortcomings. The overhearers, for all their sharpness of wit, know that the *comments* have some truth, and naturally accept the rest as also true. Thus the introduction of love-thoughts into both results from a species of misapprehension. They take the *sense* of the words, but totally fail to apprehend their *intention*. The two gulling scenes belong to the comedy of advertisement. Even the advertisers' nice touches of flattery are not lacking. The criticism is spiced with proper appreciation, as when Don Pedro hints—a very subtle inducement—that he would quite like to have Beatrice himself.

That the 'main' plot of Hero and Claudio turns on misapprehension leading to the misprision of violent disprizing, is too obvious to need commentary: but much of the play's total effect hangs on the structural mainness of this plot being displaced. As in Mannerist pictures sometimes, the emphasis is made to fall on what appears structurally to be a corner. This displaced emphasis helps to maintain the sense that the 'Ado' is about 'Nothing' (it is only through the distortion that reading gives, that much attention is given to the 'character' of Claudio).

But though the misapprehension from judging by appearances is quite obvious, it is easy to overlook the incidental touches by which the theme of false report, misunderstanding and jumping to conclusions is strengthened. Not logically strengthened: the 'incidents' are not necessary to the *story*; but the whole sub-episode of the proxy wooing does chime in cleverly with what is to follow. Don Pedro agrees to woo Hero; *immediately* Leonato's 'good sharp fellow' overhears and misreports (I.ii.5ff.); the correct report gets into the wrong ears, Borachio's; he tells Don John, who straightaway uses it malicously on Claudio (pretending to think him Benedick behind the masque-vizor). And Claudio at once anticipates his later violent and self-regarding impetuosity by assuming that Don Pedro *has* cheated him of Hero. Call this 'atmosphere', if you like; say, perhaps, that Messina is no place to trust any man's word; whatever you say, it strengthens the theme; and the ready *and perhaps drastic* misapprehensions of quick and apprehensive minds appear as of major importance in the play, as a play and not as a merely logical story.

I say 'perhaps drastic' to suggest how the matter of this part is balanced neatly on a tonal frontier: not between comedy and tragedy, but between comedy and tragi-comedy. Hence the 'limited' of my description of the play at the beginning: the drastic possibilities are so lightly touched that there is a sense of withholding—as if the author, in another mood, could give these incidents quite another tone: but not now; not yet. This feeling is most evident in the Church-scene, which is *not* tragic. T. W. Craik's line here is mainly sound; and his interpretation that *all* the passions are presented to be viewed with comic detachment is preferable to the conventional explanation, that 'the audience is throughout in the know', etc.

Without striving to make too much of it, the dance in II.i. is beautifully apposite. The couples walk their round, two by two, all masked; and all are using words to back the disguise of false faces with trivial deceit. The play-acted defamation of Hero, by means of a false dress on the wrong woman and names used falsely, is exactly parallel. In both, the truth is *behind* the looks and words. The *bal masqué* is only a game of seeming; yet it is a most apt symbol of the whole. The vizor is half deceit, half no deceit: you can never be sure. Believe it, and you make ado about what is nothing. And in the social order and shared delight of the dance—all moving to the controlling rhythm, in their appointed patterns—there is too the emblem of the harmony in which all will conclude: as the play does, with another dance, all the vizors laid aside. The real play is not ended with 'Strike up, pipers'. The very movement of II.i., where all the main misapprehensions started, is repeated and completed; and even the professed misogamists are dancing to the same tune. It is as neat and pretty as 'Sigh no more, ladies, sigh no more'.

The third plot—Dogberry, Verges, and Watch—though mainly Dogberry, is not a mere farcical variety-turn: there *is* a threat of connected episode. The Watch overhear Borachio's scheme and hear it correctly enough (their invention of a thief named 'Deformed' is a nice touch: he has arrived at official constabulary existence by the end). They only over-hear because they carry out Dogberry's ridiculous orders and make the policeman's lot a not-unhappy one by, as far as possible, doing nothing whatever. Despite their superb stupidity they do disentangle the plot: though only because, Don John having fled, Borachio tells everything, and gives them the game hands down. This is very natural and well-managed. For had Borachio set out to bluff, the Watch would have been utterly bamboozled in no time. *Superb* stupidity, however, belongs more rightly to Dogberry alone. One side of him is his art of 'comprehending vagrom' *words*: there a more 'senseless and fit man' could not be found. But this is not the whole of him; though a part entirely harmonious with the whole. Dogberry is a perfect instance of the comic mirth which Plato explained in *Philebus*: 'mirth', he says, 'is generally evoked by the sight of self-ignorance or self-conceit, as when a man fancies himself richer, more handsome, more virtuous or wiser than he really is; and this mirth must be present in one who is powerless to inflict hurt on others, otherwise he would cease to be a source of mirth and become a source of danger instead'. As a *real* official Dogberry would be a terror. Conceited igno-rance and vast self-importance in local government officers is—and was, in the time of Elizabeth—as good a joke in fiction as a very bad joke in fact.

But misprision and misapprehension are present here too, in a different guise. The incomprehension of the stupid ass is a limiting case of failure to apprehend; and over and above his miscomprehensions of language, Dogberry's own view of Dogberry is a vast misprision. To himself a superb creature, a wise fellow, as pretty a piece of flesh as any in Messina, he is superbly asinine in the Messina of wit and word-play. Yet, while apparently an *opposite* to the wit-crackers, he is also a parallel: in that pride of self-opinion and a nice appreciation of one's own wisdom and cleverness is as much theirs as his. There is no caustic correction of self-love in Benedick or Beatrice. But the parallel gives another common term, showing on analysis how the three plots have their implicit correspondences, how they genuinely belong together.

'Nothing can permanently please, which does not contain in itself the reason why it is so, and not otherwise.' I have been trying to probe down to the nervous system of those interrelations which *Much Ado* contains within itself, and which give it, as comedy, the poetic unity Coleridge there demands. I find a complex harmony of interdependent themes, some parallels, some direct oppositions; and it seems to me that misapprehensions, misprisions, misunderstandings, misinterpretations and misapplications are the best names for what the comedy *as a whole* is 'about'. The misapprehensions of language are one side of the play; those of human beings and states of affairs the other. At root the two are one; and both you can regard with Dogberry's formula for obdurate drunks: 'You may say they are not the men you took them for.' A step or stage beyond this, and what a different pattern of seemings might result: where neither looks nor words are to be trusted, but everything distrusted. . . . But *Much Ado* touches that for only a moment, and that unsymptomatic of the whole: for a few lines of Claudio's in the Church-scene. They only point to what *might* be thought and felt: in the real tragi-comedies it *will* be. Yet even in *Much Ado*, all appearances *are* equivocal.

Before leaving the plots, mark how deftly they are intertwined. Benedick and Beatrice misapprehend themselves and misprize each other. Claudio's contrived misprision of Hero, the result of intrigue, is finally dissipated by the *coup* of the Watch, which reduces all the ado to nothing. But at its zenith this same disprizing is the catalyst which liquidates the mutual misprisons of Benedick and Beatrice in the Church-scene. But the reactions to that scene (the confessions of love and Beatrice's implicit admission that she needs a man—to 'kill Claudio') only occur because Benedick and Beatrice have been prepared to 'apprehend': prepared by intrigue, which, like Don John's, is dependent on hearsay and overhearing, taking appearances at their face-value, and being led or misled by words.

Words I must stress, because Dogberry is no essential part of this intertwining as I have summarized it. I suppose you could formulate it all again by saying that the controlling theme might be styled 'mistaken identities'; for, in their pride or conceit, all the principals in some degree mistake themselves: as they mistake or wrongly take situations, and mistake or wrongly take words, on purpose and wittily or accidentally and absurdly. Leonato and Antonio, the two old men lashing themselves back into a youthful fury, and threatening duels, equally mistake themselves: they are pathetic and laughable at once. And, in a way, they reflect on Benedick's sternly assuming the role of truculent executioner to Claudio—and having a comical difficulty in maintaining the part. This is a good example of Shakespeare's detachment in this play: of the amused distance at which his creations should be held, if we are to take *Much Ado* as an artistic whole.

Despite Coleridge's too often quoted comment, 'The interest in the plot is always in fact on account of the characters, not vice versa, as in almost all other writers; the plot is a mere canvas and no more', I still think that plot (in a deeper sense than 'story') is here even more important. His implied contention that the 'interest' in the main plot is 'on account of the characters' (Hero and Claudio, chiefly; and I suppose Don John) seems to me simply untrue. Against Coleridge and his echoers we might set Jonson, putting Aristotelian principle in his own words, and answering the question 'What is a Poet?': 'A poet . . . is a maker, or a feigner: his art, an art of imitation or feigning; expressing the life of man in fit measure, numbers, and harmony. . . . Hence he is called a poet, not he which writeth in measure only, but that feigneth and formeth a fable, and writes things like the truth. For the fable and fiction is, as it were, the form and soul of any poetical work or poem.' In a later note, 'the very fiction itself', he says, is 'the reason or form of the work' (cxxx). 'Reason' and 'form' are abstractions from the apprehended 'felt' interrelations between distinguishable parts of a whole. Such interrelations I have made the central matter of my examination, attempting to resolve the theme to which the three 'plots' are subservient.

Much Ado is not a 'serious' play: it is 'limited' in managing potentially serious matters with a deft nonchalance which passes by the possibility of some being sharp things that might cut. At the same time, it is a play full of themes which are to have sufficiently serious explorations and consequences in Shakespeare's later work. Othello's situation, for example, is a variant of Claudio's; just as Claudio's behaviour to Hero is a sketch of Bertram's (hurt pride turned spiteful: providing we do not see Claudio as only 'mechanical'). Deceit by words (especially words of great meaning) is a constant in the tragi-comedies; and the comedy or farce of crediting too much of what is heard, or thought to be heard, is only the other side to 'O love's best habit is in seeming trust', and the self-imposed deception by seeming and fair words which are found in the Sonnets.

Seeming and being in the later plays have a quite different serious-ness. But such a theme exists here, as it does in *1 Henry IV*; and if we say that the one is on *love* (and sex), the other on *honour*, then, looking ahead, the change in Shakespeare's playwriting is partially represented by *Much Ado* leading to *Measure for Measure*; and *1 Henry IV* leading to *Troilus and Cressida*. By this I suggest that potentially serious and distress-ing human situations (involving love and honour) are in *Much Ado* and *1 Henry IV* handled 'lightly', as we say: contrived so as to keep them amusing, diverting, stimulating; but also so as to hold them more or less insulated from the deeper and more trenchant inquisitions into values of the tragi-comedies.

The place where we can hardly not notice little *points* of contact with the tragi-comedy outlook is the Church-scene. 'Seeming' is harshly emphasized; Claudio seems on the edge of playing a part that would make it quite another *sort* of play; and the Friar's moral lines on lost affections—sad, uncomfortable thoughts—are echoed by the King in *All's Well*. But those points mark the real insulation of *Much Ado*. The disturbed feeling of *Measure for Measure*—its troubled thinking—is not here. We can hardly speak of 'lack of feeling' in so bright, lively, glittering a piece: but is there not a certain *hard* quality, as with the bright colours of some Italian painting?

It is a *Decameron*-like story (barring the Watch), with some of the *Decameron* qualities of volatility in the persons, no wasting of sympathy on victims of jests, and the expectation of swift, unreflecting volte-faces of attitudes and emotions at the call of Fortune's pipe. That usually leaves an impression of shallowness, of a lack of *depth* of emotion, in northern European minds. The people seem rather heartless, while not in the least 'cold'; and the stories are apt to leave us thinking more about 'Now what did X really feel when . . . ?' than we know we *should*. In *Much Ado*, the brushing aside of the tone of calamity, the expectations of volatile changes of feeling in Claudio, the jocular (for so it is) 'Think not on him till to-morrow. I'll devise thee brave punishments for him. Strike up, pipers', only catch up a bright hardness (the result of a *deliberate* limitation of sympathies in the author?) which runs through the play.

Much Ado is a fantasy of equivocal appearances in a glittering world of amiable fools of all sorts. As naturally as Italians talk Italian, the Messinans talk 'equivocal'; but their 'double tongues' are as harmless as those of the 'spotted snakes' in *A Midsummer Night's Dream*. This equivo-cal quality, moreover, is deftly restricted to appearances: there are only the slightest touches of suggestion of any intrinsic equivocation in things themselves (in love, for example). Ambivalence is not a term to apply here.

These qualities urge me to 'place' the play in the course of Shakespeare's writing as follows. In the breaking down of sensitive endurance, and of mental resistance to the revelation of the unfairness of human nature, there is a point where a sense of humour *fails*; where to see life and the world in humorous proportions is no longer possible: it cannot be assumed by any act of will, or, if so, the assumption cannot be maintained. At this point distresses distress, and cannot be accepted tolerantly as the world's way, muffled by an easy 'they soon get over it' and by the cant of time. (I think of John Keats, of course; but without 'Keatsifying' Shakespeare. In the *later* plays the 'miseries of the world / Are misery'; but not here in *Much Ado*). Immediately *before* that point, the besieged mind and invaded heart may defend themselves by the assumption of a certain hardness: assume the *Decameron virtu*—the trappings and the suits of *joy*—though they have it not within. They may also find a certain high-flown gaiety—not hysterical, but making the best, and most, of the farce of human misunderstanding, deception, misprision—in the comedy of language (devised, so one may suppose, to communicate: but often used for just the reverse, either in game or in earnest). It is as if the sensitive mind and heart sought to persuade themselves by demonstration that life is a jest, and that the wider the comic net the likelier it is to resolve all the unmentioned but implied and subjective troubles in one great humorous or laughable plan, in which Fortune favours the laughers. This is the point at which great clowns who are melancholic—Chaplin, Raimu, Jouvet, Fernandel—stand and abide. One step from that strange equilibrium may turn to 'cynicism' (especially in England): the cynicism where the attitudes I called 'hardness' (self-defensive) and 'farce' (offensive, debunking) combine to 'place' love, honour, truth, only to devalue them. *Much Ado* stands in the Shakespearian canon just at that point.

NORTHROP FRYE

Making Nature Afraid

Drama is an objective form of art, and we should expect a writer attracted to the drama to have an objective attitude to his art. This is particularly true of a dramatist who, like Shakespeare, refrains from trying to impose any sort of personal attitude on us, and shows no interest in anything except his play. In this Shakespeare is unusual even among dramatists. The fact that Ben Jonson was a dramatist did not prevent him from exhibiting a remarkable personality or from often imposing it on his audience. During a period of personal controversy known as the War of the Theaters he introduces an armed Prologue into his play *The Poetaster*, who says:

> If any muse why I salute the stage,
> An armed Prologue: know, 'tis a dangerous age:
> Wherein who writes, had need present his scenes
> Forty-fold proof against the conjuring means
> Of base detractors, and illiterate apes,
> That fill up rooms in fair and formal shapes.
> 'Gainst these, have we put on this forced defence:
> Whereof the allegory and hid sense
> Is, that a well erected confidence
> Can fright their pride, and laugh their folly hence.

In other words, the armed Prologue is brought in to enable Jonson to make comments on the time and on other dramatists. In *Troilus and Cressida*, often thought to be connected with the War of the Theaters, an armed Prologue also appears, who calls himself:

From *A Natural Perspective: The Development of Shakespearean Comedy and Romance*. Copyright © 1965 by Columbia University Press.

> A Prologue arm'd, but not in confidence
> Of author's pen or actor's voice, but suited
> In like conditions as our argument.

That is, he is armed purely for decorum: his armor is appropriate to a play about war. There is no way of knowing whether there is any reference to the War of the Theaters or not, but if there is, it can only mean that Shakespeare was keeping well out of it.

Such reticence, combined with such genius, is intolerable to a certain type of stock response, which refuses to try to understand poetry apart from what it knows, or thinks it knows, about the poet. Its motto is that of the critic in Shaw's *Fanny's First Play*: tell me who wrote the play and I'll tell you how good it is. Hence it cannot know how good Shakespeare's plays are as long as it knows nothing about him except that he left his second-best bed to his wife. Thanks to a great deal of patient scholarship, we now have some idea of the order in which the plays were written, and it is possible to write a fictional biography of Shakespeare as a kind of allegory of what that order suggests. Thus the period of the great tragedies was also the period of what Professor Sisson calls the mythical sorrows of Shakespeare, with *Timon of Athens* representing a moment of peculiar exasperation. This procedure is attractive, because it is easy: one may demonstrate that one is a person of sensibility and insight in an area where no evidence can get in one's way. I think of *Timon of Athens* particularly because it has attracted so much speculation of this kind, and because the critical procedure involved has been so well described by the poet in that play:

> I have, in this rough work, shap'd out a man,
> Whom this beneath world doth embrace and hug
> With amplest entertainment: my free drift
> Halts not particularly, but moves itself
> In a wide sea of wax: no levell'd malice
> Infects one comma in the course I hold;
> But flies an eagle flight, bold and forth on,
> Leaving no tract behind.

However, what was always a foolish procedure is now happily discredited as well. The critical principle which ought to replace it is that there is no passage in Shakespeare's plays, certainly written by Shakespeare, which cannot be explained entirely in terms of its dramatic function and context. We may feel that an occasional speech or scene, such as the teaching of William in *The Merry Wives*, has been dragged in merely to fill up time, but there is nothing which owes its existence to Shakespeare's desire to "say" something. I add the clause about Shakespeare's authorship only because it is natural, when we find a passage which disappoints or exasperates us or seems inconsistent with our own view of the play, to wish that we could prove it spurious. Thus a female critic decided that the line at the end of *Macbeth*, "Of this dead butcher and his fiend-like queen" was interpolated because she felt that Lady Macbeth had made her peace with God off-stage.

Everybody has his own collection of lines or passages that he would not have written if he had been Shakespeare. I myself long for evidence that the "prophecy" spoken by the Fool in *King Lear* was the insertion of an actor who was not content to act the fool in only one sense. But I quite realize that this is the kind of feeling that a more flexible view of the play normally tends to dissolve. After reading Coleridge and De Quincey on the Porter in *Macbeth*, most people would agree that De Quincey had the broader view of Shakespeare's artistry in this instance, and is therefore right. The coarseness of the brothel scenes in *Pericles* was strong evidence to Victorian critics that Shakespeare did not write them, and equally strong evidence to twentieth-century critics that he did. Here again the latter are sure to be right, as the conception of Shakespeare implied is the more comprehensive one, and the more consistent with Shakespeare's other unquestioned work.

This implies a further principle, that a critical examination of the structure of a play seldom if ever needs to take any account of speculations about authorship. This would still be true even if I felt a confidence that I assuredly do not feel in the ability of critics to disentangle Peele from *Henry VI* or Fletcher from *Henry VIII*. It is true also when there is some external evidence to be considered, as there is in the Hecate scenes in *Macbeth*. It has been proved all through the history of drama that the word "collaborator" does not have to be used in its wartime sense of traitor, and that collaboration often, in fact usually, creates a distinct and unified personality. Nobody listening to a play by Beaumont and Fletcher feels that he is being alternately addressed by two different writers. The most striking example of a stylistic break in Shakespeare is, of course, in *Pericles*, where after two acts of rather undistinguished bumble we suddenly hear the unmistakable roar of Shakespeare's mighty rhetorical engines. But the first two acts, however they got into that form, certainly contain the incidents and images that belong to that part of the Pericles story, and there is no break in structure corresponding to the break in style.

It is consistent with Shakespeare's perfect objectivity that he should show no signs of wanting to improve his audience's tastes, or to address the more instructed members of it with a particular intimacy. His chief motive in writing, apparently, was to make money, which is the best motive for writing yet discovered, as it creates exactly the right blend of detachment and concern. He seems to start out with an almost empathic relation to his audience: their assumptions about patriotism and sovereignty, their clichés about Frenchmen and Jews, their notions of what constitutes a joke, seem to be acceptable to him as dramatic postulates. Setting aside the anonymous and mysterious epistle which introduces the second issue of the *Troilus and Cressida* Quarto, he seems never to have addressed his audience with any other attitude than that expressed in the last line of *Twelfth Night*: "We'll strive to please you every day." His characters may express more highbrow views, notably Hamlet, but then Hamlet, unlike his creator, is both a minor poet and a university wit.

The assumptions of a dramatist or the expectations of his audience may readily be translated into opinions or propositions or statements. If we do this to Shakespeare's assumptions, they turn into the most dismal commonplace. Hence the feeling expressed by such a variety of critics, ranging from Bernard Shaw to T. S. Eliot, that, great poet of Shakespeare was, his philosophy of life, his opinions, standards, and values were bewilderingly shallow. The obvious answer is, of course, that Shakespeare had no opinions, no values, no philosophy, no principles of anything except dramatic structure. Why, then, is there so determined an effort to make him an incompetent thinker as well as a great poet?

The reason takes us back to the distinction between critics mentioned at the beginning of this book. Some critics think of literature as an allegory or criticism of life, hence they tend to assume that any given work of literature illustrates something that can be expressed as a truth about life as the author sees it. *Hamlet*, according to Laurence Olivier, is the story of a man who could not make up his mind, hence the action of the play is developed to illustrate the effects of indecision, including eight corpses. The other approach, associated particularly with comedy and romance, regards the story being told, the imitation of an action being presented, as a self-contained unit. The author starts with a certain kind of story: this develops certain kinds of characters, occupying the strategic positions of that story, and each character owes his characteristic features, the things that make him what he is, to his place and function in the story. The moralistic approach sees him as owing these characteristics rather to his place as a symbol of the truths about life that the play illustrates. This approach is the dominating one in the criticism of modern literature: critics of Faulkner or Graham Greene almost invariably account for a character in terms of what he symbolizes in the author's habitual attitudes. Such an approach may be more appropriate to modern writers, but it can be misleading even there if it implies, as it is often apt to do, that there are no technical or structural problems whatever involved in telling a story. If one starts to tell a story about Tom Jones, one needs such a contrasting character as Blifil for structural reasons, not merely to symbolize the author's disapproval of hypocrisy.

In any case, many of the most cherished problems of Shakespearean criticism turn into pseudo problems as soon as the critical perspective is reversed. An example is the question: "Is Falstaff a coward?" Falstaff appears in plays largely devoted to warfare: warfare of this kind is based on a heroic code involving physical courage and readiness to die. Falstaff seems to be fairly detached about most of this code, and, unlike his predecessor Fastolfe in *Henry VI*, is articulate enough to suggest alternative values connected with saving one's life and retreating from trouble. The word coward implies a moral judgment, and whether we apply it to Falstaff or not depends on whether we accept the heroic code as a value, instead of simply as a dramatic postulate. Naturally we prefer to say that it is not we but Shakespeare who accepts or rejects the value. A tough-minded critic will insist that Shakespeare did accept it and that Falstaff is a coward; a tender-minded one will insist that he did not accept it and that he made Falstaff into an ironic hero. One approach turns Shakespeare into a stupid snob; the other turns him into a dishonest snob. When we reach a conclusion like that it is clearly time to retrace our steps.

I do not think I am threshing straw here: we may have lost some of our interest in Falstaff's cowardice, but we still talk about Shakespeare's acceptance of legitimacy, divine right, order and degree, the chain of being, Christian eschatology, and the like, as though they were truths that he believed in and wrote his plays to illustrate, or at least did illustrate incidentally. But it seems a strange critical procedure to equate so skillful a dramatic use of a theme with a belief in it which was mere commonplace in his own day and is mere superstition in ours. In Dante and Milton we recognize certain anxieties peculiar to their age, along with an imaginative vision that is independent of the age and communicates itself directly to us. Shakespeare's plays reflect the anxieties of his time: they do not show that he shared those anxieties. He may have done so as a man—there is no evidence one way or the other—but it is pointless to make allowances for things that "date" in his plays where we do not need to make such allowances.

The third scene of *Troilus and Cressida* presents the Greek leaders in conference, in an atmosphere as solemn, as rhetorical, and as barbaric as an Indian powwow. In the midst of this conference Ulysses delivers his speech on degree. He wants to get the Greek leaders to try to detach

Achilles from his homosexual friend Patroclus, but he has to do this with the face-saving demanded by warrior aristrocracies, hence all the talk about the cosmic order. The return of the ruthless and treacherous Achilles will not restore the cosmic order, but it will help to destroy the city of Priam. The audience is not asked to reflect on the state of the universe; the audience is seeing how skillfully Ulysses, like a human Aeolus, is controlling his bag of wind. When he wants to put pressure directly on Achilles he lets go with another tremendous speech on time, to which the same principles of decorum apply. To use these speeches as a basis of Shakespeare's belief, or of beliefs in his audience to which he was appealing, not only reduces his poetic thought to platitude but ignores the fact that he is using it as platitude.

Shakespeare's offenses against propriety have often been deplored: that is no longer an issue that worries us much, partly because we have a different notion of what constitutes indecency in literature. In every poet there is a craftsman who is trying to put words together into a structure solid enough to communicate with audiences remote in time and space and cultural assumptions. There is also in every poet, as in every man, an ego that wants to harangue and buttonhole, to sound off and impress, to impose opinions and project fantasies, to make enemies squirm and friends glorious by association. The only indecency known to literature is the exhibition of the author's naked ego, and a great deal of literary virtue consists in the covering up of personal vices. Shakespeare seems to have had less of an ego center than any major poet of our culture, and is consequently the most decent of writers. It is an offense against his privacy much deeper than any digging up of his bones to reduce him from a poet writing plays to an ego with something to "say."

When a great dramatist shows a deep concern for the social issues of his time, as Chekhov and Brecht do, we do not feel that this concern springs from the ego. So far from injuring their integrity as dramatists, it is an essential part of that integrity, and if there were evidence that Shakespeare had such a concern we should doubtless feel the same way about him. The complacent grinning sphinx of Matthew Arnold's "Others abide our question" sonnet could only be another kind of ego. But even concern has the technical problem of preserving the dramatic tension without collapsing into the kind of direct address to the audience that instantly destroys it. It is curious that we can think of impartiality only as detachment, of devotion to craftsmanship only as purism, an attitude which, as in Flaubert, turns all simple life into an enormously intricate still life, like the golden touch of Midas. We can hardly conceive of an imagination so concrete that for it the structure is prior to the attitude, and prescribes the attitude. Shakespeare's impartiality is a totally involved and committed impartiality: it expresses itself in bringing everything equally to life.

Let us now examine another kind of problem in Shakespeare: the one in fact that the so-called problem comedies are really about. In Terence's play *Hecyra* (*The Mother-in-Law*), the technical hero, a young married man named Pamphilus, refuses to live with his wife because he believes that she is pregnant with a child who cannot be his. She had in fact been raped, during a religious festival, by some hooligan in disguise. It was not her fault, but nevertheless Pamphilus feels that his honor demands that he repudiate her. Eventually it turns out that the disguised and raping hooligan was Pamphilus himself. This satisfies his honor, and the play ends happily. Everybody in this play, apart from Pamphilus, is presented as a decent and generous person, even the courtesan, who is usually so rapacious in Roman comedy. The contrast with Pamphilus seems deliberate, and one can hardly see or read the play without reflecting unfavorably on its hero. A juvenile delinquent would have a more coherent code of morals than that. However, Pamphilus remains the central figure of a comedy which ends as a comedy usually does, and his rewards are out of all proportion to his merits.

It is extremely unlikely that Terence had anything to "say" worth listening to, straightforward or ironic, about the society or morals of his day which he was trying to illustrate by his use of Pamphilus. All our evidence indicates that he had no interest in anything beyond trying to entertain an audience with a popular, and therefore highly conventionalized, dramatic structure. This is not to say that he was necessarily unaware of the ironic overtones of his play: it is to say that any reaction to the character of Pamphilus has to be based on his dramatic function in the plot. He could not possibly act otherwise, and therefore he could not possibly be a different kind of person, if this particular story is to get told. If we have a moralistic problem, then, it is not that we demand to see poetic justice done, and less happiness handed out to Pamphilus, but rather a reflection, which has moral overtones, on the structure of the play: What is the value, as entertainment, of a story like this?

The disproportion between action and character is a common feature of highly conventionalized fiction. In detective stories, we may often feel that the person who got murdered deserved it, and that we have more dramatic sympathy with the murderer than with his victim. But the author must follow the convention or his reader will feel cheated. We should note carefully that he does not feel cheated when the convention overrides his sympathies. Yet sometimes, in popular literature, the demands of the plot impose behavior on characters that seems to us to call the whole conception of the plot in question. If the hero of a thriller miraculously gets out of his scrape, that is convention: but if he had to be invincibly stupid to have got into the scrape in the first place, we may become impatient with the convention.

In Shakespeare there are at least three comedies in which a male character is married, to great applause, whom we have been led to think is no great catch from his betrothed's point of view. We have Claudio in *Much Ado*, Bertram in *All's Well*, and Angelo in *Measure for Measure*. Claudio is perhaps the most disturbing of the three. When Hero's infidelity is first suggested to him, he makes no resistance to the suggestion, but merely says that of course he will break off with her if the case is proved. He then accepts evidence that would hardly deceive a four-year-old child, and repudiates Hero in the most public and humiliating way possible. We can rationalize his behavior in various ways, but surely Beatrice has the sympathy of most of the audience when she regards him as a worm. Hero, apparently, dies: Claudio is unaffected emotionally by this, and ridicules Hero's father for taking his daughter's death seriously. Then the action moves on to a festive conclusion in which Claudio is completely accepted, and even Beatrice seems to find everything satisfactory.

The real critical question involved here is: Does anything that exhibits the structure of a comedy have to be taken as a comedy, regardless of its content or of our attitude to that content? The answer is clearly yes. A comedy is not a play which ends happily: it is a play in which a certain structure is present and works through to its own logical end, whether we or the cast or the author feel happy about it or not. The logical end is festive, but anyone's attitude to the festivity may be that of Orlando or of Jaques. It is unnecessary to change our attitude to Claudio, by historical or other arguments, in order to make the play a comedy for us.

The didascalia on Terence's play tell us that it was not played through on its first performance. What happened was that the audience went out during the intermission to watch a rope-dancing act in the neighboring circus, and failed to return. Clearly, Terence was not writing for an audience that gave him much encouragement to analyze character very exhaustively. The Roman audience, we feel, was rather like an audience of tired husbands at a symphony: they simply had to sit there until a certain kind of action completed itself. A prologue to one of Plautus' plays expresses this briefly but poignantly: "You'd better stretch your legs: there's a play by Plautus coming up, and it's a long one." Even in Shakespeare we may sometimes have a feeling which, if not boredom, is at any rate completed anticipation. In *A Comedy of Errors*, for instance, it is clear that these twins are going to meet sooner or later, and we wait for the author to catch up with a conclusion that we have mentally reached fairly early in the play. In comedy, as in all art that moves in time, the first datum is the drive or impetus toward the working through of a certain kind of action.

The poet then has the problem of pacing the play to provide a continuity of interest. The more restless his audience, the more strongly accented the pacing has to be. On the lowest level it must be as violent as possible, with constant running around and shouting, the action described by a character in Sinclair Lewis' *Main Street* as having "some git to it, and not all this talky-talk." But even with a civilized audience vigorous pacing is easier to take in. In music this accounts for the fact that finales are almost always in high speed. The same principle in drama takes us back to our original postulates. The popular features of drama are also the highly conventionalized features, because these latter provide the continuity of expected and anticipated devices which drive the play along with a more strongly marked emphasis. Part of our feeling about the repudiation scene in *Much Ado* is that we are expecting a comic conclusion. The statement "all's well that ends well" is a statement about the structure of comedy, and is not intended to apply to actual life.

We all know Dryden's poem *Alexander's Feast* and the influence which is there ascribed to music. Timotheus sings "A present deity" and Alexander "Assumes the god"; he sings of the fall of Darius and Alexander sheds tears; he sings of revenge and Alexander bursts out of the hall to burn the city. It is a fine poem, and probably a faithful reflection of the cultural tastes of world conquerors, but it is not a definitive piece of music criticism. In fact, one would say that if this is the kind of thing music does to people, music is a most pernicious influence on society, and the sooner we get rid of it the better. What Dryden's poem leaves out, of course, is the *structure* of music. Structure is the area of what Eliot would call unified sensibility: it is the unity which balances a variety of moods, conflicting with and to some degree neutralizing one another. Any fragment of the structure may evoke, by a kind of conditioned reflex, a certain mood or association, like the "little phrase" of Vinteuil in Proust. But structure as a whole cannot act kinetically in this way, and it does not make for clarity to confuse the effect of a Purcell aria with the effect of a bugle call to lunch. The structure of a work of art makes it the focus of a community. It does not act on people: it pulls people into it. An audience with varied backgrounds, associations, and habitual perferences is drawn together by something that says the same thing to each of them.

Mood, on the other hand, does tend to act kinetically, to suggest or act as the sign for an emotion which the hearer provides. In every well-constructed work of art, not only are the moods, and the emotional responses they cause, varied and balanced, but often two or more moods may be evoked at the same time. Thus the death of Cleopatra has both an elegiac and an ironic aspect to it: one aspect is emphasized by Charmian and Iras, the other by the clown and in a different way by Octavius. Yet we feel that there is a kind of parliament of moods, so to speak: that the house divides, and that there is a final majority in favor of one mood and not another. Tragedy is the name of a structure: it describes one important typical action of plays. It rouses conflicting emotions, generalized by Aristotle as pity and terror, achieves the balance among those emotions that Aristotle calls catharsis, and yet there is a pervading mood of a tragedy which is somber, and which we tend to think of as typically tragic. Comedy is also the name of a structure, yet it has a predominating mood which is festive. Because we are more strongly attached to our own moods than to a poet's structures, the names of categories of structure, such as tragedy and comedy, come to be used in the sense of such majority moods, so that "comic" tends to mean funny and "tragic" sad.

But in literature, as elsewhere, the unified is the opposite of the uniform. If tragedy has a uniformly somber mood, it tends to become melodramatic. By concentrating on mood it also tends to act, as far as it can, kinetically, to encourage its audience to applaud the hero and hiss the villain. The audience thereby tends to break down from community into mob. If comedy concentrates on a uniformly cheerful mood, it tends to become farcical, depending on an automatic stimulus and reflex of laughter. Structure, then, commands participation but not assent: it unites its audience as an audience, but allows for variety in response. The response to dramatic action, as to social action, ought to be a majority and not a totality. If no variety of response is permitted, as in extreme forms of melodrama and farce, something is wrong: something is inhibiting the proper function of drama.

We are not surprised to find that the plays of Shakespeare that are most nearly uniform in mood, such as *Titus Andronicus*, are not the ones that command our deepest imaginative loyalties. We are not surprised either to find that Shakespeare often goes to the opposite extreme. We may have a comedy so somber that the festive conclusion seems forced, almost embarrassing; or, as in *Romeo and Juliet*, a tragedy so full of wit and tenderness that the catastrophe carries with it a sense of outrage. Here, as in most forms of intensive irony, the audience may remain divided in its reactions. Hence both criticism and performance may spend a good deal of energy on emphasizing the importance of minority moods. The notion that there is one right response which apprehends the whole play rightly is an illusion: correct response is always stock response, and is possible only when some kind of mental or physical reflex is appealed to.

There are two forms of kinetic stimulus, though they are often found together. One is the emotional response that produces gloom or cheer; the other is the more conceptualized response of sympathy or indignation. This latter expresses itself didactically, directed toward making the audience leave the theater, still in the unnatural unity of a mob, but determined to do or at least feel something about whatever is presented as inspiring or malignant. There is nothing of this in Shakespeare, and no didactic equivalent of *Titus Andronicus*, which is another reason for the importance of not translating Shakespeare's dramatic postulates into values or opinions or propositions. In certain types of drama the action could be a fable irresistibly suggesting a moral which would be its "real meaning," so that the criticism of such a play could go over the head of the play itself to the conception that the author "had in mind," the play's idea or form. But this quasi-Platonic approach will not work with Shakespeare: his plays are existential facts, and no understanding of them can incorporate their existence. Shakespeare's "meaning" or poetic thought can be expounded only through a structural analysis of the play which keeps the genre of the play in mind as an essential part of the critical context.

I labor this point because it seems to me that there is still a good deal of confusion about Shakespeare's relation to his audiences, whether contemporary with him or with us. Such a confusion may be clearly expressed by a confused phrase, the most common of such phrases being "giving the public what it wants." Any dramatist who knew his audience as well as Shakespeare would know that the important difference in it is not the difference between intelligent and stupid people, but the difference between intelligent and stupid responses to the play, both of which may exist in the same mind. In all audiences there is an attitude that comes to the theater with a mass of prejudices and clichés and stock responses, and demands that the play illustrate them, or some of them. There is nothing to be done with such an attitude except to keep it quiet, and the superficial meaning of the play is what does that: the meaning that T. S. Eliot compares to a burglar throwing a piece of meat to a watchdog, hoping that the dog will bite it and not him. There is also a more intelligent attitude that wants only to see a play, and does not know until the end whether or not that play is what it wants. One attitude is focused on the apparent meaning, or moral, of the play; the other is focused on its structure. One attitude is reassured by the fact that in the historical plays the English are the right side and the French the wrong side; that in the romances only a real princess marries a real prince; that clowns are ridiculous and gentlemen stately. The other attitude does not seek a hidden meaning in the play addressed only to it: it simply observes the dramatic tension. In the final scene of *Measure for Measure*, the Duke has the role of dispenser of justice and Lucio has his own role as a morally reprehensible scandalmonger. Yet Lucio keeps getting laughs as the Duke blusters ineffectively at him, which means that Lucio holds just enough of the sympathy of the audience to keep the scene in dramatic proportion.

Our next step is to describe the typical structure of comedy, which I shall attempt to do [elsewhere]. Here I am concerned with distinguishing the characteristics of Shakespeare's type of romantic comedy. We have seen that the two words *popular* and *conventional* have some relevance to Shakespeare, and a close relation to one another. We have not explained, however, why certain conventions should be popular: a matter of some importance when we feel inclined to question the worth or value of a convention. For that we need a third term which complements and rounds out the meaning of the other two: the term *primitive*.

By popular we usually mean what is temporarily fashionable, for reasons that can be derived from the social conditions of any given time. But there is a more permanent sense in which a work may be popular, not as a best-seller, but in the sense of providing a key to imaginative experience for the untrained. The popular in this sense is the continuing primitive, the creative design that makes its impact independently of special education. Burns is a popular poet, not in any technical or best-seller sense, but in the sense that he continues and provides modern examples for a primitive tradition of folk song and ballad. Longfellow is a popular poet for the same reason, popularizing primitive elements as varied as ballad and Indian legend. What is popular in one generation often becomes ridiculous in the next one, quaint in the third, and is finally regarded as primitive in the fourth. Various forms of popular Victorian art are now completing this cycle.

The word primitive, however, suggests, not the old-fashioned, but the archaic, the region of origins and beginnings. Nobody can reconstruct the origins of literature, but students of drama have always been aware of its development from, or succession to, certain rituals concerned with promoting the food supply by verbal magic. This primitive element was clearly recognized by Aristotle in Greek, and Livy in Roman, drama, and its memory was conserved by later commentators, notably the famous and influential Donatus. Thomas Lodge, author of the main source of *As You Like It*, paraphrases Donatus as follows:

For tragedies and comedies, Donate the grammarian saith, they were invented by learned fathers of the old time to no other purpose but to yield praise unto God for a happy harvest or plentiful year. . . . You see then that the first matter of Tragedies was to give thanks and praises to God, and a grateful prayer of the countrymen for a happy harvest, and this I hope was not discommendable. . . . But to wade further, this form of invention being found out, as the days wherein it was used did decay, and the world grew to more perfection, so the wit of the younger sort become more riper, for they leaving this form invented another, for, sonnets in praise of the gods, they did set forth the sour fortune of many exiles, the miserable fall of hapless princes, the ruinous decay of many countries; yet not content with this, they presented the lives of Satyrs, so that they might wisely, under the abuse of that name, discover the follies of many their foolish fellow citizens.

This account establishes the principle that both tragedy and the comedy of manners are relatively late, educated, and sophisticated forms of drama. Comedy is inherently more pouplar than tragedy, for obvious reasons, but comedy as practiced by Jonson, Congreve, Goldsmith, or Shaw rests on a precarious acceptance: most of these writers, we notice, scold their audiences a good deal for preferring something more sentimental or spectacular. A tradition of arrogance toward the audience runs through such comedy from the Prologue to *Every Man in His Humour* to the Prologue to *Caesar and Cleopatra*. The popular and primitive form of drama is a romantic spectacle, full of violent action, whether melodramatic or farcical (the inclusion of these elements is a different thing from making a uniformity of mood out of them), dancing and singing, ribald dialogue, and picturesque settings. Comedy preserves this primitive form better than tragedy, and romantic comedy of Shakespeare's type preserves it better than the comedy of manners.

It is consistent with Shakespeare's general attitude to his public that he should move toward the romantic spectacle rather than away from it, and that so many of his experiments should be concerned with reviving the obsolete. Thus, after completing the austere *Coriolanus* and the even more forbidding *Timon of Athens*, we can see him turning over the pages of what seem to us rather corny and simple-minded plays, such as *The Rare Triumphs of Love and Fortune* and the hardy perennial *Mucedorus*, in search of formulas for his final romances. Gower in *Pericles* is part of an interest in *trecento* culture that extends to Boccaccio and Chaucer, and *The Winter's Tale* insists on the affinity of its story to old tales and ballads. It has been suggested that Shakespeare was responding to a new trend initiated by Beaumont and Fletcher, but, aside from the fact that the influence was more probably the other way round, Shakespeare's distinctive archaizing tendencies are not to be found in Beaumont and Fletcher.

The educated or humanist view of drama assumed that unity of action required unity of time, of place, of social classes (not mixing kings and clowns in the same play) and of illusion, keeping the action on one level of plausibility. Any exception, such as Jonson's *The Devil is an Ass*, would be likely to take the form of parody. Shakespeare not only ignores all this but deliberately turns back to the expanded screen of the old romances. *The Rare Triumphs* begins, in the convention of the Prologue to Job, with the Fury Tisiphone thrusting herself into a council of gods, and this vertical extension of the action into upper and lower worlds recurs in the oracles and epiphanies at the end of *Cymbeline*. *The Winter's Tale* seems almost written in answer to Sidney's strictures in the *Defence of Poesy* about the romances of his day that show a character as an infant in one act and as grown up in the next, and Shakespeare takes the fullest advantage of the principle stated in the Preface to Fletcher's *Faithful Shepherdess* (c. 1610) that in a pastoral tragi-comedy a god is "lawful."

All four romances provide us with infants growing into adults during the action of the play, presented or recounted. The requirement that no proper romance can take less than fifteen years for its total action is met in *The Tempest* by a long and rather wooden expository harangue from Prospero to Miranda at the beginning. Shakespeare had used this device in the early *Comedy of Errors*: if we found it only in that play we might regard it as a shift of inexperience, but when we meet it again in *The Tempest* (and in *Cymbeline*) we suspect something more like, let us say, a sophisticated, if sympathetic, treatment of a structural cliché. The rest of *The Tempest* observes the unity of time so rigidly that the time seems to keep shortening as the play proceeds, this being another device, like the use of Gower in *Pericles*, for incorporating the audience into the action. The expansion of time to include the passing of a generation—a theme much insisted on in *The Winter's Tale*—seems, paradoxically, to have something to do with the sense of timelessness in which these romances move. In *Cymbeline*, as already mentioned, we enter a world in which Rome and the Renaissance exist simultaneously, and the only phrase that will date such a play is "once upon a time."

It is not only in the later romances that Shakespeare shows a preference for the old-fashioned and archaic. *A Comedy of Errors* has more in common with a primitive folk tale like *Amis and Amiloun* than with what we should normally expect from a Renaissance adaptation of Plautus. Another experimental comedy, *Love's Labour's Lost*, with its make-shift plot, its dialogue of incessant and sometimes vicious repartee and mutual baiting, and the strong sense of personal caricature, sounds almost as though Shakespeare were trying to establish an Aristophanic Old Comedy on the Elizabethan stage, or had been reading Livy on the Fescennine plays of ancient Italy that preceded comedies with a regular plot (*argumentum*). A *Midsummer Night's Dream* takes us back to the folklore and fairy world of Peele's *Old Wives' Tale* and Lyly's *Endymion*, and the matter-of-fact bourgeois society of *The Merry Wives of Windsor* goes in for ducking, beating, and burning rituals of an ageless antiquity.

The effect of these archaizing tendencies in Shakespeare is to establish contact with a universal and world-wide dramatic tradition. Shakespeare draws away from everything that is local or specialized in the drama of his day, and works toward uncovering a primeval dramatic structure that practically anything in the shape of a human audience can respond to. When we turn to, say, Kalidasa's *Sakuntala*, in fifth-century India, we are told of a king who was betrothed to a beautiful maiden but who forgot his betrothal because of a magician's curse: her ring of recognition, which was to awaken his memory, was lost, fell into the Ganges, was swallowed by a fish, which was caught by a fisherman, and so on. There is nothing here that reminds us of the comedy of manners, but the kinship with *Pericles* and *Cymbeline* strikes us at once. Shakespeare did not know Menander, but *The Winter's Tale* is incredibly close in atmosphere to, say, *Epitripontes*, which is so much nearer to myth and folk tale than the derivative Roman comedies he did know. We may say with some confidence that if archaeologists ever discover a flourishing drama in Minoan or Mayan culture, it may not have plays like *King Lear* or *The Alchemist*, but it will almost certainly have plays like *Pericles*.

Ritual acts based on what is loosely called sympathetic magic, such as pouring water on the ground as a rain charm, resemble drama in being a sequence of significant acts, but are not otherwise dramatic. Such acts are normally accompanied by a story or myth which establishes an interrelated significance among them. Literature, in the form of drama, appears when the myth encloses and contains the ritual. This changes the agents of the ritual into the actors of the myth. The myth sets up a powerful pull away from the magic: the ritual acts are now performed for the sake of representing the myth rather than primarily for affecting the order of nature. In other words, drama is born in the renunciation of magic, and in *The Tempest* and elsewhere it remembers its inheritance.

Magic attempts to repeat, on a human level and in a human context, the kind of power ascribed to God in Hebrew religion and elsewhere. God speaks, and the forms of creation are called into being: the magician utters spells or recites names, and the spirits of nature are compelled to obey. However, drama gets back the magic it renounces in another way. Once it becomes a part of literature it enters into the function of literature. This is to use words, not to operate on the nonhuman world, but to assimilate it imaginatively to the human world, which it does mainly in the two archaic forms of identity and analogy. These reappear in literary imagery as metaphor and simile. The form of metaphor is more primitive and more concentrated than the language of simile, as well as further removed from the mental categories of ordinary experience, which are closer to the distinctions of observation and reason. In its earlier stages literature is closely attached to religion, and metaphor is also at its clearest in mythology, where we have gods conceived as human in form and yet identified with various aspects of nature, sun gods and tree gods and the like. The imagery associated with such gods is magic in reverse, so to speak: the kind of magic that enables Milton to say that nature mourns the death of Lycidas, or Shakespeare that the anemone stole the blood of Adonis.

When I spoke of the importance of convention in literature in general and in Shakespeare in particular, I did not examine the question of how a convention gets itself established in literature. Superficially, it is established by vogue or fashion: a young poet will naturally write in the way that people around him are writing. But if we try to look deeper we have to consider a bigger principle than anything we can derive from social history. The young poet in the sixteenth century normally began with complaints about a cruel mistress. If we ask why, we are referred to a convention that goes back through Petrarch to the origins of Courtly Love poetry in Provence. Two unanswered questions still remain: first, how did it become a convention in the first place?; and second, how did it remain popular for six or seven centuries through so many social changes?

The aspect of the answer that concerns us here is that conventions are descended from myths. The myth preserves the primitive identity of personal character and natural object in its purest form. At the same time the myth tells a story, and the story turns its back on the original magical function of the action. A character in a St. George play may announce that he is a Turkish knight or a doctor or the front end of a lion, like Snug the joiner, but what he will never say is: "We are representing the contest of summer and winter." If he did, the myth would cease to be a story and go back to being straight magic. Yet the bumps and hollows of the story being told follow the contours of the myth beneath, and as literature develops greater variety and independence of expression, these mythical shapes become the conventions that establish the general framework of narratives. Hence the literary convention enables the poet to recapture something of the pure and primitive identity of myth. The myth of a lost paradisal garden reappears in literature as the pastoral convention, and the relation of the convention to the myth enables the pastoral poet to use a highly concentrated metaphorical imagery without any breach of decorum.

To take a different example: *Macbeth* is not a play about the moral crime of murder: it is a play about the dramatically conventional crime of killing the lawful and anointed king. The convention gives a ritual quality to the action, and the element of reversed magic to the imagery that enables the poet to identify the actors with the powers of nature. The lawful king has his place in the "great bond" of nature: he has mysterious powers of healing, and is linked to everything in nature that keeps its rightful place and order. The usurper becomes linked with all the powers of chaos and darkness: not only is his deed accompanied by prodigious portents, but he himself becomes an incarnation of tyranny, an evil spirit that Malcolm must recognize and cast out of his own soul before he can become the lawful successor.

If we keep this mythical and conventional element in Duncan's sovereignty at the center of the play, every word of it fits together into the gigantic and terrifying tragic structure that we know so well. Take it away, and Thomas Rymer himself could hardly do justice to the chaos of what remains. The witches collapse at once into laborious grotesquerie; the passage about Edward the Confessor touching for the king's evil into unctuous flattery; the dialogue of Malcolm and Macduff into a tedious and embarrassing digression. In a play so concentrated there is no possiblity of half measures, no residual quality of intensity or poetry or realistic detail or whatnot that is left over for us still to enjoy if we hesitate about the convention. Accept the convention, and the play is all right; reject it, and the play is all wrong. The same principle holds for the comedies, and is even more important in the comedies. When Pepys saw A *Midsummer Night's Dream* and pronounced it the most insipid and ridiculous play that ever was wrote, he was not failing in critical judgment; he was saying what any honest man would have to say about it if he were unable to accept its convention.

The descent of convention from myth does not wholly explain why conventions are the way they are, of course, but it does illuminate one aspect of whatever explanation is given. I spoke of Terence's *Hecyra* and of its curious plot, in which a husband is only reconciled to his wife's having been raped when he learns that he did it himself. The question of why such a story should be told is not easy to answer, if possible, but any answer must start with the convention of the calumniated wife as a feature of storytelling in all ages and cultures. And the particular form of this story that we meet in *Hecyra* is clearly a shrunken and rationalized form of a story in which the original assault on the wife was made by a god, or some representative of one: the story that the same audience could see in a less displaced form in Plautus' *Amphitryon*, and that was still going strong centuries later in such motifs as the jealousy of Joseph. In *Much Ado* we have the same theme of calumniation, but Shakespeare has put it in something much closer to a primitive context by suggesting so strongly that Hero actually dies and revives during the play: "One Hero died defiled, but I do live," she says. Shakespeare's handling of the theme is closer to the Indian *Sakuntala*, already mentioned, where the heroine is carried off to heaven after being disgraced and slandered, whence the king has to go to collect her.

The problems of the problem comedies have to be looked at first of all as conventional descendants of myths. The "problem" of *All's Well* is not any Shavian social problem of how a woman gets her man, but the mythical problem of how Helena, like her ancestress Psyche, is going to solve her three impossible tasks: first of healing the sick king, then of presenting Bertram with a son of his own getting, and with his own ring, the talisman of recognition that, in *All's Well* as in *Sakuntala*, awakens his mind to reality. We may still find it a problem that she should want to do all this just to get Bertram, but that is because we think of Bertram after the play as continuous with Bertram during it. We should think rather of the primitive reponse demanded of us, say, in Richardson's *Pamela*, when Mr. B., who has been the most sinister and menacing of villains for four hundred pages, instantly turns into a dear and beloved husband on signing a marriage contract.

Similarly, the problem in *Measure for Measure* is how Isabella's chastity, always a magical force in romance, is going to rescue both the violated Julietta and the jilted Mariana as a result of being exposed to the solicitations of Angelo. It is a problem that brings Isabella much closer to Dylan Thomas's long-legged bait than to Hedda Gabler or Ann Tanner. Again, Isabella is unlikely to be our favorite Shakespearean heroine, but militant chastity, which is seldom likable, is her dramatic role, and the condition of her quest. A more complaisant heroine could no more accomplish this quest than Pinchwife could Petruchio's. In Shakespeare's main source, Whetstone's *Promos and Cassandra*, Isabella's counterpart does yield herself to save her brother and gets cheated.

Cymbeline, a play that might have been subtitled "Much Ado About Everything," is the apotheosis of the problem comedies: it combines the *Much Ado* theme of the slandered heroine, the *All's Well* theme of the expulsion of the hero's false friend, the *Measure for Measure* theme of the confusion and clarifying of government, and many others. There are even some curious echoes of names from *Much Ado*: in *Cymbeline* we have Sicilius Leonatus betrothed to Imogen, whose name is Innogen in Shakespeare's sources; in *Much Ado* we have Leonato, Governor of Messina in Sicily, whose wife's name, though she has no speaking part, is Innogen. The former name goes on echoing in *The Winter's Tale* as Leontes, King of Sicilia. The repetition may mean very little in itself, but we notice in the romances a technique of what might be called spatial anachronism, in which Mediterranean and Atlantic settings seem to be superposed on top of each other, as Bermudan imagery is superposed on the island in *The Tempest*. In particular, there is a convention, referred to in the Prologue to Jonson's *Sad Shepherd* and prominent in *Comus* and *Lycidas*, of mixing British with Sicilian and Arcadian imagery in the pastoral.

The same technique of superposition is used temporally as well, binding together primitive Wales, Roman Britain, and Italian Rome. *Cymbeline* has at least a token connection with the history plays of some significance. History is a prominent genre in Shakespeare until *Henry V*, when it seems to disappear and revive only in the much suspected *Henry VIII* at the end of the canon. Yet the history of Britain to Shakespeare's audience began with the Trojan War, the setting of *Troilus and Cressida*, and included the story of Lear as well as the story of Macbeth. Even *Hamlet* is dimly linked with the period of Danish ascendancy over England. Alternating with these plays of a Britain older than King John are the Roman or Plutarchan plays, dealing with what, again, to Shakespeare's audience was the history of a cousin nation, another descendant of Troy. In *Cymbeline* the theme of reconciliation between the two Trojan nations is central, as though it were intended to conclude the double series started by *Troilus and Cressida*.

The reason for the choice of the theme may be partly that Cymbeline was king of Britain at the time of Christ. The sense of a large change in human fortunes taking place offstage has to be read into *Cymbeline*, and as a rule reading things into Shakespeare in the light of some external information is a dubious practice. Still, we notice the curiously oracular gaoler, who speaks for a world that knows of no other world, and yet can say: "I would we were all of one mind, and one mind good." We notice, too, the word "peace" at the end of the play, and the way that the promise to pay tribute to Augustus fits into that emperor's decree that all the world should be taxed, the decree that begins the story of the birth of Christ. But *Cymbeline* is not, to put it mildly, a historical play: it is pure folk tale, featuring a cruel stepmother with her loutish son, a calumniated maiden, lost princes brought up in a cave by a foster father, a ring of recognition that works in reverse, villains displaying false trophies of adultery and faithful servants displaying equally false trophies of murder, along with a great firework display of dreams, prophecies, signs, portents, and wonders.

What strikes one at once about the play is the extraordinary blindness of the characters in it. Imogen begins her journey to Milford Haven by saying:

> I see before me, man: nor here, nor here,
> Nor what ensues, but have a fog in them,
> That I cannot look through.

Lucius, after the battle he was so confident of winning has gone so awry, says:

> For friends kill friends, and the disorder's such
> As war were hoodwinked

and the gaoler tells Posthumus how little he knows of where he is going. Posthumus replies that "none want eyes to direct them the way I am going, but such as wink and will not use them." Yet Posthumus himself has believed an even sillier story than Claudio does in *Much Ado*. The crafty Queen wastes her energies trying to teach Cloten the subtleties of courtship; Belarius tries to persuade his adopted sons to be disillusioned about a world they have never seen. The word "election," implying free choice, is used several times, but no one's choice seems very well considered; the word "note," meaning distinction or prestige, also echoes, but distinctions are difficult to establish when "Reverence, / The angel of the world" is compelled to focus on the idiot Cloten, stepson of the weak and deluded Cymbeline. In *Cymbeline*, as in all the romances, there is a scaling down of the human perspective. Posthumus is peevishly and querulously jealous, he is no Othello; the Queen is squalidly unscrupulous, and is no Lady Macbeth.

Imogen is by long odds the most intelligent character in the play, and Imogen throughout is surrounded by a kind of atmospheric pressure of unconsciousness. The emotional climaxes of the play are the two great songs of the awakening and the laying to rest of Imogen, and in neither of them has she any notion of the context. The aubade is sung to her indifferent ear by the agency of Cloten after she has unknowingly spent a night with Iachimo; the obsequy is sung to her unconscious body by two boys whom she does not know to be her brothers while the headless Cloten is being laid beside her in the clothes of Posthumus. We feel in *Pericles* that Marina's magical chastity will get her safely through the perile of the brothel, but at least she knows it is a peril: in other words, there is much less dramatic irony in *Pericles* than in *Cymbeline*. The ironic complications of *Cymbeline* are in themselves, of course, the customary conventions of pastoral romance, where the simple childlike pleasure of knowing more than the characters do is constantly appealed to by the author. But there also seems to be a strong emphasis on the misdirection of human will, which culminates in the prison scene.

In this scene a number of characters appear who are new to us but are older than the action of the play. They speak in a naïve doggerel verse not unlike in its dramatic effect to the verse of Gower in *Pericles*, and like it they are a sign that we are being confronted with something traditional and archaic. They are ghosts from the world of the dead, who have been invisible spectators of the action and now come to speak for us as spectators, impeaching the wisdom of Jupiter for allowing things to get in such a muddle. Jupiter tells them what, in fact, we have been seeing all along, that a skillful and quite benevolent design is being woven of the action despite all the efforts of human folly to destroy it. This scene is soon followed by the great contrapuntal tour de force of the recognition scene, when the truth is torn out of a score of mysteries, disguisings, and misunderstandings; when out of all the confusion of action a very simple conclusion is reached, and one which sounds very like peace on earth, good will toward men. The difference between *Cymbeline* and the earlier problem comedies, then, is that the counter-problem force, so to speak, which brings a festive conclusion out of all the mistakes of the characters, is explicitly associated with the working of a divine providence, here called Jupiter. Jupiter is as much as projection of the author's craftsmanship as the Duke in *Measure for Measure*: that is, the difference between *Cymbeline* and the problem comedies is not that *Cymbeline* is adding a religious allegory to the dramatic action. What it is adding to the dramatic action is the primitive mythical dimension which is only implicit in the problem comedies. *Cymbeline* is not a more religious play than *Much Ado*: it is a more academic play, with a greater technical interest in dramatic structure.

A final few words. . . . All myths have two poles, one personal, whether divine or human, and one natural: Neptune and the sea, Apollo and the sun. When the world of sea and sun is thought of as an order of nature, this polarization becomes a god or magician who controls the natural machine at one end, and the natural machine itself at the other. Tragedy, irony, and realism see the human condition from inside the machine of nature; comedy and romance tend to look for a person concealed in the mechanical chess player. When Ben Jonson speaks disapprovingly of dramatists who are afraid of nature, and run away from her, we find his meaning clear enough. When he says of himself that he is "loath to make nature afraid in his plays, like those that beget tales, tempests, and such like drolleries," the reversal of the phrase is more puzzling, although the implied comparison with Shakespeare is equally evident.

Jonson's own pastoral romance is the very beautiful, but unluckily incomplete, Sad Shepherd. Here we have Robin Hood characters, a Puck, and a Sycorax figure, the witch Maudlin, who has the witch's traditional tempest-raiser role, and boasts: "I'se pu' the world of nature 'bout their ears." There is a disconsolate lover who believes his mistress dead, and who asserts that her chastity, like that of the Lady in Comus, is closely associated with the higher order of nature which Maudlin cannot reach. This conception of nature as an order threatened, but not essentially disturbed, by witchcraft is in Shakespearean romance too. What Shakespeare has that Jonson neither has nor wants is the sense of nature as comprising not merely an order but a power, at once supernatural and connatural, expressed most eloquently in the dance and controlled either by benevolent human magic or by a divine will. Prospero in particular may appropriately be said to make nature afraid, as he treats nature, including the spirits of the elements, much as Petruchio treats Katharina. [Elsewhere] I shall try to examine more closely the myth of nature in Shakespeare, and of the way in which the emphasis is thrown, not on the visible rational order that obeys, but on the mysterious personal force that commands. As a somewhat bewildered Theseus remarks, after the world represented by his authority has been turned upside down by the fairies in the forest:

> Such tricks hath strong imagination,
> That, if it would but apprehend some joy,
> It comprehends some bringer of that joy.

HOWARD FELPERIN

Undream'd Shores:
"The Tempest"

The betrothal masque Prospero stages for [Ferdinand and Miranda] is a figuration on Gonzalo's utopia and enacts on a mythological level the human action of the play. Now it is Prospero's turn to try his hand at making allegories, and the product is more sophisticated in every sense than that of Gonzalo:

> Earth's increase, foison plenty,
> Barns and garners never empty;
> Vines with clust'ring bunches growing;
> Plants with goodly burthen bowing;
> Spring come to you at the farthest
> In the very end of harvest!
> Scarcity and want shall shun you;
> Ceres' blessing so is on you.
>
> (IV.i.110–17)

In what amounts to a revision of Gonzalo's earlier vision, Prospero has made some significant changes. Whereas Gonzalo had simply banished by fiat all the nastier aspects of civilization, Prospero's working principle in the masque is that of inclusion. The traditional golden motif of eternal spring has been added, and the bans on "tilth" and vineyards have been lifted. The "foison" of Gonzalo's speech stands, but it is now seen as the fruit of tilth, of labor, of agri*culture*. The blessing that Ceres comes "to estate / On the blest lovers" (IV.i.85–6) is not a piece of choice real estate like Hughes's Bermuda or Gonzalo's island plantation but an estate of the

---

spirit; not the result of a pagan or primitivist subversion of European customs but of their fulfillment; not the spontaneous generation of nature but a collaboration of nature with nurture; not a paradise needless of moral and physical effort but one dependent on both. The "evils" of labor, vineyards, marriage are all present in a redeemed form. The dance of Nymphs and Reapers, which suddenly vanishes as Prospero remembers "the beast Caliban," represents a disciplined harmony analogous to that of Mount Acidale (FQ, VI.X), where Colin Clout pipes to his love amid a dance of naked Graces, and which also suddenly vanishes upon the intrusion of the as yet remiss and self-indulgent Sir Calidore. When Ferdinand remarks, "Let me live here ever; / So rare a wonder'd father and a wife / Makes this place Paradise," he is quickly silenced by Prospero. Ferdinand cannot live "ever" with his wife in the seeming paradise of their father's making, but like Spenser's Red Crosse and Calidore, Sidney's Pyrocles and Musidorus, Milton's Adam and Eve, and the Dante of the Comedy, must return from this ideal vision to historical reality, to the continuing labor of governing Naples and himself. The spirit Ariel may sport endlessly after summer in an ideal landscape at the end of the play, but its human beings may not.

For even though Prospero's vision is a more full and comprehensive model of the redeemed world than Gonzalo's, it too is based on some rather arbitrary exclusions: the enforced absence of Venus and Cupid, who thought "to have done / Some wanton charm upon this man and maid" (IV.i.94–5) being one. As its banishment of lust suggests, not even the masque of Ceres is to be taken at face value, so mistrustful is The Tempest, is this "ideal" drama, of the endeavors of the idealizing imagination, of Prospero's as well as Gonzalo's attempts to allegorize experience. While there is no cynical courtiers present to mock Prosper's vision of the good and natural life, as there were at Gonzalo's, there is a Caliban plotting at that very moment to destroy it. And Prospero is aware of his own limitations as a utopist, serves as his own severest critic. The masque of Ceres is framed by his own commentary on it as a "vanity of mine Art" (IV.i.41) and as an "insubstantial pageant faded" (IV.i.155). Prospero has good reason to be aware of the "vanity," the frivolousness and pride and self-indulgence, of artistic endeavor, for it was by overdoing his passion for the liberal arts that he lost his dukedom in the first place. By indulging his desire to luxuriate in the paradise of his books, a desire very close to Ferdinand's during the masque, and "neglecting worldly ends" (I.ii.89), Prospero created a power-vacuum in Milan into which Antonio stepped. In Prospero's description of the Milanese coup d'état, his passion for the contemplative life amounts to nothing less than a hedonist idyll—"my library / Was dukedom large enough," (I.ii.109–10)—an escape from the public responsibilities of office into a private and insular world of art.

While Prospero studied an art wholly benign but completely out of this world, dedicated himself to "closeness and the bett'ring of my mind" (I.ii.90), Antonio was busily exercising an art altogether this-worldly: the Machiavellian art of the player-king:

> Being once perfected how to grant suits,
> How to deny them, who t'advance, and who
> To trash for over-topping, new created
> The creatures that were mine, I say, or chang'd 'em,
> Or else new form'd 'em; having both the key
> Of officer and office, set all hearts i' th' state
> To what tune pleas'd his ear. . . .
>   like one
> Who having into truth, by telling of it,
> Made such a sinner of his memory,
> To credit his own lie, he did believe
> He was indeed the duke; out o' th' substitution,
> And executing th' outward face of royalty,
> With all prerogative;—hence his ambition
>   growing,—
> . . . To have no screen between this part he play'd
> And him he play'd it for, he needs will be
> Absolute Milan.
>   (I. ii. 79–85, 99–109)

Musical and dramatic talent seems to run in the family, for Antonio apparently possesses the theatrical gifts of setting a score, creating character, managing plots, and playing roles that Prospero displays on the island, but all to perverted ends. We see in action Antonio's talent for envisioning and casting scenes when he tempts Sebastian to play the same part with respect to his brother Alonso that he himself had played toward his brother twelve years earlier: "My strong imagination sees a crown," he tells Sebastian, "Dropping upon thy head" (II.i.202–3)—a vision of royalty that aligns him with other visionaries and dreamers in the play, Prospero, Gonzalo, and as we shall see, Caliban. The episode of the Milanese coup illustrates, among other things, how easily that art which is uncontrolled by ethical and social concern collapses into egocentricity, at best the self-indulgence of a Prospero and at worst the self-aggrandizement of an Antonio. The two brothers divide the libertine potentialities of the imagination between them.

There is an important sense, then, in which Prospero himself stands in need of redemption at the outset of the play as much as the others, whose guilt is more blatant. And he does seem to have changed during his twelve-year exile, both in his attitude toward his dukedom and in his attitude toward his art. Whereas he had previously neglected the former as a result of his total absorption in the latter—"My library / Was dukedom large enough"—he now directs his art outward onto the world. The art that had been an end in itself is now the means, not only of recovering his dukedom, but of exercising his function as governor. The art of power and the power of art have become in Prospero's hands, not divided and distinguished worlds as they were before, but one and the same thing. The first requirement, in Renaissance terms, for the prince and the theurgist alike is self-discipline, and this Prospero would seem to have achieved. Having learned the hard way to discipline himself, to keep his own aesthetic passion in its proper place, he now bends his efforts to redressing the disorder of the Milanese court and the inward disorder of the individuals who compose it, that disorder revealed in the opening storm scene, where Antonio and Sebastian see the Boatswain's honest efforts to save them as an act of social insubordination worthy of hanging, while the real subversives are the courtiers themselves; or, closer to home, the spiritual anarchy within Caliban that causes him to claim kingship of the island "by Sycorax my mother" (I.ii.333) and just as rashly to resign his claim to the besotted Stephano.

To restore spiritual and social order Prospero employs his "so potent art." As Northrop Frye remarks: "Each [group of characters] goes through a pursuit of illusions, an ordeal, and a symbolic vision." Ferdinand is led by Ariel's music into love at first sight of Miranda, and after his ordeal as log-bearer, both are treated to the vision of the betrothal masque. Prospero has Ariel present the starving and exhausted courtiers, after their vain wandering in search of Ferdinand, with a tantalizing banquet only to have it vanish like a mirage and leave them tormented by their own frustrated appetite. The banquet, whatever its significance as an allegorical emblem, works dramatically to mirror their own grasping natures, as does the Harpy form in which Ariel appears to pronounce his sentence on the "men of sin" present. That sentence, with its language of surfeit and regurgitation, arises from the physical image of the banquet and reflects the almost cannibalistic appetite of men " 'mongst men unfit to live," men who in a phrase of Shelley's have "made the world their prey" and who are actually about to prey on one another. Prospero has Ariel lead Caliban and his drunken crew on a penal trek through the nastier spots on the island:

> I beat my tabor;
> At which, like unback'd colts, they prick'd their ears,
> Advanc'd their eyelids, lifted up their noses

As they smelt music: so I charm'd their ears,
That, calf-like, they my lowing follow'd, through
Tooth'd briers, sharp furzes, pricking goss, and thorns,
Which enter'd their frail shins: at last I left them
I' th' filthy-mantled pool beyond your cell.

(IV. i.175–82)

These men (and one not-quite-man) of more than average sensuality are misled and tormented by the mutiny of their own senses, which land them in the slimy element appropriate to their gross and brutal natures. Prospero then proceeds to deceive their eyes with illusory wealth in a kind of parody of Caliban's recurrent wish-dream of "riches / Ready to drop upon me." (III.ii.139–40) When Trinculo and Stephano linger over the "trumpery" laid out to distract them from their scheme, "divers Spirits, in shape of dogs and hounds" (IV.i.254.S.D.) drive them off, the same spirits that appeared to the courtiers as a Harpy and "strange shapes" and to the lovers as goddesses and nymphs. To those who "received not the love of the truth," writes an earlier voyager to Italy, "God shall send them strong delusion." The author of *A True Declaration* had moralized upon the mutinies in Virginia by quoting St. Augustine to the effect that "every inordinate soule becomes his own punishment." In his capacity as master illusionist, and to that extent "god o' th' island" (I.ii.392), Prospero sends a rare vision or a maddening hallucination to each of the principals according to his ability and need, an idealized projection or a grotesque parody of the spiritual condition of each, their basest obsessions or highest aspirations made flesh.

Earlier in this study I tried to show how Shakespeare's tragedies could be seen as romance *manqué* and his romances as salvaged tragedy. This formulation applies particularly well, it seems to me, to *Hamlet* and *The Tempest*. For Prospero, like Hamlet, is faced with a world disjointed by a usurpation and (attempted) fratricide, and the two most intellectual of Shakespeare's heroes both have recourse to a kind of art in their attempts to set it right. Prospero, though half-tempted to follow Hamlet and pursue the wild justice of revenge, finally decides under Ariel's prompting to shape the conclusion of his play on the Christian and romantic motive of forgiveness rather than the Hebraic-Hellenic and tragic one of retribution:

Though with their high wrongs I am struck to th' quick,
Yet with my nobler reason 'gainst my fury
Do I take part: the rarer action is
In virtue than in vengeance: they being penitent,
The sole drift of my purpose doth extend

> Not a frown further. So release them, Ariel:
> My charms I'll break, their senses I'll restore,
> And they shall be themselves.
>
> (V. i. 26–32)

Whereas Hamlet had staged his "Mousetrap" to catch the king's conscience only in the sense of ascertaining his guilt, Prospero employs his art to catch Alonso's conscience in a different sense: to exploit the purgative effect of dramatic illusion as the beginning of repentance and reformation—the process that Hamlet, in his wholly external view of Claudius as an irredeemable villain, could not see at work even in Claudius's lapsed, but not quite lost, soul. By holding the mirror of his art up to the courtiers, Prospero seeks to show them their corrupted natures and the way back to "their proper selves" (III.iii.60). It is almost as if Prospero had seen *Hamlet* and were determined to do better than Hamlet had done, to close the gap between the liberal arts and life, between philosophy and action, that Hamlet had been unable to close, and thereby avoid the tragic outcome of the earlier play.

But as I have tried to show, *The Tempest* is finally intolerant of all attempts to allegorize or idealize experience, whether they be ours or those of the characters within the play. Prospero's scenario is a noble one to be sure, born of the loftiest ideals and aspirations of the Renaissance mind, and if he could successfully stage it, he would no doubt deserve the titles of god and superman, philosopher-king, and ideal Christian prince that critics have bestowed on him. But *The Tempest* is as much about the limitations of the idealizing imagination as it is about its power, and of this Prospero seems to grow increasingly aware. Why, for example, does Prospero persist in referring to his art as a "vanity" and a "rough magic"? Why does he feel that he has to abandon it at all? And finally, just how successful is his art in producing his stated objectives?

Something that Prospero seems to have missed in *Hamlet*, and that he has to learn for himself, is that any attempt to manipulate human life artistically, even in a good cause, has its attendant dangers. Hamlet's attempt to do so is at best an evasion of real action and at worst an expression of that self-righteous euphoria characteristic of stage "revengers." Not only in *Hamlet*, but throughout Shakespeare's work we find a healthy mistrust of characters who turn the world into a stage on which to mount their histrionic or directorial fancies, the "good" characters (Friar Lawrence, Henry IV, Duke Vincentio), as well as the "bad" (Richard III, Richard II, Iago). Only in *The Winter's Tale* is the power of art in human life seen as wholly positive, and there Shakespeare takes pains to establish that the art employed by Camillo and Paulina is "an art," as Polixenes unwittingly puts it, "Which does mend nature—change it rather—but / The art itself is nature." Paulina expressly disclaims all magical art in her unveiling of Hermoine's "statue," and Leontes says then that "If this be magic, let it be an art / Lawful as eating," which of course it is, since she uses no art at all. The same cannot be said of Prospero's art. "This is no mortal business, nor no sound / That the earth owes" (I.ii.409–10):

> Full fathom five thy father lies;
>   Of his bones are coral made;
> Those are pearls that were his eyes:
>   Nothing of him that doth fade,
> But doth suffer a sea-change
>   Into something rich and strange.
>   (I. ii.399–404)

The exquisite dirge presages the spiritual transformation Prospero's art does work on Alonso, but in so doing suggests the ambivalent moral status of that art. For the sea change it describes (imagine a coral and pearl Alonso) is unnatural and artificial in the extreme, quite unlike the transformation of Hermoine's "statue" in The Winter's Tale, but very like the transformations of Autolycus's fantastic ballads. Ariel's song also conjures up the kind of transformation that medieval and Renaissance alchemists, highly suspect artificers, attempted to perform, the transmutation of base substances into pure and precious ones. (Prospero associates his art with alchemy in the opening lines of the last act, and with astrology, a sister-science of doubtful repute, during his exposition to Miranda in the first.) My point is not that Prospero's art is downright wicked (Shakespeare makes clear that it is theurgy or "white-magic" he practices as opposed to the goety or "black-magic" practiced by Sycorax) but that associations of dark and prideful learning still cling to it, despite the fact that it is now directed toward a good end. For in Prospero's artistic manipulation of human life lies a danger that besets the modern psychotherapist as much as the Renaissance magician: the danger of playing God. Hamlet casts off that theatrical role, with its attendant dangers of pride and self-indulgence, only in the last act of his play, and Duke Vincentio (as I for one believe) is never sufficiently self-aware to cast it off. It is necessary, not so much to render the ending of The Tempest one of unalloyed joy, for it is not that, but to dramatize Prospero's reform of himself, that he repudiate his art and return to the ranks of humanity. To do so is to renounce the total success of his "project," to make himself vulnerable again. But it is also to renounce once and for all that untransmuted residue of self-dramatization and self-aggrandizement inherent in any effort to recreate the world after one's desires and in one's own image. So far as Prospero is concerned, his renunciation *is* his real triumph. When he resolves to "drown my book," he redeems the belated promise of an earlier magician of the Elizabethan stage to "burn my books." He redeems the Faustus in himself. The "mercy" he finally exercises and asks the audience to exercise on him is the mature and social equivalent of the adolescent and histrionic "magic" he had formerly indulged.

The "brave new world" that emerges in the final scene is neither so brave nor so new as Prospero himself could have wished, neither the paradise regained Ferdinand had seen in the betrothal masque nor the golden age restored of Gonzalo's fancy. Presented with the son he believed dead, Alonso questions whether this too is not merely one more "vision of the island" (V.i.176). But the vision of Ferdinand and Miranda at chess is made "of flesh and blood," like the man (as Alonso is amazed to discover) who made it possible. So too the "blessed crown" Gonzalo calls down in prayer on the couple is, or soon will be, literal fact, the reality of which Antonio's and Caliban's delusions of royalty and riches are mere parodies. Even Sebastian exclaims: "A most high miracle!" (V.i.177). He is referring, as Pericles had done at the end of his play, to the working out of Providence and to the old plays in which that working out was portrayed. But the pattern of the miracle play fits only Alonso's family, despite the efforts of Gonzalo to squeeze everyone into it. In his last great monologue on the renunciation of his art, Prospero speaks scornfully of that art as "this rough magic," and it is rough indeed compared with the creative activity of God—the divinity who alone, as Hamlet says in his final act, "shapes our ends, / Rough-hew them how we will."

In his appropriation and secularization of the forms of the medieval religious drama for his final romances, Shakespeare reassigns the role once played by the grace of God to the art of man: the role of raising and reforming mere nature. In the romances art is still closely associated with grace. But just as the private imaginative visions of Gonzalo, Antonio, and Caliban all fade before Prospero's higher and more comprehensive vision, so too, it is strongly hinted, Prospero's own vision fades before that of God. There is a point at which artistic transformation ends and divine transubstantiation begins, as in the Mass or the Apocalypse, and *The Tempest* stops this side of it. Intimations of Apocalypse are at hand in Prospero's speech on the ending of the revels, in which cloud-capped towers, gorgeous palaces, solemn temples, and the great globe itself—man's noblest artifacts and the material world of which they are made—are condemned to demolition to make room, in the Christian scheme of

things, for the eternal art and architecture of the New Jerusalem, suggested perhaps in Gonzalo's summarial speech by the "lasting pillars"
(V.i.208) on which this marvelous episode of human history is to be set
down in gold. That brave new world will be built on a firmer base and of a
more substantial fabric than was Prospero's vision in the betrothal masque
and is "Too high a ditty" for Shakespeare's, as for Spenser's, "simple
song" (FQ, I.X.55). Prospero's vision was dispelled because "the beast
Caliban" had literally been forgotten in its making, that hunk of brute
nature that Prospero has to "acknowledge" in the end but cannot reform.
Also outside the magic circle of raised human nature at the end is
Antonio, who willfully defies any art, however transcendent, to reform
him. Both figures perhaps suggest in different ways the ultimate resistance
that life throws up against being transmuted into art at all, and especially
into romance; that renders any human art finally no better than the world
it works with and on; and that makes Prospero's efforts at once so potent
and so limited, so fully and so merely human.

But if Prospero is not God, to what extent or in what sense may we
legitimately think of him as Shakespeare? They are clearly analogous
figures up to a point, not simply because they share a talent for putting on
shows and because the epilogue fits the stage manager and the magician
alike, but because both are directly concerned with the creation of brave
new worlds, or more precisely with transmuting old worlds into new,
brazen into golden. The Tempest is a definition in action of the poetics of
romance, a kind of commentary on the imagination that created it, for
Prospero goes about his project in much the same way that Shakespeare
goes about his. The author of "Of the Cannibals," ever divers et ondoyant,
sets forth the principle on which both Prospero and Shakespeare proceed.
"Such an Idea of Policie," writes Montaigne, "or picture of government,
were to be established in a new world; but we take a world already made
and formed to certain customes: wee engender not the same as Pyrrha, nor
beget it as Cadmus. By what means soever we have the privilege to
re-erect and range the same anew, we can very hardly wrest it from the
accustomed habit and fold it hath taken, except we break all." The
creation of brave new worlds, whether in literature or in life, is achieved
not by despising or ignoring the imperfections of this old one (as Gonzalo
does in his vision of the island or Prospero had done before his deposi-
tion), but by repairing them. Wine is a grace of civilization which may be
abused by a Stephano, Trinculo, or Caliban, but which finds a place in
Prospero's vision of abundance. The "letters," which Gonzalo would prohibit
along with wine, may be profaned by a Caliban or overindulged by an
immature Prospero, but it is the power conferred by his book that enables

the Christian Platonist to reorder his society and redeem at least one guilty soul. Any brave new world is merely an old one rehabilitated. Our initial impression of *The Tempest* as the product of spontaneous generation, of Shakespeare's own magical imagination, is finally inadequate. Prospero and Shakespeare do not, as Gonzalo and Antonio do, create out of nothing or out of themselves. Just as Prospero attempts to build a new Milan out of the ruins of its original social structure, so Shakespeare builds the play itself out of imperfect literary structures—travelers' tales, moldy old morality plays, pastoral romances—some of it second hand and shabby stuff, but capable of renovation. Even a miraculous harp like Amphion's needs stones to work on.

But here the analogy between Prospero and Shakespeare breaks down, and Shakespeare becomes, in Joseph Warton's words, "a greater magician that his own Prospero." For the vision of the play as a whole is greater than any single vision it contains, including that of Prospero. While Prospero labors, finally with only partial success, to create a brave new world, Shakespeare is creating his own, with complete success, in the form of the play itself. And Prospero's partial failure becomes the condition of Shakespeare's total triumph, for as we have seen, the ultimate validity of any romance world depends on an implicit recognition that romance is all but impossible to achieve while remaining faithful to life. To the extent that Gonzalo's word is more than the miraculous harp, that he can effortlessly bring forth utopian islands from the sea, he is an untrustworthy romancer; to the extent that Prospero's word is finally less than the miraculous harp, he is an unsuccessful one. Shakespeare's is the harp itself. For in the making of the play Shakespeare begins where Prospero ends: with the awareness that there is a fatal gap between the ideal world of romance and the real world of history, and that no act of magic can ever make them one.

At this point in our efforts toward demystification, it might be well to take our cue from Prospero and abjure magic, with its intimations of superhuman power, as a metaphor for romance and romance-making in favor of another of the play's images, namely that of chess, with its suggestion of acquired skill. The game of chess, particularly the moralized version of it described in the epigraph to this chapter, is "not only a game in *Utopia*," as Michael Holquist has pointed out, but "the game *of* utopia" and "suggests the underlying structure of almost all utopian fiction," including *The Tempest*. The important thing for our purposes about More's utopian chess, and the morality plays in which he delighted and on which he patterned it, is that the virtues always win out in the end. *The Tempest* contains several such games, but their outcomes are by no means so assured. Gonzalo plays a game of utopia in which he thinks he has swept the vices off the board, when he is actually surrounded and defeated by them. Although Prospero's more formidable tactics work according to plan until the very end, when he does win at least two of his games, he is stalemated in at least two others. By denying total victory to the virtues, Shakespeare has effectively widened play beyond the self-contained chess-board of utopia, where the virtues always win, and onto the surrounding battleground of history, where they sometimes do. The battleground of history is also the world of the audience, where we worldlings and groundlings find ourselves striving for our moral lives with a master who has anticipated all possible defenses and counterattacks in a game we can win only if he does. This is the game of *The Tempest*, and its closest analogue within the play is the chess game between Ferdinand and Miranda. There, all suspicion of deceit and fear of losing have passed into perfect trust, and Miranda's affirmation that "for a score of kingdoms you should wrangle, / And I would call it fair play" (V.i.174–5) is also ours.

The Shakespeare of *The Tempest* may be a greater master than Prospero, but the Shakespeare of the final romances as a group is not. Whereas Northrop Frye would have him "a master who wins them all by devices familiar to him, and gradually, with patient study, to us," my own patient study suggests a more fallible figure: a Shakespeare neglectful of the worldly ends of *mimesis* and verisimilitude in *Pericles*, and forgetful of the eternal conspiracy of history against romance in *Cymbeline* and *Henry VIII*. In the end, Shakespeare and Prospero resemble each other in nothing so much as their common capacity for triumph and failure, the former providing the touchstones by which we know the latter. In *The Tempest* Shakespeare reconciles the claims of history and romance by combining an historical action of a Milanese coup d'état spun out of pure fiction with a romantic action of shipwreck and deliverance grounded in recent history. When he tries in his last play to identify the real shores of his native Britain with the undreamed shores of his two previous romances, the result is a confusion of realms worthy of Gonzalo. With *The Tempest* Shakespeare leaves behind the realm of true romance, a realm, in the words of Eliot's *Marina* "more distant than stars and nearer than the eye," where victory issues from a holding action with defeat, or not at all, and total victory is always Pyrrhic.

ROSALIE COLIE

Perspectives on Pastoral:
"The Winter's Tale"

Compared to other plays by Shakes-
peare—and by any standards, indeed—*As You Like It* is extraordinarily
well-made, its elements modulated and dovetailed to satisfaction. We are
never tempted to say the same of Shakespeare's other major confrontation
with pastoral materials, *The Winter's Tale*, a play in which we miss not
only the fundamental source of delight which the pastoral myth offers its
believers, but also the structure of argument and demonstration so even-
handedly managed in *As You Like It*, where the possibilities of over-
programming are kept carefully in check by the spontaneity, lyricism, and
specificity of the incidents, confrontations, and exchanges. The play
works with other kinds of traditions, too (folkish, melancholy, satiric,
romantic), to become far richer than any mere exercise in pastoral themes.
It qualifies its pastoral thematics by counterpointing themes from other
modes in the repertory. As so often in his workings-out and workings-into
and workings-through of conventional literary syndromes, Shakespeare
manages to get it both ways—to make us realize the limits of the pastoral
artifice and at the same time to appreciate its enormous psychic promise
and solace.

As You Like It questions pastoral assumptions, often by means of
counterposing other pastoral assumptions, offers perspectives upon any of
the conventional attitudes and actions associated within the pastoral
decorum, and insists on a relativism normally denied within that decorum;
but we feel throughout that the playwright knows where his questioning

leads and where it will all come out. Not so *The Winter's Tale*, a play conspicuously ill-made, in which our attention is withdrawn from verisimilitude; in which motivations are not to be inquired into; in which the marvelous, the incredible, the impossible are so insisted upon (statue, bear, baby) that they force themselves to become subjects of critical consideration. In this late, mystifying play so deeply involved with the pastoral mode, the lovely ease of *As You Like It* has been replaced by an inconsiderate insistence upon the *invraisemblable*, a departure from mimesis and from reality so radical and so multiple as to send us back to reconsider what "possibility" and "probability" can mean as elements of a drama.

In *The Winter's Tale*, the playwright, having solved some pastoral problems to his own satisfaction, seems to have turned his attention to a wholly different range of problems in the pastoral mode, problems still unsolved (by him and by others): that is, those problems of genre and structure debated with such passion in the Italian polemic over Guarini's *Il pastor fido* and so amusingly and trivially demonstrated in Bettini's academic dramas.

In its own peculiar shorthand, *The Winter's Tale* is a truncated torso of a play. It pays no tribute to those demands for classical modulation between genres and modes that drove Guarini and his defenders so carefully to explain how to mix comic and tragic genres in one decorum. Shakespeare's play simply forces us to face what is "tragic" and what "comic" in life and in plays, forces questions of genre and decorum. The playwright makes no compromise with generic expectations or even with conventional verisimilitude: tragic and comic members of this body are not articulated, and the differences between them are not at all glossed over, but pointedly stressed.

In this respect, remembering the beautiful organization of *As You Like It* may help us: the playwright did not *have* to write this way; he obviously chose to conduct a frontal examination of the structural and thematic limits of modern pastoral drama, that is, of tragicomedy. Even the events of the play, so often considered unnecessarily bizarre or intelligible only because vaguely "allegorical"—the shipwreck, the bear, the fortuitous love of innocent teenagers, the statue—are conventional within the pastoral frame of marvel, artifice, and disguise. The themes of the play are quite as pastoral as those of *As You Like It*: the nature-nurture problem is for Perdita very like what it was for Orlando; the debates about sheepdip and civet are, after all, another version of the *paragone* of nature and art; Rosalind's smart answer to her father foreshadows Perdita's remarks on the democracy of sunshine. It is the naked, disillusioning dramaturgy of *The*

Winter's Tale that so separates it from *As You Like It*, not its themes and devices.

In as many ways as they are like each other, though, the plays differ. That there was no clock in the forest is belied by men's ripening there and rotting, but the importance of time is made clear by the subtitle of *The Winter's Tale*'s source: the timeless has been abandoned in favor of an ambivalent, ambiguous "triumph of time." Leontes' early telling of time—"wishing clocks more swift? / Hours, minutes? noon, midnight?"— points to the importance of "moment" in consequential (and therefore tragic) lives; but the end of the drama presents time's triumph within an impeccably comic decorum. Nobles are disguised in both plays, but in the early one, the girls know that they are disguised and why that had to be; in the later play, the Princess believes herself to be the shepherdess she seems to Florizel and Polixenes to be in fact. But there is a difference, in quality and intensity, between the nature-art game in *As You Like It* and the peculiarly unnatural confluence of the two themes (nature and art, reality and its imitation) in the confrontation of Polixenes with Perdita, to say nothing of the dramatic conceit of Hermione's statue. In *The Winter's Tale*, genre is "forced" by the particularly unvarnished conjunction of tragedy with comedy, and so is generic dramatic device. The play begins entirely within the genre of tragedy, so that by the end of the third act all seems lost: Mamillius dead, Hermione stricken, Perdita exposed to die, Antigonus bizarrely slain. The audience is not let in upon the playwright's (and Paulina's) secret, that Hermione lives after all, until the very end of the play. That revelation comes as a miracle for everyone onstage and for the audience.

At the same time, the throwaway death of Antigonus, with the astonishing (marvelous—and thus properly pastoral) stage-direction about the bear, suggests that in spite of its horror, the play is about to turn around to match in unpredictability Antigonus' unpredictable death. Certainly that death is just as sudden, causeless, and startling as the psychological violence Leontes has so fully displayed in the first two acts—but Antigonus' death is in an entirely different mode, that of romance. The bear is too much—the situation's very grotesqueness protects the audience from feeling the full terror of the bear's mauling the man, as Leontes' seizure, with its hideous consequences, had conspicuously failed to do. The absolute rejection of verisimilitude in this episode moves us away from tragic expectation to another mode, one which assumes as its own ground unreality, impossibility, and exaggeration. The horrible death, furthermore, is *told* in the shepherdly clown's rustic malapropisms—turned into a topic for laughter. Indeed, as we stand off from *The Winter's Tale*, the Antigonus episode comes to stand for a great deal in the play's technique, as the dramatist strips his presentation of the usual modes of dramatic persuasion to belief: in this schematic *sinopia* of a play, devices are forced beyond their own limits to point unequivocally at their thematic and technical significances, to remind us once again that any conventional literary device, however technically "fixed" it may seem, carries thematic implications. This is, then, a particularly problematical "problem play," as Ernest Schanzer has noted; it is about the problems inherent in drama generally and those of the pastoral mode and tragicomic form specifically.

Perhaps because English drama, pastoral and other, was so mixed in form compared with Continental practice, Shakespeare does not need to appeal in any polemical way to the Continental quarrel over pastoral drama, as Fletcher did appeal to it in introducing his *Faithful Shepherdess* or as Daniel, in *Hymen's Triumph*, seems to have done. In this play, Shakespeare was guileless: he simply starts his play in the tragic mode, offering us tragic figures in the grip of a characteristically tragic psychology, then works out their solution in terms conventionally comic. After we have witnessed King Leontes invaded by inexplicable jealousy, willing under its sway to destroy his family altogether, as well as his court; after we have reached the nadir of this king's emotional and social career, we are abruptly confronted by an oracle (on which Hermione, perhaps conscious of her own genre-preferences, had insisted!), that standard device of pastoral romance. At first Leontes persists in prolonging the mode of tragedy; he exposes his baby daughter, he rejects the oracle altogether, and only when his son is reported dead does he submit to the romance conventions, accept the oracle at its received rate, and prepare to atone indefinitely.

Then, in utter flouting of verisimilitude, sixteen years intervene and we see, in another country, that the wench is not dead: the anti-courtly comedy begins. The Princess exposed as a baby has turned into a shepherdess, brought up ("bred," "nurtured") as sister to a clown who cannot read. Her beauty has attracted the attention of a hunting prince, who courts her in disguise; his courtship is challenged by his father, the King, Leontes' erstwhile victim now behaving as violently as his victimizer had done sixteen years before. Romance sequence: faced with separation, the young people resolve to flee together, on the advice of the exiled Sicilian Camillo, to Leontes' court, where they are greeted with such hospitality that the sharp-tongued Paulina, afraid of King Leontes' attraction to the young shepherdess-princess, seizes the moment to bring Sicilian affairs to their climax. She invites King and all into her gallery to view a statue of the late Queen, so lifelike that the King, whose memory of his wife has been stimulated by the Princess' resemblance to Hermoine, is overwhelmed by his sense of loss, overwhelmed by the "meaning," then, of the tragic half of the play that lay at his responsibility—at which point the statue steps down from its pedestal, flesh and blood, a creature alive and feeling. The statue brings into the sharpest possible focus that element in pastoral that sets "art" (the statue) against "nature" (the forgiving, living woman): of this more below.

Other, far simpler pastoral themes surface in the play, in particular the dialogue between court and country. In this case, the "court" is far more deeply compromised than even Duke Frederick's court. In a further upside-downing, in *The Winter's Tale* the court bears the name of the never-never locale preeminently pastoral—Leontes rules in Sicily, is himself called "Sicilia," is king and center of that pastoral island. In that land of his, though he apparently spent an arcadian youth (he and Prince Polixenes were "twinned lambs"), all is utterly antipastoral. We never hear of shepherding or poetry, and even courtliness is denied in Leontes' frenzy. The King is rude beyond measure to friend and guest, tyrannical to his councillors, and monstrous to his kind—the best of that court must flee, or must die, in trying to rectify the King's brutalities. Further, the court is sick—Sicily's air is "infected"—Sicily's!—cleansed only after Perdita returns from her pastoral oasis in Bohemia.

Times and places are confused in the play. "A sad tale's best for winter," says Mamillius in a prophecy of what is to come, for him and for his family. Leontes' courtly family is utterly unlike that Baucis-Philemon, Darby-and-Joan pair in Campion's song, with its realistic pastoral set up against the anxious observances of the court:

> *Jacke* and *Jone*, they thinke no ill,
> But loving live, and merry still;
> Doe their weeke dayes worke, and pray
> Devotely on the holy day;
> Skip and trip it on the greene,
> And help to chuse the Summer Queene;
> Lash out, at a Country Feast,
> Their silver penny with the best.
> Well can they judge of nappy Ale,
> And tell at large a Winter tale. . . .
> *Tib* is all the fathers joy,
> And little *Tom* the mothers boy.
> All their pleasure is content,
> And care, to pay theire yearely rent.

Tib-Perdita is cast out, and Tom-Mamillius dies of sorrow at what his father has done to his mother. Leontes' court does not permit domestic content, and even exemplifies antipastoral and antiromance. There is no hint in his country of the greening Sicilian muse, who has, in a highly unliterary way, migrated to Bohemia. Shakespeare has turned the pattern around, both from his source and from the larger tradition, to endow an utterly unpastoral habitat with pastoral possibilities. But even this is problematical: "Bohemia" is dislocated too: it has the same mysteriousness, the same geographical neutrality, that Thomas Rosenmeyer attributes to all the names chosen as pastoral sites. Pastoral requires never-never qualities, and the common reader knows very well that Bohemia has no seacoast, nor was it a desert either, inhabited by bears and other predatory beasts.

For all its hospitality to Perdita, its harvest queens and sheep-shearings, pastoral-unpastoral Bohemia can match Sicily in pastoral unkindness: the ship that brought Perdita thither perishes (another unnecessary, exaggerated romance convention), and on Bohemian shores Antigonus is forthwith disposed of. We are not allowed immediately to see in this seacoast the antidote to Sicily that it thematically becomes, although soon enough the resources of Bohemia begin to appear.

The clown who finds the abandoned baby is a shepherd's son, and that shepherd is quick at thematics ("Now bless thyself: thou met'st with things dying, I with things new-born": III.iii.112–13). The shepherds' ethos is, we discover, like that of "Jacke and Jone" in Campion's poem, entirely opposite to Leontes' life in more ways than just rank. Perdita is allowed to grow up a part of the natural cycle, in a natural and nature-bound family, where like the "silly Swaine" of Campion's final line, men live "securer lives" than "Courtly Dames and Knights." At least, this seems to be the case. Perdita lives happily with her shepherd-family, and when courtiers break in upon the shearing-feast, country lives are threatened. But the country idyll cannot be allowed to shine without some darkening. Like Jaques in the earlier play, but far more alienated than the unmanipulative Jaques, Autolycus destroys the pastoral sufficiency. A refugee-pirate from the city, Autolycus shows us the limitations in naivete and gullibility of the shepherd's restricted life. Though he pretends to earlier connections with Florizel, Autolycus the coney-catcher is no representative of the court itself; rather, of the city's underside, whose corruptions he spreads through the countryside as Vergil's *Eclogues* make clear that city-dwellers must.

Perdita, of course, is chosen by "Jacke and Jone" as their summer queen, the epitome of the pure country life. Time has ripened her into the mistress of the shearing-feast, where she presides over pastoral harvesting, surrounded by family and friends, admired by her elegant suitor and other strangers from the town. Indeed, she seems very little less than the goddess they liken her to. In the matching of Perdita and Florizel, we find the mixing of social ranks appreciated by "modern" pastoralists experimenting with the mode's inherent democracy, and despised by stricter Aristotelian conceptions of socioliterary decorum.

Florizel, that romance-hero, reveals himself as irrevocably in love, recognizing the shepherdess' intrinsic value, ready ultimately to forgo his inheritance for her sake. And we are made to know that it is Perdita's essence which he values, even as France values Cordelia's. Florizel honors not only a pastorally benevolent human nature, but an almost perfect one, and is not afraid to celebrate it in those terms:

> What you do,
> Still betters what is done. When you speak, sweet,
> I'd have you do it ever: when you sing,
> I'd have you buy and sell so, so give alms,
> Pray so, and, for the ord'ring your affairs,
> To sing them too: when you dance, I wish you
> A wave o' th' sea, that you might ever do
> Nothing but that, move still, still so,
> And own no other function. Each your doing,
> So singular in each particular,
> Crowns what you are doing, in the present deeds,
> That all your acts are queens.
>
> (IV. iv. 135–46)

For all his discriminating praise of her individually graceful acts, Florizel is aware that they all spring from Perdita's fundamental condition: he knows that all her delightful changes owe their beauty to her intrinsic being.

Florizel's disguised father acts as a bridge between tragedy and romance, his own behavior in the sheep-shearing scene partaking both of his son's admiration for Perdita and of Leontes' jealous tyranny. He too responds to the unutterably taking girl, and expresses his delight in her loveliness in narrowly social terms, professing himself unable to believe that anyone so beautiful could possibly spring from peasant stock. Polixenes is, then, ready to recast the girl before him, to rewrite her provenance, so to speak, to cast her in another play. In the magnificent exchange between the consciously disguised Polixenes and the unconsciously disguised Perdita, the resources of an immense tradition are exploited. Disguise itself, one property of the pastoral romance-plot, is requisite for such significant confrontations. Part of Perdita's disguise is that she is disguised to herself as well as to the others: her true origins are quite unknown to her. She believes herself a fictional queen, a queen for a day, and is quick to renounce her mock-royalty when she learns of Florizel's true estate—that is, she takes Sidney's or Denores' critical position about her place, refusing to approve "grafting" either of flowers or of social class.

For the audience, both in and out of the play, though, her disguise as harvest-queen represents her essence rather than covers or discovers her true self. She is, we hear, "no shepherdess, but Flora"—a shepherdess disguised as a queen, but apparently a goddess; as Flora, she distributes Flora's attributes, chosen with care to match her recipients' condition. For the playgoing audience, still more is involved: here is a boy playing a girl who, within this fiction, is a princess. The fiction requires disguise so that she also "is" a shepherdess, real enough as far as nurture is concerned; but in the fiction, there is an inner fiction, a play within the play, in which the boy-actor playing a princess (who thinks herself a shepherdess) must play the part also of a queen. We are reminded of Rosalind, a boy playing a girl disguised as a boy, etc.—who within her own playlet plays her real role in the drama. Perdita, unknowing where Rosalind had been aware, also plays herself: we are in on the illusionism, moreover, as she is not, since we know "what" she really is. As we shall see, this incident, so important for the pastoral theme of the play, also stands in contrast to the great scene of the statue of Hermione, where the audience is *not* in on the trick and does *not* know what strain upon its credulity will be levied.

Perdita establishes the terms of her debate with Polixenes by her gifts of rosemary and rue, matching middle age "With flowers of winter." She apologizes for having no flowers "o' th' spring" for Florizel's "time of day"—like Rosalind, this girl recognizes and reminds her hearers of time's passage and, even at the height of pastoral celebration, acknowledges the natural regulation of the seasons. She can accept, then, the melancholy fact that "twinn'd lambs" can become old rams; that men mature and age. Polixenes tests her, praising the cultivated garden flowers which Perdita, now in shepherd's ideology, rejects: the gillivors are for her "Nature's bastards," for which she will not "put / The dibble in earth." That is, these flowers are mixed in kind, strive to be what they naturally are not; Perdita behaves in accord with her flower-preferences when she lays by her queen's habiliments to return to shepherdhood, and thereby supports Polixenes' actual Aristotelianism about the mixture of modes in society (and thus in the play).

Still, she cannot help remarking that she has "heard it said / There is an art which in their piedness shares / With great creating nature": the *natura naturans*, which is for her the only legitimate creator, has been said to share with men its mysterious power. Polixenes is a modern, Baconian ruler, in defending what he calls "improvement": gillivors are for him good flowers, although for Perdita they are adulterate. The topical terms of Polixenes' argument, with their wide implications beyond their literal meanings, run counter to the social theory he so violently imposes on his son, Perdita, and Perdita's family. When he speaks simply of flowers, though, Polixenes defends Guarini's view of mixing kinds:

> Yet nature is made better by no mean
> But nature makes that mean: so, over that art,
> Which you say adds to nature, is an art
> That nature makes. You see, sweet maid, we marry
> A gentler scion to the wildest stock,
> And make conceive a bark of baser kind
> By bud of nobler race. This is an art
> Which does mend nature—change it rather—but
> The art itself is nature.
>
> 　　　　　　　　　　　　　　(IV. iv.89–97)

On the face of it, Perdita argues the plain country position and Polixenes the sophisticated courtly one. She is a pastoral ideologue, pre- and anti-technological, she rejects, so to speak, Guarini's views. But in the reality of their situation, the two ideologues change places. Obviously, if we are to take this debate of kind in its specific application to the play, as well as to the broader social contexts sanctioned by literary traditions, we must face its contradictions and ambivalences.

In *The Winter's Tale*, so problematical a play, we must accept problems even in a pastoral interlude: Shakespeare faces the issues in his metaphors, made more complicated by their multitudinous traditional use. He knows that we know who Perdita is, even if she does not. True to what she thinks she is—because her essence is truth—she argues against what she really is, because she can and will settle for simplicity. Therefore she must argue against what she most desires, that is, to be matched with Florizel. Polixenes' argument, of course, provides Florizel with the theory by which he chooses to match himself; and Polixenes' *behavior* certainly argues that his family needs some such mixture as the one he praises in plants. For instead of having learned Leontes' lesson or applied his own, by blessing his son's union with this perfect harvest queen, Polixenes rejects his own reasoning, his own metaphors, as if he had never enunciated them, to disown his son as Leontes had disowned his daughter so long before. As audience, we might have expected more of this king, especially since he had felt in Perdita's carriage "something greater than herself,/ Too noble for this place." But Polixenes cannot recognize the theoretical force of Guarini's dictum that the shepherd's life is ennobling, whether engaged in by shepherds or by nobles seeking some recreation from their busy life.

Perdita (nobly) accepts the position she has enunciated in her part of the debate, with its implied corollary that shepherdesses may not marry with princes. But she nonetheless utters the equally ideological, but opposite, pastoral opinion:

> I was about to speak, and tell him plainly,
> The selfsame sun that shines upon his court
> Hides not his visage from our cottage, but
> Looks on all alike.
>
> (IV. iv.444–47)

Florizel, a prince disguised as a lordling-shepherd, accepts the shepherd's ideals of democracy and love, which he recognizes as based on notions of natural rightness if not of natural right:

> It cannot fail, but by
> The violation of my faith; and then
> Let nature crush the sides o' th' earth together,
> And mar the seeds within! Lift up thy looks:
> From my succession wipe me, father; I
> Am heir to my affection.
>
> (IV. iv.477–82)

As so often in pastoral plays, the question of rank is not pursued to its final implications. Rosalind was a duke's daughter, Orlando a knight's son: like finally matches with like. Because Perdita is in fact royal, Polixenes' views about grafting are not in fact relevant to his son's union; and Perdita's hierarchical conception of rank, expressed in terms of gillivors, is confirmed, not challenged, by the ultimate arrangement of the plot. Such practical criticism of rank as we meet in this play actually runs *against* the notion of pastoral egalitarianism, as for instance in the exchange between clown and shepherd with Autolycus over Perdita's family's new-found gentility. The clown has been, as he says, a gentleman born these four hours, thus a gentleman (*vide* Lear's Fool) born before his father, now also an artificial gentleman. Perdita, for all her new-found royalty, nonetheless still calls the old shepherd "father," the clown still calls her "sister." The natural, generous response of her foster family is now officially assimilated to social gentility; the artificiality of social conventions of rank is underlined by the clown's comments. The clown plans to take advantage of his new privilege by *not* keeping his word—a satirical moment bespeaking nostalgia for a simpler ethics. Something as Audrey does in *As You Like It*, the clown reaches out of his pastoral world to snatch at aristocratic irresponsibility; his father, truly a shepherd and thus incorruptible, remains true to his word even though nominally converted into society's, as opposed to nature's, gentleman. The playwright once again has it both ways, as Perdita's rediscovered condition confirms the gentility she has always displayed, and the members of her family remind us of the loss incurred in giving up country manners for city behavior, their artless simplicity for the artifice and lying of sophisticated society.

Perdita's exchange with Polixenes touches on the nature-art debate in terms of nurture, training, and education; the social question of "making" a gentleman, either by his own means or the means society offers, the main subject of Castiglione's great book and fully explored in other plays of Shakespeare (notably in *King Lear*), is glancingly touched on here. As we have seen, Perdita is herself socially conservative, willing to relinquish Florizel for received reasons. And yet, because she is what she is, within the play itself the critical debate turns out to have been totally irrelevant. Shakespeare explores, and makes us explore, a major problem in pastoral thematics and pastoral literary theory, has made us consider the anomalies involved in the question—and then ripped the rug out from under the whole debate. To say this more grandly, he has chosen *not* to match his literary insight with an objective correlative within the play; the debate of kind is much ado about nothing.

All the same, Perdita somehow exemplifies some of the themes of her debate. Artless though she is as shepherdess, she is an artist in a different sense, sharing something with "great creating Nature": the flowers from which she would make appropriate garlands for her guests she has not to hand, but her poetry about those imaginary flowers is the richest of the play. She so excels nature—or, at least, nature's norm—that her imagination can dispense with the objects themselves. This scene, obviously in many ways crucial to the play, is highly ambiguous in its relation to the play as a whole: in it, the pastoral terms that inform the whole play are insisted upon so overtly, set in such relief, that we must expect to rely on them for interpreting the play. And yet we cannot: the debate is thrown away, its insights rejected as the plot turns out to have no use for them. What does it mean, then? Simply, I think, that the pastoral devices underscore what is fundamental to the whole play—underscore the frippery of the mode's metaphor and attribute—and at the same time make us see that, under all the conventional metaphorical prattle about nature-and-art, nature-and-nurture, what we must consider are questions of intrinsic human personality, of individual recognition of sharing in "kind" and in kindness.

The scene of Hermione's statue, which raises the question of nature and art in terms entirely different from those of the Polixenes-Perdita debate, similarly cheats our expectation. The famous statue is a simulacrum of Hermione, an ecphrastic Hermione, Hermione transfixed into a memorial record of what she had been and symbolized in beauty, steadfastness, and integrity. Grateful for this much, Leontes accepts the figure as a statue; like another king mourning a wife lost through his own egoism. Leontes wishes to pretend that the statue is a real woman, promises to invest it with the same devotion Admetus would render Alcestis' statue. We can recognize, beyond Leontes' confusion over the statue, another myth of the artificer as god, whose creations seem to live and breathe like living creatures.

But this scene too removes from relevance the very question we are invited to rethink, for this work of art turns out to be nature after all. As in the Perdita-Polixenes exchange, our expectations of *paragone* are frustrated by the plot. The miracle Venus performed on Pygmalion's behalf is wrought for Leontes as well, as his statue moves, steps down from her pedestal, and embraces him. But this statue was never such—it was always the woman herself, "as like Hermione as is her picture," the real, restorative, forgiving Hermione, turned figuratively to stone, to linger like Persephone underground for a sixteen-year winter's tale, and warmed into reality only by her husband's repentance-quickened life: the statue's returning to life confers upon that frozen, suspended husband his full life again. The illusion here is not that art is an illusion, but that life is.

We may stop over the trick for a moment. Pygmalion offers one archetypal example in the *paragone* of nature and art, in which nature wins out: "favella, favella," Donatello is said to have said to his *Zuccone*, that almost-real figure of his invention. Why Giulio Romano, then, selected as the artist who can create "to the life"? Who "would beguile Nature of her custom, so perfectly he is her ape"? Giulio Romano's painted titans in the Sala dei Giganti in Mantua were said to have terrified viewers by their illusionism; from Vasari comes another comment on Giulio's miraculous illusionism: "a building, round like a theater, with statues of inexpressible beauty, finely disposed. Among them is a woman spinning, and looking at a hen with her chickens, wonderfully natural." It is not quite clear from the text whether this miracle was a painting of a building, depicted as adorned with lifelike statues, or was a building with an actual row of such statues. Normally, statues were not painted, as Paulina says the statue of Hermione was: the *Zuccone* is marble, Pygmalion's lady was ivory, and though he decked it with fine garments and jewels, he did not appear to have painted it. In paintings, too, statues are generally distinguished from living people (as for instance in the painting of Lord Arundel and his gallery) by their grisaille, as opposed to the flesh-colored tints of those depicted as living. But in dramas, anyway, statues *do* tend to come alive. In *Friar Bacon and Friar Bungay*, in *The Old Wives' Tale*, in Campion's masque for Princess Elizabeth's wedding, statues speak and move. (In Campion's masque a row of women, fashioned by Prometheus, turned into statues by an angry Jove, step down from their niches into real life.)

Hermione was to be played by a real actor miming a statue, a not uncommon role in the repertory; this trick, then, is simply another *trompe l'œil* of legitimate stage-illusion. In other instances of this metamorphosis or pseudo-metamorphosis, however, there is no talk of naturalist human details, no pushing past the illusion's conventional cover. By mentioning Hermione's wrinkles, Shakespeare returns us to the undisguised artifice of this whole play, with its open, unmodulated combination of tragic with comic, its resolution of impossibility by metamorphosing tragedy into comedy. At this highest point of illusionism, illusion itself is abandoned, in the claim that reality is more startling, more miraculous, than any contrivance of art—that life itself, in its most significant moments, is hardly lifelike. Beauty's perfection, exemplified in Perdita's smooth cheek, gives way before the meaning and pathos of those wrinkles— even the ideal beauty of a mode emphasizing aesthetic ideals retires before the values attributed to suffering and feeling, validated by being experienced over time.

But turning his stress away from the artist's effort at mimetic matching, the playwright makes fun of the whole doctrine of *mimesis*— and thus strips illusionism from art. Giulio Romano had tried, thus, in Paulina's fiction, to play god and to supply a Hermione as she really would have been—hence he had to add the wrinkles that were so strange to Leontes. In terms of *mimesis*, Shakespeare forces the credible to the point where it is easier to believe the conventionally incredible than the "facts" of his fiction, of this play's plot. We are warned within the play that this is so, by an anonymous Gentleman: "This news, which is called true, is so like an old tale that the verity of it is in strong suspicion" (V.ii.27–29), a theme which runs through the last act (V.ii.62, 96–101; V.iii.115–17). By calling attention to the *vraisemblable* wrinkles, the playwright underscores his *invraisemblable*, and turns us back to rethink the convention of the "marvelous" in pastoral drama, the taming of a miracle to literary device. Where, outside of sanatoria, are pastoral interludes practical solutions to human destructiveness, of others and of self? The pastoral offers its artifact in substitution for life's consequential bitterness; in the statue-episode, as in the debate of kind, the artifice of the artifice forces us back upon the human resources such artifices symbolize. Hermione comes alive because she can forgive, comes alive when she does because Leontes is ready to receive at her hands what no man has a right to expect, the forgiveness that fulfills the utmost selfishness of his dreams.

Hermione's statuedom is an outrageous device, fulfilling even more dramaturgical needs than the incredible transition from death to life. Not only is that statuedom the means by which this unashamedly artificial play is enabled to reach a proper reconciliation at the conclusion of the varied action, but the means as well by which both Leontes and Paulina can find some justification for themselves. Hermione-as-statue offers a moment of respite—the transition for Paulina from the vengeance-world, for Leontes from the wish-world, back to the world of personality and flesh and blood, where wives can be cherished and kissed without harming their fresh paint. Hermione is not painted but real (cf. gillivors), not stone but flesh. Some silence, some interlude, some symbol must stand between Leontes and the recovery of his human self, to preserve him from the total shock of joy which overcame Gloucester. He can say that he is "mock'd with art," but actually art mediates to let him speak what he feels, possible only as long as he thinks his wife a statue deaf and dumb. Of course he is in fact "mock'd," as the audience is too, by the dramaturgy: the point of the tricks in this play is that they are *not* in fact illusionistic, that stage-conventions are themselves unmasked and mocked. Of Hermione's wrinkles the playwright has made a symbol for all the failures of art to match reality. What can Paulina say, when Leontes remarks about how much older the statue looks than his wife did, sixteen years before? Only that the fabulous artificer was trying to outdo idealization to reproduce a specific natural creature. Paulina thus denies the value of the ideal in art, and undercuts *mimesis* too. The wrinkles show how simplistic are rigid distinctions between art and nature, between the ideal and the verisimilar.

The double insistence upon plausibility and actuality is symbolized by the almost-silent meeting of Perdita with her mother's statue: Perdita, that mother's child, recapitulates the mother's beauty, in her own living regenerates her mother's lost image. In that one scene then, we see before us both timelessness (statue: art) and time (living girl: nature)—and yet the statue's cheek is wrinkled and the girl's cheek is smooth. Wrinkles are the anti-romantic attributes of mature life: if Hermione is to be restored to Leontes with any significance to that restoration, she must return at time's full cost, her loss made calculable and conscious. The wrinkles are signs that suffering really *means*.

But one can also see in the wrinkles just the playwright's game with the thematics of his mode, his game with the possibilities of his theatrical and literary craft. If he sticks to verisimilitude, and it turns out that the wrinkles are on the cheek of a living woman, who can rate him for the implausibility of the statue-device? By pointing to life as it is, he points away from the illusionism of his craft to the illusions men make of their lives. By translating his pastoral into time, he can stress the imaginative value of the pastoral ideal in lives by their nature subject to the ravages of time. Only by a fiction—a statue, a play—can one immediately grasp the enriched, concentrated meaning attributed to life, drawn from life, by the imagination. The statue can become a woman, the woman can be a statue, in a fiction, in this play: the *mode* of this play is important to this particular issue of art. Within the thematics of pastoral such an examination of the relative values of nature and art is one of the mode's dictates: the relationship between the two is reversed and at the same time reaffirmed in *The Winter's Tale*, which owes its particular being to the permissiveness of the pastoral dramatic conventions, by which a woman can pretend to be a work of art, and can be one as well. With the contrivance of art's turning into life, the pastoral, so questioned and qualified throughout the play, resumes its proper habitat, as Leontes' Sicily is permitted once more to partake of all the symbolic gifts of art and nature.

Because she is so fine a piece of work as a human being, Hermione can come to life and redeem her husband, herself, the play: in her, "Dear life redeems" by means of the statue-device. Art is not what it seems in this play, where it turns out not to be art: but, as we can see in its ending at once emblematic and enigmatic, life is not what it seems either. In human crises, human beings need the resources both of their natures and their creative powers, the resources of nature and of civlization, with its arts. In this extraordinarily proud, self-confident play, which flaunts its artfulness and its sublime contempt for mere art, the interchange of art with nature is affirmed, as art offers human nature a chance to civilize its brutalities.

RENÉ GIRARD

Myth and Ritual in Shakespeare's "A Midsummer Night's Dream"

The opening scene of A Midsummer Night's Dream leads the audience to expect an ordinary comedy plot. Boy and girl love each other. A mean old father is trying to separate them, with the help of the highest authority in the land, Theseus, duke of Athens. Unless she gives up Lysander, Hermia will have no choice but death or the traditional convent. As soon as this formidable edict is proclaimed, the father figures depart, leaving the lovers to their own devices. They launch into a duet on the impediments of love: age difference, social conditions, and, last but not least, coercion by those in authority.

The two victimized youngsters leisurely and chattily prepare to flee their ferocious tyrants; they plunge into the woods; Hermia is pursued by Demetrius, himself pursued by Helena, Hermia's best friend, whom, of course, he spurns. The first couple's happiness appears threatened from the outside, but the second couple, even from the start, insist on being unhappy by themselves, always falling in love with the wrong person. We soon realize that Shakespeare is more interested in this systematically self-defeating type of passion than in the initial theme of "true love," something unconquerable by definition and always in need of villainous enemies if it is to provide any semblance of dramatic plot.

It quickly turns out that self-defeating passion dominates the relationship of not just one but both couples, involving them in a fourway

From *Textual Strategies: Perspectives in Post-Structuralist Criticism*, edited by Josue V. Marari. Copyright © 1979 by Cornell University. Cornell University Press.

merry-go-round that never seems to allow any amorous reciprocity even though partners are continually exchanged. At first the two young men are in love with Hermia: then, during the night, both abandon that girl and fall in love with the other. The only constant element in the configuration is the convergence of more than one desire on a single object, as if perpetual rivalries were more important to the four characters than their changing pretexts.

Although the theme of outside interference is not forgotten, it becomes even more flimsy. In the absence of the father figures, the role is entrusted to Puck, who keeps pouring his magical love juice into the "wrong" eyes. When Oberon rebukes Puck for his mistake, he does so with a show of emotion, in a precipitous monologue that ironically reflects the confusion it pretends to clear, thereby casting doubt upon the reality of the distinctions it pretends to restore:

> What hast thou done? Thou hast mistaken quite,
> And laid the love juice on some true love's sight:
> Of thy misprision must perforce ensue
> Some true love turned, and not a false turned true.
>
> (III. ii.88–91)

Who will tell the difference between *some true love turned* and *a false turned true?* We may suspect a more serious rationale for the four protagonists' miseries, for the growing hysteria of the mid-summer night. A close look reveals something quite systematic about the behavior of the four, under-lined by more than a few ironic suggestions. The author is hinting at something which is never made fully explicit, but which seems cogent and coherent enough to call for a precise formulation.

The midsummer night is a process of increasing violence. Demetrius and Lysander end up in a duel; the violence of the girls' rivalry almost matches that of the boys. Their fierce quarreling certainly contradicts—or does it?—Helena's earlier expression of unbounded admiration for her friend Hermia:

> Your eyes are lodestars, and your tongue's sweet air,
> More tunable than lark to shepherd's ear.
> When wheat is green, when hawthorn buds appear.
> Sickness is catching. O! were favor so,
> Yours would I catch, fair Hermia, ere I go;
> My ear should catch your voice, my eye your eye,
> My tongue should catch your tongue's sweet melody.
> Were the world mine, Demetius being bated,
> The rest I'd give to be to you translated.
>
> (I. i.183–191)

This is a strange mixture of quasi-religious and yet sensuous worship. The last line admirably sums up the significance of the passage. Desire speaks here, and it is desire for another's *being*. Helena would like to be *translated*, metamorphosed into Hermia, because Hermia enjoys the love of Demetrius. Demetrius, however, is hardly mentioned. The desire for him appears less pressing than the desire for Hermia's being. In that desire, what truly stands out is the irresistible sexual dominance that Hermia is supposed to exert upon Demetrius and all those who approach her. It is this sexual dominance that Helena envies: "O teach me how you look and with what art / You sway the motion of Demetrius' heart" (I.i.192–193). Helena sees Hermia as the magnetic pole of desires in their common little world, and she would like to be that. The other three characters are no different; they all worship the same erotic absolute, the same ideal image of seduction which each girl and boy in turn appears to embody in the eyes of the others. This absolute has nothing to do with concrete qualities; it is properly metaphysical. Even though obsessed with the flesh, desire is divorced from it; it is not instinctive and spontaneous; it never seems to know directly and immediately where its object lies; in order to locate that object, it cannot rely on such things as the pleasure of the eyes and the other senses. In its perpetual *noche oscura*, metaphysical desire must therefore trust in another and supposedly more enlightened desire on which it patterns itself. As a consequence, desire, in A *Midsummer Night's Dream*, perpetually runs to desire just as money runs to money in the capitalistic system. We may say, of course, that the four characters are in love with love. That would not be inaccurate; but there is no such thing as love or desire in general, and such a formulation obscures the most crucial point, the necessarily jealous and conflictual nature of mimetic convergence on a single object. If we keep borrowing each other's desires, if we allow our respective desires to agree on the same object, we, as individuals, are bound to disagree. The erotic absolute will inevitably be embodied in a successful rival. Helena cannot fail to be torn between worship and hatred of Hermia. Imitative desire makes all reciprocal rapports impossible. Shakespeare makes this point very clear, but for some reason no one wants to hear. The audience resembles the lovers themselves, who talk ceaselessly about "true love" but obviously do not care to understand the mechanism of their own feelings.

Metaphysical desire is mimetic, and mimetic desire cannot be let loose without breeding a midsummer night of jealousy and strife. Yet the protagonists never feel responsible for the state of their affairs: they never hesitate to place the blame where it does not belong, on an unfavorable fate, on reactionary parents, on mischievous fairies, and on other such causes. Throughout the play, the theme of outside interference provides much of the obvious dramatic structure; and we must suspect that it is not simply juxtaposed to the midsummer night which, in a sense, it contradicts: the two may well be in a more complex relationship of disguise and reality, never clearly spelled out and formalized, allowing enough juxtaposition and imbrication so that the play, at least in some important respects, can really function as two plays at once. On one level it is a traditional comedy, destined for courtly audiences and their modern successors; but, underneath, mimetic desire holds sway, responsible not only for the delirium and frenzy of the midsummer night but also for all the mythical themes which reign supreme at the upper level.

The real obstacles are not outside the enchanted circle of the lovers: each of them is an obstacle to the others in a game of imitation and rivalry that is their mode of alienation, and this alienation finally verges on trancelike possession. The outside obstacle is an illusion, often a transparent one, a telltale disguise of the real situation, constructed so that it can serve as an allegory. It even happens that absolutely nothing has to be changed in order to pass from the truth to the lie and back again to the truth: the same words mean both the one and the other. Shakespeare loves to play on these ambiguities. I have already mentioned the love duet between Lysander and Hermia: most critics would agree that it constitutes a parody of fashionable clichés, and they are no doubt correct; but we cannot view this parodic character as sufficient justification in itself. The real purpose cannot be parody for parody's sake. There must be something more, something which Shakespeare definitely wants to say and which we are likely to miss because it will appear in the form of "rhetoric." In the duet part of that love scene, the first seven lines seem to mark a gradation which leads up to the eighth, on which the emphasis falls:

> LYSANDER: The course of true love never did run smooth;
>   But either it was different in blood—
> HERMIA: O cross! Too high to be enthralled to low.
> LYSANDER: Or else misgraffed in respect of years—
> HERMIA: O spite! Too old to be engaged to young.
> LYSANDER: Or else it stood upon the choice of friends—
> HERMIA: O hell! To choose love by another's eyes.
>   (I. i. 134–140)

The last two lines can be read as only one more "cross," the most relevant really, the one we would expect to see mentioned first in the present context. The reference to "friends" is somewhat unexpected, but not so strange as to merit a second thought for most listeners. But if we isolate these last two lines, if we replace the love mystique in the spirit of which they are uttered with the present context, the context of the preceding remarks and of countless Shakespearean scenes (not only in *A Midsummer Night's Dream* but also in amost every other play), another meaning will appear, a meaning more evident and infinitely more significant.

Everywhere in Shakespeare there is a passion which is primarily the copy of a model, a passion that is destructive not only because of its sterile rivalries but because it dissolves reality: it tends to the abstract, the merely representational. The model may be present in the flesh and strut on the stage of the theater; and it may also rise from the pages of a book, come out of the frame of a picture, turn into the worship of a phantom, verbal or iconic. The model is always a text. It is Othello's heroic language, the real object of fascination for Desdemona rather than Othello himself. It is the portrait of Portia which her lover chooses to contemplate in preference to the original. This metaphysical passion is a corruption of life, always open to the corruptive suggestions of mediators and go-betweens, such as the Pandarus of *Troilus and Cressida*. The paramount role that Shakespeare attributes to such desire, in an obviously calculated way, even in relationships where we may least expect it, is matched only in the works of such writers as Cervantes, Molière, or Dostoevsky. *O hell! To choose love by another's eyes.* Since the phrase is uttered in conformity with the ideology of "true love," surely appropriate to a royal wedding (the occasion of *A Midsummer Night's Dream*), the true Shakespearean meaning must dawn upon us, prompted not only by the events that follow but by a thousand echoes from all the other plays.

Mimetic desire remains unperceived even when it is most obvious. In the very process of being denied, displaced, reified, it still manages to proclaim its own truth. Almost every time they open their mouths, the lovers unwittingly proclaim that at the same time they ignore, and we generally go on ignoring it along with them. The midsummer night is a hell of the lover's own choosing, a hell into which they all avidly plunge, insofar as they all choose to choose love by another's eyes. Hermia, talking about the turn her love affair with Lysander has given her own life, naively recognizes that the hell is all hers, and that it was already there before the appearance of the parental and supernatural bugaboos that are supposed to be its cause:

> Before the time I did Lysander see,
> Seemed Athens as a paradise to me.
> O then, what graces in my love do dwell,
> That he hath turned a heaven into a hell!
> (I. i. 204–207)

Shakespeare is making fun of us, of course. He seems intent on proving that you can say almost anything in a play as long as you provide the audience with the habitual props of comedy, the conventional expressions of "true love," even in minimal amounts, adding, of course, a ferocious father figure or two to satisfy the eternal Freudian in us. As long as the standard plot is vaguely outlined, even in the crudest and least believable fashion, the author can subvert his own myths and state the truth at every turn, with no consequences whatsoever. The audience will instinctively and automatically rally around the old clichés, so completely blind and deaf to everything which may contradict them that the presence of this truth will not even be noticed. The continued misunderstanding of the play throughout the centuries gives added resonance to the point Shakespeare is secretly making, providing ironic confirmation that the most worn-out myth will always triumph over the most explicit demythification.

If the subject persists in his self-defeating path, the rivalries into which mimetic desire inevitably runs must logically be viewed as glorious signs and heralds of the absolute that keeps eluding him. Mimetic desire breeds rejection and failure; it is rejection and failure that it must ultimately seek. The impossible is always preferred to the possible, the unreal to the real, the hostile and unwilling to the willing and available. This self-destructive character flows directly and automatically from the mechanical consequences of the first definition: *to choose love by another's eyes.* Are these consequences really spelled out in the play? They are in the most specific fashion, in perfectly unambiguous statements that somehow never manage to be heard; and even when they are noticed, a label is immediately placed on them, canceling out their effectiveness. The following lines, for example, will be labeled "rhetorical," which means that they can be dismissed at will, treated as insignificant. Recall that when Helena seeks the secret of Hermia's power over Demetrius, Hermia answers:

> I frown upon him, yet he loves me still.
> HELENA: O that your frowns would teach my smiles such skill!
> HERMIA: I give him curses, yet he gives me love.
> HELENA: O that my prayers could such affection move!
> HERMIA: The more I hate, the more he follows me.
> HELENA: The more I love, the more he hateth me.
>
> (I. i.194–199)

It cannot be denied that there is a great deal of rhetoric in *A Midsummer Night's Dream.* Rhetoric in the pejorative sense means that certain figures of speech are repeated unthinkingly by people who do not even notice their meaning. The four protagonists of A *Midsummer Night's*

Dream certainly are unthinking repeaters of modish formulas. But mere parodies of rhetorical vacuity would be themselves vacuous, and Shakespeare does not indulge in them. With him the most exhausted clichés can become bolts of lightning. When Helena calls Demetrius a "hard-hearted adamant," she speaks the most literal truth. Harshness and cruelty draw her and her friends as a magnet draws iron. The supposedly artificial figures of speech really describe the truth of desire with amazing exactitude. When an impeccably educated reader comes upon the lines. "Where is Lysander and fair Hermia? / The one I'll slay, the other slayeth me" (II.i.189–190), he feels a secret anxiety at the thought that a cultural monument like Shakespeare may be lapsing into less than impeccable taste. These lines are satirical; but, in order to be completely reassured, we have to know what the satirical intent is about. Shakespeare is not mocking a particular "rhetoric" and a particular "bad taste." Considerations of "style" are mainly relevant to professors of literature. It is rather the whole language of passion, with its constant borrowings from the fields of war, murder, and destruction, that Shakespeare is commenting upon. A book like De Rougemont's *Love in the Western World* throws more light on the type of meditation that nourishes Shakespearean satire than all stylistics put together. Shakespeare is almost contemporary in his recourse to the debased language of degraded human relations. With us, however, debased language generally remains just what it is and nothing more; the work never rises above the mire it pretends to stigmatize, or else it immediately sinks gently back into it. Not so with Shakespeare. The interest of the so-called rhetoric is its frightening pertinence; the destiny it spells for the four lovers, the destiny they unthinkingly announce, is really the one that they are busily forging for themselves; it is a tragic destiny from which they escape only by the sheer luck of being in a comedy.

This ambiguous nature of "rhetoric" is essential to the twofold nature of the play. As long as we listen as unthinkingly as the protagonists speak, we remain in the superficial play which is made up of "figures of speech," as well as of fairies and father figures. At the purely aesthetic and thematic level of "poetic imagination," we operate with the same conceptual tools as Theseus and the lovers; good and bad metaphors, true love turned false and false turned true. We understand little more than the lovers themselves. If, on the contrary, we stop long enough to hear what is being said, a pattern begins to emerge: the disquieting infrastructure of mimetic desire, which will erupt into hysterical violence a little later.

One of the most striking features in the amorous discourse of the protagonists is the abundance of animal images. These images express the self-abasement of the lover in front of his idol. As he vainly tries to reach for the absolute that appears incarnated in the model, the lover exalts his successful rival to greater and greater heights; as a result, he feels degraded to lower and lower depths. The first animal images appear immediately after Helena's hysterical celebration of her rival's beauty:

> No, no, I am as ugly as a bear.
> For beasts that meet me run away for fear. . . .
> What wicked and dissembling glass of mine
> Made me compare with Hermia's sphery eyne?
> (II. ii.94–99)

We will be told once again that such images are "pure rhetoric"; their source has been identified: most of them, it appears, come from Ovid. This is true, but the existence of a literary source for a figure of speech does not necessarily imply that it is used in a purely formal and inconsequential manner, that it cannot be given a vital significance by the second writer. It can be shown, I believe, that the animal images are part of the process which leads from mimetic desire to myth; this process is a continuous one, but a certain number of steps can be distinguished which have an existential as well as a functional significance. Far from raising himself to the state of a superman, a god, as he seeks to do, the subject of mimetic desire sinks to the level of animality. The animal images are the price the self has to pay for its idolatrous worship of otherness. This idolatry is really "selfish" in the sense that it is meant for the sake of the self; the self wants to appropriate the absolute that it perceives, but its extreme thirst for self-elevation results in extreme self-contempt, quite logically if parodoxically, since this self always meets and invites its own defeat at the hands of a successful rival.

Animal images are thus a direct consequence of the inordinate metaphysical ambition that makes desire mimetic. They are an integral part of the rigorous pattern I am trying to unravel; the law of that pattern could be defined by Pascal's aphorism, *Qui fait l'ange fait la bête*. The whole midsummer night looks like a dramatization of that aphorism. Here again is Helena, who *fait la bête* with Demetrius:

> I am your spaniel, and, Demetrius,
> The more you beat me, I will fawn on you.
> Use me but as your spaniel, spurn me, strike me,
> Neglect me, lose me—only give me leave,
> Unworthy as I am, to follow you.
> What worser place can I beg in your love—
> And yet a place of high respect with me—
> Than to be used as you use your dog?
> (II. i.203–210)

Partners in mimetic desire cannot think of each other as equal human beings; their relationship becomes less and less human; they are condemned to an angel-beast or superman-slave relationship. Helena's near worship of Hermia might be described, today, in terms of an "inferiority complex." But psychiatrists view their so-called complexes almost as physical entities, almost as independent and stable as the self they are supposed to affect. Shakespeare is alien to this substantial thinking; he sees everything in terms of relations. Helena's "inferiority complex," for example, is only the "wrong" or the "beast" end of her relationship with Hermia and Demetrius. Ultimately, everyone ends up with the same "inferiority complex," since everyone feels deprived of an absolute superiority that always appears to belong to someone else.

Being purely mimetic, this relationship is anchored in no stable reality; it is therefore bound to be unstable. The metaphysical absolute seems to shift from character to character. With each shift the entire configuration is reorganized, still on the basis of the same polarities, but reversed. The beast becomes a god and the god becomes a beast. Inferiority becomes superiority and vice versa. Up is down and down is up.

During the first scenes, Hermia, being worshiped by everyone, appears to be and feel divine. Helena, being truly rejected and despised, feels despicable. But then it is Helena's turn to be worshiped and Hermia feels like a despicable beast. After the initial moment of relative stability, the four lovers enter a world of more and more rapid reversals and inversions. The necessities of dramatic presentation force Shakespeare to be selective and somewhat schematic in his description of the process, but the principles at work are obvious. As soon as the midsummer night crisis begins in earnest, the animal metaphors are not only multiplied but turned upside down and jumbled together. As the reversals become more and more precipitous, we obviously move toward complete chaos. All this, of course, to the renewed chagrin of our guardians of "good taste," who do not see any purpose to this unseemly spectacle and view it as mere stylistic self-indulgence on the part of the author. The "rhetoric" was bad enough before, but now it is going out of its rhetorical mind. Here is Helena, once more, getting ready to chase Demetrius through the woods:

> Run when you will, the story shall be changed.
> Apollo flies, and Daphne holds the chase;
> The dove pursues the griffin; the mild hind
> Makes speed to catch the tiger.

> (II. i. 230–233)

Reversal is so pervasive a theme in A *Midsummer Night's Dream*, as in most of Shakespeare's plays, that it finally extends to the whole of nature. Titania tells us, for example, that the seasons are out of turn. Scholars assume that the weather must have been particularly bad in the year Shakespeare wrote the play; this, in turn, gives some clues to the dating of the play. It must be true, indeed, that Shakespeare needed some really inclement weather to write what he did; however, the bad weather serves a specifically Shakespearean purpose, providing still another opportunity for more variations on the major theme of the play, the theme of differences reversed and inverted:

> . . . The spring, the summer,
> The childing autumn, angry winter, change
> Their wonted liveries, and the mazed world,
> By their increase now knows not which is which.
>   (II. i.111–114)

The very pervasiveness of reversal makes it impossible for commentators not to acknowledge the theme, but it also provides a means of minimizing its significance by shifting the emphasis where it should not be shifted, onto nature and the cosmos. This, of course, is exactly what myth itself does in its constant projection and expulsion of human violence. The nineteenth- and twentieth-century mythologists who asserted and still assert that myth is mostly a misreading of natural phenomena really perpetuate the mythical dissimulation and disguise of human violence. Shakespeare seems to be doing the same thing when he inserts his midsummer night into the poetic frame of a crisis of quasi-comic proportions. In that vast macrocosm, our four protagonists' antics appear as a tiny dot moved by forces beyond its own control, automatically relieved, once more, of all responsibility for whatever harm its even tinier components may be doing to one another and to themselves. Nature, in other words, must be included among the other mythical excuses, such as the mean father and the fairies. Shakespeare certainly gives it a major poetic and dramatic role, in keeping with the principles of what I earlier called the surface play. This is true; but, as in the other instances, he also makes sure that the truth becomes explicit. The real Shakespearean perspective is clearly suggested immediately below the lines just quoted. Titania ascribes disarray neither to herself nor to Oberon nor even to both, insofar as they would remain serene divinities manipulating humanity from outside, but to the *conflict* between them, a very human conflict, to be sure, which implies the same reversals of roles as the midsummer night and which duplicates perfectly the strife among the four lovers:

And this same progeny of evils comes
From our debate, from our dissensions;
We are their parents and original.
(II. i.115–117)

Reversals in nature are only reflections, metaphoric expressions, and poetic orchestrations of the mimetic crisis. Instead of viewing myth as a humanization of nature, as we always tend to do, Shakespeare views it as the naturalization as well as the supernaturalization of a very human violence. Specialists on the subject might be well advised to take a close look at this Shakespearean view; what if it turned out to be less mythical than their own!

The lopsided view that the lovers take of their own relationships keeps reversing itself with increasing speed. This constant exchange of the relative positions within the total picture is the cause of the vertigo, the loss of balance which the four characters experience. That feeling is inseparable from the sense of extreme difference to which the same characters never cease to cling, even as this difference keeps shifting around at a constantly accelerating tempo. It is a fact, to be sure, that two characters who face each other in fascination and rivalry can never occupy the same position together, since they themselves constitute the polarity that oscillates between them. They resemble a seesaw, with one rider always going up when the other is going down and vice versa. Never, therefore, do they cease to feel out of tune with each other, radically different from each other. In reality, of course, the positions successively occupied are the same; whatever difference remains is a purely *temporal* one which must become smaller and, as the movement keeps accelerating, even tend to zero, though without actually reaching it.

Even though they persevere in difference (an ever more vertiginous difference to be sure, but difference nevertheless), the protagonists become more and more undifferentiated. We have seen that the seasons lose their relative specificity, but the true loss of differentiation comes from the crisis among men who are caught in the vicious circle of mimetic desire. Progressive undifferentiation is not an illusion but the objective truth of the whole process, in the sense that reciprocity becomes more and more perfect. There is never anything on one side of a rivalry which, sooner or later, will not be found on the other. Here and there it is exactly the same mixture of fascination and hatred, the same curses, the same everything. It can be said that mimetic desire *really works*: it really achieves the goal it has set for itself, which is the *translation* of the follower into his model, the metamorphosis of one into the other, the absolute identity of all. As the climax of the midsummer night approaches, the four protagonists lose whatever individuality they formerly appeared to have; they wander like brutes in the forest, trading the same insults and finally the same physical blows, all drugged with the same drug, all bitten by the same serpent.

The more our characters tend to see one another in terms of black and white, the more alike they really *make* one another. Every slightest move, every single reaction becomes more and more immediately self-defeating. The more these characters deny the reciprocity among them, the more they bring it about, each denial being immediately reciprocated.

At the moment when difference should be most formidable, it begins to elude not one protagonist but the four of them all at once. Characters dissolve and personalities disintegrate. Glaring contradictions multiply, no firm judgment will hold. Each protagonist becomes a masked monster in the eyes of the other three, hiding his true being behind deceptive and shifting appearances. Each points at the hypocrite and the cheat in the others, partly in order not to feel that the ground is also slipping from under him. Helena, for example, accuses Hermia of being untrue to her real self: "Fie, fie! You counterfeit, you puppet, you!" (III.ii.288). Hermia misunderstands and thinks Helena is making fun of her shortness:

> Puppet? Why so? Aye, that way goes the game.
> Now I perceive that she hath made compare
> Between our statures, she hath urged her height.
> And with her personage, her tall personage,
> Her height, forsooth, she hath prevailed with him.
> And are you grown so high in his esteem
> Because I am so dwarfish and so low?
> How low am I, thou painted maypole?
> How low am I? I am not yet so low
> But that my nails can reach unto thine eyes.
> (III. ii.289–298)

C. L. Barber correctly observes that the four young people vainly try to interpret their conflicts through something "manageably related to their individual identities," but they never achieve their purpose:

> Only accidental differences can be exhibited. Helena tall, Hermia short. Although the men think that "reason says" now Helena is "the worthier maid," personalities have nothing to do with the case. . . . The life in the lovers' part is not to be caught in individual speeches, but by regarding the whole movement of the farce, which swings and spins each in turn through a common pattern, an evolution that seems to have an impersonal power of its own.

The time comes when the antagonists literally no longer know who they are: "Am I not Hermia? Are you not Lysander?" (III.ii.273).

Here it is no exaggeration or undue modernization to speak of a "crisis of identity." To Shakespeare, however, the crisis is primarily one of differentiation. The four characters lose a self-identity which they and the philosophers would like to turn into an absolute and which becomes relative for that very reason; it is made to depend upon the otherness of a model. When Barber points out that Shakespeare fully intends for his characters, in the course of the play, to lose whatever distinctiveness they had or appeared to have at the beginning (which wasn't much anyway), he runs counter to a long tradition of criticism, the whole tradition of "realism" and of "psychology." Many critics do not find it conceivable that a writer like Shakespeare might be more interested in the undoing and dissolving of "characters" than in their creation, viewing as they do the latter task as the one assigned to all artists of all eternity. Only the most honest will face squarely their own malaise and formulate the obvious consequences of their own inadequate principles: they blame Shakespeare for "insufficient characterization."

The question is truly fundamental. The whole orientation of criticism depends on it. It is usually the wrong solution that is adopted, all the more blindly because it remains implicit. I personally believe that the conflictual undifferentiation of the four lovers is the basic Shakespearean relationship in both his tragedies and comedies. It is the relationship of the four *doubles* in *A Comedy of Errors;* it is the relationship of the Montagues and the Capulets, of course, but also of Caesar, Brutus, and his coconspirators, of Shylock and Bassanio, of all the great tragic and comic characters. There is no great theater without a gripping awareness that, far from sharpening our differences, as we like to believe, our violence obliterates them, dissolving them into that reciprocity of vengeance which becomes its own self-inflicted punishment. Shakespeare is fully aware, at the same time, that no theater audience can assume the full force of this revelation. Its impact must and will necessarily be blunted. Some violence will be made "good" and the rest "bad" at the expense of some sacrificial victim, with or without the complicity of the writer. There is no doubt that, in many instances, Shakespeare is a willing accomplice; but his is never an absolute betrayal of his own vision, because the differences he provides are always at the same time undermined and treated as quasi-allegories. An excessive appetite for "characterization" and catharsis will take nothing of this into account: it will systematically choose as most Shakespearean what really is least so, at least in the form in which it is chosen. It will thus provide not only our realistic stodginess but also our romantic self-righteousness with the only type of nourishment they can absorb.

It is in a comedy like *A Midsummer Night's Dream*, if we only agree to read through the transparence of the "airy nothing," that the truth will stare us most openly in the face. Far from lacking substance and profundity, as even George Orwell inexplicably maintained, this play provides a quintessence of the Shakespearean spirit.

Am I not "going too far" when I assimilate the midsummer night to the tragic crisis; am I not running the risk of betraying the real Shakespeare? The language of differences and undifferentiation is not Shakespeare's own, after all. This is true if we take the matter quite literally; but it is also true that Shakespeare, in some of his writing, comes close to using that same language. A case in point is the famous speech of Ulysses in *Troilus and Cressida*: it describes that very same crisis, but does so in purely theoretical language and on as vast a scale as the most ambitious tragedies, as the crisis of an entire culture. The speech is built around one single word, *degree*, which would certainly be condemned as too "abstract," too "philosophical," if it were applied to Shakespeare by anyone but Shakespeare himself. And obviously Shakespeare applies it to himself as well as to the Greeks: it is the social framework of tragedy which is at stake.

> . . . O when degree is shaked,
> Which is the ladder to all high designs,
> The enterprise is sick! How could communities,
> Degrees in schools, and brotherhoods in cities,
> Peaceful commerce from dividable shores,
> The primogenitive and due of birth,
> Prerogative of age, crowns, sceptres, laurels,
> But by degree, stand in authentic place?
> Take but degree away, untune that string,
> And, hark, what discord follows! Each thing meets
> In mere oppugnancy. The bounded waters
> Should lift their bosoms higher than the shores,
> And make a sop of all this solid globe;
> Strength should be lord of imbecility,
> And the rude son should strike his father dead;
> Force should be right, or rather, right and wrong,
> Between whose endless jar justice resides,
> Should lose their names, and so should justice too.
> Then every thing include itself in power,
> Power into will, will into appetite;
> And appetite, an universal wolf,
> So doubly seconded with will and power,
> Must make perforce an universal prey,
> And last eat up himself.
>
> (I. iii. 101–124)

The word *degree*, from the Latin *gradus* (step, degree, measure of distance), means exactly what is meant here by difference. Culture is conceived not as a mere collection of unrelated objects, but as a totality, or, if we prefer, a structure, a system of people and institutions always related to one another in such a way that a single differentiating principle is at work. This social transcendence does not exist as an object, of course. That is why, as soon as an individual member, overcome by *hubris*, tries to usurp Degree, he finds imitators; more and more people are affected by the contagion of mimetic rivalry, and Degree collapses, being nothing more than the mysterious absence of such rivalry in a functional society. The crisis is described as the "shaking," the "vizarding," or the taking away of Degree; all cultural specificities vanish, all identities disintegrate. Conflict is everywhere, and everywhere meaningless: *Each thing meets in mere oppugnancy.* We must note this use of the word "thing," the least determined, perhaps, in the English language. The meaningless conflict is that of the *doubles*. Unable to find a way out, men err and clash stupidly, full of hatred but deprived of real purpose; they resemble objects loose on the deck of a ship tossed about in a storm, destroying one another as they collide endlessly and mindlessly.

In the light of the above remarks, a precise analysis of the midsummer crisis becomes possible. The four protagonists do not see one another as *doubles*; they misunderstand their relationship as one of extreme if unstable differentiation. A point must finally be reached where all of these illusory differences oscillate so rapidly that the contrasting specificities they define are no longer perceived separately; they begin to impinge on one another, they appear to merge. Beyond a certain threshold, in other words, the dizziness mentioned earlier will make normal perception impossible; hallucination must prevail, of a type that can be ascertained with some precision, being not purely capricious and random but predetermined by the nature of the crisis.

When polarities such as the ones described earlier between the "beast" and the "angel" oscillate so fast that they become one, the elements involved remain too incompatible for a harmonious "synthesis," and they will simply be juxtaposed or superimposed on each other. A composite picture should emerge which will include fragments of the former "opposites" in a disorderly mosaic. Instead of a god and a beast facing each other as two independent and irreducible entities, we are going to have a mixture and a confusion of the two, a god that is a beast or a beast that is a god. When the polarities revolve fast enough, all antithetic images must be viewed simultaneously, through a kind of cinematic effect that will produce the illusion of a more or less single being in the form or rather the formlessness of "some monstrous shape."

What *A Midsummer Night's Dream* suggests, in other words, is that the mythical monster, as a conjunction of elements which normally specify different beings, automatically results from the more and more rapid turnover of animal and metaphysical images, a turnover which depends on the constantly self-reinforcing process of mimetic desire. We are not simply invited to witness the dramatic but insignificant birth of bizarre mythical creatures; rather we are confronted with a truly fascinating and important view of mythical genesis.

In a centaur, elements specific to man and to horse are inexplicably conjoined, just as elements specific to man and ass are conjoined in the monstrous metamorphosis of Bottom. Since there is no limit to the differences that can be jumbled together, since the picture will necessarily remain blurred, the diversity of monsters will appear properly limitless and the infinite seems to be at hand. Insofar as separate entities can be distinguished within the monstrous whole, there will be individual monsters; but they will have no stability: they will constantly appear to merge and marry one another. The birth of monsters, their scandalous commingling with human beings, and the wedding of the one with the other, all these mythical phenomena are part of one and the same experience. The wedding of Titania with the ass-headed Bottom, under the influence of that same "love juice" that makes the lovers crazy, can take place only because the difference between the natural and the supernatural is gone; haughty Titania finds to her dismay that the barrier between her and ordinary mortals is down:

> Tell me how it came this night
> That I sleeping there was found
> With these mortals on the ground.
> (IV. i. 103–105)

The conjunction of man, god, and beast takes place at the climax of the crisis and is the result of a process which began with the play itself. It is the ultimate metamorphosis, the supreme *translation*.

In that process the animal images play a pivotal role. I noted earlier that their perfect integration into the disquieting symphony conducted by Shakespeare was not at all incompatible with their identification as literary reminiscences. We must now go further. To say that these images are compatible with the role that Shakespeare himself wants them to play in his own work is no longer enough. It is evident that these animal images are especially appropriate to that role and that Shakespeare has selected them for that reason. Most of them come from Ovid's *Metamorphoses*. They are directly implicated in an earlier genesis of myth, still quite mythical, and far removed from the obviously psychosocial interpretation implicitly proposed by Shakespeare. It is no exaggeration to assert that *A Midsummer Night's Dream*, because it is a powerful reinterpretation of Ovid, also provides, at least in outline, Shakespeare's own genetic theory of myth. It is a mistake, therefore, to view the animal images as if they were suspended in midair between the matter-of-fact interplay of desires on the one hand and purely fantastic shapes on the other. They are the connecting link between the two. Thus we can no longer see the play as a collage of heterogeneous elements, as another monstrosity; it is a continuous development, a series of logically related steps that will account even for the monsters in its own midst if they are only followed to the end, if enough trust is placed in the consistency of the author.

At the climax of the crisis, Demetrious and Lysander are about to kill each other, but Puck, on Oberon's orders, substitutes himself for the *doubles* and puts the four lovers to sleep. When they wake up the next morning, they find themselves reconciled, neatly arranged this time in well-assorted couples. Good weather is back, everything is in order once more. Degree is restored. Theseus appears upon the scene. He and his future wife hear an account of the midsummer night, and it is for the duke to pronounce the final word, to draw the official conclusion of the whole episode in response to a slightly anxious question asked by Hippolyta. Then comes the most famous passage of the entire play. Theseus dismisses the entire midsummer night as the inconsequential fruit of a gratuitous and disembodied imagination. He seems to believe that the real question is whether or not to believe in the fairies. Hippolyta's later words will reveal that her concern is of an entirely different sort; but, like all rationalists of a certain type, Theseus has a marvelous capacity for simplifying the issues and displacing a debate toward his favorite stomping ground. Much of what he says is true, of course; but it is beside the point. To believe or not to believe, that is *not* the question; and, by trumpeting his fatuous skepticism, Theseus dispenses himself from looking at the remarkable pattern of the midsummer night and the disturbing clues it may contain concerning the nature of all social beliefs, including his own. Who knows if the crisis and its cathartic resolution are responsible only for the monsters of the night? Who knows if the peace and order of the morning after, if even the majestic confidence of the unchallenged ruler are not equally in their debt? Theseus' casual dismissal of myth is itself mythical in the sense that it will not ask such questions. There is irony in the choice of a great mythical figure to embody this rationalistic dismissal. Here Theseus acts as the high priest of a benign casting-out of all disturbing phenomena under the triple heading of poetry, lunacy, and love. This neat operation frees respectable men of all responsibility for whatever tricks, past, present, and future, their own desires and mimetic violence might play on them, thus perfectly duplicating the primary genesis of myth, the one that I have just noted:

> HIPPOLYTA: 'Tis strange, my Theseus, that these lovers speak of.
> THESEUS: More strange than true. I never may believe
> These antique fables, nor these fairy toys.
> Lovers and madmen have such seething brains,
> Such shaping fantasies, that apprehend
> More than cool reason ever comprehend.
> The lunatic, the lover, and the poet
> Are of imagination all compact.
> One sees more devils than vast Hell can hold,
> That is the madman. The lover, all as frantic,
> Sees Helen's beauty in a brow of Egypt.
> The poet's eye, in a fine frenzy rolling,
> Doth glance from heaven to earth, from earth to heaven,
> And as imagination bodies forth
> The form of things unknown, the poet's pen
> Turns them to shapes, and gives to airy nothings
> A local habitation and a name.
> Such tricks hath strong imagination
> That if it would but apprehend some joy,
> It comprehends some bringer of that joy;
> Or in the night, imagining some fear,
> How easy is a bush supposed a bear!
>
> (V. i.1–22)

This positivism *avant la lettre* seems to contradict much of what I have said so far. Evidence so laboriously assembled seems scattered once more. Where are the half-concealed yet blatant disclosures, the allusive ambiguities artfully disposed by the author (or so I supposed) for our enlightenment? Long before I came to it, I am sure, many skeptical readers had the passage in mind, and they will rightly want to know how it fits into my reading. Here it is, finally, an obvious ally of the traditional readings that quite naturally regard it as the unshakable rock upon which they are founded. As such, it must constitute a formidable stumbling block for my own intricate revisionism.

The lead is provided by Shakespeare himself, and the present status of the passage as a piece of anthology, a *lieu commun* of modern aestheticism, testifies to the willingness of posterity to take up that lead. The reading provided by Theseus is certainly the most pleasant, the one which conforms to the wishes of the heart and to the tendency of the human mind not to be disturbed. We must note, besides, that the text is centrally located, placed in the mouth of the most distinguished character, couched in sonorous and memorable phrases, well fit to adorn academic dissertations on the so-called "imaginative faculty."

This speech has been so successful, indeed, that no one ever pays any attention to the five quiet lines that follow. Hippolyta's response does not have the same resounding eloquence, but the dissatisfaction she expresses with the slightly pompous and irrelevant *postmortem* of Theseus *was written by Shakespeare himself*. It cannot fail to be of immense significance:

> But the story of the night told over,
> And all their minds transfigured so together,
> More witnesseth than fancy's images,
> And grows to something of great constancy,
> But howsoever strange and admirable.
>
> (V. i.23–47)

Hippolyta clearly perceives Theseus' failure to come up with the holistic interpretation that is necessary. He and his innumerable followers deal with the play as if it were a collection of separate cock-and-bull stories. To them imagination is a purely individual activity, unrelated to the interplay of the four lovers. They themselves are the true inheritors of myth when they confidently believe in their simplistic objectivity. They see myth as something they have already left behind with the greatest of ease, as an object of passing amusement, perhaps, when the occasion arises to watch some light entertainment such as A *Midsummer Night's Dream*.

There is no doubt that we are dealing with two critical attitudes and that Shakespeare himself vindicates the one that has always been least popular. When I suggest that A *Midsummer Night's Dream*; behind all the frills, is a serious genetic theory of myth, I am only translating the five lines of Hippolita into contemporary parlance. It is not I but Shakespeare who writes that the midsummer night is more than a few graceful arabesques about English folklore and Elizabethan lovers. It is not I but Shakespeare who draws our attention to *all their minds transfigured so together* and to the final result as *something of great constancy*, in other words, a common structure of mythical meaning.

I have suggested that A *Midsummer Night's Dream* might well be two plays in one. This hypothesis is now strengthened. At this point, the two plays are coming to life as individuals; they are speaking to us and to each other, one through Theseus, the other through Hippolyta. The exchange between the bridegroom and his acutely perceptive but eternally overshadowed bride amounts to the first critical discussion of the play. Representing as he does blissful ignorance and the decorum of Degree enthroned, Theseus must hold the stage longer, speaking with a brilliance and finality that confirms the dramatic preeminence of the surface play, a preeminence that is maintained throughout. Since he gives a voice to all those—the immense majority—who want nothing more in such an affair than "airy nothings," Theseus must be as deaf and blind to his bride's arguments as Shakespeare's audiences and critics seem to have been ever since. The debate seems one-sided in the duke's favor, but how could we fail, at this juncture, to realize that the real last word belongs to Hippolyta, both literally and figuratively? In the context of the evidence gathered earlier, how could we doubt that Hippolyta's words are the decisive ones, that they represent Shakespeare's own view of how the play really hangs together? If we really understand that context, we cannot be surprised that Shakespeare makes his correction of Theseus as discreet and unobstrusive as it is illuminating, visible only to the same thoughtful attention already needed to appreciate such pregnant ambiguities as "to choose love by another's eyes" and other similar gems of exquisitely direct, yet almost imperceptible revelation.

Hippolyta is gently tugging at Theseus' sleeve, but Theseus hears nothing. Posterity hears nothing. Hippolyta has been tugging at that sleeve for close to four hundred years now, with no consequence what-ever, her words forever buried under the impressive scaffoldings of Degree once more triumphant in the guise of rationalism, eternally silenced by that need for reassurance which is answered first by belief in myths, then by a certain kind of disbelief. Shakespeare seems to give his blessing to both, ironically confounded in the person of Theseus. He places in the hands of his pious and admiring betrayers the instruments best designed to blunt the otherwise intolerably sharp edge of their favorite bard's genius.

ALVIN B. KERNAN

"A Midsummer Night's Dream"

In his first decade as a dramatist, Shakespeare seems to have been on the whole optimistic about the power of playing to affect, even in less than ideal circumstances, the real world. He laughs at actors for their clumsiness and audiences for their literal-mindedness, chiding both for their inability to forget themselves and enter fully into the play; but the laughter, while it bears witness to some uneasiness on the part of the dramatist about his theater, seems in many ways merely the graceful modesty of an accomplished and self-assured professional dramatic poet continuing the proud humanistic tradition of claiming high value for his theatrical art. Nowhere is the modesty so complete, and at the same time the claim for the potential value of playing so extensive, as in A Midsummer Night's Dream, where Shakespeare dramatizes Sidney's boast that in place of nature's brazen world the poet creates a golden one, that imagination can perceive and art reveal an unseen reality just beyond the range of the senses and of the rational mind. In the *Dream*, art is no longer defined only by its ability to shape and transform an obstinate reality, as in *Shrew* and *Love's Labour's Lost*, but is shown to have an ability to penetrate the screen of the immediate world and reveal an imaginative truth that lies behind it.

Again Shakespeare glances, with an amusement that still betrays uneasiness, at the crudities of actors and stage and at the limitations of audiences. No players could be more hopeless than Nick Bottom the weaver and his mechanical friends who, in the hope of winning a small pension, perform the internal play, "Pyramus and Thisbe," to celebrate the mar-

From *The Playwright as Magician: Shakespeare's Image of the Poet in the English Public Theater.*
Copyright © 1979 by Yale University. Yale University Press.

riage of Duke Theseus of Athens to the Amazon queen, Hippolyta. Bottom's company, a parody of the amateur players and provincial touring companies who performed in aristocratic houses on special occasions, is so literal-minded as to require that the moon actually shine on the stage, that the wall through which Pyramus and Thisbe speak be solidly there, and that the actor who plays the lion assure the ladies in the audience, lest they be afraid, that he is only a make-believe lion. The deficiency of imagination which lies behind such a laughable conception of theater, carries over into the playing style of the actors as well. Their stumbling rant, missed cues, mispronounced words and lines, willingness to converse directly with the audience, doggerel verse, and general ineptitude, constitute a playwright's nightmare and completely destroy any possibility of creating the necessary illusion. As one critic describes it:

> actors do intervene between audience and playwright. The play clearly indicates that intervention, and, as Bottom demonstrates in his failure as an actor, the actor, like the playwright, must be able both to perceive and to express the imaginative idea if the play is to be successful. For Bottom's audience to imagine a credible Pyramus, Bottom the actor's Pyramus, as well as Bottom the playwright's Pyramus, must be credible. If the playlet is to succeed, both the playwright's and actor's Pyramuses must be believably dead. Long before Bottom rises with his assurances that he is alive, the imaginative expression has been so disrupted that the audience's imaginative perception is prevented. Imagination cannot amend the matter; judgment takes over, and judgment tells us that this is the silliest matter that we have ever heard.

The audience at "Pyramus and Thisbe," Duke Theseus, his queen Hippolyta, and the young lovers who attend them, are socially superior to the actors but little more sophisticated about their proper roles in making a play work. Theseus does understand that, though this may be "the silliest stuff" ever heard, it lies within the power of a gracious audience to improve it, for "The best in this kind are but shadows; and the worst are no worse, if imagination amend them" (5.1.211–12). But the noble audience seems to have little of the necessary imagination, for they violate the imaginative space of the play, which the players have first breached, by mocking the actors, laughing at their tragic efforts, and talking loudly among themselves during the performance. For them a play is only the means to while away a dull wait on their wedding night and, secure in an untroubled sense of their own substantial reality, they can laugh at what unrealistic and trivial things all plays and players are. Theseus, that champion of Athenian rationalism, has already publicly declared that the poet's imagination is no more truthful than the lunatic's delusions or the lover's belief in the perfect beauty of his beloved:

> The poet's eye, in a fine frenzy rolling,
> Doth glance from heaven to earth, from earth to heaven;
> And as imagination bodies forth
> The forms of things unknown, the poet's pen
> Turns them to shapes, and gives to airy nothing
> A local habitation and a name.

(5.1.12–17)

Shakespeare seems to have constructed in *Dream* the "worst case" for theater, voicing all the attacks on drama being made in his time and deliberately showing plays, actors, and audiences at their worst. And since "the best in this kind are but shadows," "Pyramus and Thisbe" seems to indict all plays, including *A Midsummer Night's Dream*, as mere rant of awkward actors and unrealistic dreaming of frenzied poets. But, while admitting the worst, Shakespeare has contrived at the same time to defend plays in a most subtle fashion. Even as Theseus and his friends sit watching "Pyramus and Thisbe," laughing at poetry and plays and actors, they are themselves, seen from our vantage point in the outer audience, only the "forms of things unknown" which the imagination of William Shakespeare bodied forth and gave the habitation of Athens and such odd names as Helena and Hermia, Demetrius and Lysander. The situation is the same as that in *Love's Labour's Lost*, where the scorn for plays is also discredited by showing the audience to be themselves only players, and not such very good ones at that, in a larger play of which they are totally unaware.

This is true in *Dream* in the literal sense that the stage audience is made up of actors in Shakespeare's play, and also in the sense that they have already been unwitting players in another internal play written and produced by that master of illusion, Oberon, king of the fairies. He and Titania between them have earlier managed the lives of Theseus and Hippolyta as if they were unconscious actors in a play, and during the course of *Dream*, Oberon contrives on the stage of his magical forest a little illusion which instructs the young lovers, feelingly not consciously, in the dangers of unleashed passion and brings them at last to a happy conclusion in which every Jack has his Jill. Oberon's magical forest is a perfect image of what a theater might ideally be and do, but even here the most all-powerful of playwrights is subject to the ability of the imperfect instruments through whom he must implement his art, and Puck nearly ruins the play by putting "idleness" in the wrong eyes.

As we in the audience watch Theseus watching Bottom pretend to be Pyramus, the extended dramatic perspective forces us to consider the possibility that we too may be only another player audience on another larger stage. And if this is the case, then the audience is not only once again reminded by the bad manners of the stage audience of the positive part it must play in making theater work, but it is also being told that its own sense of the real may be no more valid than Theseus's. If his rationalistic scorn of plays and players is called into question by his status as only another player, then perhaps our skepticism about Shakespeare's play is equally compromised, for we stand in the same relationship to the things unknown that the imagination of William Shakespeare has bodied forth as A Midsummer Night's Dream as Theseus does to "Pyramus and Thisbe." A forest ruled over by a contentious fairy king and queen, a magical love potion which causes love at first sight, a comic trickster like Puck, all are at least as real as a player duke who marries a queen of Amazons, rules over a city named Athens, and believes that a way of thinking called reason shows the truth of things. And they may finally be as real as that "sure and firm-set earth" we take to be our own reality. If all the world is a play, then one play may be as true as another; and if the conditions are right, as in Oberon's play but not in Bottom's, then the theater may reveal the true nature of the world and effect its transformation.

The playwright drives home his point in the final scene. After Theseus and Hippolyta and the other couples, Bottom's play finished, make their way to bed thinking that reality reigns again, the stage fills with all those fairies which Shakespeare's imagination created to embody his vision of the beneficent but tricky forces at work in nature, just beyond the range of the daylight eye. Again it is done lightly, the claim half concealed and discounted even as it is so charmingly made, but immediate reality is being heavily discounted and a visionary power is being claimed for the dramatic poet by leaving his fairies in possession of a stage which now extends outward to claim the entire theater and the world beyond as a part of its imaginative realm.

In Dream Shakespeare claims for the dramatic poet all the powers which the Renaissance conferred on art, but his image of the theater still acknowledges the crudity and accidents of stage presentation, the clumsiness of actors, the incomprehension of audiences, and the danger that plays may be mere fantasy without much relation to reality. If the play is to work, as he tries to make Dream work, and its full powers are to be realized, then actors and audience must accept that they and their "real" world are finally as illusory as a play, are simply another play called reality, and enter with their imaginations into the full spirit of creating between them on the stage an alternate fictional world of fairies and lovers which can reveal another aspect of truth.

In Shakespeare's exploration of theater in his plays of the 1590s, the poet-playwright does not himself appear openly but only in some surrogate form of creator such as the Prince of Navarre and his compan-ions, who construct an academy and a masque; or Petruchio, who writes his shrew play as he goes along; or Oberon, who commands the illusory power of the fairy world; or perhaps even the enthusiastic actor Bottom, who is always willing to stretch a part or add a piece of business to the script of the mercifully anonymous "Pyramus." The absence of any direct image of the playwright accords with the actual situation in the public theater, where the playwright and his text remained invisible behind the production of the play. It was the play in performance in the theater before an audience that was the artistic reality, and it is on production that Shakespeare focused his attention in his internal plays, showing always in these early plays a less than ideal situation.

RUTH NEVO

'Kate of Kate Hall':
"The Taming of the Shrew"

A more gentlemanly age than our own was embarrassed by *The Shrew*. G. B. Shaw announced it 'altogether disgusting to the modern sensibility'. Sir Arthur Quiller-Couch of the New Shakespeare, judged it

> primitive, somewhat brutal stuff and tiresome, if not positively offensive to any modern civilised man or modern woman, not an antiquary. . . . We do not and cannot, whether for better or worse, easily think of woman and her wedlock vow to obey quite in terms of a spaniel, a wife and a walnut tree—the more you whip 'em the better they be.

It will be noticed, however, that Q's access of gallantry causes him to overlook the fact that apart from the cuffings and beatings of saucy or clumsy *zanni* which is canonical in Italianate comedy, no one whips anyone in *The Taming of the Shrew*, violence being confined to Katherina who beats her sister Bianca, and slaps Petruchio's face. Anne Barton has done much to restore a sense of proportion by quoting some of the punishments for termagent wives which really were practised in Shakespeare's day. Petruchio comes across, she says,

> far less as an aggressive male out to bully a refractory wife into total submission, than he does as a man who genuinely prizes Katherina, and, by exploiting an age-old and basic antagonism between the sexes, manoeuvres her into an understanding of his nature and also her own.

Ralph Berry reads the play rather as a Berneian exercise in the Games People Play, whereby Kate learns the rules of Petruchio's marriage game, which she plays hyperbolically and with ironic amusement. 'This is a husband-wife team that has settled to its own satisfaction, the rules of its games, and now preaches them unctuously to friends.' In our own day, the wheel, as is the way with wheels, has come full circle and the redoubtable feminist, Ms Germaine Greer, has found the relationship of Kate and Petruchio preferable to the subservient docility of that sexist projection, the goody-goody Bianca.

With all this fighting of the good fight behind us, we may approach the play with the unencumbered enjoyment it invites. As Michael West has excellently argued 'criticism has generally misconstrued the issue of the play as women's rights, whereas what the audience delightedly responds to are sexual rites'. Nothing is more stimulating to the imagination than the tension of sexual conflict and sexual anticipation. Verbal smashing and stripping, verbal teasing and provoking and seducing are as exciting to the witnessing audience as to the characters enacting these moves. It is easy to see why *The Shrew* has always been a stage success, and so far from this being a point to be apologized for it should be seen as exhibiting Shakespeare's early command of farce as the radical of comic action, a mastery temporarily lost as he struggled to absorb more rarefied material in *The Two Gentlemen* and only later recovered. The mode, however, of the sexual battle in *The Shrew* is devious and indirect and reflects a remarkably subtle psychology. Petruchio neither beats his Kate nor rapes her—two 'primitive and brutal' methods of taming termagant wives, but neither is his unusual courtship of his refractory bride simply an exhibition of cock-of-the-walk male dominance to which in the end Katherina is forced to submit. Michael West's emphasis upon wooing dances and the folklore of sexual conquest is salutory, but Petruchio's conquest of Kate is far from merely a 'kind of mating dance with appropriate struggling and biceps flexing'. Nor is she simply 'a healthy female animal who wants a male strong enough to protect her, deflower her, and sire vigorous offspring'.

Only a very clever, very discerning man could bring off a psychodrama so instructive, liberating and therapeutic as Petruchio's, on a honeymoon as sexless (as well as dinnerless) as could well be imagined. Not by sex is sex conquered, nor for that matter by the witholding of sex, though the play's tension spans these poles. Christopher Sly, one recalls, is also constrained to forgo his creature comforts, a stoic *malgré lui*, and thereby a foil and foreshadower of the self-possessed Petruchio.

In the Induction, the page Bartholomew plays his part as Lady Sly to such effect that Sly pauses only to determine whether to call the lovely lady 'Al'ce madam, or Joan madam?' (Ind. II.110) or plain 'madam wife' before demanding 'Madam, undress you, and come now to bed' (Ind.II.117). Bartholomew must think fast, of course, and does: '[I] should yet absent me from your bed', he says, lest '[you] incur your former malady', and hopes that 'this reason stands for my excuse' (Ind.II.124). Sly clearly has his own problems: 'Ay, it stands so that I may hardly tarry so long. But I would be loath to fall into my dreams again. I will therefore tarry in despite of the flesh and the blood' (Ind.II.125–8). But Christopher Sly's 'former malady' is, of course, an imposed delusion: it is not as anamnesic lord that he is himself but as drunken tinker. Katherina's, we will finally learn to perceive, was self-imposed, and requires the therapies of comedy— 'which bars a thousand harms and lengthens life'—not the tumbling tricks of a 'Christmas gambold' for its cure. This lower level functions as foil to the higher yardstick and guarantor of the latter's reality.

The play's formal *telos* is to supply that which is manifestly lacking: a husband for the wild, intractable and shrewish daughter of Baptista. But how shall Katherina herself not perceive that this husband is sought in order to enable her younger sister to be happily married to one of *her* numerous suitors? The situation of inflamed and inflammatory sibling rivalry which the good signor Baptista has allowed to develop between these daughters of his is suggested with deft economy. Her very first words:

> I pray you, sir, is it your will
> To make a stale of me amongst these mates?
> (I. i.57–8)

speak hurt indignity, an exacerbated pride. Her response when Baptista fondles and cossets the martyred Bianca:

> A pretty peat! it is best
> Put finger in the eye, and she knew why.
> (I. i.78–9)

indicates her opinion that if Bianca is long suffering she is also extracting the maximum benefit and enjoyment from that state. Nothing that Baptista says or does but will be snatched up and interpreted disadvantageously by this irascible sensitivity:

> Why, and I trust I may go too, may I not? What, shall I be
> appointed hours, as though (belike) I knew not what to take
> and what to leave? Ha!
> (I. i.102–4)

These first glimpses already invite us to infer some reason for the bad-tempered, headstrong, domestic tyranny Kate exercises, but when we find her beating her cowering sister, screaming at her for confidences about which of her suitors she most fancies, and turning on her father with

> What, will you not suffer me? Nay, now I see
> She is your treasure, she must have a husband;
> I must dance barefoot on her wedding-day,
> And for your love to her lead apes in hell.
> Talk not to me, I will go sit and weep,
> Till I can find occasion of revenge.
>
> (II. i.31–6)

we surely do not require inordinate discernment to understand what ails Katherina Minola. It is a marvellous touch that the pious Bianca, defending herself from the wildcat elder sister (with no suitor), says:

> Or what you will command me will I do
> So well I know my duty to my elders.
>
> (II. i.6–7)

Bianca, it may be supposed, is not the only younger sister who has got her face scratched for a remark like that.

All of Padua, we are given to understand, is taken up with the problem of finding someone to take his devilish daughter off Baptista's hands, leaving the field free for the suitors of the heavenly Bianca. And this is precisely a trap in which Kate is caught. She has become nothing but an obstacle or a means to her sister's advancement. Even the husband they seek for her is in reality for the sister's sake, not hers. When she says: 'I will never marry' it is surely because she believes no 'real' husband of her own, who loves her for herself, whom she can trust, is possible. How indeed could it be otherwise since patently and manifestly no one does love her? Because (or therefore) she is not lovable. And the more unlovable she is the more she proves her point. Katherina of Acts I and II is a masterly and familiar portrait. No one about her can do right in her eyes, so great is her envy and suspicion. No one can penetrate her defences, so great her need for assurance. So determined is she to make herself invulnerable that she makes herself insufferable, and finds in insufferability her one defence. This is a 'knot of errors' of formidable proportions and will require no less than Petruchio's shock tactics for its undoing.

The undoing begins with the arrival of Petruchio, to wive it wealthily in Padua. No doubts are entertained in Padua about the benefits of marriage where money is, but it will be noted that no one is banking on a rich marriage to save him from the bankruptcy courts. All the suitors are wealthy; Lucentio, potentially at least. The contrast that Shakespeare sets up between Petruchio and Lucentio is an interesting ironic inversion of that obtaining in the Terentian tradition. In Terence the second (liaison) plot entailed tricky stratagems for acquiring money in order to buy (and keep) the slave girl. The main (marriage) plot on the other hand hinged upon the fortunate discovery of a true identity, which meant both legitimizing the affair and acquiring the dowry. Here, in the case of Bianca and Lucentio the mercenary mechanics of match-making are masked by Petrarchan ardours on Lucentio's part (or Hortensio's, until the appearance of the widow):

> Tranio, I burn, I pine, I perish, Tranio,
>
> . . . let me be a slave, t'achieve that maid
> Whose sudden sight hath thrall'd my wounded eye.
> (I. i.155; 219–20)

and by angelic docility on Bianca's part; while Petruchio's affairs are deromanticized by the unabashed, unmasked worldliness of his motivation:

> I come to wive it wealthily in Padua;
> If wealthily, then happily in Padua.
> (I. ii.75–6)

and the formidable temper of Kate.

To Petruchio's incontinent and precipitate request to draw up the 'covenant' between them, Baptista demurs:

> Ay, when the special thing is well obtain'd,
> That is, her love; for that is all in all.
> (II. i.128–9)

and the reply is unequivocal:

> Why, that is nothing; for I tell you, father,
> I am as peremptory as she proud-minded;
> And where two raging fires meet together,
> They do consume the thing that feeds their fury.
> Though little fire grows great with little wind,
> Yet extreme gusts will blow out fire and all;
> So I to her, and so she yields to me,
> For I am rough, and woo not like a babe.
> (II. i.130–7)

And again: 'For I will board her, though she chide as loud/As thunder when the clouds in autumn crack' (I.ii.95–6). Final recognitions will reverse these evaluations: the nakedly mercenary relationship will prove itself productive of affection and of spirit as well as sheer animal spirits; the romantic will prove hollow, its Petrarchanism a mere mask.

In *The Shrew*, Shakespeare's characteristic handling of multiple levels is already to be discerned. The main protagonists are the agents of the higher recognitions, the middle groups function as screens on which are projected distorted mirror images of the main couples—images in a concave mirror; while the lower orders ridicule the middle by the parody of imitation, and act as foils for the higher by providing a measure of qualitative difference.

Though *The Shrew* fails to integrate Christopher Sly satisfactorily and indeed abandons him altogether after Act I, such a function for him, as I have already indicated, is adumbrated. Shakespeare, it seems, felt more comfortable with the playlet-within-the-play of *Love's Labour's Lost* and *A Midsummer Night's Dream* for his clowns, or with the parenthetic internal comment of a cunning and a foolish servant combination like Grumio/Tranio or Launce/Speed than with the clown-frame, to which he does not return. But the flurry of disguisings and contrivings, 'supposes' and role-playings in Baptista's middle-class household, resolved finally by nothing more complex than natural selection and substantial bank balances, do set off admirably the subtler, more complex and interiorized transformations of the Petruchio-Katherina relationship.

Petruchio's first speech in reply to Katherina's haughty insistence on her full name, is richly expressive:

> You lie, in faith, for you are call'd plain Kate,
> And bonny Kate, and sometimes Kate the curst;
> But Kate, the prettiest Kate in Christendom,
> Kate of Kate-Hall, my super-dainty Kate,
> For dainties are all Kates, and therefore, Kate,
> Take this of me, Kate of my consolation—
> Hearing thy mildness prais'd in every town,
> Thy virtues spoke of, and thy beauty sounded,
> Yet not so deeply as to thee belongs,
> Myself am mov'd to woo thee for my wife.
>
> (II. i.185–94)

Ironic, mocking, amused and appreciative, it invites us to infer a certain relief, to say the least. Though he has stoutly affirmed his priorities:

> Be she as foul as was Florentius' love,
> As old as Sibyl, and as curst and shrowd
> As Socrates' Xantippe, or a worse . . .

> I come to wive it wealthily in Padua;
> If wealthily, then happily in Padua.
>   (I. ii.69–71; 75–6)

the spirited, bonny dark lass Baptista's terrible daughter turns out to be cannot but cause him a lift of the heart. She, for her part, does not of course respond immediately to his good-humoured teasing, but we may surely assume a certain vibration to be caused by this note of a tenderness which her obsessive fear of not finding has consistently put out of court. But she has built up sturdy bastions and will certainly not imitate her conciliatory sister. Combat is her chosen defence, and that these two are worthy opponents the set of wit which follows shows. Then comes the cut and thrust of the clash between her proud-mindedness and his peremptoriness. She misses no ploy, is outrageously provocative and brazenly impolite, verbally and even physically violent. He trips her up with a bawdy pun, she dares him to return a slapped face, and it is by no means certain to anyone that he will not. His strategy of mock denial:

> 'Twas told me you were rough and coy and sullen,
> And now I find report a very liar;
> For thou art pleasant, gamesome, passing courteous . . .
>   (II. i.243–5)

contains an infuriating sting in its tail:

> But slow in speech, yet sweet as spring-time flowers.
>   (II. i.246)

so that she is criticized for being what she most prides herself on not being, and consoled by being told she is what she most despises. Again:

> Why does the world report that Kate doth limp?
> O sland'rous world! Kate like the hazel-twig
> Is straight and slender, and as brown in hue
> As hazel nuts, and sweeter than the kernels.
> O, let me see thee walk. Thou dost not halt.
>   (II. i.252–6)

And poor Kate must be beholden to him for patronizing defence against the alleged detractions of a despised world, and finds herself judiciously examined for faults much as if she were a thoroughbred mare at a fair. It is no wonder that in reply to his

> Father 'tis thus: yourself and all the world,
> That talk'd of her, have talk'd amiss of her.
> If she be curst, it is for policy,
> For she's not froward, but modest as the dove;

> She is not hot, but temperate as the morn;
> For patience she will prove a second Grissel,
> And Roman Lucrece for her chastity;
> And to conclude, we have 'greed so well together
> That upon Sunday is the wedding-day.
>
> (II. i. 290–8)

she can only splutter 'I'll see thee hanged on Sunday first'; a response which is immediately interpreted by Petruchio, for the benefit of the spectators, as a secret bargain between lovers:

> 'Tis bargain'd 'twixt us twain, being alone,
> That she shall still be curst in company.
> I tell you 'tis incredible to believe
> How much she loves me. O, the kindest Kate,
> She hung about my neck, and kiss on kiss
> She vied so fast, protesting oath on oath,
> That in a twink she won me to her love.
> O, you are novices! 'tis a world to see
> How tame, when men and women are alone,
> A meacock wretch can make the curstest shrew.
>
> (II. i. 304–13)

Round one thus ends indeed with 'we will be married a'Sunday'.

Sunday, however, brings not the marriage that has been prepared for in the Minola household, but a mummer's carnival. Petruchio arrives inordinately late, and in motley. Of the uproar he produces in the church we hear from Gremio, in a lively description containing the shape of things to come:

> Tut, she's a lamb, a dove, a fool to him!
> I'll tell you, Sir Lucentio: when the priest
> Should ask if Katherine should be his wife,
> 'Ay, by gogs-wouns,' quoth he, and swore so loud
> That all amaz'd the priest let fall the book,
> And as he stoop'd again to take it up,
> This mad-brain'd bridegroom took him such a cuff
> That down fell priest and book, and book and priest.
> 'Now take them up,' quoth he, 'if any list.'
> TRANIO: What said the wench when he rose again?
> GREMIO: Trembled and shook; for why, he stamp'd and swore
> As if the vicar meant to cozen him.
> But after many ceremonies done,
> He calls for wine. 'A health!' quoth he, as if
> He had been aboard, carousing to his mates
> After a storm, quaff'd off the muscadel,
> And threw the sops all in the sexton's face . . .

> This done, he took the bride about the neck,
> And kiss'd her lips with such a clamorous smack
> That at the parting all the church did echo.
>
>   (III. ii.157–73; 177–9)

All of this is prologue to the first open clash of wills between these fiery newly-weds. He will instantly away, she 'will not be gone till I please myself':

> The door is open, sir, there lies your way:
> You may be jogging whiles your boots are green.
>   (III.ii.210–11)

> Father, be quiet, he shall stay my leisure . . .

> Gentlemen, forward to the bridal dinner.
> I see a woman may be made a fool,
> If she had not a spirit to resist.
>   (III. ii.217; 219–21)

This is Petruchio's cue:

> They shall go forward, Kate, at thy command.
> Obey the bride, you that attend on her . . .

> But for my bonny Kate, she must with me.
> Nay, look not big, nor stamp, nor stare, nor fret,
> I will be master of what is mine own.
> She is my goods, my chattels, she is my house,
> My household stuff, my field, my barn,
> My horse, my ox, my ass, my any thing;
> And here she stands, touch her whoever dare,
> I'll bring mine action on the proudest he
> That stops my way in Padua. Grumio,
> Draw forth thy weapon, we are beset with thieves;
> Rescue thy mistress if thou be a man.
> Fear not, sweet wench, they shall not touch thee, Kate!
> I'll buckler thee against a million.
>   (III. ii.222–3; 227–39)

And he snatches her off, sublimely indifferent to anything she says, insisting upon his property rights, benignly protective, mind you, of his bonny Kate, turning all her protests to his own purposes and depriving her of any shred of self-justification by his indignant defence of her.

Stage-manager and chief actor, master of homeopathy—'He kills her in his own humour' as Peter says—Petruchio's playacting, his comic therapy, provides the comic device. One of a long line of Shakespearean actor-protagonists he holds the mirror up to nature, and shows scorn her own image. The tantrums that she has specialized in throwing he throws in super-abundance, forcing her to see herself in the mirror he thus holds up.

Grumio's tale of the saga of the journey:

> . . . hadst thou not cross'd me, thou shouldst have heard how her horse fell, and she under her horse; thou shouldst have heard in how miry a place, how she was bemoil'd, how he left her with the horse upon her, how he beat me because her horse stumbled, how she waded through the dirt to pluck him off me; how he swore, how she pray'd that never pray'd before; how I cried, how the horses ran way, how her bridle was burst; how I lost my crupper, with many things of worthy memory, which now shall die in oblivion, and thou return unexperienc'd to thy grave.
>
> (IV.i.72–84)

prepares for the continuing hubbub in the Petruchean dining-hall. That Petruchio's strategy has the additional advantage of an austerity regime as far as food and sleep and 'fine array' is concerned is all to the good. Petruchio is canny and will leave no stone unturned. Also, he has tamed hawks. But it is not physical hardship which will break Kate's spirit, nor does he wish it, any more than a spirited man would wish his horse or his hound spiritless. And Petruchio, we recall, wagers twenty times as much upon his wife as he would upon his hawk or his hound. Significantly, Kate's recurrent response to his carrying on is to fly to the defence of the cuffed and chivvied servants. Crossing her will, totally and consistently, under the guide of nothing but consideration for her desires, confuses and disorients her, as she complains to Grumio:

> What, did he marry me to famish me?
> Beggars that come unto my father's door
> Upon entreaty have a present alms,
> If not, elsewhere they meet with charity;
> But I, who never knew how to entreat,
> Nor never needed that I should entreat,
> Am starv'd for meat, giddy for lack of sleep,
> With oaths kept waking, and with brawling fed;
> And that which spites me more than all these wants,
> He does it under the name of perfect love;
>
> (IV.iii.3–12)

Katherine gets the point, but fails to get from Grumio even one of the mouth-watering items from a hearty English menu with which he tantalizes her. When she, listening hungrily to Petruchio's 'sermon of continency', and knowing not 'which way to stand, to look, to speak,' is 'as one new-risen from a dream', she might well rub her eyes and say, with

Christopher Sly, . . . 'do I dream? Or have I dream'd till now?' (Ind. ii.69).

What subtle Dr Petruchio has done is to drive a wedge into the steel plating of Kate's protective armour, so that he speaks at once to the self she has been and the self she would like to be; the self she has made of herself and the self she has hidden. The exchange of roles, with herself now at the receiving end of someone else's furies, takes her, as we say, out of herself; but she also perceives the method of his madnesses. Petruchio's remedy is an appeal to Kate's intelligence. These are not arbitrary brutalities, but the clearest of messages. And they are directed to her with undivided singleness of purpose.

In Act IV the remedy comes to fruition and Kate enunciates it:

> Then God be blest, it [is] the blessed sun,
> But sun it is not, when you say it is not;
> And the moon changes even as your mind.
> What you will have it nam'd, even that it is,
> And so it shall be so, for Katherine.
>
> (IV. v. 18–22)

And then it is enacted, with considerable verve, as she addresses Vincentio, on cue from Petruchio, as 'young budding virgin, fair, and fresh, and sweet' and then promptly again, on cue, undoes all. Kate has yielded to a will stronger than her own and to an intelligence which has outmanoeuvred her, but the paradoxical, energizing and enlivening effect of the scene is that the laughter is directed not against her as butt or victim, but, through her prim performance, towards the disconcerted Vincentio. The *senex* is made fun of, in effect, by a pair of tricksters in some subtle alliance with each other not clear to him, but clear to the audience. Partly this response is structured by New Comedy paradigms. As Grumio puts it in Act I: 'Here's no knavery! See, to beguile the old folks, how the young folks lay their heads together!' (I.ii.138–9). But mainly I believe it is due to our sense of liberation from deadlock. Petruchio has enlisted Kate's will and wit on his side, not broken them, and it is the function of the final festive test to confirm and exhibit this. It is also to be noted that the arrival in Padua of Vincentio 'exhausts' Lucentio's wooing devices, just as Petruchio's taming device exhausts its function; and it is a dexterous turn of composition which balances the mock non-recognition of Vincentio on the way to Padua, and his encounter with his Mantuan proxy, with the unmasking and recognition of the true Katherina, and the true Bianca, at the banquet.

That Kate is in love by Act V, is, I believe, what the play invites us to perceive. And indeed she may well be. The man she has married has humour and high spirits, intuition, patience, self-command and masterly intelligence; and there is more than merely a homily for Elizabethan wives in her famous speech:

> A woman mov'd is like a fountain troubled,
> Muddy, ill-seeming, thick, bereft of beauty,
> And while it is so, none so dry or thirsty
> Will deign to sip, or touch one drop of it.
> Thy husband is thy lord, thy life, thy keeper,
> Thy head, thy sovereign; one that cares for thee,
> And for thy maintenance; commits his body
> To painful labor, both by sea and land;
> To watch the night in storms, the day in cold,
> While thou li'st warm at home, secure and safe;
> And craves no other tribute at thy hands
> But love, fair looks, and true obedience—
> Too little payment for so great a debt.
>
> (V. ii. 142–54)

She wins her husband's wager but the speech bespeaks a generosity of spirit beyond the call of two hundred crowns. We have just heard Bianca snap at Lucentio mourning his lost bet: 'The more fool you for laying on my duty', and it seems that the metamorphosis of folly into wisdom which the comic action performs makes an Erastian reversal. More fool the Paduans indeed, in their exploitative hypocrisies and meannesses, than this madcap pair.

The very un-Petrarchan Petruchio has been the initiator of remedies in *The Taming of the Shrew* as well as the temperamental suitor; Katherina largely a responder and a foil. These positions will be reversed in *As You Like It* but not without a number of intermediate moves. *The Two Gentlemen of Verona* which follows *The Shrew* allows very little scope for the presentation of independent action on the part of Julia (despite her notable independence) and no occasion for courtship at all. Nevertheless, the growth of perceptions which make later developments possible proceeds through this next play, and is positively advanced by its explorations in the ambivalent and mimetic rivalry of the gentlemen.

MEREDITH SKURA

Interpreting Posthumus' Dream: "Cymbeline"

Shakespeare's *Cymbeline* is an extraordinarily complicated play, even for a romance. Set in prehistoric Britain, it combines elements of history play and Roman play, but it still ranges over an Elizabethan Italy and a timeless pastoral world in Wales. By allusion, it also ranges widely over Shakespeare's own earlier plays. Its wicked Queen evokes Lady Macbeth; Iachimo evokes Iago; and the hero Posthumus recalls Othello, although Shakespeare seems to be making mere cartoon versions of those earlier complex characters.

If the external allusions are complicated, the on-stage action is even more so. There are more than twenty separate strands of action, and although sorting them out into three major plot lines helps some, the action is still confusing, even in the way that it is primarily about Posthumus' marriage to Imogen, rather than about Imogen's father Cymbeline, who gives the play its name. And finally, the play is written in a very mannered, elliptical, and self-conscious style. While most modern audiences can respond immediately to Othello, Posthumus' adventures in *Cymbeline* present many difficulties and call for an acquired taste.

These difficulties are precisely what interest me, however. This essay will be an experiment to see how a psychoanalytic bias can be of use in coming to terms with difficult works, like *Cymbeline*, which do not readily fit into expected patterns. I am not interested in trying to psychoanalyze either Shakespeare or the reader, nor in discovering all an analyst

From *Representing Shakespeare: New Psychoanalytic Essays*, edited by Murray M. Schwartz and Coppelia Kahn. Copyright © 1980 by The Johns Hopkins University Press.

might say about the "unconscious meaning" of the play, but only in trying to use some psychoanalytic categories to explain its puzzling details. I hope to *avoid* the familiar dichotomy between analyst's and critic's explanations—or between "unconscious" and "conscious" meaning. "Meaning is an affair of consciousness," says critic E. D. Hirsch, while the analyst Ferenczi claims that the conscious meaning cannot be understood until the unconscious "depths are plumbed." I think, though, that what happens as we look at *Cymbeline*, even more clearly than with the other plays, is that we can see the terms conscious and unconscious as a misleading polarity. What we really experience instead of either of these extremes is a range of different ways of being aware.

There is no such thing as a neatly separable conscious meaning, nor a meaning of which we are totally unconscious, but only a range of different ways of being aware of and representing things—different "modes of consciousness," as one analyst has called them. Locating their effect is not simply a matter of finding an unconscious meaning behind the action, but rather of finding a play between two ways of seeing the details already visible in the action. The effect, as two French analysts have described it in their revisionary essay on "The Unconscious," is like a newspaper puzzle-game in which Napolean's hat is hidden—though perfectly "visible"—in the leaves of a tree. This ambiguous interplay affects all levels of *Cymbeline*, from moral interpretation to plot to language, and it recreates for us the shifting ambiguities of experience in our own lives that we normally do not notice.

I want to begin not with psychoanalysis but rather with the simple fact that Shakespeare's plays are about families. It is remarkable how many of the plays develop out of specific moments in what we might call the cycle of generations that makes up a family. Both comedies and tragedies begin in those moments of crisis or transition that open new worlds, the *rites de passage* through Jaques' seven ages of man—or, rather, in Shakespeare, the ages of the family. Characters grow up in and then out of families; they start their own families and struggle to keep them together; they watch their children leave to set up new families; and, finally, they fall back to become their chidren's children.

The early plays, for example, are often organized around the transition from childhood to adult passion and its responsibilities. *A Midsummer Night's Dream*, its action poised on the threshold of a royal marriage, reveals the passage from a sexless spring when Hermia and Helena sat sewing together as calm as two cherries on a branch (while Leontes and Polixenes, in *The Winter's Tale*, frisked together like twinned lambs in their boyhood days), to the midsummer heat that sends the girls to the forest scrabbling at each other like animals. We watch Romeo's passage from a sexless puppy love for Rosaline—which his family could approve—to the dog days of passion that nearly tear Verona apart.

The plays written near the turn of the century often show another kind of transition, when the young heroes emerge from their boyish isolation and irresponsibility to take over leadership, whether from a literal or a symbolic father. Prince Hal leaves his prodigal days behind to become a sober king when his father dies; Hamlet moves from his student days to an even more sobering burden of leadership when his father dies, because for him it soon requires that he really must steal the crown. Brutus—historically Caesar's stepson—moves from a quiet filial devotion to a sense of authority that leaves no more room for Caesar as soon as Brutus thinks of himself as head of Rome. And even Angelo in *Measure for Measure* crosses the threshold, leaving the cloistered virtues and an "unsounded self" to confront adult responsibilities and temptations. Elsewhere we can see a movement in the other direction, when a Titus or a Lear thinks he can retire to his children's nursery.

Cymbeline and the other romances differ from the earlier plays in their scope; they present the whole cycle, often ranging over several crises in different generations. The histories present such cycles too, of course, but what distinguishes the romances is the way they focus on one particular aspect of family experience that I want to examine here. The romances make explicit a paradox about families that Shakespeare put at the center of his plays long before the anthropologists began to study kinship relations: the family is so important that characters cannot even imagine themselves without one, yet every family must bring on its own destruction. Its very success in raising children ensures that they will want to leave—or to take over in the wrong way. As the crisis recurs in each generation, both parents and children have to find the right balance between holding on and letting go; they must avoid both the threat of an ingrown family collapsing in on itself and the threat of an explosion that will tear the family apart.

The romances stage several of these crises, and in them the two threats take many forms. The threat of holding on too tightly is seen most strikingly in the threat of incest in these plays. *Pericles* opens with a story about incest; incestuous longing is just hinted in *The Winter's Tale*, when Leontes sees his daughter for the first time in sixteen years; and there may be a more obscurely implied incestuous attraction making Prospero jealous of his potential son-in-law. Shakespeare also suggests an incestuous ambition on the part of characters like Cloten and Caliban, who want to marry their lovely step-sisters, usurping their proper role within their foster families and refusing to leave.

But incest is only one form of a more general danger that family bonds will become too strong. Parents in particular threaten to swallow up their children. Mothers are quite literally ready to eat their "little darlings" during the famine in *Pericles* (reversing the threat from Lear's "pelican" daughters). More often the parents simply do not want their children to leave or to shake off parental power. Antiochus in *Pericles* delays his daughter's wedding because he wants her for his own use, but even the less perverse parents like Simonides in *Pericles*, or Cymbeline or Prospero, delay weddings. And Alonso—who lets his daughter go—is sorry: she is in another country; it's as if the wench were dead.

The opposite threat of families exploding outwards comes sometimes from parents who throw their children out, as Dionyza does in *Pericles*, or as Leontes does. Cymbeline merely loses track of his sons, but the effect is the same. More often, however, it comes from the children who try to break out of the family too soon. So Florizel refuses to ask his father's blessing on a dubious marriage, and Perdita herself denies her shepherd "father" in running off with Florizel, just as Cymbeline's sons defy their shepherd "father."

These family dramas are interesting in themselves, but they are also the outward accompaniment of an equally important inner drama that I want to look at more closely. It is a drama that each new generation feels: the conflict between family inheritance and personal individuality, between old memories and new perceptions, between being part of the family unit and being the head of a new family. This is the universal drama that Freud saw in the very specific fate of Oedipus. What psychoanalysis adds to the traditional western understanding that the past shapes us is the idea that the past works on us unconsciously and in even stranger, less direct ways than it did for Oedipus, permeating our present lives without being literally true as it was for him.

Too much emphasis on the past, of course, is reductive, and we have all read psychoanalytic criticism that reduces an ongoing drama to a perpetual repetition of the same old family drama. So the analyst finds that Prince Hal and Hamlet commit oedipal crimes—as do Brutus, Macbeth, Angelo, and Florizel. Shakespeare's plays resist such reductions—but they do so partly by taking them into account.

The plays present a uniquely balanced vision. Without ever reducing present experience to mere repetition of the past, they never leave out the shadowy resonances that the analyst finds in present experience. Indeed, Shakespeare finds a way of representing the ambiguity of *current* experience that re-creates "out there" some of the complexity of what it is like inside our own overlaid minds. We are each tied to a family with bonds stronger than any an overbearing father can impose because those bonds are part of our sense of ourselves, taking the form of memories or attitudes of mind and perception. The child can leave his family behind, but he cannot escape its influence, and in some sense he cannot know who he is until he knows where he has come from—until he knows his roots.

One way Shakespeare portrays all this, of course, is to put the literal parents onstage. Thus Hamlet really is struggling with his parents, and so is Coriolanus. No wonder the analyst takes to these plays, as Norman Holland says, like a kitten to a ball of wool. But another way Shakespeare portrays the family influence is by symbolic reenactments of the original family situations, so that a character leaves home and comes to a new world, seemingly to a new family, but we can see that he is also simultaneously working out his relationships to his old family as he tries out the new one. We can neither reduce his current to his past experience, nor can we ignore his past. The family references flicker on the surface. They are neither a psychoanalytic skeleton behind the surface, nor are they quite part of the literal meaning. And this is precisely the role they have in life. The family's role comes out most strikingly in the case of Posthumus in *Cymbeline*, and it is to his adventures that I want now to turn, to see how the cycle of family crises reverberates as part of his own separate experience as an individual, and particularly how all this emerges in the strange climactic dream he has at the turning point of the play.

Of course, to the casual audience, Posthumus in this play is primarily a husband, but we shall see that there is no way for him to find himself as husband until he finds himself as son, as part of the family he was torn from long ago. The story of Posthumus learning to be a proper son is not literally part of the main plot, and in fact it is hardly noticeable and seldom noted in discussions of the play. But it is nonetheless a shaping influence on the story of his learning how to be a husband.

No one would claim that *Cymbeline* is solely about families. It is, in fact, about several different relationships that hold men together. Its three main plots examine political, generational or familial, and marital ties, so that the story of Posthumus' marriage takes place only in this larger context. All three plots are about human bonds gone wrong—exploded or imploded—and then being righted by a new faith or mutuality of trust.

The first, or political, plot is the story of King Cymbeline of Britain, who refuses to pay tribute money to Rome and is getting ready to go to war about it. In the second or dynastic plot, we learn that Cymbeline's two sons disappeared long ago, and his good wife has died. He is now remarried to a wicked Queen with an unsavory son whose name Cloten, rhymes with "rotten." Cymbeline is foolish enough to insist that his daughter Imogen marry Cloten instead of letting her marry the orphan Posthumus, whom Cymbeline has been bringing up as his own son.

In the third plot (really the main one), Imogen and Posthumus do get married secretly anyway, but with almost disastrous results. Posthumus is banished, and while he is away he succumbs to an Iago-like villain, Iachimo, and makes a bet with him on his wife's chastity. Iachimo promptly worms his way into Imogen's bedroom by hiding himself inside a trunk so that he can come out in the night to inspect her room and see the telltale mole on her left breast—and to take the bracelet Posthumus gave her. All this ocular proof convinces Posthumus that Imogen has betrayed him, and, rashly, he orders her killed. Of course he soon repents—too late, as he thinks, to save her, so instead he vows to serve her father, Cymbeline, by fighting in the British army against Rome. (We begin to see how the plots mesh.) He makes a heroic stand with three other rustic soldiers, and these happy few save the King and win the war. Posthumus, however, gets himself arrested as an enemy to Britain, still trying to repent and now willing to die.

Although, as I said, these plots are not literally about families, all three have family resonances behind them. Even in the first plot, Cymbeline's politics are a magnification of family rebellion. He was brought up at the court of Rome where he learned a Roman honor that now teaches him to rebel against Rome itself. The second plot is literally about family conflicts, and it presents the crisis I have described. Cymbeline is Imogen's possessive father; he wants to "pen her up," as he says, and make his Queen her jailer. Such restraint takes an alternate form in Cymbeline's pastoral alter-ego, Belarius, who has stolen the King's two sons and keeps them penned up in a cave. The two fathers have opposite motives—Cymbeline wants to prevent Imogen from marrying outside the courtly circles appropriate to his dynastic expectations, and Belarius wants to keep his stolen "sons" from entering into the same courtly world. But in both cases the children are being kept at home and treated as things, not people ("Foolish thing!" Cymbeline calls Imogen, "Disloyal thing!"). Cymbeline further tightens the family circle by insisting that Imogen marry "his wive's sole son."

It is in the Posthumus plot, as I have suggested, that the family resonances are most striking, however. Posthumus' trouble at the beginning of the play is that he does not know who he is—and this is partly because he does not know who his family is. Literally, of course, everyone does know his family, but he is introduced as an orphan—his very name, Posthumus, proclaims his status as one born out of his parents' death, just as he was "ript" from his dying mother's womb. The first thing we hear about him is that he cannot be "delved to the root"—a dubious note in a play about family trees, in which every man who founds one is associated with a tree. And, just listening to Posthumus, we hear an immature young man—good, but not yet able to distinguish independence from rash rebellion. Posthumus is cut off from his elders; he himself tells us that the weakness which led him to wager on Imogen's chastity in the first place was his swaggering refusal to "be guided by others' experience." If Cymbeline imposes his own experience in too stifling a way, Posthumus tries too soon to break free from the experienced elders—as perhaps he broke free too soon from his mother's womb when he was "ript" from it.

Though his real family is dead, Posthumus' story is a sequence of substitute-family adventures. It is not at all obvious, but we can see that he associates himself with two new families and works out his relation each time to a new father and two older brothers, all as part of his other adventures. His first foster family is Cymbeline's, and here he makes a mistake and usurps his proper place when he elopes with Imogen. We may certainly sympathize with his desire to marry Imogen, but it is at best precipitous and at worst tainted with the disrespect and incest that show most clearly in the stepson Cloten. For, in a sense, Cymbeline's degenerate stepfamily is a symbolic reflection of Posthumus' actions, and Cloten is a parody of Posthumus himself. Cloten is of course Posthumus' opposite in so many ways: mean, proud, and cowardly—and he smells. Yet there are similarities, and these lie in more than their common passion for wagers and gambling. Imogen mistakes Cloten's *body* for Posthumus', and as for the spirit, Cloten's potential for selfish possessiveness is the very thing Posthumus must come to terms with. In fact, it is a Clotenish trait that nearly kills Posthumus' marriage, when he makes that bet and gives in to a boorish rage.

So Posthumus' mistakes with his first family coincide with his mistakes in his marriage. But he goes on to a second foster family, and this one leads to the healing of his marriage. Having killed Imogen (or so he thinks), Posthumus repents by joining Imogen's father's army, as we saw, and he promptly winds up fighting beside an unidentified father and two sons. (We of course know that these are really Cymbeline's own sons and their kidnapper, in disguise, and we can appreciate the ironic play among various levels of "real" and only apparent family ties.) This time Posthumus takes his proper place: brave, but not overbearing; accepting his position as nameless third son; subduing his own ends to those of the little family. He stands with Belarius in the "narrow lane," but instead of killing "the old man" in a repetition of an oedipal crime at the crossroads, he defends him selflessly, and the group single-handedly saves Britain. It is only when he has become a proper son that he becomes a man and takes his father's place, for Posthumus' father was known and named for his brave defense of Britain. Significantly, it is only when Posthumus goes into battle that he invokes his family's protection and takes on its name.

It is only when Posthumus moves from the older, suffocating family bonds, in which members are imprisoned and imprisoning, to this more generous conception of what it means to be part of a family, that he can establish a new and more mature relationship with his wife. At first he himself had been like a possessive parent, jealously guarding Imogen; when exiled, he left her with a "manacle of love," the bracelet he comes to believe in more than he believes in Imogen herself. Finally he winds up in his own prison, manacled and doomed. But once the characters find the right way of giving themselves to each other, the manacles of love become living, strengthening bonds. And when Imogen and Posthumus finally find each other at the end of the play, whether we hear "rock" or "lock" in the disputed word of Imogen's greeting, her words transform all the rocky prisons, bonds, bolts, and locks we have heard about earlier. Posthumus, not recognizing her, had pushed her away, but she embraces him, saying:

> Think that you are upon a [l]ock, and now
> Throw me again.
>
> (V.v. 262–63)

All the strongholds in the play are similary transformed: the British island, "paled in with rocks unscalable," or the "temple" Imogen, whose "lock" Iachimo did not pick after all.

Posthumus' prison is itself transformed by the dream he has there, in which his family forms a strong, unbroken circle around him and we see the bondage of the prison walls replaced by family bonds. (The stage directions are perfectly clear: beginning with a call for *solemn music*, they specify each family member and then order them all to "circle Posthumus round as he lies sleeping" [V.iv.28].) For Posthumus' achievement as a husband and a son is crowned by this vision of his family. Dead though they are, they appear physically on stage, breaking into the current action and revealing their implicit presence all along. They appear just when Posthumus finds himself, and the dream is a perfect climax to his story.

The dream is a climax for the whole play as well, and I want to turn finally to it now to see more clearly the general role of the family in the play. The dream comes at the moment when the action has gotten more tangled than we ever see it elsewhere in Shakespeare, and when the levels of duplicity and sheer misunderstanding have multiplied so that even the audience, which sees everything, has some trouble sorting them out. The dream reassures both the characters and the audience that the complexities will be made simple and the separations will become re-unions, and that the "extraordinary blindness" of the characters has been countered all along by the insight of an all-seeing god.

What sort of dream can achieve all this? The critics have come to call it the vision of Jupiter, and so it is. I have left out the best part of the dream, actually, in my first description. The great god comes down from the sky in a marvelous flourish: "Jupiter descends in thunder and light-ning, sitting upon an eagle. He throws a thunderbolt. The Ghosts fall on their knees" (V.iv.). And when he leaves, "The marble pavement closes; he is entered / His radiant roof" (V.iv.90–91). But the more homely aspect of the dream, which is a vision of Posthumus' family, is just as important, if not more so. The family frames Jupiter's appearance and is responsible for it. They are the ones who summon him and ask him to account for himself. (Why has he been treating their son this way?!) And they remain behind to have the last word after he leaves.

The dream can be interpreted either as a revelation of the divine forces in human affairs, or as a revelation of the familial matrix that underlies all human experience. We can name the force that guides the action in Cymbeline's world, either by interpreting "from above" and calling it Jupiter, or by interpreting "from below" and calling it the effect of family.

The two phrases "from above" and "from below" allude purposely to Freud's account of the interpretation of dreams, in which he distinguishes on the one hand between traditional dream interpretation, which looks to the bizarre images in dreams for prophecies and god's word, and Freud's own more mundane interpretation, which looks for derivatives of early infantile complexes. Freud would not be surprised to discover that a dream about God was "really" about the dreamer's father. Of course, Freud's answers to questions about how gods and fathers were related were often reductive answers: the "illusions" of art and religion derive from the forgotten mundane truths about the family. But the play insists on both interpretations. What is revealed in the dream is a guiding force that comes out of the family and is associated with it but is as "rare," to use a recurring word from the play, as a divine power would be.

My point is that while Shakespeare avoids the Freudian reduction of the divine vision, he still "psychologizes" or internalizes it. Shakespeare's originality lies not only in joining gods and fathers, combining two different aspects of experience, but in joining and transforming two familiar literary traditions so that each takes on new meaning. The first of these is the divine epiphany, the entrance of a *deux ex machina*, who was expected in the narrative romances on which Shakespeare drew and who literally appeared in machines of various subtlety on the sixteenth-century stage, including Shakespeare's own plays: Hymen in *As You Like It* and Diana in *Pericles*. What is extraordinary about Posthumus' epiphany, however, is that while Jupiter does indeed descend, he neither does nor says anything of substance—no rescues, no revelations, and only the flimsiest, most circumstantially creaky, of oracles. Essentially all he does is say "I am here."

The same is true of Shakespeare's transformation of the second tradition that he drew upon for the dream—the family recognition scene. For just as Shakespeare gives us an intervening god who does nothing, he gives us a recognition scene in which nothing is recognized. Posthumus is not literally reunited with his family, the way children in romances always are, and he does not learn anything literally new about his identity. He is not a prince and was not meant to be; he is merely his father's son. After the dream, nothing has changed except his state of mind; Posthumus has simply recognized his past and therefore recognized himself. Here, as with the divine epiphany, what is usually staged as an outward movement of the plot—and what appears as such in Shakespeare's other romances—has become instead an inward movement of the mind. Other young heroes (or more often heroines) in the romances must also find their parents in order to find themselves. What is different here is that Posthumus cannot find his parents in the flesh; he must find the idea of his parents. "Sleep, thou hast been a grandsire and begot /A father to me," says Posthumus when he wakes: he is the child of his own vision (V.iv.93–94). Shakespeare is not Sophocles, and he has not written another *Oedipus*. What he has done in this play is just what Freud did in his theory *about* Oedipus: he has rationalized a myth by making it into a psychological truth.

I want now to suggest that this semi-psychoanalytic insight about the family's presence can help us to understand and cope with the difficulties, obscurities, and ambiguities in *Cymbeline*—because the family's ambiguous presence in the characters' lives is closely related to the remarkable degree of confusion unique to this play, and to the pervasive uncertainty about just what is going on. Of course, no one finally trusts appearances in any Shakespearean world—at least we do not usually trust those characters who trust appearances and demand ocular proof. But in this Shakespearean world, appearances are almost never right or even determinable; the characters are literally nearsighted and otherwise inclined to misinterpret or overinterpret. But even more unsettling, not only do we mistrust external appearances here but also internal ones. We mistrust even those overwhelming inner passions that seem to be the rock-bottom reality of life.

This is the kind of distrust more familiar to the psychoanalysts, and *Cymbeline*, more than any other Shakespearean play, comes closest to the strange unsettling revelation of depths below depths unearthed in psychoanalysis. It presents a world where identities shift—and so do loyalties (Posthumus dresses like a Briton to defend Britain and then puts on Roman clothes and is arrested); where past suddenly overtakes present; where one emotion turns into its opposite. *Cymbeline* shows us what it is like to be a creature of the past, a creature with a latency period and latent meanings in everything we do. The play shows what it is to be an individual whose identity paradoxically depends on being part of a family in which that identity is threatened; an individual whose conscious experience is colored by *un*conscious, and whose current life is always shaped by a quiet, or not so quiet, symbolic force from the past.

Cymbeline has been called a history play, but it is a history play of the individual too, and it shows that what we are now comes out of what we *were*. Like Oedipus, its characters keep meeting their past and must give it a place, just as Cymbeline must finally "pay tribute" to the Rome that generated him and his ideals, even though he has outwardly defeated the Roman army. The play presents a world in which a "posthumus" child finds life only by recreating his dead parents, and where people who had seemed dead come alive in strange ways. Interestingly enough, the play also ensures that we in the audience also keep meeting figures like Iachimo/Iago from our past lives with Shakespeare, and it forces us to find a way of incorporating that past without letting it take over.

There are many scenes in *Cymbeline* where Shakespeare demonstrates the family resonances enriching—and confusing—the characters' experience, but I will mention only one here. The scene comes just past the middle of the action, when everyone is moving to Wales. In the political plot, the Roman forces are gathering there; in the second, or dynastic plot, Cymbeline's kidnapped sons are living there; and in the marriage plot, Imogen is heading there (in disguise, of course) to find her husband. In addition, when Imogen arrives in Wales (disguised as the boy Fidele), she accidentally wanders into the cave where her kidnapped brothers have been living for the last twenty years with their kindly kidnapper, though neither they nor she realizes anyone else's true identity. The scene I am talking about comes after Imogen, alias "Fidele," has been living with the brothers for a while and is suddenly discovered "dead" by one of them, though *we* know she isn't really dead but only drugged.

The scene begins when the young man, whose real name is Arviragus but who is known as Cadwal, comes onstage carrying the dead body of what he thinks is the boy Fidele. This death makes the young man remember the death of their mother (rather, of the woman they have taken all along to be their mother, but whom we know was merely the kidnapper's wife). But this is not all the death evokes. For us in the audience, the scene evokes Lear's entrance with the dead Cordelia in his arms, and, if we are loose enough, it evokes the *pietà* behind Lear's posture. Behind the *pietà*, it evokes an original image of the mother with a living child in her arms. In addition, when we hear Fidele called a "lily" in this scene, we may remember an earlier scene in the play—a time when Imogen was not dead but asleep and Iachimo spied on her in order to get information to mislead Posthumus. Then too she was called a "lily" as she lay senseless.

Now Fidele is not Fidele, of course—"he" is Imogen; nor is he dead. He has merely taken a potion that the wicked Queen gave to his friend thinking it was poison, but which we know is a harmless sleeping medicine. For that matter, not only isn't this Fidele dead, but Arviragus' mother, whom he mourned before, was not his mother either. Nonetheless, all these confusions do not invalidate Arviragus' emotion—any more than they invalidate the audience's esthetic and even playful appreciation of the scene. We take it for granted that we who are watching can bring something to our experience of this scene: other scenes in the play, scenes in other Shakespearean plays, a whole cultural matrix, and all our common human experience as well. What Shakespeare shows, in addition, is that even the characters most directly and least esthetically involved in the experience also bring things to it, making it richer and more complicated that it "really" is.

But experience is always richer than it "really" is, so long as there are people to observe it. The exaggerated complications in *Cymbeline* make us realize with even more force than usual that "reality" finally lies in the enrichment, and the truth lies in the excess. Arviragus' "excessive" or mistaken emotion, we finally realize, is appropriate after all: Fidele really is his sister. Arviragus is responding to a larger truth than the literal—just like Freud's patients, whose literally false *déjà vu* experiences are yet true representatives of their "psychological constellation" of the moment.

Partly because the play's twists and self-consciousness encourage our detachment, they also encourage us to consider curiously those things we usually take for granted, and to ask not only "Who is that?" but "How do I know?"—to wonder about the nature of identity. The action suggests and discards several answers to that question and leaves us, I think, with a more amorphous and unsettling one—one more like the psychoanalyst's. We already knew that identity is more than a surface phenomenon. Only in the case of a sham like Cloten do clothes make the man and give him a lineage (his "tailor" was his "grandfather" [IV.ii.81–82]). And only a promiscuous Italian "jay" (whore) finds her beauty's "mother" in her painting, as Imogen says (III.iv.50–51). But identity is more than skin deep too, in this play. A mole identifies Guiderius at the end, but it was just such a mole that misled Posthumus about Imogen's true nature earlier. And not only moles but whole trunks can mislead; the trunk in which Iachimo hides to observe the mole is only a prelude to the more spectacular confusion of identities when Imogen mistakes Cloten's headless trunk for Posthumus'.

To discover his identity, Posthumus must look not only at the present trunk but at the roots. He must look to his family—but he must look in the very special, imaginative way we have seen. Instead of literally discovering his family, he must simply reimagine them; he must make what he can of the past, recreate his family in his dreams. And if the puns on which I have partly based this argument seem tenuous already, I will add one that is even more far-fetched and seemingly peripheral. There are some literal or vegetable "roots" that appear in the play during Imogen's pastoral interlude as Fidele. For she takes on the job of cooking for her hosts and makes them dishes, as they say, fit for the gods, when she "cut[s] our roots in characters" to make her brothers' broth (IV.ii.49). I am not suggesting that Shakespeare here is giving away *his* recipe for making characters out of their roots (for one thing, "character" did not yet mean quite what it means for us). But I am suggesting that the farcical misunderstandings in this play are matched by its seemingly trivial puns. And that it is in just such flickering, uncertain, off-center signs that the unconscious meaning of our love manifests itself, and the unconscious depths of character, which are always *felt*, make themselves *known*.

A. D. NUTTALL

"The Merchant of Venice"

Shakespeare saw that Rome was not England. He also saw that Venice was not London.

Venice, to the Elizabethans, was in some ways what Hollywood was to the rest of the world in the 1930s, or perhaps it would be better to say a mixture of Hollywood and Paris: *the* glamorous, daring, brilliant, wicked city. Even today as the senile, jewel-encrusted Bride of the Adriatic sinks malodorously beneath the waters of the Lagoon, one can glimpse, in the real city, what the effect must once have been. The rest of the world is black, white and grey and here alone, among gilded lions, rosy brick and white marble stained with green, is the Coloured City. The most neutral description of Venice begins to sound like overwriting. Many things, to be sure, have changed. The city of sexual licence has become oddly puritanical; notices in the *vaporetto* stops alert the visitor to the possible indecorousness of his or her costume. Meanwhile the frescoed walls still blaze with the great Venetian scenes of social splendour, ruffs, brocade, fruit, wine and amazing people. Here is the only adequate equivalent in visual art to the Shakespearean mode of, say, *Antony and Cleopatra*. The painters of his own land, Isaac Oliver or Nicholas Hilliard, lacked the necessary physical amplitude and much more besides. In Shakespeare's time travellers' reports of the city abounded and moralists debated whether it was better, in the name of Experience, to send one's son to Venice (with all its attendant perils) or to provide him with suitable books about the place instead.

But the strangest thing of all, to the Elizabethan Englishman, is

From *A New Mimesis: Shakespeare and the Representation of Reality*. Copyright © 1983 by A. D. Nuttall. Methuen & Co., Ltd.

still unsaid. In 1597 (the probable date of *The Merchant of Venice*) the cycle by which we are sustained was plainly visible to any inhabitant of this country. The food he ate he saw first in his own or his neighbour's fields. Even in the nineteenth century Thomas Hardy tells in the four-teenth chapter of *The Mayor of Casterbridge* how from the streets of an ordinary English country town you could actually nod to the men cutting corn in the fields. Corn, bread, beans, pigs, cows, sheep, wool, cloth, all made a natural sense, authorized and watched over by the seasonally changing English sky. But Venice is actually built in the sea. Salt, undrinkable seawater flows in its great streets. Again and again the traveller to Venice must have thought, first, 'How can anyone live in this barren place?' and, next, 'How can these people be so rich?' No trees, no grass, but everywhere brick, marble, porphyry, bronze and gold. Here was a people living in a way that in Shakespeare's time must still have seemed partly unnatural, for they appeared to live on money alone. Money, traditionally defined as the medium of exchange, itself barren, had here proved strangely fruitful and multiplied itself hourly in the market place.

To put the case in this simple way involves both exaggeration and some distortion. The English practised usury and Venice had her subject territories. Yet the fundamental contrast retains a certain force. Venice was the single, most spectacular example of the power of wealth to beget wealth, and its miraculous setting in the sea is emblematic of that power. Venice is the landless landlord over all.

The crucial part of this finds expression in Shakespeare's *The Merchant of Venice*. It is in a way futile to search for the sources of Shakespeare's knowledge of Venice. By the time he came to write *Othello* he was able to consult Contarini's *The Commonwealth and Government of Venice*, perhaps in Lewis Lewkenor's translation of 1599. But meanwhile London was full of vigorous talk and Venice was an excellent subject of conversation. For all we know Shakespeare may have visited Venice himself in 'the missing years'. The word 'merchant' alerts us first. In his plays set in England merchants hardly figure. We may revive the original impact of the title if we substitute 'the Capitalist' for 'the Merchant', but such 'equivalents' are never truly equivalent. Then, the imagery of money, the chink of coins pervades this play as it does no other. Moreover, this golden imagery is in places pointed very sardonically; it is applied with an almost brutal directness to the central romantic love story of the play. There was of course a convention of applying the language of finance to love, but the point of the convention lay in a paradox, the paradox of applying the lowest and most contemptible terms to the highest and at the same time most human situation, love. Thus the usual thing is to set the metaphor at odds with its application. The lady 'out-values value', makes wealth into poverty as long as she is lacking, and so on. In place of this serviceable and well-worn ingenuity *The Merchant of Venice* offers a disquieting simplicity. Bassanio tells of his love in these words:

> In Belmont is a lady richly left,
> And she is fair and fairer than that word,
> Of wondrous virtues.
>
> (I. i.161–2)

First he tells us of the money and then, in simple, joyous juxtaposition, of her beauty and virtue. Bassanio is not an out-and-out fortune-hunter who is after Portia for her money. He really loves her and her wealth is simply a component of her general attractiveness. There is a certain repellent ingenuousness about Bassanio. He can trust his own well-constituted nature. It would never allow him to fall in love with a poor woman; for, after all, poor women are not attractive. After such a start a strange light is cast on the rest of his speech:

> her sunny locks
> Hang on her temples like a golden fleece,
> Which makes her seat of Belmont Colchos' strond,
> And many Jasons come in quest of her.
>
> (I. i.169–72)

The Golden Fleece in another context would have been a paradox of love language. Here it is uncomfortably close to the centre of Bassanio's interest.

Shakespeare deliberately involves Bassanio's love from the outset in a faintly humiliating financial atmosphere. But he plants no overt stylistic signals of what he is about so that the effect is faint indeed. The flow is as smooth as that of any poem by Drayton or Daniel and one almost begins to suspect Shakespeare of a cynical contempt for his audience ('I'll make them drink this and they'll never know what they swallowed') were it not for the fact that, in the trial scene, he plainly relies on the fact that some of this, at least, has stuck in the mind. Bassanio's first move in his courtship is less than heroic. It is to touch his friend Antonio for a loan so that he can improve his sartorial image.

It is curious how wit can consist in the very avoidance of an expected complexity. One may compare the conversational practice known in the slang of forty years ago as 'kidding on the level'; the speaker makes a remark which sounds ironic but the real joke lies in the fact that every word is literally intended: 'Hello darling, you know I hate your guts.'

Shakespeare with his strangely bland coupling in this play of the language of love and the language of money is in a manner kidding on the level. Even Portia, who is generous in her love, speaks of her own money as one of her attractions in a strangely unconscious manner when she says to Bassanio,

> You see me, Lord Bassanio, where I stand,
> Such as I am. Though for myself alone
> I would not be ambitious in my wish
> To wish myself much better, yet for you
> I would be trebled twenty times myself,
> A thousand times more fair, ten thousand times more rich,
> That only to stand high in your account
> I might in virtues, beauties, livings, friends,
> Exceed account. But the full sum of me
> Is sum of something which, to term in gross,
> Is an unlesson'd girl.
>
> (III. ii. 149–60)

Notice how wealth is twice placed at the summit of an ascending rhetorical scale involving character and beauty. The accountant's language, 'to term in gross', is uncomfortably close to what is actually going on. An imprudent director—I could not call him perverse—might well have Bassanio surprised by these words in the very act of appraising with his eye the value of the room's hangings.

But Portia is not really unconscious. She understands Bassanio with that peculiar, pitiless clarity of love which characterizes all the great Shakespearean heroines, these women who so utterly transcend their contemptible lovers. After she has said that she will pay off Antonio's debt for Bassanio, she says to her betrothed,

> Since you are dear bought, I will love you dear.
>
> (III. ii. 315)

The play on 'dear' is not wholly comfortable and, at the same time, the love is real and unstinting.

It is perhaps not surprising that this speech should help to make one of the principal 'echoes' of the play:

> 'Tis dearly bought, 'tis mine, and I will have it.
>
> (IV. i. 100)

This time it is not one of the nice people who speaks. It is Shylock and he is talking about a pound of flesh cut from the breast of Antonio.

The Merchant of Venice is about the Old Law and the New; about the low Jewish justice of an eye for an eye and a tooth for a tooth and the way this justice is transcended by Christian charity and mercy. The climactic trial scene is archetypal. The black-clad Jew haggling for the flesh of the fair-skinned Christian, the supervening figure of Justice who is also Love, all this is the stuff of legend. It recalls the medieval *Processus Belial*, as has often been observed, in which the Virgin Mary defends Man against the Devil who lays legal claim to his soul. Behind this analogue lies the doctrine of the atonement itself, in which God paid the legal price for man with his son who was also himself. In the fact of such powerful patterning all ethical ambiguities, we shall be told, must surely fall silent. The Jew is wicked, unhappy, usurious, greedy, vengeful. The Christians are happy, generous, forgiving. This, it might be said, is the plain meaning of the play, and it takes a determined 'Transparent' critic to darken it. In fact it is not difficult to do so. For as soon as we enter the fiction and treat the figures of the drama as possible human beings in a possible, great mercantile city, everything feels slightly different.

It is true, of course, that certain archetypes operate powerfully in the play. But it is not true that they are the only thing there, that the mind should be arrested at their level of generality, that there is nothing behind them. It is Shakespeare's way to take an archetype or a stereotype and then work, so to speak, against it, without ever overthrowing it. Shakespeare himself darkens the pristine clarity of these ethical opposi-tions and he does so, in the first instance, with allusions to money. To this he adds the figure of Antonio, about whom shadows gather from the beginning. If Bassanio's love for Portia sounds uneasily shallow and merce-nary, Antonio's love for Bassanio is disquietingly intense. The stereotypi-cal impression of Christian society in *The Merchant of Venice* is of a world of felicity, conviviality, parties, easy commerce of like spirits, harmony. In all this Antonio is from the first incongruous. He is melancholic. Later, when he is in great peril, he sees himself as in some way polluted and wishes to die:

> I am a tainted wether of the flock,
> Meetest for death; the weakest kind of fruit
> Drops earliest to the ground, and so let me.
> (IV. i. 114–16)

In the first scene of the play Antonio is left alone with Bassanio and says, with an air of one coming to the point,

> Well; tell me now what lady is the same
> To whom you swore a secret pilgrimage,
> That you to-day promis'd to tell me of?
> (I. i. 119–21)

Bassanio does not answer, but dwells at length on his lack of cash. Antonio with extreme generosity places at his friend's disposal,

My purse, my person, my extremest means.
(I. i.138)

The reference to 'person' and 'extremest means' evidently looks forward to the horror so narrowly averted in Act IV. The 'Opaque' critic will feel an impulse at this point to arrest the structure of allusion at the level of thematic motifs: Antonio's words 'pre-echo' the situation in Act IV as an early musical phrase may 'pre-echo' a major development in the last movement of a symphony. The 'Transparent' critic will not be patient of such impediments to humane inference; he will at once begin to wonder if Antonio, aware of the dangerous extremity of his own love for Bassanio, senses the obscure likelihood of a violent outcome. Some may go further, and surmise a kind of deathwish in Antonio. None of this is verifiable or has the force of necessary truth. A moderate alliance of Opaque and Transparent criticism might tell us that Antonio speaks with sudden violence because of the strength of his love, but neither foresees nor deliberately invokes the later horror; that is 'inadvertently' alluded to, by a species of dramatic irony. But what happens to the ordinary spectator, sitting in the audience? It is possible that the majority of spectators, since 1597, had no conscious reaction at all; simply did not separately 'notice' the connection between Antonio's words. But those who did, explicitly, notice the connection will have construed it in terms of character, to a greater or lesser extent. For the bias of theatrical apprehension, oddly enough, is to 'Transparency'. The figures on the stage are apprehended as people. The very tawdriness of the visible means of presentation in a theatre renders this compensatory exercise of Transparent interpretation the more necessary. Otherwise all audiences would see as Natasha saw in Tolstoy's *War and Peace* (VIII. ix) and drama would die. In the history of drama Brechtian alienation is very much the special case, but even it is not fully Opaque, entirely formalist. Brecht, admittedly, deliberately arrests the apprehension of the spectator at the level of the ostentatiously artificial means; he 'foregrounds' the mechanisms of his art. But he counts on a residuum of unused imaginative sympathy, which he is able to channel the more efficiently in the direction of 'doctrine'. In so far as this channelling occurs (and it is essential to his enterprise) his art is neither abstract nor formalist. Meanwhile it is manifestly, *creakingly* unlike other forms of dramatic experience. It may resemble the drama of 'primitive' societies as that drama appears to a cultural outsider, but the *Towneley Play of Noah*, say, never felt to its first observers as Brechtian drama feels to us.

The most natural inference from any or all of the Transparent interpretations of Antonio's words, from the most modest to the most speculative, is that Antonio loves Bassanio with a love so intense as to throw Bassanio's more decorous love for Portia into unhappy relief. Some may feel that this secondary inference is merely monstrous and inherently improbable. But in a manner the thought of Antonio in love occurred to Solanio within the play before it occurred to any spectator or reader outside it, for at I. i.46 he suddenly says to Antonio,

Why, then, you are in love.

Antonio answers, 'Fie, fie!' Solanio treats this as a negative but, strictly speaking, it is not. The New Arden editor J. Russell Brown notes with admirable precision that it is 'an exclamation of reproach rather than a clear negative'. Of course Solanio does not suggest that Antonio is in love with Bassanio. He merely plants the idea that Antonio's melancholy is connected with love and then the play itself, with overwhelming single-ness of purpose, directs us to a single love object. Antonio's love is exercised against the bias of financial interest. Setting aside the more obvious impediments, one could not imagine Antonio speaking of Bassanio in the unconsciously self-interested way Bassanio spoke of Portia. Bassanio sees Portia as the centre of his future happiness and wealth. Antonio looks very differently at Bassanio; he sees the beloved extinction of both wealth and happiness.

A seed is thus planted at the back of our minds and the progress of the drama brings it to an obscure flowering. In II. viii Solanio describes the parting of Bassanio and Antonio, in which Antonio was unable to hold back his tears, and comments, 'I think he only loves the world for him' (II. viii.50). While the dapper Bassanio seeks joy and a fortune in Belmont, Antonio, for mere love, faces mutilation and death in the city. When all seems to be over Antonio says to Bassanio,

> Commend me to your honourable wife;
> Tell her the process of Antonio's end;
> Say how I lov'd you; speak me fair in death;
> And, when the tale is told, bid her be judge
> Whether Bassanio had not once a love.
>
> (IV. i.268–72)

What gives the business of the ring-begging in V. i its extraordinary tension if it is not the half-buried conflict between male love and hetero-sexual love? Here formally—and not so formally—a brief dramatic 'min-uet' enacts the rivalry of Antonio and Portia. At its end, although we are in a comedy and the figures are pairing off in the soft Italian night, Antonio does not get a partner. We may remember that great, drab line from the Sonnets:

> I may not evermore acknowledge thee.
>
> (xxxvi. 9)

Given this 'transparent' psychological intuition the story of the caskets ceases to be an inert, decorative centerpiece and becomes charged with latent irony. Bassanio, dressed up to the nines with someone else's money, is mockingly rewarded with the gift proper to plain virtue. The leaden casket bore as its legend,

> Who chooseth me must give and hazard all he hath.
>
> (II. vii. 16)

W. H. Auden in one of the most brilliant critical remarks of the century observed that this requirement is met by two people in the play, neither of whom is Bassanio. It is met by Antonio and Shylock. That is where the real *agon* lies.

I have granted that the stereotype gives us a mercenary Shylock and merciful Christians (the Christians being 'above' vengeance) and that this stereotype is observed in the play. But we have already seen how Shylock's savage ''Tis dearly bought' was pre-echoed, in a more elevated setting, by Portia. 'My daughter! O my ducats!' cries the grief-stricken, confused, mercenary Shylock (II. viii. 15). 'Like a golden fleece', says Bassanio (I. i. 170).

> I will make fast the doors, and gild myself
> With some moe ducats, and be with you straight.
>
> (II. vi. 49–50)

says Jessica to her Christian lover, as they make off in the night with the turquoise Leah gave to Shylock when he was a bachelor (III. i. 105). All of which gives added force to Shylock's plea at the trial, where he says, in effect, 'Remember me? I'm the usurer, the man who makes deals. So where is the pound of flesh which is owed me?'

In the course of the play we are told certain things about the state of Venice. The Christians have among them 'many a purchased slave' (IV. i. 90). Jews are employed when ready capital is needed. They are considered as aliens (as emerges when Shylock forfeits his goods and places his life at the Doge's mercy, on the ground that he sought the life of a *Venetian* citizen). All this Auden brings out in his admirable essay. Shakespeare is clearly aware of the covert manner in which Christian merchants make money breed, which is by the ancient doctrine a kind of usury ('usury' originally referred to any form of interest and was later— very revealingly—restricted to *excessive* interest). Shakespeare is likewise aware of the lower, 'coarser' kinds of interest for which Shylock and his kind are needed. He shows with great clarity the almost exclusively mercantile character of the Venetian economy:

> the trade and profit of the city
> Consisteth of all nations.
>
> (III. iii. 30–1)

Here it is Antonio who speaks. The tenor of his argument is that justice must be maintained because if it is not foreign investors may withdraw their money. It is hard to imagine a similar subordination of justice to the profit motive in one of the English histories. In this way Shakespeare shows both the separateness and the economic symbiosis of Christian and Jew.

In I. iii Antonio tells Shylock that he makes no use of usury (line 65) and Shylock in reply tells the curious story of Laban, who agreed with Jacob that he (Laban) should have any particoloured lambs that were born while Jacob could have the others. At conception time Laban set peeled wands before the ewes, who subsequently gave birth to particoloured lambs. Antonio in reply eagerly distinguishes 'venturing' from 'usury'; Laban, he insists, merely trusted in God, he had no power of his own to affect the outcome of the bargain. Or are the ewes to be understood as themselves signifying gold and silver . . . ? Shylock, sardonic, uncoopera- tive, turns the question aside (91):

> I cannot tell; I make it breed as fast.

Antonio, one senses, is not confident that he has won the argument (it is hard to be sure that Laban did not intervene, with his peeled wands, for had he simply wanted to accept God's dispensation he could surely have waited till it became evident at lambing time). Antonio's words 'The devil can cite scripture for his purpose' are the words of a man who is holding fast to a conviction that his opponent must be wrong, but cannot quite see how. Meanwhile we sense that Antonio's money (whether by 'venturing' or indirect usury) may breed as fast as Shylock's. He is the merchant, after all.

We thus have a curious situation in this play. Shakespeare em- ploys throughout a latent system of allusions to the economic character of Venetian society and this system of allusions, instead of corroborating the stark opposition of good and evil proposed in the play's main action, subtly undermines it. The economic allusions tell us—against the simple plot—that the Jews and the Christians are deeply similar, for all are mercenary. The general vice which Christians ascribe to the Jews is one of which they are themselves—in a less obvious manner—guilty. The Jews therefore perform a peculiar ethical function in that they bear the brunt of the more obvious dirty work necessary to the glittering city. This counter-system of allusions is organically joined to the drama as a whole and therefore exhibits artistic form. But at the same time it is mimetic of reality, in a pretty specific manner. For it can hardly be pure coincidence that Venice really was thus. A recent historian of Venice in the sixteenth century, Brian Pullan, notes, 'Jews were deemed to be there for the purpose of saving Christians from committing the sin of usurious lending', and again, 'The Venetians had consistently combined the attitude of ritual contempt for the Jews with a shrewd and balanced appreciation of their economic utility.' He quotes the diarist, Marino Sanuto, 'Jews are even more necessary than bakers to a city, and especially to this one, for the sake of the general welfare.' It is quite obvious that Shakespeare, Sanuto, Pullan are all discussing a single, real object.

As commonly with Transparent criticism there is a penumbra of unverifiable, remoter possibilities. Since these also compose a relevant system they are worth noting. Shakespeare's sense of background may be very detailed indeed. Anyone who knew anything about Jewish religion would be aware that Shylock, no less than Antonio, was out on a limb. First, the practice of usury is, in the Jewish religion also, tainted with moral dubiety. *Leviticus* 25: 35–7 simply forbids usury, but *Deuteronomy* 23:19–20 permits the exaction of interest from a stranger, though not from a brother (hence the title of Auden's essay). Thus as the Christians need the Jews, so the Jews need the Christians to practise usury on. The symbiosis is more perfectly symmetrical than we may have thought. Shylock, however, breaks with his religion, in particular with *Deuteronomy* 24:6, when he agrees to take Antonio's *life* as a pledge. The passage in *Deuteronomy* uses the metaphor of a millstone: 'No man shall take the nether or the upper millstone to pledge: for he taketh a man's life to pledge'; the metaphor suggests that 'life' is here equivalent to 'means of living'. We may compare *Ecclesiasticus* 34:22, 'He that taketh away his neighbour's living, slayeth him.' Shylock makes precisely this equation at IV. i.371–2:

> you take my life
> When you do take the means whereby I live.

This pattern of scriptural reference would tend to reinforce an impression, already subliminally present in the play, that the Christians, in taking away Shylock's capital, are doing to him what he wished to do to Antonio. The act of mercy has an inner likeness to the act of revenge. Shakespeare completes the ironic pattern by making Antonio say to Portia, 'Sweet lady, you have given me life and living' (V. i.286). It is typical of Shakespeare's genius that in his great comedy of economic reality he finds the single point where language most powerfully asserts the interdependence of economics and humanity, in the etymological affinity between a person's *life* and a person's *living*. This is in its turn analogous to the economic and ethical meanings of *worth* and *value*.

One effect of Shakespeare's economic subtheme is to make one suspect that the high-minded talk of the Christians is a luxury available only to the dominant class. Old money can afford to talk in this way. We notice that Portia speaks of mercy when Shylock is sharpening his knife for Antonio, but as soon as the tables are turned and Shylock is on the run, Gratiano cries out again and again that Shylock must hang. Shylock is in fact forgiven and the central ethical plot is clearly dominant at this point. Yet even here one senses something less than ethical, a faint smell of patronizing contempt in the very exercise of mercy. Again, though Shylock's money is new and the Christian's old, the misfortune of Antonio the merchant shows us that we are now in a world in which even old money can be horribly at risk. Portia alone has so much old money that she rises above the rest, as Belmont rises above Venice in the sweet summer night. In this way a cruel reductive pun is worked, dramatically rather than verbally, on the notion of transcendence.

That Shakespeare's picture of Venice is not one of minute, documentary accuracy is obvious. The law shown in this play, for example, is fairy-tale law, not real law. But Shakespeare's art in this play remains— not only in the obvious triumphs of probable human motivation at the level of individual character, but also at the less accessible level of influences and conditions—cognitive, with a breath-taking intelligence. He saw the economic peculiarity of Venice and then made the second, greater leap of perceiving how an economic fabric may condition the very nature of moral action: mercy and charity lose their primal simplicity; in the new order personal loyalty, bereft of traditional feudal support, is both sharpened and made more dubious. The ancient stratagem of the Atonement, whereby God sends his substitute to take on himself our sins and save the world, fascinated Shakespeare both in this play and in *Measure for Measure*. There a figure of Christian mercy discovers that his city needs not mercy but rigorous justice, finds a substitute to do his dirty work for him and, when the substitute is drawn into evil of the worst sort, forgives him with a charity at once generous and insulting. In both plays

Shakespeare admits what others might have wished to exclude, the ugly anthropological ancestor of the Atonement, the scapegoat, the unhappy creature on which a society vents its bad conscience.

But the most difficult point remains. These half-buried echoes and subauditions in the play really do compose a structure, and an exciting subversive thesis. But they are not the play. After years of pious criticism the views of A. D. Moody and H. C. Goddard are very seductive. Moody says, 'Shylock avows the moral sense by which they actually live. We can see that in condemning Shylock they are condemning their own sins. It would seem then that they are making him literally their scapegoat . . . or, as H. C. Goddard puts it, "They project onto him what they have dismissed from their own consciousness as too disturbing." ' But in agreeing with this we are in danger of forgetting the real generosity, however produced, of the Christians, the real ferocity, however explained, of Shylock. They did forgive Shylock. Shylock would have torn open the breast of Antonio. These are things which no theatrical experience of the play will ever let you forget. As William Empson says, we must view the Bassanio-Portia relationship with 'a generous scepticism which can believe at once that people are and are not guilty.' So Shakespeare will not let us rest even here. The subversive counter-thesis is itself too easy. We may now begin to see that he is perhaps the least sentimental dramatist who ever lived. We begin to understand what is meant by holding the mirror up to nature.

Chronology

1564	William Shakespeare born at Stratford-on-Avon to John Shakespeare, a butcher, and Mary Arden. He is baptized on April 26.
1582	Marries Anne Hathaway in November.
1583	Daughter Susanna born, baptized on May 26.
1585	Twins Hamnet and Judith born, baptized on February 2.
1588–90	Sometime during these years, Shakespeare goes to London, without family.
1590	*The Comedy of Errors.*
1593–94	*The Taming of the Shrew, The Two Gentlemen of Verona.* Shakespeare becomes a sharer in the Lord Chamberlain's company of actors.
1595–96	*A Midsummer Night's Dream, Love's Labour's Lost.* Son Hamnet dies. Grant of arms to father.
1597	*The Merchant of Venice.* Purchases New Place in Stratford.
1598–1600	*As You Like It, Much Ado About Nothing, Twelfth Night* and *The Merry Wives of Windsor.* Moves his company to the new Globe Theatre.
1601	Shakespeare's father dies, buried on September 8.
1603–04	*All's Well that Ends Well, Measure for Measure.* Shakespeare's company becomes the King's Men.
1607–08	*Pericles.* Marriage of daughter Susanna on June 5. Mother dies, buried on September 9.
1609	*Cymbeline.* The King's Men move to Blackfriars Playhouse.
1610–11	*The Winter's Tale, The Tempest.* Shakespeare retires to Stratford.
1616	Marriage of daughter Judith on February 10. William Shakespeare dies at Stratford on April 23.
1623	Publication of the First Folio edition of Shakespeare's plays.

Contributors

HAROLD BLOOM, Sterling Professor of the Humanities at Yale University, is the author of *The Anxiety of Influence*, *Poetry and Repression* and many other volumes of literary criticism. His forthcoming study, *Freud: Transference and Authority*, attempts a full-scale reading of all of Freud's major writings. He is the general editor of *The Chelsea House Library of Literary Criticism*.

ELMER EDGAR STOLL was Professor of English at the University of Minnesota. His books include *Shakespeare and Other Masters* and *Art and Artifice in Shakespeare*.

G. WILSON KNIGHT was Professor of English at the University of Leeds. His books include *The Wheel of Fire* and *The Imperial Theme*.

M. C. BRADBROOK was Lecturer in English at Cambridge University. She is the author of *Themes and Conventions of Elizabethan Tragedy* and *The Growth and Structure of Elizabethan Comedy*.

HAROLD C. GODDARD was Professor of English at Swarthmore College. He is the author of *The Meaning of Shakespeare*.

REUBEN BROWER was Professor of English at Harvard University. He is the author of *The Fields of Light: An Experiment in Critical Reading*.

ANNE BARTON is a Fellow of New College and University Lecturer in English at Oxford University. She is the author of *Shakespeare and the Idea of a Play*.

JOHN HOLLANDER is Professor of English at Yale University. His criticism includes *The Untuning of the Sky*, *Vision and Resonance* and *The Figure of Echo*. His poetry is most readily available in his *Spectral Emanations: New and Selected Poems*.

C. L. BARBER was Professor of Literature at the University of California at Santa Cruz. He is the author of *Shakespeare's Festive Comedy*.

A. P. ROSSITER was Lecturer at Durham University and at Cambridge University. His books include *Angel With Horns* and *English Drama*.

NORTHROP FRYE is University Professor at the University of Toronto. His books include *Anatomy of Criticism*, *Fearful Symmetry* and *Fools of Time*.

HOWARD FELPERIN is Professor of English at the University of Melbourne. His books include *Shakespearean Representation* and *Shakespearean Romance*.

ROSALIE COLIE was Professor of English at Wesleyan College. Her books include *The Resources of Kind: Genre Theory in the Renaissance* and *Paradoxica Epidemica: The Renaissance Tradition of Paradox*.

RENÉ GIRARD is University Professor of the Humanities at Stanford University. His books include *Mensonge romantique et vérité romanesque* (*Deceit, Desire and the Novel*) and *La violence et la sacré* (*Violence and the Sacred*).

ALVIN B. KERNAN is Mellon Professor of the Humanities at Princeton University. His books include *The Plot of Satire* and *The Imaginary Library*.

RUTH NEVO is Professor of English at Hebrew University at Jerusalem. She is the author of *The Dial of Virtue* and *Comic Transformations in Shakespeare*.

MEREDITH SKURA is Professor of English at Rice University. She is author of *The Literary Use of the Psychoanalytic Process*.

A. D. NUTTALL is Professor of English at the University of Sussex. His books include *A Common Sky* and *A New Mimesis*.

Bibliography

Arthos, John. *The Art of Shakespeare*. New York: Barnes & Noble, 1964.

Barber, C. L. *Shakespeare's Festive Comedy*. Princeton: University Press, 1959.

Barton, Anne (Anne Righter). *Shakespeare and the Idea of a Play*. London: Chatto & Windus, 1962. Reprint. Harmondsworth and Baltimore: Penguin Books, 1967.

Bradbrook, M. C. "Authority, Truth and Justice in *Measure for Measure*." *Review of English Studies* 17 (1941): 385–99.

———. "Dramatic Role as Social Image: A Study of *The Taming of the Shrew*." *Shakespeare Jahrbuch* 94 (1958): 132–50.

———. *The Growth and Structure of Elizabethan Comedy*. London: Chatto & Windus, 1962.

Brower, Reuben A. *The Fields of Light: An Experiment in Critical Reading*. New York: Oxford University Press, 1951.

Brown, John Russell. *Shakespeare and His Comedies*. 2nd ed. London: Methuen & Co., Ltd., 1962.

Brown, John Russell, and Harris, Bernard, eds. *Later Shakespeare*. London: Edward Arnold, 1966, and New York: St. Martin's Press, 1967.

Bryant, Joseph Allen. *Hippolyta's View: Some Christian Aspects of Shakespeare's Plays*. Lexington: University of Kentucky Press, 1961.

Campbell, Oscar J. *Shakespeare's Satire*. 1943. Reprint. New York: Gordian Press, Inc., 1971.

Chambers, E. K. *Shakespeare: A Survey*. New York: Hill & Wang, 1958.

Champion, Larry S. *Evolution of Shakespeare's Comedy: A Study in Dramatic Perspective*. Cambridge, Mass.: Harvard University Press, 1970.

Christensen, Jerome. "The Mind at Ocean: The Impropriety of Coleridge's Literary Life." In *Romanticism and Language*, edited by Arden Reed. Ithaca: Cornell University Press, 1984: 146–52.

Clemen, Wolfgang. *The Development of Shakespeare's Imagery*. London: Methuen & Co., Ltd., and Cambridge, Mass.: Harvard University Press, 1951.

Coghill, Nevill. "The Basis of Shakespearian Comedy." *Essays and Studies of the English Association* (1950): 1–28.

Craig, Hardin. *The Enchanted Glass: The Elizabethan Mind in Literature*. Oxford: Basil Blackwell, 1950.

Danby, John F. *Poets on Fortune's Hill: Studies in Sidney, Shakespeare, Beaumont and Fletcher*. London: Faber & Faber, 1952.

———. "Shakespeare Criticism and *Two Gentlemen of Verona*." *Critical Quarterly* 2 (1960): 309–21.

Edwards, Philip. *Shakespeare and the Confines of Art.* London: Methuen & Co., Ltd., 1968.

————. "Shakespeare's Romances: 1900–1957." *Shakespeare Survey* 2 (1958): 1–18.

Ellis-Fermor, Una. *The Jacobean Drama: An Interpretation.* London: Methuen & Co., Ltd., 1936.

Empson, William. *Some Versions of Pastoral.* Norfolk, Ct.: New Directions, 1950.

Evans, Bertrand. *Shakespeare's Comedies.* Oxford: At the Clarendon Press, 1960.

Felperin, Howard. *Shakespearean Romance.* Princeton: Princeton University Press, 1972.

Fergusson, Francis. *Shakespeare: The Pattern in His Carpet.* New York: Delacorte, 1958.

Foakes, F. A. *Shakespeare: The Dark Comedies to the Last Plays—From Satire to Celebration.* Charlottesville: University Press of Virginia, 1971.

Frye, Northrop. *Anatomy of Criticism.* Princeton: Princeton University Press, 1957.

————. "The Argument of Comedy." In *English Institute Essays* (1948), edited by D. A. Robertson. New York: Columbia University Press, 1949: 58–73.

————. *A Natural Perspective: The Development of Shakespearean Comedy and Romance.* New York: Columbia University Press, 1955. Reprint. New York: Harcourt, Brace & World, 1965.

————. *The Secular Scripture: A Study of the Structure of Romance.* Cambridge, Mass. and London: Harvard University Press, 1976.

Garber, Marjorie B. *Dream in Shakespeare: From Metaphor to Metamorphosis.* New Haven and London: Yale University Press, 1974.

Gesner, Carol. *Shakespeare and the Greek Romance.* Lexington: University Press of Kentucky, 1970.

Goddard, Harold C. *The Meaning of Shakespeare.* Chicago: The University of Chicago Press, 1951.

Granville-Barker, Harley. *Prefaces to Shakespeare.* 2 vols. Princeton: Princeton University Press, 1946–1947.

Hartwig, Joan. *Shakespeare's Tragicomic Vision.* Baton Rouge: Louisiana State University Press, 1972.

Hunter, Robert G. *Shakespeare and the Comedy of Forgiveness.* New York: Columbia University Press, 1965.

Kermode, Frank. *English Pastoral Poetry: From the Beginning to Marvell.* London: Harrap, 1952.

————. *William Shakespeare: The Final Plays.* London: Longmans, Green, 1963.

Kirschbaum, Leo. *Character and Characterization in Shakespeare.* Detroit: Wayne State University Press, 1962.

Knight, G. Wilson. *The Shakespearean Tempest.* London: Oxford University Press, 1932. Reprint. London: Methuen & Co., Ltd., 1971.

————. *The Wheel of Fire: Interpretations of Shakespearean Tragedy.* 4th ed. London: Methuen & Co., Ltd., 1949.

Lawrence, W. W. *Shakespeare's Problem Comedies*. London: Macmillan, 1937. Reprint. Harmondsworth and Baltimore: Penguin Books, 1969.

Leech, Clifford. "The 'Meaning' of *Measure for Measure*." *Shakespeare Survey* 3 (1950): 66–73.

————. *Twelfth Night and Shakespearean Comedy*. Toronto: University of Toronto Press, 1965.

Levin, Harry. *The Myth of the Golden Age in the Renaissance*. Bloomington: Indiana University Press, 1969.

Levin, Richard. *The Multiple Plot in English Renaissance Drama*. Chicago: The University of Chicago Press, 1971.

McCary, W. Thomas. *Friends and Lovers: The Phenomenology of Desire in Shakespearean Comedy*. New York: Columbia University Press, 1985.

McFarland, Thomas. *Shakespeare's Pastoral Comedy*. Chapel Hill: University of North Carolina Press, 1972.

Muir, Kenneth. *Last Periods of Shakespeare, Racine, and Ibsen*. Detroit: Wayne State University Press, 1961.

————, ed. *Shakespeare: The Comedies: A Collection of Critical Essays*. Englewood Cliffs, N. J.: Prentice-Hall, Inc. 1965.

Nelson, Thomas Allen. *Shakespeare's Comic Theory: A Study of Art and Artifice in the Last Plays*. The Hague and Paris: Mouton, 1972.

Nevo, Ruth. *Comic Transformations in Shakespeare*. London: Methuen & Co., Ltd., 1980.

Palmer, D. J. *Shakespeare's Later Comedies: An Anthology of Modern Criticism*. Harmondsworth and Baltimore: Penguin Books, 1971.

Parrott, Thomas Marc. *Shakespearean Comedy*. New York: Oxford University Press, 1949.

Peterson, Douglas L. *Time, Tide, and Tempest*. San Marino, Ca.: Huntington Library, 1973.

Pettet, E. C. *Shakespeare and the Romance Tradition*. London and New York: Staples Press, 1949. Reprint. London: Methuen & Co., Ltd., 1970.

Phialas, Peter. *Shakespeare's Romantic Comedies: The Development of their Form and Meaning*. Chapel Hill: University of North Carolina Press, 1966.

Quinones, Ricardo J. *The Renaissance Discovery of Time*. Cambridge, Mass.: Harvard University Press, 1972.

Rossiter, A. P. *Angel with Horns*. London: Longman Group, Ltd., 1961.

Schanzer, Ernest. *The Problem Plays of Shakespeare*. New York: Schocken Books, 1963.

Shell, Marc. *Money, Language and Thought*. Berkeley: University of California Press, 1982.

Smith, Hallet. *Shakespeare's Romances: A Study of Some Ways of the Imagination*. San Marino, Ca.: The Huntington Library, 1972.

Spencer, Theodore. "Appearance and Reality in Shakespeare's Last Plays." *Modern Philology* 39 (1942): 265–74.

Stoll, Elmer Edgar. *Art and Artifice in Shakespeare*. New York: Barnes & Noble, 1951.

———. *Shakespeare and Other Masters*. Cambridge, Mass.: Harvard University Press, 1940.

Tillyard, E. M. W. *Shakespeare's Early Comedies*. Atlantic Highlands, N.J.: Humanities Press, Inc., 1983.

———. *Shakespeare's Last Plays*. London: Chatto & Windus, 1938. Reprint. 1964.

Toliver, Harold E. *Pastoral Forms and Attitudes*. Berkeley: University of California Press, 1971.

Traversi, Derek. *Shakespeare: The Last Phase*. London: Hollis & Carter, 1954.

———. "*Troilus and Cressida*." *Scrutiny* 8 (1938): 301–19.

Welsford, Enid. *The Court Masque: A Study in the Relationship Between Poetry and Revels*. Cambridge: Cambridge University Press, 1927.

Wilson, John Dover. *Shakespeare's Happy Comedies*. Evanston, Ill.: Western University Press, 1962.

Yates, Francis A. *Shakespeare's Last Plays: A New Approach*. London: Routledge & Kegan Paul, 1975.

Young, David. *The Heart's Forest: A Study of Shakespeare's Pastoral Plays*. New Haven: Yale University Press, 1972.

Acknowledgments

"Shylock" by Elmer Edgar Stoll from *Shakespeare Studies: Historical and Comparative in Method* by Elmer Edgar Stoll, copyright © 1927 by Macmillan Publishing Co. Reprinted by permission.

"The Writing of *Pericles*" by G. Wilson Knight from *The Crown of Life* by G. Wilson Knight, copyright © 1948 by Methuen and Co., Ltd. Reprinted by permission.

"Virtue is the True Nobility: A Study of the Structure of *All's Well that Ends Well*" by M. C. Bradbrook from *The Review of English Studies* 26 (1950). Reprinted by permission.

"*Measure for Measure*" by Harold C. Goddard from *The Meaning of Shakespeare* by Harold C. Goddard, copyright © 1951 by The University of Chicago. Reprinted by permission.

"The Mirror of Analogy: *The Tempest*" by Reuben Brower from *The Fields of Light: An Experiment in Critical Reading* by Reuben Brower, copyright © 1951 by Oxford University Press. Reprinted by permission.

"*Love's Labour's Lost*" by Anne Barton from *Shakespeare Quarterly* 4 (1953), copyright © 1953 by Folger Shakespeare Library. Reprinted by permission.

"*Twelfth Night* and the Morality of Indulgence" by John Hollander from *Sewanee Review* 2, vol. 68 (1959). Copyright © 1959 by The University of the South. Reprinted by permission.

"The Alliance of Seriousness and Levity in *As You Like It*" by C. L. Barber from *Shakespeare's Festive Comedies* by C. L. Barber, copyright © 1959 by Princeton University Press. Reprinted by permission.

"*Much Ado About Nothing*" by A. P. Rossiter from *Angel with Horns: Fifteen Lectures on Shakespeare* edited by Graham Storey, copyright © 1961 by Longman Group Ltd. Reprinted by permission.

"Making Nature Afraid" by Northrop Frye from *A Natural Perspective: The Development of Shakespearean Comedy and Romance* by Northrop Frye, copyright © 1965 by Columbia University Press. Reprinted by permission.

"Undream'd Shores: *The Tempest*" by Howard Felperin from *Shakespearean Romance* by Howard Felperin, copyright © 1972 by Princeton University Press. Reprinted by permission.

"Perspectives on Pastoral: *The Winter's Tale*" by Rosalie Colie from *Shakespeare's Living Art* by Rosalie Colie, copyright © 1974 by Princeton University Press. Reprinted by permission.

"Myth and Ritual in Shakespeare's *A Midsummer Night's Dream*" by René Girard from *Textual Strategies: Perspectives in Post-Structuralist Criticism* edited by Josue V. Marari, copyright © 1979 by Cornell University. Reprinted by permission.

"*A Midsummer Night's Dream*" by Alvin B. Kernan from *The Playwright as Magician: Shakespeare's Image of the Poet in the English Public Theater* by Alvin B. Kernan, copyright © 1979 by Yale University. Reprinted by permission.

" 'Kate of Kate Hall': *The Taming of the Shrew*" by Ruth Nevo from *Comic Transformations in Shakespeare* by Ruth Nevo, copyright © 1980 by Ruth Nevo. Reprinted by permission.

"Interpreting Posthumus' Dream: *Cymbeline*" by Meredith Skura from *Representing Shakespeare: New Psychoanalytic Essays* edited by Murray M. Schwartz and Coppelia Kahn, copyright © 1980 by The Johns Hopkins University Press. Reprinted by permission.

"*The Merchant of Venice*" by A. D. Nuttall from *A New Mimesis: Shakespeare and the Representation of Reality* by A. D. Nuttall, copyright © 1983 by A. D. Nuttall. Reprinted by permission.

Index